HISTORY

OF THE

Rise, Difficulties & Suspension

OF

ANTIOCH COLLEGE

A RECORD OF FACTS.

BY IRA W. ALLEN, A. M.

LATE PROFESSOR OF MATHEMATICS, ASTRONOMY AND CIVIL ENGINEERING IN ANTIOCH COLLEGE.

COLUMBUS:

PRINTED AND PUBLISHED BY JOHN GEARY & SON.

1858.

A COLLECTION OF FACTS.

HISTORY

OF THE

Rise, Difficulties & Suspension

OF

ANTIOCH COLLEGE.

CONTAINING LETTERS AND STATEMENTS

From Professors HORACE MANN, W. H DOHERTY, T. HOLMES, A. L. McKINNEY and H. D. BURLINGAME. Elders D. MILLARD, JOHN ROSS, IRA ALLEN, ISAAC C. GOFF, J. D. CHILDS, D. P. PIKE, N. SUMMERBELL, D. LONG, J. E. CHURCH, D. E. MILLARD, J. H. CURRIER, J. McKEE, J. T. LYNN, J. WM. BROWN, A. BRADFIELD, B. SEEVER, H. SIMONTON, M. CUMMINGS, JAMES MAPLE, E. FAY, &c. Dr.'s W. H. BELLOWS and R P. STEBBINS. W. L. SCHENCK, M. D., and H. C. FOSTER, M. D. Messrs. JOHN GEARY, A. M. MERRIFIELD, F. A. PALMER, G. L. SALSBURY, W. MILLS. AARON HARIAN, PETER COOPER, M. H. GRINNELL, J. E. BRUSH, O. H. ROBERTS, A. S. DEAN, &c,

BY IRA W. ALLEN, A. M.

LATE PROFESSOR OF MATHEMATICS, ASTRONOMY AND CIVIL ENGINEERING IN ANTIOCH COLLEGE.

COLUMBUS:

PRINTED AND PUBLISHED BY JOHN GEARY & SON.

1858.

PREFACE.

Just one year ago to-day, D. P. Pike, of New England, said to the world, through the "Herald of Gospel Liberty":—"I hope some day a full and truthful expose or history of Antioch's misfortunes may be known and justice done to all." This was the expression of a noble aud generous soul, and thousands of our ministers and brethren have doubtless cherished, if not expressed, the same hope.

Four years ago to-day and our confidence in Horace Mann was almost boundless; yet step by step he has forced us to change our opinion. His course at Antioch College has been marked with cruelty and injustice, and has caused great suspicion and wide spread distrust. His venomed javelins have been hurled at all, or nearly all, he representative Professors and Teachers of the Christian Church, ever connected with the Institution; and he has finally succeeded in wresting the College itself from its Denominational basis; and yet no Pope at Rome, perhaps, ever concealed himself so much behind priests and bishops and cardinals, as has the President of Antioch College behind committees, and agents and spies.

Within the last few months also, (and for the first time in our life) our character has been ruthlessly assailed by Mr. Mann and his clique, in a variety of ways, and especially through the "Gospel Herald." The columns of the "Herald," however, the only avenue of approach to the masses of our people throughout the Great West, have been closed against any full and fair reply to their false and libelous charges, as the reader will find by perusing the "Introduction to Part Second." Horace Mann and his co-workers are therefore responsible for the appearance of this work. They have called it into existence. They have left us no other honorable course; and for whatever praise or blame may attach to the work, they must be held primarily accountable. Yet we will not knowingly sit in judgement on their motives. These we leave to the great Judge of all the earth. Their deeds, however, will form a part of history, and will be criticised by the world.

The object of this volume is to meet the expectations of Bro. Pike and others; to do justice to Mr. Mann and his coadjutors by a statement of facts which ought to be known: to inform the great masses of the Christian Denomination and render them more self-reliant in their educational enterprises; to benefit Antioch College by redeeming it, if possible, and placing it upon a Christian basis, and to vindicate the holy cause of truth and justice.

Our aim has been to injure no one; but to benefit all concerned by a statement of the truth: for "*The truth shall make you free.*"

No mere personal interest could have induced us to prepare and publish this book. We had hoped to be excused from such a task; and, were it possible, we would now gladly be relieved from presenting it to the public; for we well know that the age of persecution is not yet passed, and we expect that this little "messenger of truth" will call down upon our head the most bitter anathemas of which our assailants are capable; but come what may, commendation or persecution, life or death, our decision is made. We will discharge what we believe to be our imperative duty to the Founders and Patrons, to the Scholarship holders and Trustees of Antioch College; to the whole Christian Denomination, to the world and to high Heaven; and then leave the results in the hands of an all-wise and omnipotent Providence.

This volume has been made as full and complete as the limits of the work would allow. It covers a period of eight years, and is divided into three parts. Part First treats of the leading events from the Marion Convention, 1850, down to Oct., 1857: and Parts Second and Third, with the conclusion, embrace the leading facts from the latter date down to the present time.

The work is made up, to quite an extent, of letters and statements from our leading men, for which they are, of course, responsible.

The remaining portions have been drawn from official records and other reliable sources, and for their arrangement we are responsible, errors excepted, which will be cheerfully corrected when they are made to appear: and we hereby request all persons who may peruse these pages to notify us of any inaccuracies which they may find; for we do not claim perfection. Indeed, it cannot reasonably be expected that a work covering several years, and embracing such a variety of incidents and circumstances, could be wholly free from errors. The works of the wisest men are imperfect. Nor have we, in the composition of this volume sought for historical allusions, nor labored to give a classical finish to the style; yet the book has not been hastily thrown together. It is no ignus fatuus, no air castle, as every careful and candid reader will be convinced, We have given much time to the examination of records and statements, and much labor to the clear arrangement and accurate presentation of the facts. Our aim has been to give the plain truth in plain English; and to effect this no pains have been spared.

Our enemies, we think, are not numerous, and they have our most hearty good wishes and our prayers. We have not the slightest desire to injure them. We have prepared these pages for their benefit, as well as for the benefit of our friends; and in the discharge of this duty we have received much aid and encouragement from ministers and brethren, several of whom have read, or heard read, considerable portions of the manuscript copy of the book, and advised us to publish it. For their valuable counsels and deep interest in this matter, they have our most sincere thanks.

As in all our intercourse with Students and Teachers and fellow Professors in Antioch College, we have endeavored to manifest a Christian spirit; so also in discussing the various topics and events which form the present volume, have we striven to exercise kindness, charity and justice, and if these pages are received in the same good spirit; if they accomplish the objects for which they are intended; if they fulfill the noble mission on which they are sent forth, our highest expectations will be realized, and we shall feel richly rewarded for all our efforts.

IRA W. ALLEN.

Yellow Springs, O., Sept. 10th, 1858.

HISTORY

OF THE

Rise, Difficulties and Suspension of Antioch College.

Previous to the year of 1850, much had been written and published in our Denominational papers, on the subject of Education ; and on the 2d day of October of that year, the largest General Convention of the Christians which ever convened, assembled at Marion, N. Y.

It was a *delegated Convention*, composed of 82 delegates, representing 26 Conferences and 521 votes, or ordained ministers ; and never, perhaps, since the beginning of time has so large a religious body come together in a kinder, more earnest spirit, and held a Convention of three days in which greater harmony and love were witnessed. They came with noble purposes and for a noble object. The work upon which they were entering was one on which angels might smile, which God could approve ; for it was no other than the establishment of a great Seminary or University in which young men and women were (we hoped) to be educated for the highest usefulness in this life, and the highest happiness in "the world to come."

One of the results of that Convention was Antioch College, for which we have hoped; and prayed, and paid our money. But where is Antioch to-day ? Does she exhibit and diffuse the spirit which the Marion Convention breathed into her ?

Is she preparing our sons and daughters for great usefulness on earth and for glory in Heaven ?

Soon after the Convention, soliciting agents, for various sections of the United States and the Canadas, were appointed and entered upon the work.

Eld. J. Phillips, of Ohio, in a few months, succeeded in raising in money and approved notes, nearly $100,000 ; and this entirely within the bounds of his own state. The palm was therefore adjudged to Ohio ; and the locating committee after visiting several places and receiving proposals, determined Jan. 21st, 1852, to locate the Institution at Yellow Springs, O., widely celebrated for its charming glens and "yellow springs."

This small town and vicinity gave 20 acres of land for the College Park, and $30,000 to the Building Fund.

The College was incorporated on the 14th of May following; and on the 23d of June the corner-stone was laid with appropriate ceremonies. The concourse of people on the occasion was very large; and after music by the Springfield brass band, and prayer by Eld. D. F. Ladley, singing of a hymn, &c., Judge Probasco, of Lebanon, delivered an address; after which an ode, written for the occasion by Eld. J. Ellis, was sung; an address delivered by Dr. Freeze, of Philadelphia; when other exercises befitting the occasion closed the day.

On the 15th of Sept., 1852, the Faculty of the College was elected. Mr. Mann was chosen as President with the privilege of selecting two Professors. Prof's. Doherty, Allen, Holmes, and McKinney were also elected. The persons selected by Mr. Mann proved to be C. S. Pennell, A. M., his nephew, and Miss R. M. Pennell, his niece; so that the original Faculty was as follows, viz.:—

FACULTY.

Hon. HORACE MANN, LL. D., President,
and Professor of Political Economy, Intellectual and Moral Philosophy, Constitutional Law and Natural Theology.

Rev. W. H. DOHERTY, A. M.,
Professor of Rhetoric, Logic and Belles-Lettres.

IRA W. ALLEN, A. M.,
Professor of Mathematics, Astronomy and Civil Engineering.

Rev. THOMAS HOLMES, A. M.,
Professor of Greek Language and Literature.

C. S. PENNELL, A. M.,
Professor of Latin Language and Literature.

Miss R. M. PENNELL,
Professor of Physical Geography, Drawing, Natural History Civil History and Didactics.

——————
Professor of Chemistry, and Theory and Practice of Agriculture.

——————
Professor of Mineralogy and Geology.

——————
Professor of Modern Languages.

Rev. A. L. McKINNEY,
Principal of Preparatory School.

Early in November the first Faculty meeting, of several days' continuance, was held at Mr. Mann's residence, near Boston, at which important questions touching the College were discussed, and the curriculum of studies mapped out, which soon after was published to the world. There seemed to be a unity of purpose. The meeting was harmonious. The Professors exhibited a noble enthusiasm, and left, on the adjournment of their pleasant sessions, with high anticipations for the future.

The second meeting of the Faculty convened at the same place on the 23d of March, 1853. Differences of opinion were fr quently manifested during the session, but all passed off harmoniously; and no one could have predicted, I think, from anything which transpired on that occasion the unpleasant and unjust transactions which have followed.

Soon after this meeting I sailed for Europe, and from what transpired during my absence I must rely upon testimony or history.

The school opened October the 5th, 1853, by the Dedicatory Exercises, which were interesting and impressive. Many were the hearts which beat strong on that day, and were big with hope for the future prosperity and glory of the College. Among the actors on that occasion were Elds. John Ross and Isaac N. Walter, the former of whom still lives to instruct and guide the church over which he has presided for thirty-five years, an able defender of a free Christianity; but the latter "has gone the way of all the earth;" has "fought the good fight," and exchanged the "sword of the spirit" for a "crown of glory."

The number of young persons assembled to enter the institution was as large as the buildings, in their unfinished condition, would accommodate, for the Gentlemen's Hall was not yet in a state for occupancy, nor was Antioch Hall fully completed, as the immense scaffolding, the ring of the mason's trowel, and the almost incessant strokes of the carpenter's hammer, unequivocally testified.

The candidates for admission were examined in the Dining Hall; recitations went on; and, notwithstanding the discomfort of unfinished edifices and grounds strewn with building materials, the number of students throughout the year was as large as could well be accomodated.

Early in September, 1854, I arrived in New York, direct from Europe, and calling on Eld. Eli Fay, he took occasion to give me a brief history of the College during my absence; and I was greatly surprised to learn that troubles had already arisen.

He reflected on Mr. Mann as the chief cause of them, represented him as opposed to prayer meetings in the College, and Prof. Holmes as a firm advocate of them.

Mr. Fay said he deemed it his duty to tell me these things ; hoped I would stand up firmly for the right for prayer meetings and a Christian influence, and requested me to keep him posted on College matters.

Such statements were wholly unexpected; for although I supposed Mr. Mann to be a cool-headed Unitarian, and his religious views to differ considerably from those of the Christians, and although I had had some forebodings that religious differences between himself and the Christian Denomination might, perhaps, at some future time, occasion trouble, yet I did not consider it *probable;* for however much Mr. Mann might differ from the Christians in religious matters, inasmuch as he had been elevated by them to the Presidency of their first great College, I presumed he would let differences of opinion alone, and labor to build up a large university and their own educational interests.

Selfish considerations alone, it seemed to me, if no higher motives, would induce him to pursue such a course.

I listened to Mr. Fay's story, but determined that my mind should not be prejudiced, for I was a great admirer of Mr. Mann.

I had perused his lectures, and they were polished, instructive, popular in their character, and seemed to be pervaded by a high moral, if not Christian, spirit. For mere dogmas or opinions, so long as they are not unseasonably presented or unduly urged, I care nothing. A pure heart and a Christian spirit are the great desiderata—the grand essentials.

My personal acquaintance with Mr. Mann was slight, yet I believed him to be just the man for the Presidency of our College ; and be his views and practices what they might, I was fully determined that my admiration should not be cooled, nor my faith weakened, except by seeing and hearing for myself.

With such a determination I arrived at Antioch College, September 14, 1854, and entered at once upon my duties.

Prof. McKinney was absent, *pro tempore*, acting as soliciting agent for the Institution, and in his place was another gentleman, so that all the teachers of the Preparatory Department, seven in number, were strangers to me. Indeed this was my first visit to Ohio, and being by far the youngest member of the Faculty, and the duties of my extensive department being weighty, I engaged but little in the general administration of the College. I was, however, vigilant and observing.

In Faculty meetings my voice was not often heard, except on questions of importance and when duty called; and then, whether my views were coincident with or opposed to those of Mr. Mann or any other member of the Faculty, I endeavored to present them with courtesy and decision.

It did not require many weeks to convince an observer that some of the Professors and Teachers sympathized fully with the founders of the College and labored for their interests, while the others had little or no regard for them, other than as paymasters. Profs. Doherty, Allen, Holmes and McKinney, were of the Christian connection, and labored for its interest. Mr. Burlingame, Mrs. Holmes and Miss Shaw, of the Preparatory Department, were true to the interests of the Christians, but the four remaining teachers of said Department, brought there through the influence of Mr. Mann or Miss Pennell, or of both, seemed to have decided proclivities in other directions.

It soon became clearly and painfully evident that a spirit of partiality was active in the Institution. Mr. Mann and Miss Pennell seemed to be very desirous of obtaining all the teachers possible from Massachusetts, or New England, and especially those who had attended the Normal School at West Newton, the former residence of Mr. Mann, and the scene of Miss Pennell's labors; and unless teachers had been down to this modern Mecca they were looked upon as deficient in the divine art of pedagogy!

The lines were sharply drawn. It seemed that Mr. Mann or Miss Pennell could not say enough in praise of the teachers whom they had brought up from New England. Faculty meetings, parties, and other occasions, appeared too few and far between for their fulsome panegyrics of their relatives and friends in the school, while those Professors and Teachers sent to Antioch by the Christians as their representatives, were criticised or passed over in silence.

In October, 1854, there was a special meeting of the Trustees. But few were present, yet important resolutions were passed, one of which is "Resolution No. 17,"—viz.

"*Resolved*, On motion of John Phillips, that Dr. H. A. Warriner, of Cincinnati, be appointed Professor of Chemistry in Antioch College, whose duties shall commence and be performed at such time and for such terms as shall be decided on by the Faculty, and whose salary shall be in proportion to the number of terms in a year for which he is employed."

It is said that Dr. Warriner was recommended to Mr. Mann by one or more Unitarian clergymen, and by him to the Board of Trustees! It is also said that Mr. Warriner connected himself with the Christian Church of Cincinnati, in accordance with Mr. Mann's advice, a short time before his name was laid before the Trustees for a Professorship!

There are not many men, it is to be hoped, who would connect themselves with a church for the sake of a Professorship!

Why was not this matter attended to at the annual meeting of the Board? Why have so many important resolutions been passed, at the special meetings of the Trustees, when so few were present? Was it not because a few men can be managed more easily than a larger number? because measures could be executed at these side meetings which would doubtless have been rejected at the annual meetings; and which, once passed, could not be reconsidered without much opposition and great trouble?

How very convenient for some persons have these side meetings been!

The absence of Prof. McKinney was much regretted by the friends of the College, for he was a zealous instructor and much liked by the students. Besides, Mr. Mann had now a majority of votes in the Faculty by counting his own.

But another revelation was at hand. A feeling against Prof. Holmes had been cherished in a certain quarter, and in March, 1855, at the close of the Winter Term, it broke out. Some of the students signed a petition for the removal of Prof. Holmes! Whether Mr. Mann directly favored this movement, and how much, I will not say; but that he did indirectly encourage it is evident.

To one of the leading students (H. C. Badger) in the College, and of the chief actors in this movement, I heard Mr. Mann talk one evening, and I know not how he could have given better encouragement in a transaction of this kind.

After he had closed, and at his request, I spoke with said student and reprimanded him severely; so much so, that after he had retired, Mr. Mann said—"Professor Allen you take very strong ground against the right of the students to petition, far stronger than I should dare to take."

Replying that I had only briefly expressed my views of *right* in the matter, I withdrew. Mr. Mann brought up the matter before the Trustees who were then in session, thought Mr. Holmes would have to leave a while, and advised that the Board grant him leave of absence to go to Europe. This was granted; but Professor Holmes was not allowed, as is customary to be a member of the committee to select a person to fill his chair during his absence!

Who had so deep an interest in the Greek Department as Prof. Holmes? and why was he not allowed a voice in naming a substitute?

There were things connected with this transaction which may perhaps be concealed until the "great day of reckoning;" but enough was known to produce a deep sensation throughout this and other communities.

Many of the friends of the College were not only amazed but deeply indignant at this transaction; and it was whispered around that the heads of Professors Doherty and Allen would fall next!

It was believed that Mr. Mann and his accomplices would be satisfied with nothing short of the removal from the College of all true representatives of the Christians, the founders of the Institution! No Professor or Teacher who was a member of the Christian Denomination, and who had the courage to advocate and labor for its interests could long be safe. But more of this on another page.

The Winter term closed on the 13th of March, and the meeting of the Trustees closed some two days later. It was in contemplation by some of the Board, to give Mr. Burlingame a more prominent position in the Institution; and Mr. Fay accordingly took occasion to ask Prof. Pennell some questions about Mr. B.; whereupon Prof. P. dropped some remarks prejudicial to Mr. B. touching his method of teaching. Mr. Fay laid the matter before Mr. Burlingame; and after the Trustees had dispersed, Messrs. Pennell and Burlingame happened to meet in my room, when a lengthy conversation sprung up between them, in which Mr. Burlingame demonstrated the folly of Prof. Pennell's remarks, and pinned him to the wall. After dining the conversation was continued during a walk through the glen, the result of which seemed to be beneficial upon Prof. P., at least for a time.

In writing to Mr. Fay on the 20th of March, I alluded to the above mentioned conversation, and intimated that Mr. Burlingame had signified his intention of resigning his post, to take effect at the close of the year. In reply Mr. F. penned the following letter, in which he also takes occasion to allude to communications from Prof. Holmes and others:

MR. FAY'S LETTER.

New York, March 25th, 1855.

Prof. Allen:—Dear Sir:—Your excellent letters stating affairs at Antioch and explaining your relation thereto have just come to hand, and though I have but little time in which to reply to the whole, yet I dare not delay, and must write what I can. I sincerely hope you will maintain the independence of your position, and defend your rights at all hazards. I also hope that you will never for one moment lose sight of the fact that Antioch College is the property of the *Christians*, and should be under *their control*. No man should stand between them; and all attempts to divorce them should be at once rebuked, and by all that is worth defending at Antioch, and all that is noble in the position we occupy as a denomination. I hope you will resist to the last any indignity offered to us by any of the teachers. I hope you will bring before the Faculty those subordinate teachers who openly deride our people or treat with disrespect the Western students. Submit to no insults for your own sake, and for our sakes, and for the sake of Antioch. Why pay our money to those who insult us?

I also hope you and others will stand side by side in trying to make Antioch what its founders and patrons desire it might be. If you do so openly and on all occasions, you will *conquer*. I know it and can give my reasons. Don't fear to tell Mr. Mann plainly just what you think of the whole affair, and that partiality shown to teachers and disrespect shown to our own will result in an explosion, as it certainly will if it is not stopped.

Now, sir, I desire to write to Mr. Mann myself, and tell him that you and Prof. Holmes and lady, and Mr. Burlingame and Miss Shaw, agree in thinking that partiality has been shown to those teachers which were recommended by himself and Miss Pennell, (now Mrs. A. S. Dean,) also that it is the belief of the whole that teachers from the Christians are treated with disrespect, that they do not intend longer tamely to submit to it, and give it as my own opinion that the Christians must be more largely represented in the corps of instruction, or there will be uncontrolable trouble. * * * *

I learn by telegraph from Mr. Mann that Dr. Siedorff has not been heard from. Have Mr. Burlingame put in his place by all means. Can't you work with Doherty so that he will assist you in bringing that about?" * * * "You need have no fears about the extent of Mr. Dean's labors as agent hereafter. He will hardly get a new appointment. *

This letter is in confidence† except you think best to show it to Mr. Burlingame. *He must not leave the school.* You see plainly that a crisis is coming, and the Christians will as certainly be victorious in an open war as God reigns. If he will stand by he will have a noble place. Write me immediately and inform me what is now doing.

Very respectfully, E. FAY.

The Spring term opened on the 28th March, and a few days thereafter the typhoid fever laid me on my couch.

My classes in Mathematics and German, each appointed one of its members to fill my vacant chair and conduct the recitations; and their action was well pleasing to me, for they had selected the very persons whom I would have chosen. In a day or two, however, Mr. Mann called on me, and wished to know if it would not be best to have Mrs. Mann take charge of my German class during my sickness. I told him that I had the fullest confidence in all my classes, believed that they were doing well, and thought that the German class would get along finely under the direction of Miss S., whom the class had selected for its teacher during my illness; that Miss S., had studied the German previously and was far in advance of the other members of the class; yet did not know as I had any special objections to Mrs. Mann's taking

† The above is the only confidential letter which appears in this review. And this would not now be presented had not Mr. Fay violated the most sacred obligations of a man to man.

the class, if he thought best. Not many days elapsed, however, before some members of the class called on me, and wished me a speedy recovery, for said they—we have no ambition to study or carefully prepare our lessons under the direction of Mrs. Mann!

It had not occurred to me that my classes in Mathematics would be troubled; for it is well understood that, in our Colleges and Universities, each professor has the direction and control of his own department, under no other arrangement would men of ability and integrity consent to occupy Professorial chairs. Judge then of my surprise when a member,of the class in Differential and Integral Calculus, who, calling on me, was asked, how they were progressing, said that they were doing well, and did not wish to leave the study.

What do you mean? asked I. Why, continued he, Mr. Mann informed us the other day that the Faculty thought we had better leave Calculus and take French, accordingly our class held a meeting and after consultation declined to take French, for we feared that Mrs. Mann would be placed over us; but supposing it was your wish that we should leave the Mathematics, as Mr. Mann said "the Faculty thought," &c., we concluded to defer the Calculus until the following term, and take one of the studies of that term (Tacitus) in its place, provided Prof. Pennell could hear us recite, which proposition however we hoped would not be accepted, for we much preferred to go on with the study of Calculus! Their proposition was however accepted by Prof. Pennell.

Soon after a member of the class in Trigonometry and Surveying called, and on being asked, how they were advancing, said finely, and showed me how much they had accomplished, adding that several members of the class did not wish to leave the study. I remarked that I did not know what he could mean by *leaving the study*. Why! we supposed you did! We thought it was your wish! said he; and added that a member of the Faculty had been conversing with some one or more of the class, advising them to drop Mathematics and take French; and that four members of the class were rather in favor of the change.

I told him my wish was, that the class go on with the Surveying, and that I hoped to be able to resume my duties in a short time. The class then held a meeting, voted unanimously to go on with their Mathematics; and were not further disturbed.

Not a word was breathed to me touching the proposed changes in the Mathematical Department, until, as above stated, I learned what was going on from members of the classes; and the better to effect said changes it was whispered that "Prof. Allen will not, probably, be able to take charge of his classes again this term."

The plea that I was not able to converse on such matters is far from the fact, for I received calls daily from Mr. Mann and others, and talked freely with them on various topics.

The scheme, however, failed. No French class could be drummed up; and Mrs. Mann did not win laurels in the German Department, as was fully evident when I again took the class on the 10th of May, about five weeks after I was taken sick.

In writing to Mr. Fay I made mention of this matter, as a friend to a friend, in reply to which Mr. F. wrote as follows:

MR. FAY'S LETTER.

New York, June 12th, 1855.

Prof. Allen—Dear Sir:—Yours of the 6th inst. is just received. I hasten to reply; though I can only indicate in general terms the condition of affairs as they exist between Mr. Mann and myself. Mr. Mann heard by way of Mr. Dean that I was not well pleased with many things at Antioch, for I have not hesitated to speak my mind on that subject. Mr. Mann immediately wrote me a very long letter, inquiring what I had heard and asking my authority. I replied at great length and reviewed the whole ground. I told him that there were three leading complaints made to me from various sources.

1st. That there was partiality shown towards those teachers who were brought there by his or Miss Pennell's influence.

2nd. That Miss Pennell is President of the College.

3d. That some of those teachers who are not of us are in the habit of speaking contemptuously of the Christians and the teachers whom they have placed there.

I presented with these complaints all the evidence which has been presented to me, not giving any names. In support of the first complaint I stated distinctly that there had been a *general* uneasiness among *all* the teachers ever sent there by the Christians, and that not more than one, and indeed I knew not there was one, who was satisfied with the administration of affairs.

After mentioning the names of Mr. and Mrs. Holmes, I said, "Prof. Allen, Mr. Burlingame and Miss Shaw do not consider their positions pleasant or desirable." * * * Now, my dear Brother, if things are there as you say they are (and I do not doubt it, as all your statements are corroborated by others,) if your rights have been infringed and you feel injured, I cannot see why you should be afraid to meet Mr. Mann face to face in defence of the right. Certainly I cannot act as a mediator if I must withhold all the facts. How can parties ever be reconciled while they seek concealment with smouldering fires in their bosoms? My only hope of a satisfactory adjudication is in the *plainest* and *strongest* statement of all the facts in the case. I am by no means afraid to tell Mr. Mann what I think of his course. I hope you are not.

Why not go to him, then, with all your grievances, and demand restitution, or, at least, an explanation?

I do not know what will be done with the Preparatory Department. I am tired of this care and almost discouraged.—Very truly yours,

E. Fay.

As to "a mediator," I did not ask Mr. Fay or any other man to act as such, I was by no means "afraid" to talk with Mr. Mann ; and was surprised that Mr. F. should draw any such inferences from my letter. I communicated the leading facts touching my sickness and the treatment of my classes to him in compliance with his oft-repeated request that I would keep him advised of College affairs.

I was intending to talk with Mr. Mann and others at the close of the term, and this I did do.

I have had interviews with Mr. Mann at different times on matters connected with the administration of the College, in which I have given him my views in plain, unequivocal language. Most of these interviews too have been at my own request, thus practically showing that I was not "afraid to meet Mr. Mann face to face in defence of the right ;" and had he exhibited any spirit of concession and equitable adjustment, had he not insisted on my coming over to his stand point, or at least, on my silent submission to his views and acts, our interviews would have been more frequent and of a more pleasant character.

Our differences were no mere personal matter, but involved general, important and sacred principles, I regarded the interests of the Christian Denomination at stake; and although I was willing to make large concessions, yet I could not consent to sacrifice those principles which I considered vital to our present well-being and future prosperity.

The reader will notice that the above letters of Mr. Fay are not only replies to my communications to him, but that they are also of a more general nature, embracing the general administration of the College, and containing the names of four other Professors and teachers who were displeased with the ruling influence in the Institution.

This state of things had commenced, and progressed to some extent during the first collegiate year, and hence before my return from Europe. It was quite a common expression at that time "that Miss Pennell is President of the College," and the reader will not be greatly surprised at that remark when he is informed that Mr. Mann, in conversation with one of our ministers a few months since, said—"*I do think that Mrs Dean knows more than all the other members of the Faculty put together, myself included.*"

The reader will further notice that Mr. Fay informed Mr. Mann "that there had been a *general* uneasiness among *all* the teachers ever sent there by the Christians," &c. ; and also that "all your (my) statements are coroborated by others. How different from Mr. F.'s recent statements in the "Gospel Herald !"

The above letters contain the advice and instruction of at least one of the Trustees, and a member of the "Committee on Instruction," **and** this was without doubt, the right spirit, for as the Christians had founded a great College, it was not only their right but *their duty* to direct and control it; and had they neglected this duty they would justly have merited the scorn and condemnation of the world. They looked to me as one of their representatives, and desired me to stand firm in the defence of their rights. This I have endeavored to do in a Christian spirit, and for this consistency of action, this discharge of my duty, I am now reviled and persecuted by the very man who wrote the above letters!

The Spring Term closed June 25th, 1855, after which Miss Shaw resigned, being determined that her name should not be connected with an Institution professedly under the control of the Christians, but in reality governed by a foreign influence. And does any one wonder that the accomplished daughter of Eld. Elijah Shaw, one of our oldest, ablest, and best-beloved ministers, could not endure the dominant influences at Antioch?

Mr. Burlingame also left for the East with the intention of not returning; but meeting Mr. Fay and other Trustees who urged him to remain at Antioch, and held out flattering inducements, he finally consented to return for one year; and in the mean time should they execute their purposes he would continue on.

During the preceding year, W. H. Knapp, a Unitarian clergyman of the Theodore Parker school, I believe, was steward of the College.

He had been secured by Mr. Mann who desired to have a gentleman of more polish and refinement in the stewardship than Bro. F. Applegate, who filled that office during the first year of the institution, and who, under all the drawbacks of unfinished buildings and the lack of conveniences, gave, it is thought, universal satisfaction, save to Mr. and Mrs. Mann, and perhaps a few others.

Rev. Mr. Knapp was liberally provided for. His salary was $800 per annum, besides various other valuable perquisites worth probably $800 to $1000 more.

He had the use of the College funds and the College credit, and was backed by Horace Mann's powerful aid and influence, yet he could not sustain the credit of the Hall. From about 250 boarders in the Hall when Mr. Knapp first came to the College, the number dwindled down to about 50, I believe, before the close of the year.

After the close of the year Mr. Knapp was requested to leave, and the services of Mr. Geo. L. Salsbury and lady were secured for the next year.

And now what is not a little remarkable is that while I write, and after the lapse of four years, news comes that Mr. Mann's clique is laboring earnestly to persuade Bro. F. Applegate to go back into the Hall as steward! and A. S. Dean is active in the matter!

Why is this? Has Bro. Applegate become highly polished and refined during these four years? or has the College retrograded so that he will now answer!

We have always regarded Mr. Applegate as a gentlemanly and honorable man, and fully capable of carrying out whatever he undertakes; and who is so dull as not to see the significance of this new move?

Mann, Dean, Fay & Co., know full well that great suspicion rests upon them throughout the country, and hence their desire to secure the services of Bro. Applegate as an important aid in overcoming the distrust of the people.

Mr. Mann is shrewd and pulls the wires cunningly, but will he not have to pull them a great many times before he brings his clique into favor with the public?

The third Collegiate year opened Sept. 5th, 1855. Prof. Holmes had now been absent over five months; but he did not leave until both Mr. Mann and Mr. Fay (the two most active members of the Committee on Instruction,) had given him positive assurances that Mrs. Holmes should be retained, during his absence, as a teacher in the Institution. This was an important condition, for, since Prof. Holmes had finished his course of Academical, Collegiate and Theological study of nearly ten years, he had given his time to preaching; and like most ministers had not received much of this world's goods. Mrs. Holmes had likewise passed through the same lenghty course of study with her husband, and was one of the most thorough teachers at Antioch. She gave good satisfaction to her classes the previous year, and instead of spending the Summer vacation of ten weeks, as did others at popular places of resort, she remained in Yellow Springs, like a dutiful and devotedwife, to save money for her husband who was far away over the broad Atlantic.

That she would be retained in the Institution, she probably had not the slightest doubt, for she was aware of the assurances of Mann and Fay to her husband. Judge therefore of her utter astonishment and disappointment on receiving a note signed by Mr. Mann and one other member of the committee, on the evening of the 4th September, informing her that her services were no longer desired in the Institution!

Thus on the evening before the third College year commenced, and after all her preparations to go on with her classes had been made, were the bright hopes of Mrs. Holmes suddenly blasted.

Does the reader ask what were the reasons for this fiendish act?

I answer that no true and valid reasons have ever been or can be adduced. Attempts were made to create an impression abroad that Mrs. Holmes had done some terrible thing, too horrible even to be mentioned! but the truth is, *she had done no such thing.*

The matter came up before the Trustees a few weeks later, Oct. 11th, 1855, when it was stated by Mr. Mann, or with his consent, that she had been dismissed at the request of the Faculty. Prof. Doherty arose, and said that the statement was false, that the Faculty knew nothing of the matter until after the deed was done; (Mr. Mann has often found it convenient, it is said, to screen his acts under the expressions "The Faculty desires," &c., "The Faculty has decided," &c.)

Some of the Trustees wished to know the reasons why Mrs. Holmes had been dismissed; but Mr. Mann thought they ought to have enough confidence in him, in the committee, to believe that the act was necessary without a statement of the reasons.

If the call for the reasons is persisted in, Mr. Mann thought they should be stated in private; that the reputation of a woman is her all, and he did not wish to injure Mrs. Holmes! The trustees accordingly went into *secret session*.

After said session was over, however, some of the Trustees told me what had been said and done, and that not one single valid reason had been adduced for dismissing Mrs. Holmes!

The Board, under the lead of a modern Jeffrey, would not receive petitions from Mrs. Holmes' classes that she be retained as their teacher. Ah! No. The petitions were on the wrong side. They were for, not against her! Eld. Summerbell and Bro. Salsbury went over with Mrs. Holmes to the Trustees' room, but the Board would not allow her to come before them and plead her own cause, and as Mr. Mann thought that Mrs. H. should be required to vacate her rooms in the Ladies' Hall, the Trustees passed a decree to that effect, and appointed a committee to carry it into execution!

The committee called on Mrs. H., but their courage failed them, and after quite a little visit they retired without alluding to the object of their mission!

Some of the Trustees informed me that it was very hard to thus ostensibly sanction Mr. Mann's proceedings; but the College was heavily in debt, and they feared that a contest at that time might prevent the raising of money!

To such an extent were the claims of right and justice ignored and baffled by a determined man, aided by the financial condition of the College!

But we say, under all circumstances, "Fiat Justicia;" "Let justice be done though the heavens fall." We believe, as Elder D. P. Pike said in the "Herald of Gospel Liberty," of Aug. 30th, 1855, speaking of College affairs, "Let there be no appearance of any design or underhanded movements; no favoritism; no *one-man power* anywhere.

Let everything be in open daylight, and then there will be no trouble about collecting money to save Antioch."

When the College opened in the Autumn of 1853, there being no regularly appointed College Chaplain, and nearly all the members of the Faculty being clergymen and lecturers, they voted to take turns in conducting religious services in the College chapel on the Sabbath.

On my return from Europe, in 1854, they desired me to enter into this arrangement, but I declined, for the very important reason that I was not a clergyman, and did not believe it to be my duty to enter the pulpit. And, had I been a minister, I could not have consistently discharged the duties of the sanctuary, for my Professorship embraced the whole course of *pure* Mathematics together with the *applied*, including Astronomy and Civil Engineering, which in most colleges are divided between two professors, and in our best institutions they are distributed among three, and sometimes four, professors. My Professorship, therefore, claimed my whole energies.

Mr. Mann, however, spoke to me several times during the year, urging me to preach or read book sermons.

I declined, of course, and stated, among other reasons, that I had conscientious scruples against turning the sacred desk into a rostrum for lectures on Physiology, Astronomy and Politics. I thought the great and glorious truths of the Bible should be expounded and enforced on the Sabbath, and that lectures on purely scientific subjects should be delivered during the week.

But on the second Sabbath of the third Collegiate year, Sept. 16th, 1855, after Prof. Doherty had conducted the afternoon service and the audience was leaving the chapel, Mr. Mann intimated to me that it would be *my turn* to preach next Sabbath.

I replied that I had *no turn*, no "part or lot" in the matter, and I thought the Faculty so understood it.

He thought not! Said that Prof. Pennell and Mr. Zachos would not go on this year unless I would take a part; said he had not conversed with them on the subject, but he had good reason to think so!

With the duties and engagements of the other professors, I replied, I have nothing to do. My business is with my own department. Besides, I do not think that Dr. Warriner, who is daily expected from Europe, will take part in the Sabbath services.

Mr. Mann thought he would; said he was very confident, from his acquaintance with him, that he would preach. (Mr. Warriner, however, down to the present time, has not preached, nor even taken part in morning prayers during the week!)

Mr. Mann, now seeing that his logic nor his weak sophistries moved me, endeavored to intimidate me by threats; but his persistent and menacing conversation of more than two hours did not effect his purpose.

What did Mr. Mann mean? His object, doubtless, was twofold.

1st. To cause *his turn* to come round less frequently. (He had expressed this wish more than once in Faculty meetings; said he found it a great task to prepare his lectures for the Sabbath!)

2d. To overload me, and thus injure my influence.

Mr. Mann well knew that I had already assumed more than one man ought to attempt; for I now had the entire charge of the highest (Junior) class in the College, except in essay reading once a week to Prof. Doherty.

The studies of said class were:

1st. Mechanics, Dynamical and Statical.

2d. Calculus, Differential and Integral.

3d. Dramas of Schiller and Gœthe.

4th. Spherical Trigonometry, Navigation and Civil Engineering.

These four recitations, of an hour each, mingled with considerable oral instruction, were my daily duties; in addition to which I also took part in morning chapel exercises and other general duties of the Faculty. The charge of the German dramas was by no means a light task, for they were historical, requiring much research, and were also among the most difficult of the plays of Gœthe and Schiller. Furthermore, I took charge of this recitation in German, to save the College additional expense, (more than $100 per term,) and for which I neither charged nor received a single penny.

Of all these things Mr. Mann was well aware. He knew that I was doing much more than was required of my Professorship, and more than one man should attempt; and yet he wished to force me to preach or lecture as often as himself, and that, too, when he had not had a single recitation since the College opened.

Let us now look upon the other side of the picture.

Mr. Mann was much pleased with Eld. Austin Craig's religious opinions, and had desired, ever since the College opened, to get him into Antioch as an instructor.

After Prof. Holmes left for Europe, and after Dr. Siedorf declined to take his place, Mr. Craig was requested to become his substitute. Mr. C. declined coming that term, but he would think of it.

Mr. Burlingame, therefore, as the last resort, was urged by some of the Faculty (especially by Mr. Mann,) to take Prof. Holmes' classes. He did so at a few hours' notice, and, although a young man, discharged the duties of his new position to the satisfaction of all concerned.

But, after about five months' deliberation and preparation, Mr. Craig consented to take charge of Prof. Holmes' classes, and commenced at the opening of the Fall Term, Sept. 5th, 1855.

In a short time, however, President Mann called on Mr. Burlingame and desired him to take one of Mr. Craig's classes. Told Mr. B. that Mr. Craig was the most like Jesus Christ of any man whom he had ever met! that he was a profound Greek scholar; that he had written a Greek book, which, when published, would prove of great value, &c., but that his health was failing and he could not carry on his three classes in Greek! Mr. Burlingame declined.

Mr. Mann called again, but without obtaining the consent of Mr. B.; and, as the meeting of the Trustees was near at hand, the matter was *hushed* and rested. As soon, however, as said meeting was past and the Trustees had dispersed, Mr. Burlingame was again urged to take one of the Greek classes! Mr. Craig himself called on Mr. B. and stated his case, that he could not perform the amount of study necessary to carry on the three classes, &c.

Accordingly Mr. B., notwithstanding his own duties were onerous, he having charge of the Freshman Class in Higher Algebra, in addition to classes in the Preparatory Department, accommodated Mr. Craig by taking one of the Greek classes.

Now, why was Mr. Mann so much more tender of Mr. Craig than of Prof. Holmes? Was it not on account of Eld. Craig's peculiar religious or theological views? on account of his not laying any particular stress on church organization or church ordinances, and thust differing from all, or nearly all, members of the Christian Church or connection and from other evangelical denominations? If this was not the reason, pray what was it? Will Mr. Mann enlighten the public on this point?

The people have had an interest in Antioch College, and they doubtless now desire to know what Mr. Mann's policy is? Why not draw the curtain aside and let the truth appear? Christian ministers and Christian churches, at least, have an interest in the Institution, and they should know the facts, and to present these is the object of this work.

Previous to the commencement of this same term, the Committee on Instruction engaged a Miss A. J. Chamberlain, (a lady of New York, of considerable and successful experience as a teacher in N. Y. Central College and other schools,) to teach French, German and English studies, Mr. Mann writing the letter informing her of her appointment with his own hand.

Miss Chamberlain entered upon the discharge of her duties at the opening of the year, Sept. 5th, 1855, one of her classes commencing the study of the German language.

On the 11th of October the Board of Trustees convened, and on the 13th they appointed a new "Committee on Instruction" of five members, of which Mr. Mann was chairman as before; and three of the five were citizens of Yellow Springs.

This committee passed a resolution to the effect that no assistant teacher should be appointed without an examination; and this was done, I was informed, on account of the known incapacity or unfitness of some of the lady teachers (Misses Wilmarth and Ballou,) from Massachusetts, brought here by Mr. Mann's influence; and so that no incompetent teachers might be engaged in the future.

Soon after the Trustees had dispersed Miss Chamberlain received a note one evening from Mr. Mann, informing her that the committee desired to see her at his house.

She went over immediately; and what was her surprise when informed by the committee (a bare majority,) that a resolution requiring the examination of all assistant teachers had been passed, and they desired her to go to Cincinnati, O., (a distance of 75 miles,) and be examined in French and German by a competent professor. They had no doubt but that she was abundantly qualified to teach those languages, but it was necessary to go through the formality of an examination! They further told her that it could be kept quiet; she could slip down to Cincinnati on the cars and return without the students and others knowing it!

Of course Miss Chamberlain declined doing any such thing.

At a subsequent meeting of the committee it was proposed that, if Miss C. would not go to Cincinnati, that she be examined by Prof. Allen; and Mr. Mann came to my room and requested me to examine Miss Chamberlain in German, and also in French, if I would.

I then replied to Mr. Mann that I was fully aware of the action of the committee touching Miss Chamberlain, and that I regarded the whole scheme as most extraordinary, that I regarded the endeavor to give the resolution (passed several weeks after Miss Chamberlain had been engaged and had entered upon the discharge of her duties) an *ex post facto* application with abhorrence; that no teacher having the least self-respect could submit to such an indignity, and that I would not examine Miss C., nor take any part in a transaction of such inhumanity!

Mr. Mann seemed astonished at my knowledge of the affair and hardly knew what to say. He, however, still requested and begged that I would examine Miss C., and did not retire until I assured him most positively that no amount of persuasion could induce me to take part in a transaction which I considered wholly uncalled for and unjust. Mr. Mann was, therefore, baffled in this scheme for the time being, but as Mr. Craig would not consent to teach the Greek another term, Mr. Mann set about finding a person to teach both the Greek and Modern languages, and thus force Miss Chamberlain wholly into the department of English studies. He at last succeeded in securing the services of a gentleman, who came at the opening of the Winter Term.

Why, I ask, were Mr. Mann's tender mercies wholly expended on himself, his relatives and *obsequious* friends? Why could he not afford to be impartial? Why must he deceive the other members of the committee in order to get their votes?

"Honesty is the best policy;" at least, in the long run.

Mr. Craig remained in Mr. Mann's family during the winter, preaching in the College Chapel a part of the time, but left in the spring, very well satisfied, no doubt, that the post of Greek instructor in Antioch College was not the post for him.

Towards the latter part of the Winter Term the Junior Class also, which was reciting in German to the new Greek and German teacher, and which had been under my direction in that language during the two previous terms, held a class meeting, and, by a unanimous vote, appointed and instructed a committee to call on me and request that I would take charge of their German recitation for the coming term.

I thanked them for the compliment, inasmuch as their present instructor was a native European and a man of extensive attainments in the whole field of Philology as well as in other departments of knowledge, and told them that my own extensive Department demanded my whole time, and, even if there were no other reason, that I could not think for a moment of taking charge of that recitation so long as there was a regularly appointed teacher for that branch of study.

On Jan. 30th, 1856, there was a convention of the friends of the College in Hope Chapel, N. Y. City, at which bonds to the amount of $85,000 were drawn up and signed by responsible parties.

New England pledged herself for $25,000; the Central States and Canada pledged $30,000; and the Western States $30,000; it being understood that some one or more of the Unitarians would be responsible for $25,000.

On his return, Mr. Mann made a speech before the assembled school, and reported fine success.

He spoke of one denomination (Christian) as founding Antioch College and not paying for it, and of the unparalleled generosity and magnanimity of another denomination (Unitarian) in coming forward and meeting its indebtedness, and that, too, without asking to control it!

But did not Mr. Mann well know that, at that very time, a very strong, if not the dominant influence, at Antioch was *virtually*, if not in name, Unitarian?

The Unitarians had given only about $20,000, and of the bonds amounting to $110,000, they proposed to give only $25,000, while the Christians pledged $85,000, and this $25,000 was, I am informed, pledged by two wealthy Unitarians of New York City, who had large amounts of money invested in land and town lot speculation in and near the village of Yellow Springs, and besides, if the Unitarians did not formally claim a voice in the control at that time, they knew that course to be their best policy; for the Unitarian doctrines are far below par at the West, and hence the desire to keep the Christian flag flying over the College, while the Unitarian leaven is working quietly, yet powerfully, beneath!

Thus things moved on; and those who were laboring and longing for the realization of the wishes and intentions of the founders of the College, were often made to feel that strong Foreign influences were at work against them; yet they endured these things as patiently as possible and said but little about them, hoping that the Trustees would soon see their way clear before them and rectify these abuses of trust and power.

During the Spring term Mr. Burlingame, seeing but little prospect for the speedy triumph of right, resigned his post, to take effect at the close of the College year, July 1st, 1856, when he left not to return.

Miss Chamberlain also resigned and left.

Some eight days later, July 9th, a forced examination, touching Miss Wilmarth, took place before the Faculty.

Mr. Geo. S. Salsbury had now served the College as steward, and Mrs. Salsbury as matron, for the year 1855–6, and they were much rejoiced that the time covered by their contract had expired.

They were intelligent and enterprising, and among the most active, devoted, and influential of our Church members in Central Ohio, and situated as they were, coming into daily contact with students and teachers and citizens, they had a fine opportunity for learning the views and feelings of various persons both in and out of the College.

Believing therefore that a statement from Bro. Salsbury must of right, and justly, have great influence with our brethren throughout the whole country. I requested him to send me his impressions and the facts which he had obtained while connected with the College.

He replied by the following statement:—

LETTER OF GEORGE L. SALSBURY, ESQ.

CARDINGTON, Ohio, July 13th, 1858.

PROF. IRA W. ALLEN,

MY DEAR BROTHER—In your letter to me of the 9th inst., you request me to state my impressions of Antioch College and its affairs, as obtained during my residence there as steward during the years of 1855-6, and also any facts connected with my stay and between myself and the College, as in relation to the College.

I comply most cheerfully with your request, but can only briefly indicate some few of the leading events or occurrences, for were I to write out a history of my experience and observations here it would occupy volumes.

First, then, I will state that during the long vacation at the College in the years 1854-5, I was written to by Eld. Ladley, a member of the committee, and others, strongly urging me to come and take the stewardship of the College, and through their influence, and with the influence of many others of my brethren, I was induced to write out and send a proposition containing the terms upon which I would go, which was, I now think, tendering the services of myself as steward, and of my wife as matron, for $500. I soon received flattering letters, saying that my proposition would no doubt be accepted, and that I had better place myself in readiness to come. Consequently, I wrote to Mr. Gray, my son-in-law, who was keeping a public-house at Ontonagon, on Lake Superior, to come and take my public-house during the year that I should be at the Springs. He left his business there and came to Ohio to do so. But a few days before the school was to commence I received a letter from Eld. Ladley, stating that Mr. Mann had been East, or written East, I will not now say which, and had made an arrangement with a Mr. Knapp, a Unitarian minister, to take that station (the stewardship) unknown to him and those who were making arrangements with me, consequently I would have to abandon the idea of coming. I had made every arrangement to go, besides having got Mr. Gray to leave his business to come and take my hotel, which, in fact, damaged me full $200; but I could not blame Eld. Ladley or others with whom I had acted, for it seemed that Mr. Mann had made the arrangement with Mr. Knapp without their knowledge, and that, too, when Mr. Mann was not a member of the committee. But when I heard that they were to pay him $800 and board him and family, consisting of himself, wife and five children, and school his children, when I had proposed to perform the same services for $500, I thought they had not consulted the interest of the College, at least so far as the finances of the College were concerned. However, it passed by, and some time in the spring of 1855 I was written to again by various persons to come and take the stewardship of the College. I finally went to the Springs, and found that Mr. Knapp had failed to give satisfaction, and that there was a determination on the part of a majority of the committee, having his case under consideration, to have him removed, although he strongly desired to stay, and claimed that Mr. Mann had held out inducements to him that he could retain the place for a term of years, also that Mr. Mann strongly desired to retain him, although there were a large number of persons connected with the Christians and their interest, and the best interests of the College, who wished him removed. They wished me to leave an offer with them to rent the Boarding Hall for the coming year, and that they would lay it before a committee upon that subject, which was to meet in a few days. I did so; left my proposition and returned home. On my way home, and after I returned, I had frequent conversations with friends upon the subject of price that I had offered. They induced me to send a new proposition offering $50 more rent, two of the Committee going so far as to say to me, if I lost money by it, they would get the Executive Committee to remit the rent, and, if I still lost money, they would have the College make it up to me, for they were determined to root out that Unitarian clique that was ruining the Christian cause at the College and eating up and filching away its finances at the tune of thousands of dollars.

The Committee met at the appointed time, and a majority decided in favor of my offer, and in a few days I was notified by letter to go to the Springs to complete the written contract. I went, and after hearing of the violent opposition of Mr. Mann to having my contract accepted, and of his being strongly in favor of retaining Mr. Knapp; and seeing the disordered and distracted state of affairs at the College, and the two parties, the one in favor of Mr. Mann and his herd of relatives and Unitarian friends, who were sponging the College out of some eight or ten thousand dollars per year; the other, the members of which were truly Christians in sentiment and feeling, and who were acting honestly for the best interests of the College; and learning that with the same hall for which I had agreed to pay rent Mr. Knapp had sunk the College in debt some $2,500 or $3,000, and he having Mr. Mann's influence in his favor, and feeling confident from what was then said to me (and as I afterwards found to be true) that his influence would be brought to bear against me, to make my success an up-hill business or entirely doubtful, I then went to two of the committee, King and Crist, and told them that if they would let me off from the contract I would give them $100 and go home. They objected, and said that they would stand between me and Mr. Mann and his influence; that the rules of the College should be lived up to, let that party say or do what they might, and again reassured me that the rent should be remitted if I lost money; and further, that, if I lost, the College would make it up to me; that they wished to get clear of that Unitarian influence from the Institution and have a good Christian atmosphere pervade the place; and, in view of all these things, they could not excuse me on any terms. Supposing them to be true and honorable men I removed my family to the College, and entered upon the discharge of my duties.

I soon found to my cost that my suspicions had not been ill-grounded, and that very little confidence could be placed in some men connected with the College, however lofty their position or loud their professions. Suffice it to say that no part of my written or verbal contracts were lived up to where there was a possibility to avoid them; that in many instances the plain and express rules of the College were violated, and, as I have good reason to believe, to make it an up-hill business for me; and that students were given the privilege by Mr. Mann to board themselves in their rooms, in the Hall, in open violation of the express rules of the College, which had always been forbidden before. They were given the liberty to take rooms there and board elsewhere; to take their supper and breakfast in their rooms and dinners out, where there were young men boarding (I mean young ladies who had always been forbidden before;) and, in short, there was a boarding room in nearly one-half of the rooms which were occupied in the Hall!

When this system first began I called on the young women to know why they were violating the rules of the College. They informed me that they had received permission from Mr. Mann to do so. I then went to Mr. Mann and he most positively denied having given such liberty. They again and again assured me that he did, and that it was talked between Mr. Mann and themselves what they should eat in their rooms. They said if Mr. Mann had made the least objection to it, they should not have done it, and still if he raised an objection they would abandon it. Several of them went the second time to see him, and he again renewed the privilege to them as they told me, (and as I have not the least doubt.) I then had the second interview with Mr. Mann upon the subject; and he again denied to me having given those privileges; (but being convinced from what I knew of the character of many of the students that he had so done, I let the matter drop;) and they were permitted to continue the practice of boarding themselves in their rooms during the last two quarters that I was there; and even in several instances to do their washing in their rooms; and the thing became so general that during the last two quarters there were as many as twenty-five to thirty, most or all the time, engaged in the practice. The result was that very frequently nearly half of the dishes and tumblers belonging to the house would be taken off and frequently found, tumblers, plates, &c., broken and thrown out of the windows, and on several occasions we have hunted up about the rooms as many as forty or fifty articles, and frequently found them thrown about the empty rooms, behind the wood-boxes, &c.

Thus you see that there were really twenty-five or thirty boarding rooms in the same Hall that I was paying rent for, and that, too, while I was compelled to keep up all the expenses of the house; and I think it will not be difficult for any unprejudiced mind to see the difficulties that must necessarily arise where there are so many different interests involved. But yet I was compelled to submit to all this; and why? I answer because I had advanced some four or five hundred dollars in furniture and other things for the College, which, by the terms of my contract, the College was to take at the expiration of the year and allow me for. They were not bound to pay for them until the year was out, and had I left before, I would have been under the necessity of yielding the possession of the property and of looking only to the College for it; and I had learned the College was bankrupt and under mortgage and debts for more than its value. So my only safety was to hold on, till, by the terms of my contract I could compel them to make the payments. Furthermore, when I first arrived there I found that there was no cooking apparatus which would answer to cook for more than twenty-five or thirty persons; and thus it ran on to near the commencement of the school, I frequently calling on the Executive Committee to see to it, and furnish some further necessary cooking arrangements. Finally, two of the Executive Committee agreed with me, that if I would go to Cincinnati and purchase a large steamboat cooking-stove and make the first payment, which was to be one-third of the price, and give my notes payable in three and six months for the balance, when I returned the one-half of the first payment should be refunded to me; and then the College should pay the one-half of the other several notes as they became due; and at the expiration of the year the College should take my part off of my hands and refund me my money. I purchased the stove for one hundred and eighty dollars, I think; paid the one-third down, and gave two notes payable in Bank for the balance, in three and six months; paid the transportation on it to the Springs, and set it up. I soon called on the Committee for the one-half of the advanced money. Excuses and promises were made from time to time, but no money paid before the second payment became due. Then I again called on them to make that payment, which would make their part, as I had paid the first third. They again made promises until the day before the last day of grace. I then expressed my own money and paid the note. I still waited on promises until the third and last note became due. Again they agreed to pay it, but let it run till about the last day of grace, when they told me to let the Bank sue the note and take the stay! I readily told them that my credit was worth something to me, and that that was not my way of doing business. So I expressed my own money again and paid the third and last note. These things necessarily diverted my money from its proper and rightful channel, and compelled me to borrow money at ruinous interests to keep my business along; and still throwing the College further in my debt; thus further compelling me to stay on and try and secure my pay from the College!

Now, this transaction is a fair specimen of about all their dealings with me!

As to my opinion about the influence exerted by Mr. Mann and a majority of the Faculty and teachers of the College in favor of the Christian connection, I am free and frank to say that I believe, from my own observations there, that they have no sympathy in common with the Christian connection; but on the contrary they exercise a baneful influence against the Christians, as a body; and that the College under its present and past administration has been nothing more nor less than an incubus, dragging the denomination down to disgrace, and will so continue as long as the present faction rules it; and further, that it has never been really owned or governed by the Christian denomination, nor ever will be; and further, that the Christians and the scholarship holders have been basely deceived and swindled out of their money; and that their confidence has all been betrayed by a certain set of wire-workers who have become rich out of that which rightfully belonged to the College. I feel, for one, that I have been wronged out of one hundred dollars which I paid for my scholarship, some fifty dollars donation to the College, the services of myself and wife one year, the loss of some two hundred and fifty dollars through the chicanery and manœuverings of those having the control of the College, together with the use of my property here for one year, and the expense of moving to and from the College, bleeding me at the tune of about one thousand dollars. Taking my scholarship and all into the account with what I had to give in to get my pay on what they honestly owed me; and finally taking a note of forty-five dollars to close up with them; and leaving that with one of the Executive Committee to collect and pay some small debts; and he going off with that without settling those debts, a part of which I have since paid: *under all these circumstances I have concluded to graduate.*

Now, let me ask any candid member of the denomination to look at things which exist and have existed there, and answer whose college Antioch is or has been—the Christian Denomination's or Mr. Mann's? He first secured the Presidency there with a salary of two thousand dollars per year and the use of a house, that was made to cost over ten thousand dollars, while he himself did not spend at the College for the first three or four years actually much more than three months per year; but was off attending to his own business, and lecturing at fifty dollars per lecture. Besides this, before he would accept the Presidency he must reserve to himself the privilege of choosing one-third of the Faculty. And who has he chosen as said members? His nephew, Mr. Pennell, at one thousand dollars per year, and Miss Pennell, his niece, who is now Mrs. A. S. Dean, at one thousand per year; and through his (Mr. Mann's) influence Mr. Blake, a relative, was Deputy Treasurer, at a salary of eight hundred dollars, and Miss Wilmarth, who is also a connection, was a teacher at a salary of four hundred dollars per year; and Mr. A. S. Dean, who married Miss Pennell, was agent of the College, receiving as high as fourteen and sixteen per cent. on subscriptions to the College and on scholarships; and who, on coming to the College, was not worth five hundred dollars in the world, but who now boasts of being worth thirty-five or forty thousand dollars! In view of all these things need I ask whose College is Antioch? The answer is No. It does not belong to the Christians, and I fear not to say it never will be theirs. Indeed, I hesitate not to declare that the first fatal step of the Christians was in choosing Horace Mann as its President, let his educational qualifications be what they may; although I think we have many men who will compare with him in that respect. Again, let me ask what has been the course pursued at the College towards those of the teachers and Faculty who were truly of and with the Christians in heart and feeling? Where is Bro. Holmes and wife? Where is Eld. A. L. McKinney? Where Bro. Burlingame and wife? And where is Eld.

Doherty? A purer or better man the sun never shone on, nor a man better qualified for his station. And where, finally, let me ask, is Prof. Allen? and, in short, any and every one having the true interests of the College and of the Christians at heart? Let Elds. Weston and McWhinney, who have became the white-washers and backers of Mr. Mann and his faction, answer these questions; and let them answer, in view of their previous words and declarations upon this subject; not after their bread and butter depended upon their answer; or answer in view of truth and eternal justice. Where are they all? and at whose instance and chicanery have they been removed? and for what good reasons?" When I was there Prof. McKinney was away, and Prof. Holmes was in Europe; and Mrs. Holmes had just been dismissed; and my mind was clearly convinced during my stay in the College, that Mr. Mann had laid his plans to get both yourself and Prof. Doherty out of the institution; and I at the time so expressed my opinion to my confidential friends.

Since I left the College (or graduated) I have been quite still, saying but little; but I must say I have been not a little surprised in reading the "Herald" to see in some letters of some of our professed Ministers of the Gospel the great change that has come over their vision within the last year or two; especially when I take into consideration their previous declarations to me and others, and their written declarations published in the "Herald!" Many things which have appeared in the "Herald," I know from personal knowledge, not to be true. In short, I confess I have lost confidence in many of our Ministers, in whom I once had the fullest confidence.

But I do not mean by any means to include in the above statement such men as Eld. Ladley, Eld. Lynn, Eld. McKinney, and hosts of others, whom I know to be men of honor and integrity, and true to our cause.

But it has been charged by some of that faction that the Christians had given but little towards building the College. Let me refer all such to a circular published some four years since by A. S. Dean, (for whose veracity I do not feel willing to vouch), in which, speaking of the College finances, he says: "The Christians, though a comparatively poor body, have raised among themselves $150,000, already paid into the Treasury. This has been collected under two forms, viz: one hundred thousand dollars towards the Endowment Fund and fifty thousand dollars towards the Building and Apparatus Fund. The Institution still requires, to support its Professors and to complete and pay for its buildings and apparatus, $100,000." Now, take his word as good, that they had actually paid $150,000, some four years since: then add the large amounts they have paid since, to the $150,000 paid before, and then ask Mr. Dean to inform the Christians where this large sum of money has gone, together with the large sums given by the people of Yellow Springs, some $30,000, I believe, to get the College located there, and also the large amounts given by those outside of the Christian denomination. When he can give a satisfactory answer to these questions, and show that all this money has been faithfully and honestly expended for the College, I fear not to pledge my word for the Christians that they will again unloose their purse strings and hand out their hundreds and thousands to redeem the College. But until that is done and they have some assurance that the College is to belong to the Christians when paid for, and that the future monies shall be faithfully expended, Mr. Dean had better provide himself with spending money before he starts out to get further subscriptions.

I have already, perhaps, spun out this letter to too great a length, although I have spoken of only a few of the many things which I desired to say. But I must close for this time, subscribing myself

Your brother in Christ, G. L. SALSBURY.

Still later in the vacation Mr. Mann desired an interview with me. The day and hour were appointed; and at the designated time Mr. Mann called at my study in Antioch Hall.

He commenced the conversation by charging me with "publishing to the world grave charges against him," and wished to know why I had done so? Why I did not first call on him? I replied that he was mistaken, that I had done no such thing; that to the world I had invariably presented the bright side of college affairs, and to that extent which might perhaps be called almost deception, yet I did it with pure motives, hoping that the errors and abuses of trust might soon be stopped and the institution made what it was designed to be; that he had done things and conducted transactions which I deemed to be highly unjust, and that I had written concerning some of them, under the seal of confidence, to two or three persons whose right and duty it was to know what was going on in the College; that this was my right and privilege and I should exercise them, that he was a public man and he must not expect that his acts, especially when highly unjust, would be passed by without at least some private notice.

He wished to know what he had done that was wrong. I replied that of those things he was quite as well aware as myself, and saw no particular good to be obtained by rehearsing them. He wished and urged me to mention some of them.

I then spoke briefly of the injustice done by him to Prof. Holmes, to Mrs. Holmes, to Miss Chamberlain, and to others; most of which acts he endeavored to explain away by such expressions as the following:—"Now, Prof. Allen, if you only knew the facts in the case you would think differently." "If you only knew *all* the facts in the matter I am sure you would exculpate me." But he did not give me such facts! Now if there were mitigating circumstances, if there were facts which, if known, would clear Mr. Mann of suspicion and blame, why did he not present them?

The probability is strong that there were no such facts.

Mr. M. again pressed the question—"Why did you not come and

consult and advise with me about these things, before mentioning them to others?"

Because I did not see what good could be accomplished in talking with you after the deeds were done, especially as you are so set in your own way; and besides I feared you would consider me too officious. I knew that you had been many years in public life and must be fully aware that, as formerly so even now as President of our College, you would be held accountable for your official acts; and that, if you desired my advice on any proposed measure, it was your duty to consult me, I should have been most happy to have aided you in any laudable undertaking.

If my advice would have been so acceptable to you, why did you not ask for it before dismissing Mrs. Holmes? or, at least try and explain the matter to me after it was done, as did Mr. ——, one of the members of the Committee on Instruction?

But he would not have called on you, *had I not requested it*, said Mr. Mann. Ah! I understand it now! The mystery is solved! His calls at my study were a part of your dark plot, the after plot, of the banishment of Mrs. Holmes from Antioch College!

But Mr. Mann, will you please answer one question, viz: "Why is it that all the Professors and Teachers ever sent to Antioch College as the representatives of the Christians have been more or less criticised, and some of them most grossly abused, while the other Professors and Teachers brought here by your influence have been praised and extolled, and their faults and errors sedulously concealed? Why has such marked partiality been shown?

"It is no such thing." "It is all moonshine," said Mr. Mann.

But all the representative Professors and Teachers of the Christians are agreed in this matter. They came from different parts of the United States, were strangers to each other, and had exalted opinions of Antioch and of its President; and yet all have been compelled to change their opinions after living in the College a few months; and what is remarkable is, that they all, without one exception, have *come to the same conclusion! Remarkable?* Not at all; for stern facts, unmistakeable and clear, have driven them to this conclusion against their own inclinations! They all believe that marked partiality has been shown; and that an influence foreign to the wishes and intentions of the founders of the Institution has been largely influential if not *dominant* in the College.

To which Mr. M. replied—"It is not true." "It is all imaginary;" and reiterating again and again *"It is all moonshine,"* he left my room.

On the 1st of Sept., 1856, the Trustees assembled in annual session. Prof. McKinney's leave of absence having expired, he resigned, notwithstanding he was urged to resume his chair in the institution, saying no amount of money could tempt him to re-enter the Institution under existing circumstances. This vacancy was now to be filled. The Trustees took an informal vote; Mr. Burlingame receiving two-thirds of all the votes cast, and Mr. Zachos, who had been acting as Prof. McKinney's substitute for two years, the remaining third.

Speeches were then made by Mr. Mann and others warmly advocating Mr. Zachos and urging his election. Mr. Zachos was himself present at times during the meeting, and gave the Board a specimen of his oratorical powers on some question which came up.

But little was said concerning Mr. Burlingame. The question came to a final vote, by ayes and noes, which resulted as before in giving Mr. Burlingame two-thirds of all the votes cast!

This result struck consternation into that clique which had mainly controlled the College, and which was now struggling desperately to control every department of it, the Finances, the Trustees and the Faculty. Efforts were therefore immediately made to get a reconsideration of the vote electing Mr. Burlingame, but no one who had voted in the affirmative could be induced to make such a motion. For one evening and a day were these exertions kept up. Prof. Pennell was quite active in lobbying; and some students seemed to be thought necessary to influence the minds of the Trustees. Thus hour after hour moved on, the Board keeping up some show of business a part of the time, until the evening of the next day, when this matter was again brought up, and one of those who voted against the election of Mr. Burlingame, moved a reconsideration of the vote! every man who had voted for him remaining firm.

This motion was objected to, as being contrary to parliamentary usage which requires that *a motion to reconsider* shall be made by one who voted with the majority. To this it was replied by Mr. Mann and the President, Hon. A. Harlan, that although this was the general rule, and practiced in this country, yet there had been some cases in England, where persons, voting with the minority, had offered motions to reconsider and hence that it would be allowable in this case, and so decided! The question of reconsideration was therefore before the Board which at the request of some member went into secret session!

Speeches were made on both sides yet the remarks of Mr. B.'s friends were quite brief and made to parry the thrusts of the opposition. Mr. Burlingame needed no eulogy. He was known to be a young man of unbending integrity and an able instructor.

The chief speaker against Mr. Burlingame's election was Horace Mann who threw his whole energy into the contest. His speeches were quite lengthy. He made use of every resource of rhetoric and tried every art at his command, to warp the judgments and melt the feelings of his opponents; and in the effort wrought himself up to that pitch of real or feigned emotion that his handkerchief was put in requisition!

In order that the reader may know of what kind of material Mr. Mann's speeches were made, I will mention two of his principal objections to Mr. B.

1st. He objected to Mr. B'.s ability and experience. Now what are the facts? Mr. B. had been an instructor in different High Schools and Academies in the East; had received $800 per annum; and was at the time he was engaged to come to Antioch, Principal of a flourishing Academy in N. Y. State.

He had served in Antioch two years, teaching chiefly Latin, Greek and Mathematics; had filled Prof. Holmes' chair one term, and aided me also by taking charge of the Freshman Class one session in Mathematics; was besides a graduate of Union College; and yet after all this Mr. Mann represented him as unfit for the Principalship of the Preparatory Department of Antioch College. Who is so *dull* as not to see through such sham pretences!

2d. Mr. Mann said it would be unpleasant to have Mr. Burlingame here on account of his wife! Whereupon Mr. Merrifield arose and moved that the Trustees require President Mann and all the married Professors to obtain divorces immediately ! ! [Laughter.]

Why this grave objection of Mr. Mann? Simply because Mr. B. had recently married Miss A. J. Chamberlain whom Mr. Mann (as the reader has seen on a previous page) had treated with most despicable injustice !

Thus certain fault-finding busy-bodies were never at a loss for some pretext in their opposition to the Professors and Teachers sent to Antioch by the Christians. If they were married men, how very easy to throw out unjust insinuations against their wives, as did Mr. M. against Mrs. Holmes and Mrs. Burlingame. If they were unmarried men, and happened to look a second time at a lady; why! they were making love, &c., or if they attended strictly to their duties and took little or no notice of the ladies; why then, some other beautiful stories must be manufactured out of nothing. It must be stated that they had abused Mr. Mann's hospitality, or had "*positively* falsified the record," or had instigated the removal of a brother Professor from the Institution, &c., &c.! Such myths would be so ingenious and beautiful and plausible!

But to return, Mr. Mann finished his long and *very able* speech at a late hour of the night; the question was called for; the vote taken; and the result declared that every man had remained firm in his convictions of right!

Thus were Mr. Mann's gigantic efforts wasted upon the air! and that tyrannic power which had so long controlled the College was sharply rebuked. Not one vote had been gained! Mr. Mann seemed for the time completely wilted down.

The Board completed its business and adjourned.

Mr. Burlingame, who was residing in Michigan and engaged in business, was immediately notified of his election, but declined to accept it.

The Principalship was therefore still vacant and the duty of filling it now devolved upon the Committee of Instruction of which Mr. Mann was chairman.

The result therefore was that Rev. Alvin Coburn was transferred from the post of Assistant Treasurer to that of Principal of the Preparatory Department.

Mr. Coburn had been brought on from New York during the meeting of the Trustees, by A. S. Dean & Co., for the purpose it is said of running him into the Principalship; but that not proving practicable, he was slipped into the office of Assistant Treasurer at a salary of about $700. He had hardly taken up his quill, therefore, before he was tilted into the Principalship at a salary of $1,000 per year. But the reader may be a little curious to know the qualifications of the new incumbent, as Mr. Mann was so particular in the case of Mr. Burlingame.

Well, Mr. Coburn's history, as told me by himself, is this: He was a schoolmaster for 16 years in the State of Vermont, teaching common and select schools. He then entered the Theological Seminary (Unitarian,) at Meadville, Pa., where he studied with A. S. Dean and others, after which he preached about 8 years in Western New York, and then rode into the great Antioch on the influence of Messrs. A. S. Dean and Horace Mann!

Mr. Coburn had never received a Collegiate education, yet the fact that he was either pledged to go, or would probably go, with Mr. Mann was, no doubt, a sufficient virtue to cover up all deficiencies!

The office of Assistant Treasurer was now vacant, and the duty of filling it rested with the Executive Committee, of which Mr. Dean was a member; yet, notwithstanding his efforts to seat himself in the Treasurer's office, the other members of the committee desired an honest man, and accordingly appointed Eld. J. C. Burghdurf, a gentleman of high respectability and unbending integrity, and that, too, in direct opposition to Mr. Dean's insinuations that Mr. B. was incompetent, &c.

Possibly the members of the committee were influenced in some degree by a fear of the rats in Mr. Dean's house, and a determination not to feed said rats longer with College books!

A word of explanation may here be necessary.

Some three years ago Mr. Blake, brother-in-law of Mrs. A. S. Dean, was Assistant Treasurer, and while in the office he made out with great care and labor an alphabetical list, in a large blank book, heavily bound, of all the Scholarship-holders' names which could be obtained.

After Mr. Blake returned to New York City, Mr. Dean occupied the office, and before long this large book was missing. The matter was inquired into, it is said, when it appeared that Mr. John Kershner, a member of the Executive Committee, had last seen the book in Mr. Dean's house. Mr. Dean was then asked where the book was.

He replied that he did not know; did not know *certainly* what had become of it; but, *probably, "the rats had eaten it up!"*

Since that time, when anything disappears, it is jocosely hinted *"that the rats have eaten it up."*

But seriously. Will not every scholarship holder ask, "Why did A. S. Dean destroy this valuable book, or keep it concealed? Why did he commit it to the flames or other destructive forces, unless it was to aid himself in swindling the College out of hundreds and thousands of dollars?

How much of the funds intended for the College Mr. Dean has kept back and applied to his own uses may, perhaps, never be known; but be that as it may, *it is known* that several paid scholarships have come to light during the last two or three years, of which no mention could be found on the College books!

But how easy to smooth over such little delinquencies! Mr. Dean, of course, forgot to note them down when the money was paid him, and they had not occurred to him since!

But why have not the College officers been more careful of its funds? Why was Mr. Dean allowed to have $40,000 or more of Scholarship notes in his hands for collection, without giving security to the amount of a single dollar?

Was it because he had become by marriage Mr. Mann's nephew?

After Mr. Mann's defeat by so large a majority of the Trustees, he seemed to wear a more subdued, yet determined, countenance. An effort was now made to create suspicions in different sections of the country against myself, by representing that I had planned and carried through the election of Mr. Burlingame; that I was determined to depose Mr. Mann from the Presidency of the College and seat myself in his chair! and by other utterly absurd and false insinuations and statements! Yet of these things I took no notice, believing that persons of good common sense would not be affected by them.

Thus affairs passed on; and, as the year wore away, it became more and more evident by Mr. Mann's sullen and overbearing manner, especially in the Faculty meetings, that he was planning some scheme to be executed, if possible, at the close of the College year.

The Trustees assembled in Annual Meeting on the 26th of June, 1857, and it was

"*Resolved*, On motion of Eli Fay, that a committee of five be appointed to arrange business to come before the Board."

A committee was accordingly appointed, consisting of F. A. Palmer, D. P. Pike, H. W. Bellows, Wm. Mills and John Phillips. The next day, June 27th, the committee reported as follows—viz.:

"That in a general estimate of the debts of Antioch College they are not less at this time than $130,000, of which $40,000 is due to the Scholarship Funds, leaving $90,000 now to be cashed. That upon the supposition of the bonds being all paid in April 1st, 1858, with two years' interest, and the expected contribution from Unitarian friends received, and after the remaining scholarships ($75,000) are collected, (supposed not to be worth more than $30,000,) there would remain, after all debts were paid, only $41,000, which, at 8 per cent., would produce an income for the College of $3,280, just about one fourth of the sum absolutely necessary for the annual support of the Institution.

"That this is the most favorable view of our assets, and that, in all probability, the actual realization of our anticipated resources would be far less than is here supposed; that Antioch College is running in debt at least $50 every day; that in this state of things the committee see no wisdom or justice in struggling longer with our irresistible fate, and recommend that the law should be permitted to take its course by assignment or otherwise, and the debts of the College be liquidated by the sale of its property.

"In making this recommendation the committee do not fail to consider the possible rescue of Antioch. Indeed, they propose this course as a means of arousing the friends of education to come forward and buy the College, and carry it on upon the same educational footing and under the same religious auspices under which it has hitherto been conducted.

"It is plain to the committee that the grand cause of the unsuccess of Antioch is the Scholarship system, the undertaking on the part of an Institution, with a very poor endowment, to educate at rates next to nothing, several hundred youth.

"This is the millstone around the neck of the Institution. Failure is the only means of throwing this millstone off, and the loss falls where it ought to fall, upon those who, for four years, have been enjoying the benefits of the Institution, and who voluntarily undertook whatever risks belonged to an Institution which was an experiment.

"Whatever enemies among the scholarship-holders the failure of the College might occasion, it is believed that a position sweeping away the debts of the College would arouse new friends, who, in time, when a proper system of tuition was established, would place the College upon a broader footing, and under circumstances of greater prosperity than ever.

"We should anticipate a great falling off of students at first; but our faith is, that the four years' experiment has already raised the educational reputation of the Institution to a heighth which will secure it favor in spite of the use of tuition fees, and that a few years will see the number of youth now here back again, and bringing the means of sustaining the Professors, to a great degree, in their pockets.

"Once down on the solid rock, the College in the hands of independent, liberal men, and placed, not on a denominational, but a thoroughly liberal basis, it is believed that those whose past interests has made them personally acquainted with the educational wants of the West, would bestir themselves to get a new fund, which should not be wasted to keep the College alive from day to day; which would not run away, but be permanent and safe.

"The committee believe that a strictly denominational basis is not suitable for Antioch College; that its new friends would desire that the name, the honor, and the essential control of the Institution, purchased, if such should be the case, by the mutual contributions of Christians, Unitarians and others, should be permanently in the hands of the Christian body, as its founders, and the chief among its patrons, pupils and friends. In behalf of the Committee,

"F. A. Palmer, *Chairman.*"

PREAMBLE AND RESOLUTION.

"*Whereas,* The foregoing report of the committee of five, consisting of—

F. A. Palmer, H. W. Bellows,
D. P. Pike, William Mills,
John Phillips,

On the subject of the finances and available resources of the College, and of its liabilities and annual expenses, in the opinion of the Board of Trustees, presents substantially the true condition of Antioch College; and inasmuch as it appears by said report that the College has not the means of paying its present indebtedness; and that the salaries of the Professors and Teachers, together with the interest annually accruing, and necessary expenses, exceed the annual income of the Institution by at least $10,000 or $12,000 annually; and the Institution at the end of each year finds itself at least $10,000 more in debt than at the commencement; and to continue thus to increase the debts of the Institution from year to year would be dangerous to the Trustees, unjust to the creditors, unjust to scholarship holders and donors, unjust to all friends of the Institution and those interested in its welfare; therefore—

Resolved, That the President of the College, Professors, Teachers, officers, employees of the College, now receiving compensation for services, be and they are hereby discharged from further service. *Provided*, this resolution shall not affect their right to receive their salaries, or the possession of rooms which they now occupy, until the 7th day of September next.

Said preamble and resolution were passed unanimously, sixteen members of the Board of Trustees being present at the time, viz: Aaron Harlan, Horace Mann, F. A. Palmer, D. P. Pike, A. Stanton, John Phillips, W. H. Bellows, John Kershner, William Mills, Eli Fay, J. P. Corly, J. C. Burghdurf, A. S. Dean, William R. King, James Maxwell, S. Stafford.

On motion of F. A. Palmer,

Resolved, That A. Harlan and A. Stanton be a committee to obtain legal advice on the best mode of closing up the affairs of the College.

"On the adoption of the foregoing report, D. P. Pike arose and said, 'that by the adoption of the report he considered the New England Bond at an end, and that its obligation ceased, and he could not pledge New England for this or any amount. He would, on his return, make a statement of the Board's action, and use his influence just as if the Board was still in full force, while the new arrangement continued in harmony with the original design of the College;' which statement, by the request of Mr. Pike, was ordered to be entered on the minutes of the Board."

Two days later, June 29th, it was voted to assign all the College property, all voting "Aye" except the President of the Board, Hon. A. Harlan, who recorded his vote "Nay." The assignment was made to F. A. Palmer, of New York City.

The careful reader has noticed that the above report is a remarkable document, and *revolutionary* in character; and being adopted—

1st. It cuts off all the rights and prerogatives of the scholarship holders.

The Committee says: "It is plain to the Committee that the grand cause of the unsuccess of Antioch is the scholarship system." Now, although I have never been an advocate of such a scholarship system as that adopted by the managers of Antioch, yet I cannot agree with the Committee in believing that to be the chief cause of the downfall of the College. There have been other powerful causes which have led to the suspension of the Institution, as will be seen from the preceding and following pages. Indeed, had this system, however defective it is, been well executed and controlled, it would never have given the College any trouble. In truth, this scholarship system has been greatly abused, and from its abuse rather than from its rightful use, has the trouble spoken of partly arisen. The fact is that the troubles at Antioch have arisen from the violation of both the letter and the spirit of the *resolutions* passed at the Marion Convention (1850) and soon after, and from a disregard of the College charter. (See appendix.)

From the "Herald of Gospel Liberty" I clip the following reply of Prof. Holmes to some injudicious and incorrect statements of O. J. Wait. Most of the article bears directly upon the point under consideration:

"ANTIOCH COLLEGE.—O. J. W. says, 'the greatest trouble, the plan excepted, has been in our sectarianism.' In this, 'after closely scanning all parties,' I am prepared to say I think O. J. W. as much mistaken as he was when he thought 'Prof. Holmes missed it' in not accepting the invitation to a seat in the present Faculty.

'The greatest trouble' has been neither in the plan, (if I understand to what he refers by plan,) nor 'in our sectarianism,' but almost solely in the fact that money paid in on scholarships, for the endowment, was paid out for building and other purposes, regardless of Article 14th of the 'Articles of Incorporation of Antioch College,' which reads: '*No part of the funds, which now or hereafter may be raised, by gift, grant, or otherwise, as permanent endowment of this Institution, shall ever be expended, but shall be kept at interest on good bond and security, and the interest thus accruing shall be appropriated to the educational expenses of every student sent to it by the owners of scholarships.*'

"Had the endowment money been sacredly appropriated as it should have been, instead of being paid out as it was, all other mistakes would be regarded as minor points and side issues, and as such, would fail entirely to thwart the original and excellent 'plan.' Be assured there is no plan for the endowment of a literary Institution that possesses so many advantages as the *scholarship plan.* By this plan large endowments may be secured with but slight sacrifice on the part of individuals, while at the same time a general interest is created in the Institution, and its halls filled with students, also, who are thus obtained, and being more generally drawn from the laboring classes, are endowed with better physical constitution, appreciate more the advantages they thus obtain, and make more substantial, efficient men in the end. These are advantages which, in my opinion, find no parallel in any other 'plan' of endowment. Of course the money obtained in this manner is just as good, just as available, as if it had been furnished by the munificence of a millionaire.

"I 'recommend' as earnestly as O. J. W. that 'minor points and side issues' be forgotten; but we must not mistake side issues for main issues, nor main issues for side issues.

"Let us not blame the plan for our disregard of its provisions, nor fancy that the cry of 'our sectarianism' will draw off attention from the blind, reckless, impetuous zeal which has driven our beloved Antioch to the extremity in which we now see her.

"'By-gones' must of course 'be by-gones,' and I pray too, most ardently, for 'the restoration of the property,' *if it may be restored to us*, but 'if worst comes to worst,' I will *not* 'go for what we can get, if it be less than two-thirds,' *nor if it be less than the whole.'*

"THOMAS HOLMES."

2d. This report is a remarkable document also in its religious leanings.

Did the committee suppose that the following statement early in their report, viz.—"They propose this course as a means of arousing the friends of education to come forward and buy the College and carry it on, upon the same educational footing, and under the same religious auspices under which it has hitherto been conducted"—would blind the Christians to the whole concluding portion, in which they recommend to place the College, "not on a denominational," but what they are pleased to call "a thoroughly liberal basis, in the hands of independent liberal men"—("new friends?")—yet these new friends would desire that the *name* be "Christian"—*i. e.*, that our colors be kept flying over the College, so that our numerous churches all through the West may pour into the treasury their thousands and tens of thousands of dollars annually, and send in their sons and daughters by hundreds, while the liberalistic (Theodore Parker) leaven is slowly but surely leavening the whole mass!

Some of our restless, unstable young ministers may snap and, perhaps, swallow such a bait, but they will be mostly graduates of Meadville Theological Seminary. Our cool, clear-headed men—and many such we have—will not be allured into such a snare!

Does not this report make a direct thrust at the spirit, if not the letter, of the Marion Plan? (See Appendix.)

Was it the intention of the delegates to the Marion Convention to go into partnership with Unitarians, Universalists, or any other denomination in building up a College? or was it not rather, to found a FREE CHRISTIAN INSTITUTION to be under their own control and direction. 1st. For the education of their own sons and daughters, and 2d. For the education of all other suitable persons who may seek its halls?

Will not Eld's. John Ross, David Millard, Jasper Hazen, D. F. Ladley, and other members of the Convention, who were especially concerned in drafting a plan for the College, tell us what their intentions were? Did they intend that the College should belong to and be controlled by the Christians? Or was it their wish that it should be a Babel of all the foolish and ranting-isms which might be invented?

Will our able and reliable men speak out on these questions?

But every person only partially acquainted with the history of the Institution will doubtless ask, why this assignment of all the College property? Was this assignment a necessary and laudable transaction, especially when good Bonds to the amount of $110,000 had been executed by responsible parties, and would be due, principal and interest, in about nine months?

Why this haste to place all the College assets in the hands of one man? Was it not the wily scheme of a designing man or clique?

Was it not because Horace Mann feared that the Bonds would be promptly met, and the College controlled by the Christians? Because he could control one man more easily than many individuals?

For my own part, from the very first breath of the proposed assignment, I have not doubted *the design* of the movement. I have never believed that such a transaction was called for or wise; and had not that step been taken, the College would have been freed from debt before this day. To prove this let us look for a few moments at

THE FINANCES OF THE COLLEGE.

STATEMENT OF THE FINANCIAL CONDITION OF ANTIOCH COLLEGE AS SHOWN BY THE BOOKS, NOV. 14th, 1854.

Received - - - - - - - - -	$120,921.28
Of this amonnt there is credited to Board, Rent, Tuition and Incidentals - - - - - - -	$11,458.14
All other sources, including Donations, Loan, Agents' accounts not settled, articles sold, &c., - -	$109,463.14
	$120,921.28
Construction account is charged, including Lumber, Freight, Wages, Contracts, Insurance, &c., &c. -	$90,411.75
Library, Apparatus, &c., - - - - - - - -	5,500.00
Expenses for Salaries, President, Professors and Tutors	7,763.59
Steward's account not settled - - - - - -	8,643.65
All other accounts - - - - - - - - - -	8,168.94
	$120,487.93
Cash on hand, Nov. 14th, - - - - - -	$433.35
	$120,921.28

The Liabilities of the Institution as Notes and Bills payable including Mortgage to Conn. M. L. Insurance Company - - - - - - - - - -	$46,608.26
Balance due Contractors - - - - - - -	$11,000.00
Sundry accounts in Cincinnati, Dayton, Boston, and N. Y. City, - - - - - - - - -	$9,175.00
	$66,783.26

Such was the statement of the book-keeper who was employed to examine carefully all the books and accounts, and it is as accurate doubtless as it could well have been made. The reader will notice that the debt at that time was not quite $70,000.

In April following a circular was sent out to the holders of scholarships who had not paid their notes, from which I extract the following:

"ANTIOCH COLLEGE, YELLOW SPRINGS,
Green Co., O., April 16, 1855

"SIR, At a meeting of the Trustees of Antioch College, held March 7th, 1855, it was ascertained that the current expenses of the Institution far exceed its income. At present, the notes given for scholarships constitute the only permanent endowment of the College.

"These notes bear an interest of only six, or at most seven, per cent., according to the law of the State where they were given.

"Whatever the legal right may be, it is very generally supposed that each scholarship entitles its holder to keep one pupil at the Institution, constantly, free of all charge for tuition. But it is plain that six or seven dollars a year, (the income on a scholarship note,) will defray but a small part of the expense of educating a pupil at the College. But, could the scholarship money be paid in, it might be legally loaned in several of the Western States at ten per cent. interest, and thus the income of the Institution be very much enlarged. * * * *

"It will of course be understood that no holder of a scholarship can, after the said first day of October, next use his scholarship for the education of any pupil at the College, unless the requirement of the subjoined Resolution is complied with.

"*Resolved*, On motion of Rev. Eli Fay, of New York, that all owners of scholarships in Antioch College, who, on the first day of July next, shall be in arrears for interest on their scholarship notes, shall be reqnired to pay the whole of said notes, (both principal and interest,) on the first day of October next; and that all others who owe the College on scholarship notes, shall be required to pay one half of the principal of the same on said first day of October, and the remainder in one year from that time.

Resolved, Unanimously, that the above Resolution be printed in the form of a circular, and a copy sent to each scholarship holder, and this shall be deemed and taken to be sufficient notice of their being called upon to pay such notes.

"The above is the substance of two Resolutions passed by the Board of Trustees of Antioch College, March 7th, 1855.

"WM. R. KING, *Secretary.*
A. S. DEAN, } *Com. on*
J. F. CRIST, } *Printing.*"

This circular created quite a sensation among the drawers of the notes, for large numbers, if not the most, of them had given these notes on the assurances of the agent, that they would never be obliged to pay them, but only the interest annually and perpetually.

A few persons paid their notes in part or in full, but a large majority took no notice of the circular. Early in April also appeared a circular by J. E. Brush which was sent from the offices of our Eastern papers to their readers. The object of this circular was to arouse the people to action, and by the collection of small sums to meet the current expenses of the Institution. From a somewhat lengthy article in the *Messenger* of April 12th I clip the following:—

"ANTIOCH CIRCULAR.

"BRO. CUMMINGS—As a friend of our cherished institution, I thank you for the promptness displayed at your office in getting out the circular. * * * To avoid a burthensome tax on a few, and at the same time enlist the sympathies of a numerous class of friends who are scattered over the entire Union and Canada, we propose to ask from each a DOLLAR for Antioch annually for a few years, or if they please TEN DOLLARS in one payment; the first to constitute them a privilege of credit in one pamphlet to be hereafter issued by the College, or in the latter case to have their names appear in such issues for life. Now it does appear to me that we have friends enough who will feel it a pleasure to say to the world, "I am a friend of Antioch; my name shall be enrolled among those who are to constitute its early benefactors." * * It is said that the College stands on the highest ground, and is the largest building in the State. Surely it ought to, and will *(if the dollars are forthcoming,)* become the *highest* in point of usefulness to the whole country. * * * "J. E. BUSH.

NEW YORK, April 7, 1835."

From an article in the "Herald of Gospel Liberty," I also clip the following extract:—

"BRO. CARTER—You have probably received an 'Antioch Circular' from Camptown. Before getting out a similar one from your office allow me to suggest that you should incorporate in it the following as a leading feature of the movement.

The object of this Circular is to awaken, if possible, an interest sufficiently extensive to secure for the College donations of one dollar each from ten thousand donors, whose names will be collected in alphabetical form for convenient reference, and each donor will receive an acknowledgment of his or her present in a neat pamphlet, with an article on the condition of the College. The question naturally arises, for what purpose is this solicited? We answer, to sustain the Institution and help its revenue, so that its indebtedness may not increase. A few figures will illustrate more clearly.

The current expenses for Teachers, &c., is about - - -		$11,000
The interest (at present) on the debt is about - - - -		6,000
		$17,000
Its revenue from room rent, about - - - - - - -	2,000	
Its revenue from scholarships, - - - - - - - -	5,000	
	——	7,000
		$10,000

"Leaving this amount, $10,000, to be otherwise provided for the *present time.* The agents in the field, and those who are to be put in commission, will constantly pair down this sum; first, by the reduction of the debt; second, by increasing the endowment fund. Then, again, the action of the Trustees of the last meeting will call in scholarships, and instead of 6 per cent. the College will in a year or two realize 8 or 10 per cent. on the capital. Thus for a few years at most a deficiency of some thousands per annum will be experienced. Now, if the people will step in and fill the gap, Antioch need feel no fears on the score of finances. Ten thousand names look large; yet when it is remembered how extensively the Christian denomination has spread itself, it should not be regarded as a mark beyond the reach of the two papers to influence. Just look at it: suppose Bros. Pike and Goff, with their able associates, succeed in moving only 500 ministers or lay members in so many different sections to do something; we would say such a minister or layman must have quite a limited influence in his village, town or city, if he could not find 20 persons willing to subscribe one dollar for the best and most liberal College in the United States. * * * *

"Now if our brethren in all directions will set at work and aid the movement by their personal efforts our people will do a deed for Antioch that will be remembered with gratitude by those who are to succeed in the great work of enlightening the rising generation. J. E. BRUSH.

"NEW YORK, April 9, 1855."

The responses to this call were not very numerous, and but few hundreds of dollars, at most, were obtained. And why? The treatment which Professor Holmes had just before received at the hands of Horace Mann and others tended to chill the feelings of many of the friends of Antioch. Prof. H. was quite widely known among our people and much beloved.

Early in May following, F. A. Palmer published a statement in our papers, entitled "Extract from the Trustees' Report of Antioch College," from which I take the following, viz:—

* * * "From a careful and conscientious survey of the College property, including land, buildings, water works and fixtures, together with the library, apparatus, furniture, &c., the Trustees of the College estimate or appraise its value at one hundred and forty-six thousand dollars. This estimate has also been confirmed by component public officers of the connty in which the College is situated.

The College owes as per statements made and examinations had at this meeting not more than seventy-five thousand dollars, leaving, therefore a balance of assets of not less than seventy-one thousand dollars in real estate and other property. There are also seventy-seven thousand eight hundred and eighty 92-100ths dollars in scholarship notes as an endowment fund." * * * * F. A. PALMER, *Treasurer.*

"NEW YORK, May 4th, 1855."

This statement was accompanied by a communication beginning as follows:—

"MR. EDITOR—Dear Sir:—Believing that the friends of liberal Christianity will be interested in anything concerning Antioch College, I will make the following statement in addition to the above. During the last meeting of the Trustees, held March 7th, they received reports from the College agents laboring in the East and West. Rev. J. T. Lynn and A. L. McKinney, Agents for the West, reported that the subscriptions in Ohio and Indiana amounted to $6,000, with a fair prospect to increase the same, $30,000 during the present year. These brethren are laboring zealously for the welfare of the College in their respective fields."

He then goes on to speak of Mr. A. S. Dean's services as agent; and that the Trustees residing in New York City had "appointed the Rev. Dr. Stebbins to labor in Boston and other Eastern cities as agent for the College," the Rev. John Phillips, "agent for the Christian Churches in New England," and the Rev. John Ellis "agent for the State of New York;" and concludes by saying:

"We have $11,000 subscribed conditionally and a good prospect of its being much increased in this city and Brooklyn, which we hope soon to be able to collect, and with the present appointment of agents and promises of liberal friends, we expect soon to be able to raise the full amount of funds necessary to pay all the indebtedness of the College and also to raise an Endowment Fund by the sale of Scholarships and donations of at least $200,000. * * *

"If we will but unite in this noble work, Antioch will soon become the pride of the Christian Church, useful in truly developing the human mind, and the greatest blessing to the growth of our true and glorious country. Truly Yours, "F. A. PALMER,

"*Treasurer of Antioch College.*"

Eld'.s Phillips and Ellis went on to their appointed fields of labor, but for some reason they did not succeed in raising much money. Dr. Stebbins, so far as we know, did not attempt to fill the Agency assigned to him; but he did make a proposition, the substance of which is expressed in the following extract from a circular put out about this time by the Treasurer of the College:

"Our esteemed friend and brother, Dr. Stebbins, President of the Meadville Theological School, has very kindly and generously pledged himself to pay into the College Treasury, before January 1st, 1856, $25,000, provided the scholarship owners will pay in, or pledge to pay, an equal amount by the 1st of July next. He also suggested the following plan, viz: for each scholarship holder to pay $25, and as much larger sum as he can contribute, to pay off our present indebtedness. This is a very simple and sure way to liquidate our debts, and do, at the same time, a great good. The scholarship owners are the real parties who are immediately benefitted by this movement, as they are the *bona fide* owners of the College property, and are *personally responsible* for all its debts; now, by availing themselves of this very generous offer on the part of Dr. Stebbins, they can secure $50,000 by paying the small amount of $25, and upwards, upon each scholarship. This may be the means of saving our cherished Institution, removing the disgrace it has so long been laboring under, and save it to the Christian denomination—to *liberal christianity*.

"By a valuation made in March last by Mr. Mann, our President, together with the Treasurer and Surveyor of Green county, Ohio, the whole value of our College property was $146,000, scholarship notes about $82,000, making together $228,000, besides nearly $30,000 of pledged subscription, which we are in hopes of having paid in within a few months, while our whole indebtedness, at the last examination had in March, was about $75,000; leaving a suplus above debts of $71,000, which, added to our scholarship notes and subscriptions, will give us a gross surplus of $183,000; and this whole property is owned entirely by the scholarship holders. These statements, we think, are as correct as it is possible to make from the College books.

"Now, the first thing for us to do is to pay off this debt, which hangs as an incubus over all our operations for usefulness, and then to increase our endowment fund, to at least $200,000, which can very easily be done if we all do what we can in responding immediately to this call. * * * * * * * * *

"We hope and trust that whatever feelings of dissatisfaction from different causes may have arisen, will now be laid aside, and that every scholarship owner from Maine to the Mississippi will unite and make a common cause to save Antioch by liquidating its debts; and *consent*, by return mail, to pay the $25 or more, as Dr. Stebbins' proposition is only open until July 1st, 1855, and he will require all the time thereafter, this year, to raise the $25,000, which, if you comply with his proposition, he is pledged to do.

"Friends of liberal unsectarian education in the West, in the name of God in whom we trust, and who has blessed our labors thus far in establishing our noble Antioch, we solemnly entreat you, if you have any desire to spread right principles, any love for the rising millions in the Mississippi Valley, or any interest in the first-born Institution of the Christian denomination, to respond nobly and promptly to this call; God requires a sacrifice to-day as much as in former days, and he loves the cheerful giver. All who are willing to give the $25, or more, (and we trust there are none who will not,) will please sign the annexed circular and return it *immediately* to G. S. Blake, Esq., Assistant Treasurer, at Yellow Springs, Green county, Ohio.

"F. A. Palmer, *Treasurer*."

This circular, and especially the proposition of Dr. Stebbins, created quite a stir, and new efforts were put forth to raise funds to sweep away the debt of the College.

From the "Messenger" of June 28th I clip the following brief extracts:

"I wish our people to remember that we have a splendid College at

Yellow Springs, Ohio, in full operation, that not only gives satisfaction, but does honor to the people called Christians.

* * * "One Methodist member says if it is sold, he will give of his private funds to buy it $50,000. The Catholics have $200,000 ready to buy it when sold, so that if this debt now against us is not paid, we may safely conclude that our beloved Antioch will pass into the hands of the Roman pontiff, and become a powerful agent in establishing the 'man of sin' in the United States.

* * * "This money can be raised in our own ranks, without any brother or friend being burdened in the least; and I mistake the character of our people entirely if they do not respond to this call.

* * * "I want all the friends of education, and lovers of a free and rational christianity, in this State, to think this matter over, solemnly before God, and be ready to do something praiseworthy, when I call at your place Some are able to give one thousand dollars, others five hundred, and a great many can give one hundred each, and still many more can and will, I trust, give fifty dollars each, to relieve us in this distress. And then again, I presume we have more than five hundred good brethren who can and will give twenty-five dollars each rather than to have our College sold. * * *

"One poor minister told me the other day he would give half his salary this year for Antioch; another will give all he gets as marriage fees; a third will give a gold watch-guard worth $30; and so our ministers make offers to aid what they can at this crisis. And will our brethren be less liberal than our poor ministers? I think not.

* * "What I have said about Antioch is no fancy sketch. It is mortgaged, and will be sold unless the money is raised, and it is for you to say whether it shall be ours or go over to the Catholics. I know you will say when I call upon you by your liberal subscription: *Antioch is ours, now and forever.* "J. Ellis.

"Albany, N. Y., June 8, 1855."

In the "Messenger," of July 26th, appeared an article from "Incognito," (alias Eld. Eli Fay,) which ought, in my opinion, never to have been set up in type; and of which I should now take no notice could a true and impartial history of the College Finances and the methods of raising them be given. He commences his most ungenerous and uncalled for article as follows:

"Imprudent Management.—I learn from various sources, but especially from traveling agents, that there is great dissatisfaction among our people in regard to the amount of compensation which the agents of the College receive for their services, and also to the manner in which the money contributed has been expended."

And then goes on at some length to defend the agents. Why is Mr. Fay so very sensitive about the agents? Is it because a part of the large per centage which he was instrumental in according to A. S. Dean went into his own pocket?

The Rev. Mr. Incognito then begins his most cowardly and unjust attack upon the Christians in the following words, viz:

"But how stands the case with the Christians as a body—the legel owners and sensitive controllers of Antioch? How much interest have they in it? How much have they really paid towards it?

"After availing themselves of all the means of information within their reach, the Trustees unanimously agreed at their last meeting that the College in its present condition did not cost more than $120,000. Probably considerably less. Certainly not more. Our present indebtedness is $75,000. Subtract from this sum $15,000 for interest paid on money hired and amount due to teachers, and we have $60,000 left which has been invested in the property. This $60,000 of indebtedness subtracted from the entire amount which the property cost, leaves $60,000 as the sum which has been donated to the College. Of this amount $30,000 were given by the people of Yellow Springs and vicinity, and $18,000 by the Unitarians of New York City—making $48,000. This subtracted from the $60,000 of donations, leaves $12,000 as the sum contributed by the Christians. In addition to this, a number of thousand dollars have been paid to agents. But after making a wide allowance for discrepancies, the entire amount donated to Antioch College by the Christian denomination cannot exceed $25,000."

* * * "Think for one moment how ridiculous is the complaint that our College, costing $120,000 is not paid for with the$ 25,000 which we have contributed. Think what its present condition would have been if the advice of some of our wise ones had been followed and reliance exclusively placed upon our own people. The foundation would not yet have been laid, at all events with the pastrate of liberality it would not have been opened for the reception of students in ten years."

Let us now extract briefly from a circular by A. S. Dean, Mr. Fay's boon-companion, which was published about a year previously:

"ANTIOCH COLLEGE.

"1st. ITS PATRONAGE.—Antioch College is the child of the Christian Denomination, &c."

"2d. ITS ORGANIZATION.—The enterprise was received with hearty enthusiasm by the Christian Denomination. The subscriptions soon warranted the laying of the corner-stone on a beautiful site, at Yellow Springs, Ohio, a central position, about 74 miles North of Cincinnati, celebrated for salubrity, beauty, and fertility. A ch rter was obtained from the State of Ohio, the Hon. Horace Mann, the most distinguished edu ator in the country, called to the Presidency, and a corps of Professors appointed, of whom two are Unitarians, four Christians one a Baptist, and one a Dutch Reformer, a set of College buildings erected, of economical yet attractive character; and the Institution opened with about three hundred pupils in Oct. last, being unable to receive a hundred more applicants, on account of the yet unfinished state of its accommodations.

"3d. ITS FINANCES.–To accomplish this gratifying result, the Christians, though a comparatively poor body, have raised among themselves $150,000, already paid into the Treasury. This has been collected under two forms, viz—$100,000 towards the endowment Fund, and $50,000 towards the building and aparatus fund, &c."

Now who is correct, Eli Fay or A. S. Dean? I should not dare to vouch for Mr. Dean's veracity; yet I fear that he is nearer the truth in this matter than Mr. Fay. Two such intimate friends should be careful that their stories harmonize!

Mr. Incognito continues—"But there is another fact to be chronicled in the history of this enterprise equally interesting to all parties. We have a perfectly reliable promise from the Unitarians of $25,000 more, if we will at once remove all indebtedness from Antioch. This, with the $30,000 given at Yellow Springs and the remainder of the $25,000 pledged by the Unitarians of New York city, will make $80,000 received from abroad to aid in our noble undertaking. Though it must be admitted that such generosity from others was not anticipated, yet it should be stated that our plan from the first was intentionally so formed as to reach the sympathies and purses of the unsectarian and benevolent. In obtaining aid from abroad, we challenge comparison with any similar movement ever made in America. Our satisfaction in that respect is equalled only by the deep chagrin and burning mortification with which we view the unpardonable penuriousness of our people."

Does Mr. Fay intend to say that no part of the $30,000 subscribed by the citizens of Yellow Springs was paid by the Christians? If so; it is not the truth. Members of Christian Churches in and near Yellow Springs gave something towards this fund; although we know that the major part of it ($20,000 or $21,000) was given as a speculation, viz.—to obtain the location of the College, and by Judge William Mills alone, who was at that time a member of the Methodist Church.

Mr. Fay seems to exult "in obtaining (so much) aid from abroad." Is this laudable? Where is that $80,000? Has it been received? We answer that not one dollar of that "perfectly reliable promise from the Unitarians of $25,000 more" has ever we believe been received; and that of the other "$25,000 pledged by the Unitarians of N. Y. City," only about $20,000 have been paid.

Thus we see that most of the $30,000 location fund was given simply as a good monied investment. And what about the $20,000 from the Unitarians? Was this the result of disinterested benevolence? or was it not given because President Mann and some of the Faculty were known to be Unitarians in sentiment?

If the truth were known, we fully believe, that it would appear that the Christians have paid by far the largest share of the money used in building and carrying on Antioch College.

As a body they have not gone abroad for donations, nor solicited foreign aid. Whatever has been received from such sources has either been volunteered, or sought for by such persons as A. S. Dean and Eli Fay who seem to think "a prophet is not without honor save in his own country."

Rev. Mr. Incognito also says: The College has been greatly embarrassed for the last year and a half, and more than once would have been closed if it had had no stronger friends than the Christians. I know full well that the monetary crisis of the past year has made it difficult to raise money. But I know equally well that ten men might be named in the Christian Denomination who could have paid off the indebtedness of Antioch at any time without injury to themselves or to their families."

And without doubt, too, "ten men in the Christian Denomination" might be named, any one of whom might pay the entire indebtedness of the College without injury to himself. But what does this prove, Mr. Fay? Does it not show that our people of means, at least, are not pleased with the administration of College affairs? Does it not indicate that they prefer to pay for and carry on their schools without let or hindrance from other associations, that they choose to manage their own Colleges rather than to engage in partnerships which are the sources of so much trouble? Some of our leading men have more than once told me that the Christians would pay for Antioch College very quickly and endow it, if certain persons would only leave the premises; but that so long as they remained, they feared that nothing could be done, and that the Institution would pass from our hands altogether.

Does not Mr. Fay, therefore, see that we have small cause to congratulate ourselves, even over the small amount received "from abroad;" and that it has proved a much greater curse to us than blessing?

Eli Incognito concludes:—"We have now the last opportunity to retrieve our reputations and save Antioch. Hard times cannot be urged during the ensuing year as a reason for withholding. Every member of the Christian Denomination should know that the fate of Antioch and the question whether it is to continue *their* College will be decided during the next three months(!) * * *

"I have not one word of importunity or entreaty to offer. If our people think they can afford to lose Antioch let them try it, and they will very soon find themselves growing beautifully less, as many of our strong young men will at once be convinced that they are '*in the wrong pew.*' We shall be shunned and scorned by all the noble and benevolent, as the blind, ignorant and heartless things which we shall have proved ourselves to be. What minister of ordinary ability and laudable ambition would *unite* or *remain* with us after such an event? * * *

"As a deeply interested looker-on I will for the present remain,

INCOGNITO."

I have omitted the more objectionable portions of this article, and would have been glad to have omitted the whole could I have done so in justice. Every denomination, doubtless, has several such nervous, fault-finding, hypochondrias; and it should not be thought a wonderful thing that the Christian connection, numbering some 1,200 to 1,500 churches, and about as many ministers, has one such nondescript.

We have used this signature "Incognito" as synonimous with "Eli Fay," and presume he will not question the propriety of the synonym! If so, we shall be under the necessity of referring him among others to A. S. Dean, who some three years since volunteered the assurance that Incognito's article was written by Eli Fay; that it was submitted to him in manuscript by said Fay in New York city for his advice on the question of publication; and that after carefully reading and considering it, he advised Mr. Fay not to publish any portion of it.

Such assurances, however, from A. S. Dean or any other person, were not necessary; for I had not read said article half through before I made up my mind that Eli Fay was the author of it. But this fact was not very generally known, and some of our people still continued to labor for Antioch. In the "Messenger" of Aug. 2d, 1855, an article appeared written by Dr. Stebbens from which we extract briefly—

"BOSTON, MASS., July 25th, 1855.

"*Friends of Antioch College*—I have received letters from agents and others requesting me to give them more time to raise the money which will hold my pledge for the College. I can assure you I have no disposition to take advantage of the shortness of the time to avoid meeting my pledge. Nay, I shall glory rather in being required to fulfill it. But how long must we *wait? Work*, WORK; this must be our cry. Six months delay gives us six thousand dollars more to raise. Think of that, friends of Antioch. It will be an everlasting disgrace to let Antioch go out of our hands. Do you wish to have it remain *ours*, so that we can say our Antioch? Then up, and work, and give freely. We have money enough. * * * *

"*Friends of Antioch*, I will give more time as you desire; but how *much* more will depend upon the returns made at the annual meeting of the Board of Trustees at Yellow Springs the first Monday in September. If I am satisfied, at that time, that the friends of Antioch are doing their duty, at work as they ought to be, I *may possibly* yield *a very little* more. But we *ought to be ashamed* if we do not pay that debt before that day, and all the people will say, '*Amen. Shame! shame!*'

"RUFUS P. STEBBINS."

In the same issue is an excellent article from Bro. J. E. Brush, which contains the following extract from a private letter of Eld. Childs to Bro. Brush:

"Elders J. Weeks and myself have agreed to raise *two thousand dollars* in this Conference provided Mr. Stebbins is taken at his offer. We shall enter the field as soon as we learn that fact, and not stop till the work is done. We hope you will find the man in the East who will come out Stebbins-like and stand in the gap to pledge the balance. The denomination must and will provide the funds, only give them time. (Signed) "J. D. CHILDS."

From Bro. Brush's spirited article we also make the following brief extract:

"I would say to Bro. Childs that Dr. Stebbins has been assured that the Christians will not stop on $25,000; that we mean to keep to work till the endowment fund is made large enough to handsomely sustain the College. I would further say that no fears need be entertained now relative to expenditures, every dollar will be accounted for. The evidences multiply that our people are able and willing to place the Institution on a solid basis; all they want to know is, that their gift is not to be jeopardized. I have great pleasure in assuring all that *the safety of the College is now beyond a question.* To show that this assurance is well grounded, I would say that four gentlemen have advanced twelve thousand dollars as a temporary loan to meet those pressing claims which have of late so much annoyed the operations of the College. I need not add that as prudent, far-seeing men they would not be likely to do this if the property could be taken from us. While we make this statement to relieve the minds of our friends, we hope it will in no wise have a tendency to abate exertion. It should, in fact, increase our ardor to prove to those who have so generously advanced capital that their confidence will not be misplaced. We earnestly appeal to all who feel interest in the matter to follow the example of Messrs. Childs and Weeks. If the entire connection will do as well as they pledge for their conference in proportion to its means, the 1st of January next will see Antioch out of debt. The present is a most favorable moment to do up the work; all we need is men who have a mind and will to act. Let those who would like to leave an honored name to posterity now step forward and help the most free and liberal educational enterprise of the age. * * *

"I trust the above will be a sufficient assurance to Messrs. Childs and Weeks to go ahead. J. E. BRUSH.

"NEW YORK, July 21, 1855."

In the same issue, also, appears the accompanying card:

"BRO. CUMMINGS—*Sir:*—We have just commenced a subscription for Antioch College, and have obtained near $200—six individuals subscribing $25 each—to be paid by the 1st of January next, if enough is raised to secure R. P. Stebbins' pledge. We shall continue our efforts, and hope to get considerable more by the 1st of October. Yours, &c., "IRA ALLEN."

The editor of the "Messenger" says in the same issue:

"On last Sabbath Bro. E. Fay, one of the agents for the College, presented its condition and claims to our people, and informed us that in his judgment the Church and friends of the cause in Camptown ought to pay $500 towards liquidating the debt on Antioch. We are happy to say our friends most cheerfully responded to the call, and in a few minutes pledged the amount desired, and seemed to be glad of the opportunity."

Quite a general interest was again awakened in Antioch, and in the payment of its indebtedness; and thousands of the aged and young, of parents and children, were ready to give aid, awaiting the call of the College Agent. There was quite an enthusiasm among the ladies.

In the "Messenger" of August 16th appeared the following card from Mrs. Ira Allen:

"Bro. Cummings—I feel it my duty to write a few lines to my sisters in the Christian Church in these United States. I do not know but many of them have done much towards paying for Antioch, yet there may be many more who feel small and feeble like myself who have not given their pledge for what they are willing to give. I would say to my beloved sisters, let us make a free-will offering to our God, a sacrifice that will be acceptable. I will give my pledge for $10, to be paid the first of January, on condition that the Christians secure the College. May our prayers go with our donations that the King of Heaven may preside over Antioch, and all who feel an interest in the cause of Christ. Betsey Allen."

"Potsdam, Aug. 8, 1855."

From a spirited communication by Bro. Brush, in the same issue, I clip a few lines:

"'The Work Goes Bravely on.'—*Bro. Cummings:*—I have the pleasure to say that the Stanfordville Church, under the care of Eld. Roberts, has proved itself a worthy associate of the Camptown Society, in responding to the call to save Antioch. Bro. Fay laid before the people last Sabbath the claims of the College, and plainly expressed his opinion as to their duty. The draft was duly honored in the sum of *six hundred and fifty-three dollars*, which you will please enter on the list as the subscription of that Society. Also, *one hundred and twenty-five dollars* more, for the present as 'from a friend.' An eye-witness says it was a pleasure to observe the good feeling produced by this effort."

Such were the people whom Rev. Mr. Incognito had villified and grossly maligned; and, so far as he was able, had held them up to the scorn and derision of the public. The scorn and derision and contempt, however, have chiefly, if not wholly, alighted upon himself, who so richly merits them.

In the "Herald of Gospel Liberty," of August 30th, 1855, appeared an editorial of five columns, by D. P. Pike, commencing as follows:

"ANTIOCH COLLEGE.—I have not refrained from writing upon this subject because I have any less attachment for education or our College enterprise, than I had when I urged the arrangement at the Marion Convention against the assaults of denominational discontents, who have since found a home with other sects, but who have not yet entered the first class of cars in those denominations.

"I there advocated a College *for the Christian denomination;* a College of our own, not to be owned in company with any one; a College entirely under our control, managed for our own interests and purposes. In that Convention Antioch College had its conception. From that Convention we began to talk about OUR College *then to be.* At that Convention Elders John Ross, David Millard, John Phillips and Jasper Hazen and Bro. A. M. Merrifield were appointed a committee to report on a plan for a College. They reported the following, which was adopted, viz:"

Bro. Pike then gives the Marion Plan, the transactions of the Sub-Committees in New York and Ohio, and the College Charter, (see appendix,) and says:

"I regard it important to give this history at this time, that our New England churches may know the just position of Antioch College.

"In the first place, I wish it distinctly known what rules were adopted to govern the Treasurer and Agents."

Here Bro. Pike refers to the resolutions touching this matter, showing how carefully the Sub-Committee guarded the funds "so far as resolutions were concerned," that the Sub-Committee continued in office until the Board of Trustees was chosen, September 4th, 1854, and gives the names of the Trustees.

"When these Trustees were chosen by the owners of scholarships, the work of the sub-committee ceased, and the servants created by the Christian Denomination, were responsible to the denomination for nothing beyond the transfer of the College property into the hands of the Trustees. They were members of a Provisional Committee, and as such, the whole committee through their sub-committee were bound to make a report of their doings from the time they where chosen up to the hour they transferred the property into the hands of the Trustees, the servants of the holders of scholarships.

"The Christian Denomination is not responsible for the acts of the Trustees, but for the acts of the sub-committee up to the time of the transfer. I wish this point distinctly understood. It may be of use some future time.

"The next point worthy of attention is the fact that our servants have not reported. We have no report whatever from our Provisional Committee. They have not told the denomination how much property they received, how much they expended, nor what was the state of the finance when they transferred Antioch College to the Trustees. They have not presented any papers of that transfer nor given the denomination a settlement as public servants generally do. Therefore, what does the denomination know of Antioch College from the reports of their servants? Just nothing; yet 'INCOGNITO' is ready to condemn the slowness of our liberality, and hold up the denomination in a very unpleasant aspect. 'Let justice be done though the heavens fall.'

"Again, where are the reports of the sub-committee's agents, and the treasurer's report contemplated by the resolutions adopted at Marion?

"Did their agents report 'every three months, in tabular form, the name of every donor and subscriber for the College, with the amount that each individual may have donated or subscribed?'

"Did the Treasurer 'cause to be published, in at least one of our periodicals, a faithful account of the returns of our soliciting agents?' If so, who has seen it? I mean only up to the time of the transfer. I will venture to say if those two things had been faithfully done Antioch College would have had 50,000 dollars of which it is now *minus.* I censure no one; but I say that there has been a general complaint for this neglect. Persons who contributed wanted to see their money publicly credited according to these published resolves. Thousands were looking for a full and clear report of our committee at the Convention at Cincinnati; but they were doomed to disappointment, and it cooled their interest. These things are Antioch's misfortunes; and they have very seriously affected the donations of our denomination. The sub-committee also saw fit to remove the Bibical Department. Hundreds were dissatisfied at that arrangement, who had made up their minds to contribute largely in that direction. They were disappointed and discouraged. The sudden death of the New England agent had stirred up their sympathies, but unexpectedly that channel was closed. I think the denomination deserves some consideration from these undeniable facts.

"The College is in debt about $77,000, perhaps less, and one writer says to the public that it is running in debt $12,000 per year, a thousand dollars per month. Another writer tells us that Antioch is to be sold within a short time; and another that when Antioch fails the denomination is done, and of course some one must be prepared to preach the funeral sermon. A thousand Antiochs may be blown to atoms, and still the denominations's funeral may not be necessary. She was born and progressed, to the honor of God's name be it spoken, before Antioch was thought of being necessary. That is not the string to pull if we would raise money and redeem Antioch. Such logic is defective. Men who have the dimes in high latitudes among the snow of the mountains, are not frightened by such inuendoes. We must change such tactics if we would redeem Antioch College.

"But can Antioch College be redeemed and saved? Most certainly. I do not desire such a failure as the sale of our College, by any means. I know the things I have named are serious obstacles; but they can be immediately overcome. Let some good man or men immediately be employed to carry into effect the resolutions of the sub-committee at Marion; take the books and find every dollar donated and by whom;

make out the list and let us see who and how much has been donated. Let us see the cash received in that form. Then let us have item by item of the expenditures up to the time of our committee's transfer, and then you restore confidence.

"Secondly, let it be fairly understood that owners of scholarships own, to all intents and purposes, 'Antioch College;' that after they took the property by their Trustees, the denomination was no longer responsible for the success or failure of Antioch College. If our servants have abused the trust reposed in them and made contracts beyond their instructions, then let us see it. If they have done as we desired and the College is in debt from our direction, then let us wake up as men and relieve our sub-committee or any of our servants by settling the bills as by agreement. It is not best to stigmatize the denomination in this matter until we have seen both sides. It takes two parties to make a bargain. If I am accessory by my vote at Marion for any of our College liabilities, as a member of the denomination, tell me the amount and I will settle the bill if possible. Place the College upon its own merits, and let the denomination have full sea room, and the College will be paid for. Let by-gones be by-gones, only have a fair statement of the affair. Let there be no appearance of any design or underhanded movements; no favoritism; no one-man power anywhere. Let everything be in open daylight, and there will be no trouble about collecting money to save Antioch. * * * * *

"D. P. P."

That the Treasurer and agents of the College did not live fully up to their instructions, and that the sub-committee did not make a full report of its doings and of the doings of its servants to the denomination is without doubt true; yet we are inclined to think that more blame has been heaped upon them than they, or the most of them, deserve. What could the Committee and the Treasurer do? They at first had confidence in their agents. They were brethren together, members of the same household of faith, and believed that each would do his utmost for the establishment and prosperity of the College. When, therefore, the time came round for the reports, and the agents were not ready, and made many and plausible excuses, the Committee and Treasurer exercised patience and waited on them. Their confidence inclined them to the belief that the agents would have their accounts all in order in a few weeks, or months at most; and thus time ran on until it was too late to obtain full and complete statements. It is a very easy thing to say that the committee ought to have dismissed those agents who did not report promptly according to instructions; yet if we go back several years, and place ourselves in the position of the Committee and Treasurer, I think we shall find less cause to find fault than we now imagine. Had they dismissed the agents where could they have found others in time for the work? The buildings were going up rapidly and money must be had; hence they wished to avoid those interruptions necessarily consequent upon a change of officers.

I do not say these things to excuse the Committee or its agents from any just censure; for they all, doubtless, have committed errors, and that A. S. Dean has been guilty of the grossest carelessness, if not dishonesty, is certain. Let them be censured as much as they deserve, but no more.

These delinquencies referred to by Bro. Pike have probably arisen from the fact that this College movement was regarded too much in the light of religious and friendly transaction, rather than a strict and rigid business matter. The agents were looked upon more as friends and brethern than as officers strictly amenable for the prompt discharge of their duties.

The appointing power was therefore lenient towards them and overlooked or winked at their shortcomings; and now we and they look back and see where they missed it.

The friendly and religious feelings and sympathies are truly desirable in such a movement, indeed they are indispensable; but they should never blind and lead the judgment astray. All monied transactions should be conducted in a strict, business-like way; and had the agents been placed under bonds, and held strictly to the resolutions, defining their duties, or, in case of delinquency, been promptly dismissed, much of Antioch's misfortune would have been avoided. That the sub-committee ought to have made a report of all their doings down to the expiration of their office, September 4th, 1854, when the Trustees were elected, we think is evident; and we deeply regret their neglect of this duty.

"Experience is a dear schoolmaster," it is said; and it may now be too late to retrace our steps and rescue the College; yet if our people will hereafter follow the teachings of this "schoolmaster," if they will now and hereafter labor unitedly and earnestly to establish, direct and control free Christian Seminaries and Colleges for the education of their own sons and daughters, and all other suitable applicants, we shall not consider the lesson too dearly purchased.

In the "Messenger" of August 30th, also, appeared an article from E. Fay, from which we take the accompanying lines:

"Bro. Cummings—I am devoting my entire time to the raising of money for Antioch. My success, I think, is the true index of the interest which our people feel in regard to it. It shows plainly that they intend to save the College, and are all ready for decisive action. Let timid and penurious souls put their hands upon their hearts while I make the following report from a few churches. The church in

Camptown has pledged over $600; in Stanfordville, N. Y., $603; in Freehold $500; in New Baltimore and vicinity, $800; in South Westerlo and vicinity, $800.

"I find the people all ready and panting for action. In some places the interest was so great that farmers left their harvest fields, and took me in their carriages and rode with me two or three days, as the case required, to facilitate my labors. * * *

"We hope to have so many efficient agents in the field that every church east of Ohio will be canvassed during the next four months, and if our people will now act in harmony, each do what he can, all will be safe. * * *

"If we could raise a few dollars more than what is needed to pay our debts it could be used to great advantage for chemical, mathematical and philosophical apparatus. Prof. Allen writes me that he is very much in want of additional apparatus to teach Civil Engineering. Let every man make arrangements to respond nobly when the agent calls. E. Fay."

Well, Rev. Eli Incognito, did you find any "unpardonable penuriousness" among these brethren? Did you find any "strong young men" "*in the wrong pew*" in these churches? "What minister of ordinary ability and laudable ambition would" not be pleased to "*unite or remain with*" such noble souls?

We doubt whether any churches of equal ability in any denomination ever showed a more liberal and praiseworthy spirit than these Christians. Will you not, therefore, Mr. Incognito, take back your low, cowardly flings, retract your unjust charges against the Christians, and make the "amende honorable"?

In the same issue of the "Messenger" appeared the accompanying card:

"Eastern Friends of Antioch—I had despaired of Antioch until our Eastern friends took hold of the work. Now there is much to encourage us. The moment Mr. Palmer began to take an active interest, things began to wear a different aspect. I shall ever remember the earnestness with which Bro. Brush has urged on the work of redemption. His has thus far been a great work. Also the "Palladium" has accomplished much. To my brethren East I would say, the College is worthy the efforts you are making—and greater efforts. If you save it, yours will be a greater glory than Ohio's in starting it, and Ohio will not envy you the praise. Yea, the whole denomination will rise up and call you blessed. N. Summerbell."

Eld. Summerbell had just removed from Cincinnati to Yellow Springs, and, like most of our ministers who lived at a distance from the College, thought that the affairs of the Institution were, on the whole, conducted quite impartially and wisely; but a residence of a very few weeks in Yellow Springs convinced him that "it is not all gold that glitters," that Antioch was rotten at heart!

At the very opening of the Fall Term, a few days later, Mr. Mann dismissed Mrs. Holmes, without giving a single reason for the act, and this transaction, coupled with the treatment of Prof. Holmes, created a great stir in some portions of the country where it was known, and without doubt retarded the inflow of money. Why did Mr. Mann do this unjust thing? Did he suppose that he had obtained such a complete control over the Christian Connection that, do what he would, they would submit to his mandates, pour their money into the College Treasury, and munificently endow himself, his family, and his friends?

Why did Mr. Mann disregard the request of Eld. Pike—"Let there be no appearance of any design or underhanded movements, no favoritism, no one-man power anywhere?"

These transactions in the College, and the decision to have no Biblical Department connected with the Institution, injured the feelings of large numbers of our brethren and friends. One of the chief inducements to found a College was to have a good Biblical school attached to it, in which our young men might be instructed in the free, sublime and inspired truths of the Holy Bible without the accompaniments of human devices and creeds. The reader can, therefore, easily perceive how the decision, not to allow any Biblical Department in connection with the College, would dampen the ardor and check the zeal of our people. The result was, that notwithstanding the eloquent and numerous appeals of some of our ministers, the money came slowly, and principally from small sections of the country.

In the "Messenger" of December 13th, 1855, came another stirring article on Antioch from Bro. J. E. Brush, from which our limits will only allow the following quotation:

* * * * "Accounts from New England are encouraging—our brethren there are at work with a will, and I think can be relied upon for the portion promised from them by Bro. Pike—viz., $25,000, and if they could add a few thousand more so much the better. Our State beyond the Eastern Conference *has not done its share*. I am very sure we have many societies that are quite as able to roll up $600 to $800 as the Stanfordville, Freehold, or Westerlo and other churches. How will those brethren and friends feel when they reflect at some future day, 'if we had done our duty as nobly, the College would have been saved?' I hope Bros. Stanton, Marvin, Childs, Weeks, Welton, Allen and other good friends will be unremitting in their efforts to reach every church and obtain all that can be raised. If they do this, New York, New Jersey and Pennsylvania will be good for $30,000. If to this we add the conditional pledge of $25,000 on the part of Dr. Stebbins, which, however, cannot be relied upon except the balance of the debt is made up—then we have $40,000 more to raise, which will not only pay the debts, but restore the $17,000 or $18,000 of scholar-

ships used up in building, and cover all deficiencies for teaching through 1856. The Trustees being made free from embarrassment, can at once place themselves in a position to secure an endowment income that will in a few years sustain the Institution without any help beyond bequests; and until that point is reached, a few energetic agents can go out among the churches each year in advance, and quickly secure contributions enough to provide for the coming year's deficiency, as for instance, during 1856 obtain enough for what will be required for 1857, and so on.

"But how about the $40,000? Will the West come up to the scratch and raise it? Here lies the issue. If Antioch goes down, Ohio will be mainly responsible for the disgrace." * * * *

"J. E. BRUSH."

A week later, and an editorial from Eld. I. C. Goff appears in the "Messenger," which commences with these lines:

"SHALL ANTIOCH BE SAVED?—The buildings, grounds and endowment fund are valued at $250,000. The location is surpassingly beautiful and healthy—the character of the Institution is of the highest order, and its success for the time it has been in operation is without a parallel in the history of literary institutions in any country. The debt against Antioch, including salaries of Professors and all other expenses, up to the 1st of April, 1856, will not exceed $85,000, not including about $18,000 of the endowment fund, which has been used in paying the debts of the Institution. We have enough pledged, including the $25,000 pledged conditionally by Dr. Stebbins, within $30,000 to $40,000, to redeem the Institution and pay the last cent of its indebtedness; but unless the balance is pledged before the 1st of March next, Dr. Stebbins withdraws his proposition, and in all human probability the Institution is lost to us forever."

Bro. Goff then goes on with a stirring appeal to our people, whom he represents as "a denomination of 300,000 *liberal Christians*," and eloquently exhorts them to come up to the rescue, raise the money, and redeem the College; and concludes with these words:

"We write on this subject zealously, because we feel deeply. We have been identified with the ministry of the Christian denomination for thirty years; have 'seen the rise and fall of many in Israel,' and are too much interwoven with our whole denominational fabric to walk coolly out, if Antioch fails, with *'Incognito's'* 'ministers of ordinary abilities and laudable ambition,' or with his 'strong young men, suffering only the mortification of having got into the wrong pew,' to 'seek intercourse with classes who know how to appreciate education.' With us, *the Christian denomination or nothing!* 'Their people is our people, their God is our God—where they die there will we die and there will we be buried.' "G."

Notwithstanding these stirring appeals the money came slowly at this time, no large sums being received except from Eastern New York and New Jersey. But the reader asks why were not more munificent responses made? Let us go back two or three years, and we shall find some of the causes. We shall find that it had been heralded through the country, in newspaper pœans, that large amounts of money had been raised and paid into the College Treasury—nearly $100,000 from Ohio alone! Mr. A. S. Dean said, in a circular, "The Christians, though a comparatively poor body, have raised among themselves $150,000, already paid into the Treasury."

The impression, therefore, became quite general that the College Treasury was overflowing with gold and silver, (not with $100 notes!) and the immediate result of these flaming announcements was, that large numbers of friends who desired to give something concluded to retain their money until it might be needed, or until an agent called. Very soon, however, the tune changed, and in the very same papers it was announced that the College was heavily in debt!

This, of course, caused great surprise, and the question was very naturally asked, "What has become of those oceans of money?"

It soon became known abroad, also, that the principal College agent, A. S. Dean, who was a poor young man in New York, had engaged extensively in trade and speculation in and about the Springs, and that he had purchased thousands of dollars worth of town property, lots and farms!

This, of course, deepened the suspicion, and the friends of the College only drew their purse strings the tighter. Mr. Dean could operate anywhere in the United States, and by virtue of a written contract he possessed, it is said, the sole agency of all New York and New England, and, for a long time, would not allow other agents to operate in those States, although he gave the most of his time to speculation! The result was, that but little money was raised in that territory except in New York City, and by our largest churches, where but little time of the agent was required and large profits secured.

Indeed, it was said that Mr. Dean received 16 per cent. on all moneys which came through his hands! that Eli Fay had been chiefly instrumental in appointing Mr. Dean agent, and giving him a written contract for the Eastern territory and the *sixteen per cent.* What share of the profits Mr. Fay was to have we do not know.

Another thing which displeased many of our people was, that the agent, instead of spending his whole time in visiting our churches and Conferences, and obtaining their money, goes direct to New York City and lays the matter before Dr's. Bellows and Osgood.

These liberal-hearted ministers would very naturally desire to aid a College to the Presidency of which a Unitarian brother had been elevated, and they therefore called on their parishioners to aid in the noble enterprise. The result was that $25,000 were subscribed, and about $20,000 paid in, on which Mr. Dean's per centage was $3,200!

Elated with this success, Mr. Dean went heavily into speculation, and gave but little attention thereafter to the raising of money, except to make an occasional sally into the East to obtain a "big haul" from some of our wealthy churches and friends, or from the Unitarians.

It is claimed that about $50,000 have come through Mr. Dean's hands, on which his fees, at 16 per cent., would amount to $8,000; but a part of this $50,000 consisted of Scholarship-notes, some of which have not been collected to this day, and those which have been collected have, perhaps, been nearly swallowed up by the collection fees Had Mr. Dean retained nothing more than his large per centage there would have been less complaint.

Eld. John Phillips, who obtained nearly $100,000 of Scholarship notes in Ohio, was allowed only 6 per cent., but it required another 6 per cent. to induce persons or agents to go out and collect the said notes; and, as is seen by the preceding articles, only about $18,000 of all the Scholarship-notes had been thus far collected!

The distrust occasioned by these things was also increased by a growing, if not already dominant, Unitarian or foreign influence in the College.

Eld. Pike, speaking of the Marion Convention, said: "I there advocated a College for the *Christian Denomination*—a College of our own—not to be owned in company with any one; a College entirely under our control, managed for our own interests and purposes. In that convention Antioch College had its conception; from that convention we began to talk about OUR College *then to be.*"

These were the feelings of many; no doubt, of the most of our people. They desired a free Christian College for the education of their sons and daughters, a College under their own direction and control. And was not this the right spirit? the part of wisdom? Why rush into partnership with any association or church, so long as we are abundantly able to found and endow colleges of our own? Is it not our imperative duty to provide, at least, for the education of our own sons and daughters?

Add to all these things the unjust treatment which Prof. Holmes, Mrs. Holmes, Miss Chamberlain and others had received, at the hands of Horace Mann & Co., and does the reader wonder that the Christians could not have much heart to pay their money into the College Treasury? The surprise is that they should continue to pay in any amount, unless they could be allowed to control their own College, without "let or hindrance." And this, doubtless, would have been the case, were it not for the fact that "distance lends enchantment to the view." In order to wake up a greater interest, and to increase the inflow of money, some of the Trustees and friends at the East determined to call a convention in New York City, which was done by publishing the following circular in our papers:

"TO THE FRIENDS OF ANTIOCH COLLEGE.

"NEW YORK, Dec. 17th, 1855.

"In consideration of the great importance of sustaining, by paying off the debts of this Institution, the undersigned Trustees, together with a number of friends, have decided to call a General Convention in this city, to be held at Hope Chapel, January 30th, at 11 o'clock A. M., and it is hoped and expected that the friends of Antioch will attend, as this will be a meeting which will decide the future existence of the College.

"This Institution has been established and conducted by the friends of religious liberty; and if it is to continue to bless the rising generation with its holy principles, and stand as a glorious monument to liberal and unsectarian Christianity, let them but decide and come boldly to the rescue.

"The College property is estimated at $146,000. Its debts upon the 1st of October last were $85,000. In addition to this, it was found upon examination that about $18,000 of the Scholarship funds had been expended, thus making the aggregate of indebtedness at that time $103,000. This has been increased, and is continually increasing, by the accumulation of extra interest, cost of law suits, &c. To meet all this, and clear the whole indebtedness from the College, the Trustees, at their last session at Yellow Springs, received conditional assurances from the friends in New England that they would furnish $25,000; from Dr. Stebbins, $25,000; from New York, New Jersey and Pennsylvania, $30,000. These assurances were made upon the condition that the West would furnish $30,000, which sums, amounting to $110,000, would cover every contingency of liability.

"We appeal to every friend of the Institution, in all the sections named, to decide the fate of an enterprise whose object you so highly appreciate and deeply love.

"This Convention will be a combined, powerful and decisive effort to rescue Antioch from its heavily impending dangers, the accomplishment of which would be a cause of joy to every liberal Christian, who now watches with solicitude its embarrassed position.

PETER COOPER, ELI FAY,
M. H. GRINNELL, F. A. PALMER.
D. P. PIKE,

"P. S.—Every agent is expected to be present at this meeting with their reports of subscriptions."

In the same issue of the "Messenger," containing the circular, appeared an editorial from which we extract briefly:

"For nearly a year past, agents and friends have been at work arduously, to secure means by conditional pledges for the discharge of the debt, hoping to raise enough to pay all indebtedness by receiving $25,000 offered on this condition by Dr. Stebbins. Our hopes through the year have been high. In various directions much has been accomplished, and in some, much remains to be done or *all* is lost. Limit is set to the generous offer of Dr. S., and that is the 1st day of March next. Unless the balance is pledged before that time, we *shall not* receive this proffered assistance. If we cannot raise the balance, we certainly could not raise the whole, and all our fond expectations will go to ruin and wither before our eyes."

Bro. Cummings then goes on at length to state the object of the proposed convention and to urge our brethren and friends generally to attend and make up a LARGE CONVENTION.

An article from Bro. Ross, of New York, entitled "The Crisis" also appeared in the "Messenger," and closed in these words:

"Antioch is there. And *there* it will probably remain an efficient 'Sebastopol' to be used for the promotion or destruction of the great principles we labor to inculcate. If it is lost to us, there is not only the loss of the money then expended, which we are illy able to bear, but we shall not be allowed even to spike the guns of that strong fortress, and may expect them turned against ourselves. This is a thought for the whole connexion, but more especially for our brethren in Ohio, and the rich and fertile valleys of the West. How can any of our people stand and look on with indifference in this struggle that our spirited and generous-hearted brethren are now making to promote our holy cause? I envy not—such cold unfeeling hearts. And if the College is lost these will be the cause of it, and stand alone in their glory. Brethren, one and all, to the rescue. Let the contemplated Convention in New York city on the 30th of Jan. inst. be as fully attended as possible. J. Ross."

Charleston 4 Corners, *Jan.* 12, 1856."

Two weeks later, the Editor of the "Messenger" speaking of the action of the Convention, said:

"The people of the West were well represented; among the number were Hon. Horace Mann and Judge Mills, of Yellow Springs, who brought with them a bond acceptable to the Convention for the $30,000, apportioned to the friends of the College, west of the east line of the State of Ohio, towards paying the outstanding debts. Their money was all subscribed but about $8,000, and with good securities these pledges were all endorsed and made safe to the College upon the condition that the Central and Eastern States make up their apportionment.

The Central States, New York, Pennsylvania, New Jersey and the Canadas, were expected to raise a like sum with the West—$30,000—only about half of which was found to be pledged and absolutely reliable. But quite a number of the friends of the Central division relying upon the sympathies and co-operation of the friends of the College, bound themselves in a bond like the Western people, for the whole $30,-000, and directed the continuance of the present Agents, with the addition of as many more as the Committee on Agents should deem proper, to secure by subscription at the earliest possible period, the balance of the $30,000.

"The Convention considered the securities ample, and so far all was safe. New England was ably represented by Elders D. P. Pike, T. Cole and others, and like true friends to the College secured the sum of $25,000, as the Western people did, while only about $10,000 ot the amount was pledged. They did nobly, and, we think, more so than any other section, considering their distance from the College and their numbers. So far we considered Dr. Stebbins' proposition fully met. Only one thing remained to be done to render the College safe, and that was to provide for its contingent expenses for the next five years, which, it was thought, would be about $5,000 annually, unless the means of sustaining it should be increased."

After making arrangements for said contingent expenses, the Convention adjourned.

The bonds could be paid at any time; but matured on the 1st April, 1858, at which time they were to be cashed in full, principal and interest.

Of this amount the Christians of New England pledged -	$25,000
The Christians of the Middle States and the Canadas. -	30,000
The Christians of the West. - - - - - -	30,000
One or more Unitarians of New York City. - - -	25,000

Two weeks later still, Feb. 21st, 1856, the "Messenger" contained the accompanying card, together with the announcement of the names of the newly-appointed agents:

"ANTIOCH.

"The Committee on Agencies for this Institution in the Middle States and Canada are most happy to announce to that portion of the church, and friends of this great enterprise, whose liberality they represent, that *Antioch is safe, beyond a contingency.* The Committee, with others, are now bound in behalf of the friends of this enterprise, in New York, New Jersey, Pennsylvania and Canada West, to pay to the Trustees of the College, within two years from the 1st of April next, the full sum of $30,000, this being their distributive share of $85,000, its aggregate indebtedness, minus the $25,000 otherwise provided. In behalf of the Committee, I. C. Goff."

It was also announced from other sources, that *Antioch College is now safe;* that our churches and friends can now make their donations, and pay up their subscriptions—"without further misgivings or delay."

On March 6th, the Editor of the "Messenger" commences an article in these words:

"THE PROSPECT FOR ANTIOCH.

"We are informed by the Treasurer of Antioch, F. A. Palmer, Esq., of New York, that Dr. Stebbins declines furnishing the $25,000 which he proposed to do conditionally, for the reason that he does not consider his proposition fully met by our people. This information would cause us to feel almost hopelessly sad, were it not for the fact that two of our Unitarian friends, who are abundantly responsible for hundreds of thousands of dollars, have nobly come forward and agreed to give the $25,000 in the place of Dr. Stebbins to save Antioch. We have now everything to encourage us to pour the funds into the Treasury like a flood on the first of April next. The friends referred to reside in New York city—we know them well, and have no fears of their flinching a hair's breadth. Antioch is now safe, and let her scattered pledges be collected as soon as possible."

A few of our churches in Eastern New York and in New Jersey, aided perhaps by Eastern Pennsylvania, had raised some $15,000, with instructions to the agent not to pay it into the College Treasury until it should be certain that the whole debt would be liquidated. The agent, however, being assured that all was right, paid over the money, which was immediately swallowed up in the great vortex! and the debt went on increasing!!

The following circular was issued by the Executive Committee, viz.:

"ANTIOCH COLLEGE, YELLOW SPRINGS, O.

"WHEREAS, the entire indebtedness of Antioch College is $110,000, which amount is guaranteed to be raised in different sections of the country, by responsible individuals pledging certain amounts from certain portions of the same; and as the amount pledged for all that portion of the country West of the East line of the State of Ohio is $30,000, with interest at 7 per cent. on all unpaid after the first day of April, 1856, the remainder being guaranteed by individuals East of said line of Ohio; the Executive Committee of Antioch College would therefore request all the Christian Churches West of said line, (and those East of it, should those interested wish it,) to appoint an efficient person of their number to act as agent for the College, to solicit and collect moneys for the College and forward the same to the Treasurer of the College with all due dispatch.

"*Resolved*, That the agents appointed by churches shall be allowed a reasonable per centage on all moneys collected and paid into the Treasury by them, and that said agents be requested to enter immediately upon the work.

"*Resolved*, That the several churches are requested to forward the name and post office address of the person appointed agent by them, to

Wm. R. King, Secretary of the Board of Trustees, at Yellow Springs, Greene Co., Ohio.

"*Resolved*, That all editors friendly to Antioch College be invited to publish the foregoing preamble and resolutions.

"The foregoing resolutions were adopted unanimously.

"Adjourned till Monday next at 2 o'clock, P. M.

WM. MILLS, *Chair. of Ex. Com.*

"March 29th, 1853. WM. R. KING, *Secretary.*"

The efforts of the Western bond signers to obtain agents to canvass the country were not successful. They solicited and *urged* Eld. N. Summerbell to take an agency; but he believed that Antioch College was proving a curse to the Christians; indeed, that it was *dead* so far as the interests of the denomination were concerned, and would consequently have nothing to do with it. He felt confident that he could raise large amounts of money and fill his own pockets well, even at a low per centage, but he believed that the Christians would ultimately be defrauded or tricked out of their money and the Institution; and hence he declined all solicitations. How soon have his predictions been verified!

But money must be had to meet current expenses; and hence the scholarship notes were parcelled out among several men; A. S. Dean of course receiving the lion's share, some $50,000 worth, and giving no security.

He put out a circular, and that too without submitting it to the other members of the Executive Committee as they testify; which produced a blaze of indignation in different sections of the country.

Those who received it felt insulted and many declared that they would never pay a single dollar to A. S. Dean.

Indeed, the excitement ran so high in some counties of the State, that they threatened to handle Mr. D. in a manner not very mild or genteel, if he should venture into their neighborhood.

From his circular I make the following brief extracts:

"YELLOW SPRINGS, Greene Co., O., July 1856.

"DEAR SIR: The Trustees of Antioch College, at a meeting in March last, unanimously resolved, in view of a *former* resolution, and the pressing wants and financial embarrassments of the College, that 'the scholarship notes be collected immediately, and that an agent be empowered to collect each scholarship note due, and unpaid, in the most expeditious manner possible, not prolonging the time,' &c.

"Accordingly your note has been left with me for immediate collection. You are hereby duly notified that we look to you for its prompt payment. * * * You were notified by a circular a year ago that your note must be paid. * * *

"The amount of $85,000 in good bonds, drawing 7 per cent. interest, is secured to the Scholarship Fund and placed in the hands of the Treasurer; hence the College has a right to use the avails of these notes to pay off its debts to that amount. Therefore do not say the money cannot be used if paid, and excuse yourself in this way!

"Do not flatter yourself that the note can not be collected on account of any verbal promise of the agent. Your written contract, the note, supersedes all others previously made. Here it is: 'On the first day of October, A. D. 1853, for value received, we, or either of us, promise to pay to the Treasurer of Antioch College, or order, one hundred dollars, with six per cent. interest, payable in advance, for a term of years, *discretionary* with the Trustees of said College.' Hence there is no alternative left you but to pay the note; for pay it you must, whether the College remains in the hands of its present owners, or is sold to Catholics. * * *

"No students hereafter will be admitted into the Institution, on any scholarship, of which any part remains unpaid, after the commencement of the next term, Sept. 10th, 1856. * * *

"Address Treasurer of Antioch College, Yellow Springs, Greene Co., Ohio. As soon as the amount is received, your note will be sent by return of mail. A. S. DEAN."

Notwithstanding the great offence given by this circular, some of the collectors of the notes were quite successful; and at the meeting of the Board of Trustees about a year later, June 26th, 1857, it was found that about $45,000 of the scholarship notes had been collected and paid out on the liabilities of the Institution. At this meeting the Trustees also found that the entire "debts of Antioch College are not less, at this time, than $130,000, of which $40,000 is due to the Scholarship Funds," and that the College is running in debt about $10,000 or $12,000 each year!

Will the reader now pause a moment and compare these figures with the balance sheet of Nov. 14th, 1854?

At that time the liabilities of the College were about - - -	$67,000
About two years and one half later, when the assignment was made, they were said to be, including the $40,000 of Scholarship Funds paid out on debts - -	130,000
Increase of debt, therefore, in about two and a half years, was - - - - - - - - - - -	$63,000
But, during this time, there was received, on the bonds of the Central and Western States, &c., about - -	$20,000
Real increase of debt, therefore - - - - - -	$83,000

Which would be at the rate of about $33,000 per annum! instead of $12,000, the highest amount allowed by the Trustees.

For the result will be the same, if we suppose the $20,000 received on bonds, &c., to have been used in reducing the liabilities from $67,000 down to $47,000, which, taken from $130,000, leaves $83,000 as before.

The proper increase of the debt for two and a half years, at $12,000 per annum, gives - - - -	$30,000
By this estimate there are unaccounted for - - -	$53,000

But Messrs. Mann and Dean may say that the entire $40,000 of scholarship notes was not received since Nov., 1854.

In the autumn of 1855, it was only claimed that about $18,000 of the Scholarship Fund had been collected; and doubtless a part of this had been received during the year, or since Nov., 1854; but we will be generous with Mr. Dean, and allow that the whole $18,000 was received previous to Nov. 14th, 1854.

The liabilities of the College, at that date, were then $67,000, plus $18,000, or - - - - - - - -	$85,000,
June 26th, 1857, the liabilities were - - - - -	$130,000
Increase in two and a half years - - - - - -	$45,000
Received on Bonds, &c., - - - - - - -	20,000
Real increase in two and a half years - - - -	$65,000
Allowable increase, at $12,000 per annum - - - -	30,000
By this estimate there are unaccounted for - - -	$35,000

Will Mr. A. S. Dean, who has handled so much of the scholarship money, come forward and tell the holders of Scholarships what has become of this large amount of money? this $35,000, or of the $53,000 obtained by the first estimate?

The reader will also notice, by the balance sheet of 1854, that $5,500 were appropriated for library and instruments. This money was handed to Mr. Mann, who doubtless passed over a large share of it to Mr. Dean for the purchase of books; but can either, or both, of these financiers, account for every dollar of that money, and *produce vouchers therefor?* The people, and especially the scholarship holders, would be glad to see such a statement.

Perhaps the most of this money was properly expended; yet, being present when the matter was talked over before the Trustees, and the report made, my mind was not fully satisfied. One reason why an accurate report could not be made was, said Mr. Mann, or A. S. Dean, that a large box of books was knocked open after its arrival at the College, the books scattered, and the bill or invoice lost!

But, we would ask, could not a duplicate bill have been obtained of the publishers or dealers who put up the books? We fear there were other things in the way of a clear and accurate report.

Of course the report was drawn up in as favorable a form as possible, and recorded on the records of the Trustees as follows:

"March 18th, 1856.—The committee appointed to inquire into the expenditure of the library and apparatus money placed in the hands of Mr. Mann, report that Mr. Mann has exhibited to them vouchers for nearly all the money deposited with him; that some orders for books are now out, the amount of which cannot be estimated, and they have not time at present to investigate the case more fully.

"They ask, therefore, to be discharged from the further investigation of the subject.

"Committee, { JACOB REASOR, JOHN KERSHNER, S. STAFFORD."

Report adopted.

Is it honorable for any man, and especially for the President of a College, in whose hands money has been placed for a specific purpose, to defer making a report of its expenditure for years, and until a committee is appointed to inquire into the matter? Is it praiseworthy for the President of a College to keep such a loose account of moneys entrusted to him for the benefit of the Institution, that an Investigating Committee cannot find time "to investigate the case more fully?" Is it complimentary to the President of a College to have a "committee appointed to inquire into the library and apparatus money placed in his hands, beg to be discharged from the further investigation of the subject?" I do not wonder that the committee prayed to be discharged from such an unpleasant and fruitless task!

Does Mr. Mann imagine that he has acquired such an ascendancy over the Christian Connection and churches that they will pour their treasures into his hands and ask no questions?

Of course this imperfect report was accepted and adopted! The Trustees swallowed the pill with wonderful composure! And why not, after so many larger ones had been forced down their throats?

Several of the Trustees must, however, be excepted, for they were very indignant that some members of the Board should rush through important measures, as the appointment of Dr. Warriner, &c., &c., at small special or side-meetings of the Board!

But why talk about $5,500, when so much larger sums have been tossed about like playthings? Is it not decidedly vulgar, in these "Young America" times, to observe the good old maxim, "Take care of the pennies and the dollars will take care of themselves?"

But to return to the main subject; why was the assignment made?

The bonds amounting to $110,000, had not yet matured; but the intervening 10 months, to April 1st, 1858, would soon pass. The signers were responsible and honorable men. D. P. Pike and A. M. Merrifield, representatives of the New England bond signers were on the ground with several thousand dollars, and with positive assurances that New England would pay the entire $25,000, with interest, for two years, on or before the maturity of the bonds, and they further stated that, if the other bondsigners would pay off their bonds in full immediately, they themselves would borrow money and do the same.

The representatives of the signers of the Central Bond ($30,000,) on which about $15,000 had already been paid, said that they would pay the balance with interest; and the West was far more able to pay its bond ($30,000) than either of the other sections.

Indeed, when the bonds were executed, it was said, speaking of the Western States, "their money was all subscribed but about $8,000, and with good securities these pledges were all endorsed and made safe to the College upon the condition that the Central and Eastern States make up their apportionment."

Why, therefore, did the Western bondsigners now repudiate their bonds, and thus release the Central and Eastern States, and make the payment of the College debt an open question again?

Had not the assignment been made, the whole $110,000 of bonds, with more than $10,000 of interest, would have been paid on the 1st of April, 1858, and the whole debt swept away—that is, if the Unitarians of N. Y. City had paid their $25,000. But suppose they would not have paid this, the remaining bonds from the Christians were $85,000, and counting the interest, more than $90,000, enough to have cancelled all the debts save a part of the money ($40,000) borrowed of the Scholarship Fund? Why then, I ask again, was the assignment made, and the validity of all these bonds destroyed?

Was Mr. Mann afraid that the Christians would pay these bonds and control the College? Was he still smarting under the rebuke received from the Trustees a year previous in the election of Mr. Burlingame, and determined to avenge it? Or was it to carry out one of his hobbies, to try the new and wonderful experiment of turning a great Denominational College into a "Union School?"

From the report laid before the Trustees on the 26th June, 1857, written by Dr. Bellows, and recommending the assignment of the College property, especially when taken in connection with remarks made by Mr. Mann in Faculty meetings; it is evident, we think, that Mr. Mann's intention was to take Antioch College from *its denominational basis*, and place it upon *"a thoroughly liberal basis,"* in the hands of "*new friends,*" so that himself, his relatives, and particular favorites might have full control of the Institution.

In order to execute this great scheme it seemed necessary—

1st, To assign all the College property.

2d, To cut off all the rights and immunities of the scholarship holders, except the right to pay their notes!

3d, To form a "Joint Stock Company," (of which wealthy Unitarians and others might be controlling members,) to purchase the whole College property of the assignee.

4th, To repudiate the $40,000 borrowed of the Endowment Fund and paid out on debts.

5th, To collect in the outstanding or unpaid scholarship notes ($75,000,) and use the money for the benefit of the "Joint Stock Company," by paying old debts or forming a new endowment for said Company.

6th, To exclude from the Board of Instruction, Profs. Doherty, Holmes, Allen, and all other true representatives of the Christians by—

7th, Keeping up a temporary school during the suspension of the College, the Professors and Teachers in which should be mainly relatives and peculiar friends of Mr. Mann and Mrs. Dean, with a light sprinkling of obsequious and non-Denominational Christians to take off the curse; and, after the purchase and re-establishment of the College, by the "Joint Stock Company"—

8th, To slide the temporary Faculty, with perhaps some slight modifications, into Antioch as a permanent Board of Instruction.

9th, To pretend to the Christian Denomination that most of the Teachers are members of their church, and hence the school is theirs, while they whisper to the Unitarians that Unitarianism is really after all controlling the whole concern.

How far Mr. Mann has been able to execute his plans may be seen from the following pages.

As I have said above, the vote to assign was taken on the 29th June, and on the following day there was a meeting of the scholarship holders. Several of the Trustees came in, one of whom was called to the chair, and others reported what they had done—viz. assigned the property, discharged the Faculty and Teachers, &c.

Dr. Bellows also made a speech, in which he stated that the Unitarians did not want Antioch; that they were not such fools as to desire to purchase the college and bring it under their control, for what could they do with it? They have but few churches in the West and but few children to send to College; but they have money; and if the Christians will take hold, pay for and patronize the institution, the Unitarians will endow or aid in endowing it. But if the Christians desert Antioch, depend upon it the Unitarians will do the same.

This was a sensible speech. We have used the name "Unitarian" several times in the preceding pages, but with no feeling of disrespect. We believe the Unitarians, as a body, to be honorable men, and do not believe that they have laid plans or would countenance schemes to wrest Antioch from the hands of the Christians; yet it is quite evident that some persons, *professedly* members of the Christian Church, are very desirous that the Unitarians should have a large, if not a controlling influence in the College, and are laboring for that end! Besides, it is very natural for the Unitarians to desire the Christians to go on with Antioch and patronize it largely with money and pupils, and allow them to come in and aid in its finances, being satisfied with several Unitarian Professors and Teachers in the Board of Instruction, although they are nominally members of the Christian Church. By thus sailing under our flag they can the more surely Unitarianize our sons and daughters, and build up their cause in the West. Of course they would not touch the College, if the Christians desert it! They have no desire for empty brick walls!

Mr. Mann followed in a forcible speech, by which he endeavored to convince the scholarship holders that he was *really* a member of the Christian Church! A certain minister whom Mr. Mann had under his wing, then arose and made a sentimental speech and offered the following resolution—

"*Resolved*, That the thanks of this meeting be and they are hereby tendered to the Unitarians and all other liberal minded Christians and friends who have heretofore aided us in our efforts to establish and maintain Antioch College, by their sympathies and money; and we hereby return to them our Christian sympathies, and invite their alliance upon terms of perfect equality in the enterprise of building up and maintaining a College upon the great and liberal principles of Antioch College." Passed without a dissenting vote!

The formality of electing a new Board of Trustees was then attended to. From the old Board some were dropped (being too Denominational, or too Evangelical!) but most were retained. Adjourned.

Thus one act in Mr. Mann's drama had, no doubt, been played to his satisfaction.

The Trustees, now retired to their room to look into the great future! It was proposed that a school be kept up during the suspension of the College to prevent the students scattering to other institutions. After a discussion of this matter, it was decided, it is said, that the Trustees could not carry on a school in their corporate capacity. Some of the

Trustees in their individual capacity, therefore, and visiting friends, started a subscription, to be binding when $6,000 were pledged, for the purpose of carrying on a school during the ensuing year. Dr. Bellows, of New York City, put down $500; Dr. Gannett, of Boston, $500; Judge Mills, $500, and others smaller sums to the amount of $3,000. They then selected Mr. Mann as the head of this temporary school, and appointed a Committee of Arrangements consisting of Dr. Bellows, Hon. A. Harlan and Eli Fay, to rent the buildings of the assignee, appoint Teachers, and attend to all other business necessary to the success of said school.

On the next day, July 1st, the commencement exercises took place, consisting of orations from the gentlemen and essays from the ladies of the Graduating Class, the conferring of degrees, the Baccalaureate address, &c. In the midst of these exercises, Dr. Bellows stepped forward and announced to the large assembly that the school would go on next year, essentially under the same auspices as heretofore. After the public exercises of the day had closed, the Faculty, Graduating Class and invited guests sat down to the Commencement dinner which was followed by a dessert of witty and interesting speeches for some two hours.

The Graduating Class of fifteen persons, for high scholarship and thorough discipline, would have done honor to the oldest Colleges of the land. Antioch College had done much for the intellectual growth and strength of its pupils, but had failed to advance their spiritual interests to that degree which had been so devoutly desired by the friends of the Institution.

Thus closed the fourth, and it is feared the *last* year of Antioch College under the patronage and direction of the Christians. I say "*direction* of the Christians," for they were the founders of the Institution, and doubtless morally, if not legally responsible for its acts, although there were foreign influences within and around its walls which stoutly opposed, and to a great extent, frustrated their intentions and blasted their hopes.

Many were the persons who returned to their homes with hearts saddened by the recent transactions, (the assignment of the College property, &c.,) and with dark forebodings of the future. Some of the Trustees, and, perhaps most of them, were opposed to these measures, yet felt compelled, by the force of existing circumstances, to vote for them ; for, said they, if Mr. Mann is determined "*to rule or ruin,*" the sooner the crisis comes the better; then the Christians will see more clearly where they stand and where Mr. Mann stands, and can shape their future course accordingly.

A few days later I met Mr. Harlan, President of the Board, in Antioch Hall, and remarked to him that I intended soon to leave for the East; that numerous friends would inquire concerning the future of the Institution as well as the past, and that it would give me pleasure to be able to answer them as definitely as possible.

Mr. H. then said he would like to talk with me a while, and we walked up to my study. He remarked that the Committee of Arrangement had taken no action on appointments, except in one case, and then at the urgent request of the individual; that he had not consulted the other members of the committee, but he was ready to state frankly that he desired me to remain as a Professor for the ensuing year; that he had not heard the slightest intimation against me from any quarter, and should be very sorry to have me think of not returning.

He then spoke of Prof. Doherty; said that some of the students did not like his method of teaching, and had signed a petition against him, although they spoke of him in very high terms as a man and a Christian, and he could not therefore vote for him.

On the right of students to petition against officers of the College, and the duties of Trustees in such cases, we then had quite a discussion; when Mr. Harlan passed to a consideration of various other matters touching the College, and hoped that affairs could be so managed as to please both the Christians and the Unitarians. After a conversation of some two hours, Mr. H. arose to leave, saying, it is highly proper that you should know the mind of the committee touching yourself; I will therefore see Mr. Fay immediately and let you know. It will not be necessary to await a reply from Dr. Bellows.

I added that I had no desire to hurry the committee; that I had never asked for a position in Antioch College, and did not *now* at all request an appointment in the proposed school for the coming year; that my simple object in speaking to him was, to be able to answer the inquiries of Eastern friends as definitively as possible. He left, saying he would see Mr. Fay immediately.

Some ten days later, passing through Antioch Hall, I met Mr. Harlan, who was taking an invoice of the College property for the assignee, and remarked that he would like to speak with me a few moments. He apologized for the delay, and said that during the last few days he had had several interviews with Mr. Mann, and had learned of an objection to my appointment. Mr. Mann finds no fault at all with your ability and qualifications for your Professorship, but thinks that you purposely oppose some of his wishes.

If he means by this, was my reply, that I have sometimes differed from him as to the best method of doing business, and the justice of certain transactions, and have occasionally voted differently from him. I acknowledge it; but I supposed a man had a right, in this Republican government, to an expression of his own honest convictions and to his own vote.

O, yes—yes—certainly. Mr. Mann does not stand on so narrow ground as that; but he thinks you take delight in causing him trouble and contesting his plans.

If Mr. Mann has *really* any such belief; if he has so deceived himself, or been deceived by others, I am sorry. I have never harbored any such feeling towards him. In our business transactions I have expressed my honest convictions of right; and, in casting my vote, I have always had in view the prosperity of the College and the best interests of its founders.

Mr. Mann intimates, added Mr. Harlan, that he will resign if you are appointed; and as he was chosen by the same power (the subscribers of the $6,000,) which appointed us a "Committee of Arrangements," we have no power to remove him, and must engage those instructors whom he nominates or approves. We do not know, therefore, how the matter will turn, and as there seems to be some objection, it may be best to consult Dr. Bellows. He further added, that he knew no objection to my appointment, other than the one above stated from Mr. Mann.

Mr. Fay was, at this time, carrying around in his pocket the petition against Prof. Doherty, and endeavoring to create a prejudice against him. He was also endeavoring to poison the minds of persons against me by the most malicious insinuations. For instance, one of the mildest was the following: Prof. Allen, probably, never belonged to the Christian Church until he joined at Springfield last spring! Now, Mr. Fay knew better. He knew that he was practicing downright deception, or ought to have known it. The first letter which he ever wrote me, while yet a stranger, we never having met, begins and ends as follows:

"Honeoye Falls, Aug. 2d, 1852.

"Mr. Allen—*Dear Sir:* I write officially to inquire if you would accept a Professorship in Antioch College; and, if so, which Chair would you prefer. * * * * * * Please inform me at your earliest convenience, &c.

"We meet for the election of the Faculty on the 15th of September next. We intend to have the Hon. Horace Mann for President, if we can get him. Very respectfully yours, E. Fay."

"I. W. Allen, A. B."

"P. S.—Direct to Honeoye Falls, Monroe Co. N. Y.

"Permit me also to inquire if you are a professor of religion; and, if so, of what church you are a member. The committee are very anxious that the Faculty be composed of truly pious and devoted men. E. F."

Now, it so happens that I have registers of the dates, &c., of all letters received, and all letters written by myself, for the last twelve years, and it stands Mr. Fay in hand to be careful what he says on Antioch matters.

In the copy of my reply, dated Potsdam, Aug. 10th, 1852, to the above letter of Mr. Fay, I find answers to his questions; and, touching my church relations, I said briefly, but explicitly, "I made a public profession of religion in 1841, and am a member of the Christian Church of Potsdam, N. Y." Of this church my father, Ira Allen, has been pastor some 30 to 40 years.

On the 4th of November next ensuing, Mr. Fay met us at our first Faculty meeting, at Mr. Mann's residence, West Newton, Mass.; and, during our recesses from Faculty business, several occasions offered on which I conversed freely with Mr. Fay, touching my church relations and preferences, and various other matters.

In the spring of 1853 also, before I sailed for Europe, we had several interviews in New York City, in which our acquaintance was extended. Mr. Fay, therefore, had both my verbal assurances and my written statement on this point; and what reason had he for throwing out his insinuation, in 1857, that I had been a member of the Christian Church for only a few weeks? Did Mr. Fay doubt my word? or did he question the character of the Christian Church of Potsdam, N. Y.? This church, it is true, has not adopted Mr. Fay's "constitution," nor any other creed except the Bible; yet it has been, and perhaps is, the leading church in the Northern N. Y. Christian Conference, and is one of the oldest of our churches in the Empire State.

But here is a card which shows what Mr. Fay believed touching this matter in September, 1852:

"CERTIFICATE OF ELD. D. F. LADLEY.

"*To All Concerned:*—We would state that about the time we elected the Faculty of Antioch College, the name of I. W. Allen was mentioned among a number of others as a man suitable every way for a Professorship; but being a stranger to some of us in the West, and as we were bound to have a majority who were members of the Church, the question was asked, 'Is Mr. I. W. Allen a regular member of the Christian Church?' It was answered in the affirmative by several.

"Eld. E. Fay said (in substance) that Mr. Allen was the son of Eld. Ira Allen, a venerable and reputable minister in the Christian Connection; and that he was brought up in a Christian family, and under Christian influence, and was a member of the Church.

"So said Mr. Merrifield and others; and the whole conversation concerning Mr. I. W. Allen was such as to warrant the conclusion that he was not only a member of the Christian Church, but that he was a scholar, a gentleman, and a Christian of the right type, and a graduate of Hamilton College, New York.

"June, 1858." D. F. LADLEY."

Soon after the conversation with Mr. Harlan above alluded to, I left for the East, knowing nothing further of the intentions of the Committee until the following editorial, by Eld. James Maple, appeared in the "Gospel Herald" of August 13th. It is a strong, pointed article, and its truth cannot be successfully controverted; for truth is mighty, and will ultimately triumph. Read this article with care:

"ANTIOCH COLLEGE—A WARNING.—Our readers have long been expecting that we should say something concerning the miserable and discreditable position of this Institution, on which the fondest hopes of the Christian denomination have long rested. We are almost daily receiving letters of inquiry from our brethren in all parts of the West, calling upon us to speak out and let them know the true condition of the College, and what have been its practical results. So sad is the story of its failures and misfortunes that we have refrained, perhaps too long, from writing them, until now we have reached a point where a sense of duty impels us to speak out with that earnestness and sincerity which the cause demands. It is with a trembling hand and bleeding heart, but with a firm determination to discharge our duty to our brethren and the cause of Christ, that we now take up our pen to write the sad history of the failure of our first great effort to establish an institution of learning worthy of our position in the religious world, and commensurate with the wants of the age. Antioch College is the result of an impulse from above, and properly managed, would have been a blessing to us and the world; but we fear that it is an entire failure. Its whole history has been a round of disaster and disgrace.

"1st. It has ended in a failure of a most disagreeable kind to all concerned in a commercial point of view. Every rule and law promulgated by the Marion Convention for the regulation of its expenditure and the publication of its accounts has been violated. It was provided by that Convention, that all its accounts should be published quarterly in our papers, but instead of this, no correct account of the business exists. All that we know now is that the chief Agents are rich, and the College is bankrupt, and an enormous sum sufficient to build two large Colleges—remains to be paid. We are very sorry to be under the necessity of writing this, but it is true, and our brethren should know it.

"2d. But we regret to say that Antioch College is a still more complete and miserable failure in a religious and denominational point of view. We have, as a people, looked to it with fond hope as a means by which we were to be supplied with a more numerous and efficient ministry—a ministry such as our wants demanded. For this our brethren have prayed and sacrificed their money; but what has been the result? Some powerful influence has been at work among the students ever since its opening, preventing all religious power from operating on them, and turning them away from vital piety and every spiritual motive, so that no revival season has ever been enjoyed in this College—no conversions made during the whole period of its existence. What a melancholy thought! A College with hundreds of students in operation for four years and not one single soul converted to God in all this period. This is a thought over which the angels in Heaven would weep if they are capable of weeping. There has not only been no conversions to God, but on the contrary, many students who entered its halls as professing Christians have been turned aside from the religion of their parents, and become careless or sceptical, if not positively infidel, in their views. This is a sad story to write, and we feel like exclaiming in the language of the prophet: 'Oh that my head were waters, and mine eyes a fountain of tears, that I might weep day and night for the slain of the daughter of my people!'

"What a sad thought that our College has, thus far, been rather an injury than a benefit to us as a denomination. It may also be remarked that all our best ministers who have been connected with the College, or who have labored with the unfortunate church under its shadow, have been discouraged and driven away by some malignant influence. One even sent into exile, and the wife soon dismissed in her husband's absence, although petitioned for by the students—others driven into the far West, where their God has abundantly blessed their labors, others retired indignant; and now we hear that the only two remaining Professors in whom our denomination has confidence are assured that they will be dismissed under various pretenses from the Faculty about to be constituted for us by Messrs. Fay, Harlan and Dr. Bellows. Why are these things so? What strange power has been at work to produce this most unfortunate result? Every effect has an adequate cause, and there has been some enemy to vital godliness and to the Christian denomination at work. Where and what is it?

"Under these circumstances demands are being made on the purses of the Christian people of the West.

"1st. To pay up all unsettled scholarships. What the purpose of Mr. Palmer, the assignee, is, may be learned from the following notice, published in the 'Herald and Messenger':

"'Antioch College—*Notice.*—The scholarship notes of Antioch College are now in the hands of F. A. Palmer, at the Broadway Bank, who was appointed by the Board of Trustees at their late meeting sole assignee of all their property. The makers and endorses of the said scholarship notes can have the privilege of paying them by remitting their several amounts with interest to the assignee on or before the first day of September next, after which time they will be put into the hands of counsel for collection, which will add expense to all parties.

"'F. A. Palmer, *Assignee.*'

"'Broadway Bank, New York, July 24, 1857.'

"This, it seems to us, is a very unwise and injudicious course, to say the least we can of it. It is stated in the report of the committee appointed to make the assignment that the College is no longer to be a denominational one, and this has been confirmed by the President of the present Board of Trustees, who is also the President of the Committee to select a Faculty. If this is to be the case, we have nothing more to do with it, and why collect the unsettled scholarships until the other property is disposed of? for if it is sufficient to pay the debts of the Institution, there is no use for it.

"2d. To advance money for the support of the new-made Faculty, *from which our best known and esteemed men have been excluded.* If we are to have no substantial and real representation in the Faculty, and it is to be no longer a denominational institution, why call upon us for aid? We have already thrown away enough money.

"Under these circumstances we feel it our duty to warn our people in this matter, and for ourselves we think it better to wait for more light upon the designs of the present managers, before pledging ourselves to a useless and discreditable Institution, which must be cured or killed so far as the denomination is concerned."

In the latter part of August a circular was sent forth by the "Committee of Arrangements" which begins and ends as follows:

"CIRCULAR.

"Antioch College will be opened for the ensuing year on Wednesday, the 9th day of September next, (1857.)

"The Committee of Arrangements hereby announce some of the provisions which have been made for the coming year.

"The services of the President, (Mr. Mann,) of Mrs. Dean, Prof. Warriner and Prof. Carey will be retained.

"In the Department of Rhetoric, Logic and Belles Lettres and of Mathematics there will be a change.

"The Rev. Austin Craig, D. D., will be a member of the Faculty.

"The Preparatory Department will be under a new head.

"The old scholarship system being abolished, a Tuition Fee will be substituted for it, which, for the College Classes, will be $24.00 a year, &c. * * *

"It is believed that the College will open under better auspices than ever before.

"*Committee of Arrangement,* { Rev. H. W. BELLOWS, D. D.
Hon. AARON HARLAN.
Rev. ELI FAY."

Now, why is it said that "Antioch College will be opened on the 9th of September;" "the College will open under better auspieces," &c.? Why is this downright deception practiced upon the public?

Mr. Harlan told me in October last, in a lengthy conversation on Antioch affairs, that the present temporary school is not legally "Antioch College," that the College is in existence, but in a torpid state, *asleep*, its entire assets having been assigned. Judge Mills and other professional and business men have told me the same in substance. The counsel of the assignee also declared in court in this village, in a suit to recover a scholarship note, that "Antioch College is not now in operation or in existence."

This circular called forth the following article from Eld. James Maple, editor of the "Gospel Herald," in which it will be seen that Messrs. Mann, Craig and Warriner, and Mrs. Dean, (although they are nominally members of the Christian Church,) are not considered "representatives of the Christian denomination." And "Dean, Fay & Co." probably were never more concisely and *truthfully* depicted than by Eld. Maple's definition—"a little scheming, selfish, greedy clique." This article was, without doubt, the honest expression of both the head and heart of Mr. Maple. It appeared in the "Gospel Herald" of September 3d, 1857. *Read it carefully:*

"ANTIOCH COLLEGE AND ITS NEW FACULTY—TOTAL EXCLUSION OF THE REPRESENTATIVES OF THE CHRISTIAN CHURCH.

"The article which it was our painful duty to write and publish in our paper of the 13th ult., has opened the eyes of our people to the dreadful failure, both in a financial and religious point of view, of this Institution. We mourn over its present condition, and have no confidence either in the wisdom or piety of its present managers. Nothing but the deepest conviction of the absolute necessity of speaking out in the plain language of truth could induce us to return again to the sad story of Antioch College. But we have determined that we will discharge our duty to the Christian denomination and to God, whatever may be the consequences. There are but three questions with us: 1st. What is the truth? 2d. Is it necessary for it to be spoken? 3d. Does the cause of Christ demand it? These points being settled, we have no choice left. We must speak out, and we pause not to inquire what will be the result to us personally. We are willing and ready to make any sacrifice and to endure any amount of persecution for our beloved Zion. We have laid over all on the altar of the Christian Church. She has her faults, but, with all her faults, we love her still.

"We have received, by the kindness of a friend, a copy of the circular issued by Messrs. Harlan, Fay & Bellows, 'the Committee of Arrangements,' from which we copy the following: 'The services of the President (Mr. Mann,) of Mrs. Dean, Prof. Warriner and Prof. Carey, will be retained. In the Departments of Rhetoric, Logic, Belles Lettres, and of Mathematics, there will be a change. Rev. Austin Craig, D. D., will be a member of the Faculty. The Preparatory Department will be under a new head. The old scholarship system is abolished,' &c.

"Now it will be observed here that a clean sweep has been made of all the representatives of the Christian denomination. Not one of them is even named in the above list. We ask, then, can our people be expected to patronize it under such management? We desire to use only mild and becoming language, such as we will not regret when we come to answer for the deeds done in the body in the great day of judgment; but we must say that a more imprudent course of action could not have been chosen, a more wanton and high-handed outrage could not have been committed, than that to which we refer, and it must alienate and mortally offend every true and honest member of the Christian Church in every part of the country. We can assure Messrs. Dean, Fay & Co., that our people will not be the tame and spiritless tools of their little scheming, selfish, greedy clique. There is some self-respect and denominational honor left in the Christian Church, and the course pursued by the managers of the College will call them out. This monstrous invasion of all our rights, this contemptuous and insulting expulsion of our best men from their places in the Faculty, will teach our people the necessity of acting in future by themselves alone, and avoiding all compromise with those who are the open or secret enemies of our denomination. We have learned one valuable lesson from our experience in building Antioch—the importance of self reliance. This is worth, to us as a people, all the College has cost.

"The following gentlemen were chosen, with the full approbation of the Christian denomination, as our representatives in the Faculty of Antioch College. They are still available, and have, by the most sedulous culture, been making constant improvement in every qualification necessary for their offices; and now all their names are omitted from the list of the Faculty: Prof's. Allen, Doherty, Holmes and McKinney.

"In these circumstances, therefore, we feel compelled to say that Antioch College is, under its present arrangement, unworthy of the confidence of the Christian Church."

On the 25th of August, an Educational Convention was held in Haverhill, Mass., by which various resolutions were passed. Some of these were expressive of the views of the New England friends on Antioch College, and their relations thereto; and others recommended the patronage and endowment of the New England Christian Institute, and the founding of a Biblical School in connection with it. In the next issue of the "Herald of Gospel Liberty," the following brief statement touching the College was published:

"MEETING OF THE BOND-SIGNERS AND FRIENDS OF EDUCATION.

"At a meeting of the Signers of the Bond, and others friendly to our educational interests, in New England, held in Haverhill, August 25th, a report was submitted by D. P. Pike, presenting a comprehensive statement of the present condition of Antioch College, which, on motion, was accepted, and so much of said report as relates to the New England Bond adopted; by which, in view of the original plan having been abandoned, and the College property transferred, it was resolved that the signers of the New England Bond were released from all further legal or moral obligation. The Treasurer of the Bond-Signers was then instructed to call for the return of the Bond, that it may be cancelled, and the Executive Committee instructed to ascertain of the donors if the money in the Treasury can be used for the promotion of our evangelical interests in New England.

"O. H. ROBERTS, Pres.
"B. F. SUMMERBELL, Sec'y."

In copying the above into the "Gospel Herald," Eld. Maple says:

"Our readers will remember that, some time since, our brethren in New England pledged $25,000 towards paying off the debt on Antioch College. This was secured by a Bond. Since Antioch College has ceased to be a denominational College, and our brethren have been turned out of the Faculty, they have held a meeting on this subject. It met at Haverhill, Mass., August the 25th. There were some thirty ministers at the meeting, besides other friends of education."

From the same number of the "Herald of Gospel Liberty," Eld. Maple copies an editorial on Antioch College, from which I clip the following extract:

"If the College could become emphatically ours, denominationally, by the raising of $60,000, we think something might be done towards effecting that object in New England. * * * New England is in favor of a denominational College. The plan adopted at Marion is our plan. And, looking at Antioch as we now do, we prefer not to discuss its claims. In the meantime, we would call the attention of our readers to the New England Christian Institute at Andover, N. H.

"We have received a circular from Antioch, with a request that it be published; but it appears so decidedly aimed against the original plan that we doubt the expediency of publishing it. Prof's. Allen and Doherty are not retained. No mention is made of Prof. Holmes or J. B. Weston, and we fear, from the present aspect of Antioch, that it has lost much, if not most, of its denominational character. We assure our friends, however, that should any prospect arise favorable to its redemption, under circumstances which shall secure it to our own denomination, we shall not hesitate to give it our support."

On this editorial, Eld. Maple remarks as follows:

"Bro. Carter says, 'New England is in favor of a Denominational College. The plan adopted at Marion is our plan.' We say the same of the West. We are in favor 'of a Denominational College,' and, had Antioch not ceased to be such, it would have had our hearty support, and, we have no doubt, but the West would have paid her portion of the debt promptly and honorably.

"Again Bro. Carter says, 'If the *College could become empatically ours, Denominationally*, by the raising of $60,000,' &c. This is our view of the West. If it '*could become emphatically ours, Denominationally*,' it would have the united support of all the West; '*but, as it now appears, there will probably be but little disposition to do much in that direction.*' Antioch '*has lost much, if not most, of its Denominational character*. This has wounded the feelings and alienated our brethren in the West, and those who have brought about this state of things are responsible for their results.

"Our brethren in New England are not discouraged in educational enterprises, but are now hard at work to build up a Christian Institute at Andover, N. H. This is the right spirit, and we rejoice to learn that their efforts are being blessed."

In the "Gospel Herald," of Sept. 3d, is an article from Elder J. Jacobs, who has resided here for several years, and been a member of Antioch for three years. He has, therefore, enjoyed very good opportunities for observing the influences at the College. He says:

"* * * My soul has been made to burn within me, when I saw that Antioch did not, by far, meet its original design; also when I have read articles from professed Christian ministers averring that there is no Unitarian influence exerted over the College.

"There has always been an antagonism between a part of the Faculty and the Christian Church in this place, and this was exhibited to the students in the following manner: Students belonging to the Methodist or Presbyterian Church could obtain permission to attend their places of worship without any difficulty; but it was with great difficulty that students having their standing in the Christian Church in this place could get permission to attend the ministrations of that church, when Profs. Holmes and Doherty were pastors, also when Summerbell was pastor.

"Again, students have been refused the privilege of attending the weekly prayer-meeting of the church.

"* * * Now these are facts, and this is the influence that students have had thrown around them; yet, men at a distance will aver that there is no influence in the College operating against the Christians. The word *repent* has never been taught there in my hearing by any of the Faculty but those who have been removed.

"But is it any better now? The circular that is now in circulation states that it is about to open under better auspices than ever; no doubt it will be decidedly Unitarian, if we may judge by the committee chosen to select the Faculty, Messrs. Bellows, Harlan and Fay. The Christians have not a representative in this committee. Bellows and Harlan do not profess to belong to the Christian Denomination, and experience has proven that Fay has no sympathy for us. Besides this, since he has been Pastor of this church he has declared against denominational distinction. * * * JESSE JACOBS."

An article by Eld. D. P. Pike, of Newburyport, Mass., published in the "Herald of Gospel Liberty," speaks of a revival of religion in the New England Christian Institute. The following is an extract:

"How cheering to know that the Great Head of the church is willing to bless in the conversion of the youth who come to our Institute. Seek first the kingdom of heaven, then education and refinement will be committed to the trustworthy, to those who, under God, can be useful, a blessing to the world.

"Brethren of the Christian Denomination in New England, here is a school under our control, to be managed without the interference of those who design us no good. Please send us your sons and daughters. We will soon have this Institute equal to any in New England.

"We hope to have a large increase of pupils, and the benevolence of New England in this direction."

Eld. Maple copied this article into an editorial on Antioch College in the "Gospel Herald," and commented on it as follows:

"This is the kind of a school that we need *"under our own control; to be managed without the influence of those who design us no good."* Thank heaven! God has already blessed this Institute with a revival of religion, and precious souls have been converted. An Institution of learning, baptized with the spirit of God, will prosper. The conversion of the soul is the 'one thing needful,' and this object should always be kept supreme. Our only hope of success is in God and the omnipotence of truth. It is in vain to look to any other cause for aid; they must fail us in the end. The Israelites once went down to Egypt for aid instead of looking to the Lord the only true source of help, and they got more than they bargained for. Brethren, let us learn wisdom from the experience of the past, and put our trust in God. Let us be sure not to look to Egypt for aid."

Let the reader mark this paragraph and compare it with what Mr. Maple said a few months later concerning his Egyptians, Horace Mann and Mrs. Dean, *"those who design us no good."* "The conversion of the soul should always be kept supreme." Has Mr. Maple received so much light since he wrote the above sentence, as to be fully convinced that "the conversion of the soul" is the *supreme* object in Mr. Mann's school? If so, we would like to know what kind of conversion Mr. Mann advocates. Is it a conversion effected by the study of Mathematics, the classics and the sciences? We fear that this is the position of Eli Fay as well as Mr. Mann; and we wish to know why they do not come out and advocate their doctrines in our papers, so that our brethren and friends who live at a distance from Yellow Springs may also know their views.

The following clear statement from Eld. Millard, of New York, appeared in the "Gospel Herald" of Sept. 17th:

"THE FAILURE.

"The disastrous failure of our College enterprize has filled with gloom the minds of many who had been looking to it, as the future hope of the denomination.

"The disclosure of the fact that Antioch College had failed financially was *bad;* but to learn that it has proved a most signal and disgraceful failure to the denomination by whom it was founded, is still *worse.*

"The College it seems, has now passed into the hands of those from whom, as they have no sympathy with us as a religious body, we can expect no favors. Can our people then be expected to patronize it? Indeed, it comes with ill grace from the present managers—after having removed from the Faculty *all* the members who were chosen with the full approbation of the Christian Denomination, as our representatives there—to ask it of us. The truth is, the College has gone from us. And, as 'there is some self-respect and denominational honor left in the Christian Church' we say—Let it go—but do not insult us by asking us to go with it.'

"'We have learned,' says Bro. Maple, in a recent spirited and truthful article on this subject—'one valuable lesson from our experience in building Antioch—the importance of *self-reliance.*'

"Let us profit then by the lesson thus dearly bought, withdrawing at once our sympathy and patronage from a College no longer *ours*. Let us rally to the support of *our own* institutions, and strive to make them what we had hoped of the once 'great' but now *fallen*, 'Antioch.'

"West Bloomfield, N. Y., Sept. 1857." D. E. Millard."

At the close of a long article by Eld. D. P. Pike on his last visit to Antioch College and the West, concluded in the "Herald of Gospel Liberty" of Sept. 10th, and copied in the "Gospel Herald" by Eld. Maple, he says:

"Antioch College in its finances and progress was not satisfactory to me, seen from any point. I look back to our Marion Convention and think of the plan there proposed, and what was there designed. I compare what has been attempted, and I see no resemblance whatever. I now wish we were at Marion with our present experience, and about to make a beginning for a college of our own. I think we might do something to our credit as a denomination, independent of all other aids or influences. I cannot have much courage. Plan after plan may be devised, but there is a worm wasting at the root, or there is something working against us denominationally at Antioch College. No teachers of our denomination can long succeed there; some trouble must arise, from some cause or other, to make them unpopular or not acceptable. It cannot be that our professors are *all* to blame. These and some other things sicken me, and render void my hopes. It is possible that a better state of things may exist, and these causes may be removed. I hope they may, but the blame is not all on one side. I hope some day a full and truthful exposé or history of Antioch's misfortunes may be known, and justice done to all."

In the same number of the Gospel Herald, appeared the following from Elder Summerbell, who has resided in Yellow Springs, and hence speaks from his own knowledge:

"ANTIOCH COLLEGE.

"Antioch College being now dead to us, beyond the possibility of a resurrection, a reasonable regard to our own health demands that she be buried out of our sight. Therefore, I suggest that very little be said about her in our papers in future. It is now two years since I saw the last signs of life in her, and this accounts for my silence upon the subject. * * *

"Let those keep the walls who now have them. All we ask of them is, that we may be delivered from the body of death; and that the cold carcase be not drawn across our path in future. We have been injured, deeply injured, but it is not too late to recover; yet, let none be deceived—Antioch has never been under our control, and now that she is acknowledged dead, let her be buried. N. SUMMERBELL."

Professor Holmes, who had been in Europe more than two years, landed in Boston on the 13th day of August, 1857. His return was warmly welcomed by his numerous friends in different parts of the United States. He was at the Educational Convention in Haverhill, Mass., August 25, and at the annual session of the Miami Christian Conference, Ohio, which opened Sept. 1st, 1857. Before this body he made a statement of the circumstances attending his departure for Europe, which stirred deep emotions in many a heart, and strengthened many a person in the belief that Horace Mann is not *above* richly-merited and dark suspicion. He showed how persistently and determinedly Mr. Mann had pursued him, and labored with him, to induce him to consent to go to Europe; how he had held out inducements, and assured him that his wife should be retained as a Teacher in the Institution; but Mr. Holmes replied that he could see no light in that direction, nor could he deem it duty to go; when Mr. Mann added, if he did not go—if he remained in the College—large numbers of students would leave, and the Institution would be deeply injured!

The climax was now reached. Prof. Holmes was touched in a most tender place. He had labored, and prayed and sacrificed much for Antioch; and nothing perhaps in this world was so near and dear to his heart, save the cause of Christ. Indeed, he had hoped, as one of the founders of Antioch, that the Institution would be largely influential in advancing the cause of the Redeemer, and publishing the doctrine of the cross of Christ. He therefore told Mr. Mann, that *if Antioch was to suffer* by his remaining, he would leave—would consent to go to Europe.

As these last words were spoken, delight lit up Mr. Mann's countenance, and the exultation of triumph thrilled through his whole frame. His immediate object was accomplished. Time and circumstances would doubtless aid him in the future. He immediately disappeared from the College chapel, whose broad spaces were dimly lighted by the moon, and whose walls had witnessed and recorded the scenes of that hour of night—leaving Mr. Holmes to his own reflections.

How strangely and significantly to Bro. Holmes must have been the sounds of those retreating footsteps as they echoed and re-echoed along the silent and spacious halls of Antioch! How often, and vividly must memory have called up this scene, as he moved through the vast, dim and chill cathedrals of the Old World!

Prof. Homes went from the conference meeting to Yellow Springs, where, it appears, he heard some statements concerning himself not altogether true or pleasing. These statements came from Eli Fay, or grew out of what he had said early in the vacation—viz: that they intended to invite Mr. Holmes to fill the Greek chair for *one* year, so that he might leave the Institution with more honor, &c.

It was clear, then, that if they invited Mr. Holmes back, it would be for only a short time, and chiefly to soften or do away with the suspicions of the Christians.

A few days later, Prof. Holmes wrote from Michigan to the "Gospel Herald," as follows:

"Bro. Maple—Before leaving Yellow Springs, it reached my ears several times that some one in that place was endeavoring to fasten the detestable crime of equivocation upon me, by stating, that while I averred that I knew nothing of the intention of the committee appointed to supply Antioch College with Teachers the coming year, to invite myself to a seat among them 'there was a perfect understanding between me and that committee.' I quote the words as they were reported to me by several persons, and in this manner to make known 'to all whom it may concern' that *'there was no understanding at all between me and that committee.'* At the time I made the statement before the Miami Conference, I had received no invitation from that committee, verbal or written, direct or indirect, to occupy such a place. On my arrival at Yellow Springs, I was informed that the committee had appointed me to the Greek chair, and had requested a third person to inform me of the fact, immediately on my landing in Boston; but that was positively *the first intimation I had* that the committee intended to do or had done any such thing. Equivocation is a contemptible crime that I despise, only resorted to, in my opinion, by those who dare not face upright truth. Let the serpent, the scriptural emblem of the devil, squirm and wind his tortuous way at our feet; let beasts of prey crouch and skulk in secret that they may spring unobserved upon the unwary; but let those whom 'God hath made upright' act uprightly and openly.

Thomas Holmes."

"Ann Arbor, Mich., Sep't 15, 1857."

In the "Messenger" of Sept. 17th, the editor says:—"As to the Faculty for the present year, it is almost useless to speak; it is ephemeral at best. More wisdom, we think, could have been displayed, and the Faculty should have been named in full in the circular recently published. We do not believe there are sufficient reasons for the changes made for one brief year."

In the "Herald" of Oct. 1st, J. B. Weston published a highly colored article in which he endeavors to do away with the suspicion resting on

Mr. Mann's "ephemeral Faculty;" but his article has injured himself more than any one else. He says:

"It is true that Prof. Holmes did not accept his appointment, because he thought another field offered him better opportunities for usefulness; but this is not to be charged to the committee."

Mr. Weston gave no other reason for the absence of Prof. Holmes; and one of two things must be true, either Mr. W. meant to decieve our people or he was extremely short sighted and careless.. Will the readers of the "Herald" give Mr. Weston the benefit of "stupidity," or will they charge upon him "equivocation" which Bro. Holmes calls "a contemptible crime?" However much Mr. W. may strive to cover up his equivocation, *we do know* that he is aware of several reasons for Prof. Holmes' absence.

From the latter part of the lengthy article by Eld. Jacobs, in reply to Elders Craig and Weston, I clip the following lines relating to the above brief extract from Weston's statement:—

"* * * Why did he not tell us the manner in which Professor Holmes was treated, that the world might know who was to blame for his declining a seat in Antioch? Does he not know that when he professed to state facts, that the people were looking for the whole truth, but he has left false impressions on the minds of the people * * * that it was Prof. Holmes' voluntary desire to go and preach the Gospel. True, he preferred to go and preach under the circumstances, but why did Mr. Weston not tell the circumstances, and let others form their own opinion on the subject; instead of trying to form opinions for them * * * to the injury of Prof. Holmes' reputation, and that of the Denomination?

"Why did he not tell you the kind of treatment Prof. Holmes received? Why did he not tell you that before Prof. Holmes started for Europe, he obtained a promise that his wife should have a situation in the College till he returned? and that she stayed through a long vacation the ensuing summer on expense waiting for her place in the College the ensuing term, but when the term opened another took her place? Why did he not tell you that Prof. Holmes had not enough respect paid him by the committee, who selected a Faculty, to have his name inserted on the circular which was sent throughout the land?

"Why did he not tell us that Prof. Holmes had no knowledge of his being an appointee till he had made arrangements to preach, and came to this place for his books?

"Surely Prof. Holmes has had just causes for doing as he did; he has fought a sore battle, he has been in peril both by land and sea, but his face always to the enemy, and surely if he falls in battle, he, like the old Roman veterans will have no wounds in the back.

"Yellow Springs, O., Oct. 12th." JESSE JACOBS."

A few weeks later Bro. Holmes wrote an account of the powerful revival in Portsmouth, N. H., and of the numerous and glorious baptismal seasons; and said "ninety seven have been added to the church, and more than one hundred souls hopefully converted to God in our meetings, and probably as many more among other denominations. Some of the seasons of baptising were the most impressive I ever witnessed. Several times three churches have been at the water's side at once, and their three ministers harmoniously uniting in the most solemn and interesting services, while the spectators were numbered by thousands, and the deepest solemnity prevaded the vast assembly. Portsmouth is a regular *Baptist* city so far as this ordinance is concerned. But few converts can be satisfied here without attending to this duty in the manner that most people acknowledge the Savior himself performed it." But at the close of his lengthy and stirring revival letter he adds:

"P. S.—In view of the above facts, I wonder if those who were sure that I "missed it" when I refused to return to Antioch, will re-consider their judgment in the case, and admit that I was the best judge of what the Lord would have me do. By the way, the reason I assigned for not returning to Antioch was not that I thought I should "be more useful" in another field, but that "I thought I should *enjoy* my labors more in some other place." The reasons why I did not "enjoy" my labors there are quite numerous. I did think at one time I would make a statement of *some* of them for the benefit of those who thought I "missed it," but my excessive labors here prevented it, until a stop was put to the discussion of the subject in the "Herald." Perhaps it is just as well. T. H."

If these statements of Bros. Holmes and Jacobs are not satisfactory to Mr. Weston, there is other testimony of a very pointed character on this subject. But the readers of the "Herald" are well aware that "a stop was (*not*) put to the discussion of the subject in the "Herald," as noticed in Bro. Homes' letter, for although Mr. Maple *did shut down the gate several times,* he raised it again *as often* to some individuals! Why did the editor break his promises so often? Why did he exhibit such gross partiality?

It is perhaps, not generally known that, contrary to the usual custom in this country, the Faculty of Antioch College has "authority to confer such honors and degrees as are usually conferred by Colleges;" and that just before the Trustees voted to assign the property and suspend the Institution, Mr. Mann conferred the degree "D. D." upon Eld. Austin Craig! I say "Mr. Mann conferred;" for he brought the question before the Faculty without a minute's warning, and in the face of a strong opposition, he carried it in the affirmative *only* with the votes of those members of the Faculty who were under his influence or control!

In the "Gospel Herald" of Oct. 15th, Eld. J. Ellis, writing on the College, says:

"And furthermore, as a closing or crowning work just before she went down, she made for us a "Doctor of Divinity," so that if in process of time our divinity should become enfeebled with age, or should meet with a sudden attack of disease, we can apply to a doctor of our own for medical aid. Yet as we have no divinity but the "Scriptures of eternal truth," and as they are not sick, or even sickish, nor we sick of them, I suppose Dr. Craig will receive but few professional calls. It may be possible, however, that the Theology of Antioch may need his medical skill, and so prove that there is nothing made in vain."

A few weeks later, and the following article appeared in the "Messenger:"—

"THE FIRST CHRISTIAN DOCTOR OF DIVINITY.

"Some paper says that Antioch College, at its late Commencement, manufactured for the Christians their first Doctor of Divinity, out of Bro. Austin Craig. And is this verily true? Have we not had titled men in Israel before this? Did not 'Bennett's College' make Bro. Simon Clough a D.D. and an LL. D.? And did we not a year or two back, borrow a Doctor, to cure some of our young Ministers, here in Pennsylvania? Did not Doctor Stebbins come and join our Israel for a time, and thus take away the reproach of our condition? We have not heard a word from Bro. Craig, how he bears his heavy honor, but infer that he takes it easy. It is doubtless very opportune, for, according to the symptoms indicated by the papers, our divinity was sick at Yellow Springs. "*The doctor*" has gone to its relief. PEN POINT."

Whether "The Doctor" found "our Divinity at Yellow Springs" *so* "sick" as to be incurable, and hence concluded not to return; or whether he thought that one year's service was an equivalent for the "D.D.," we cannot say; but we do hope that he may find sufficient comfort in his "Dr." to compensate him for all his exertions in behalf of Mr. Mann and the "Joint Stock Company," and for his long journey through the East, and his efforts to alienate our friends in that section from us. For all these distinguishing labors, and especially for the last, we hope that Eld, Craig *may live long upon the earth*, or as the old Roman expressed it—" SERUS IN CŒLUM REDEAS."

PART SECOND.

REVIEW OF THE REPORTS

OF THE

So-called "Self-Constituted Committee,"

CONSISTING OF

T. M. McWHINNEY—J. G. REEDER—O. J. WAIT.

SELF-CONSTITUTED COMMITTEES.

What can be more blame-worthy than the ex-parte manner in which some men feel called upon to cast their influence in favor of suffering favorites, and to the manifest injustice of honorable men, and this with the greater boldness, from the fact that defence is almost impossible under the circumstances. In the case of the false claim made before the youthful Solomon, by the untrue mother, there was no defence for the true mother, but to save the life of the child if possible by yielding it up to the other. Such is precisely the case with the Christians now. They who have wisdom can discern the true from the false.

N. SUMMERBELL.

INTRODUCTION.

The following note from Eli Fay reached me through the post office:

"Yellow Springs, Oct. 14, 1857.

"PROF. I. W. ALLEN—*Dear Sir*:—I would inform you that on Saturday, the 17th inst., at 1 o'clock P. M., I shall present to a committee of five gentlemen the reasons which induced the Committee appointed to employ a Faculty for our College, for the current year, to fill the chair which you had occupied with another person. There will be an opportunity to confront my witnesses if you desire to do so. The meeting will be held in Antioch Hall or at the President's house.

"Yours, for truth, E. FAY."

With all my knowledge of Mr. Fay's restless character and officiousness, I was not a little surprised at the cool impudence of this letter, especially when taken in connection with his recent action in College affairs. The question arose at once, who are the members of Mr. Fay's "committee of five gentlemen"? By what body, religious or secular, have they been appointed?

I had no knowledge of the appointment of any such committee by the Board of Trustees, by any convention of the Christian Connection, or by any of our Conferences.

Besides, it was evident that if a committee had been thus officially appointed, it would give me due and timely notice of its official character and proposed investigations.

It was also highly probable that if the other members of the "Committee of Arrangements," Messrs. Harlan and Bellows, had had any hand in the appointment of said "committee of five gentlemen," due information of the same would be given.

I therefore determined to take no notice of Mr. Fay's impertinent communication; or of his "committee of five gentlemen," for if they were gentlemen, they certainly would hold no meeting concerning myself without giving me suitable notice of the same; nor would they take any action touching myself without an interview or consultation with me. I did not believe that *gentlemen* would consent to act on a committee, simply on the invitation of an interested party.

Time passed on, and no intimation reached me that a "committee of five gentlemen," or any other committee, had held a meeting concerning myself, until the "Gospel Herald," of Nov. 12th, 1857, came to hand, containing a report of a "committee of three," the so-called "self-constituted committee."

Of such a committee I had received no notice from any living soul, not even from Eli himself! What further proof is needed to show the strictly partizan character of this whole transaction. Said committee was composed of Elds. T. M. McWhinney, J. G. Reeder and O. J. Wait; and most singular and deceptive was their statement! I deemed it my duty to inquire into the facts of the case; and accordingly called on several of the professors and students, and on Messrs. McWhinney and Reeder, and from the resulting revelations, it was evident that Eli Fay had brought the said committee together, that he was at the bottom of the whole scheme, and was doubtless the mere tool of Horace Mann!

I also wrote to Eld. Maple, editor, and to John Geary, Esq., publisher, of the "Gospel Herald," asking how said "report" found its way into the paper. They replied as follows:

"FRANKLIN, O., Nov. 21st, 1857.

"MY DEAR BRO. ALLEN—Yours of the 14th inst. has just been received. The report of that Smelling Committee was got into the 'Herald' by a trick. At the close of the Convention here (at Franklin, Oct. 28th 1857.) Bro. McWhinney came to me and asked if I would publish their report.

"I answered that I did not know, for I was not acquainted with its nature. He said that it did not reflect on the character of any one in the least, nor do any injustice to any person. I told him that if he would send me such an article, I would publish it. He replied, that as soon as he went home, he *would write it out and send it to me;* but instead of this he took it to Mr. Geary and stated that I had authorized its publication. This is how it found its way into the 'Herald.' * * *

"I have many things to say, but must close for want of time to add more. Yours in love, JAMES MAPLE."

"COLUMBUS, O., 5th, Dec. 1857.

"MY DEAR BRO. ALLEN—Since the receipt of yours of the 1st inst., I have been obliged to be absent from my business some time, consequently could not answer sooner.

"At the Franklin Convention, Bro. McWhinney and myself had a conversation with regard to the affairs of the 'Herald.' He asked me if it was necessary to send articles intended for publication to Eld. Maple, or could such be sent to me direct. I told him it depended entirely on the subject; that, if it was merely a matter of religious news or such like, he might send it to me; if otherwise, it should be submitted to Eld. Maple. I was not advised at the time that anything would be sent, nor was I aware of the existence of the 'Report.'

"A week, perhaps, after the Convention, the 'Report' was received at this office from Bro. McWhinney, with a few lines written at foot, stating that it had been submitted to Bro. Maple, and that he had given direction as to its insertion in the 'Herald.' * * * * Hoping that this may be satisfactory—I am, Dear Bro. Allen,

"Yours very truly, JOHN GEARY."

These letters speak for themselves, and place Mr. McWhinney in as favorable a light, doubtless, as the truth will warrant. Who can envy him his position?

As the Committee's "Report" contained only assertions and insinuations, and professed to be "gratuitous," I was for some time in doubt whether or not it would be best to notice it with a reply. In the mean time, several short articles appeared in the "Herald," either ridiculing or correcting the self-constituted Committee's statements, one of these articles was signed "☞;" another, "A Student;" another "Ironical," &c.

In a few days a letter arrived from Mr. Maple, at the close of which he says—"The Student puts that Smelling Committee through on the short line. I have some other good things for them, if they do not make any reply to '☞' and 'A Student' soon. If you have anything to say, the paper is at your service."

I, took up my pen, therefore, and sketched a somewhat lengthy review of the Committee's "Report," which I read a few days later to Eld. Maple. He seemed to be pleased with it, said he had thought that it would not be worth while for me to notice the "Report," but on hearing my reply, he said it had better be published.

I asked him if it was too severe. He thought not; that if any change was made, it had better be made still more pointed. He further remarked that, if the Committee did not soon reply to the questions proposed to them in the "Herald," a certain gentleman who was acquainted with the case would publish the facts. I determined, therefore, to withhold my review until the said gentleman (whose name Mr. Maple did not give me) had published his article; and while awaiting its appearance, my attention and time were wholly engaged in another direction until the first of February.

For some reason said article did not appear, and the *why* was quite evident, from the tone and style of Mr. Maple's conversation on the 2d of Feb'y. It was quite evident to my mind that Fay & Co. had embraced him, and breathed into him their poisonous breath, unbalancing his mind and obscuring his vision. I saw that he had swerved from, if not wholly deserted, the noble position which he had occupied, Bro. Maple was now another man. What he before denounced and detested, he now lauded to the skies! He now declined the publication of my review unless the Executive Committee of the "Gospel Herald" would express their assent; said he would consult them and write me immediately. Such a letter never reached me. Time passed on, and the frequent editorials of the "Herald" confirmed my opinion concerning Mr. Maple.

The first of March removed every vestige of doubt on the subject; for on that day the contents of a letter written by him to that small but determined clique, "Mann, Dean, Fay & Co." which has ruined our College, were made known to me.

This letter was written on the 18th of Feb'y, and contained that, which numerous citizens of this place and vicinity can prove to be false.

In it Mr. Maple had betrayed private and confidential trust! He had deserted his true friends and defenders, and gone over to the embrace of his most inveterate enemies!

This letter it is true, was directed to Eld. Austin Craig; but his previous and subsequent acts have shown that he is in the interest of the clique above alluded to, notwithstanding his protestations to the contrary. "Ye shall know them by their fruits."

On the 18th of March the "Herald" contained the "second report" of the "self-constituted Committee," and a more thoroughly reckless and blackly false article, probably, never appeared in print!

Of course, methought, the "Herald" will now be open to a reply. Accordingly, I prepared a brief and pointed card, to be followed by a full review of the Committee's assertions, and dispatched it at once to Dr. Schenck, of Franklin, requesting him to read it to Mr. Maple, and hasten its insertion in the paper. I sent this article to Dr. Schenck because Mr. Maple, while professing to be my true friend, had in an underhanded and cowardly manner betrayed my confidence. How could I have had any further communication with him, until he had at least attempted to explain his course? A few days later, the article came back with the announcement that Maple would not publish it.

It was now painfully evident that Eld. Maple had not only prostituted himself, but also our Denominational organ, to the interests or dictation of a clique. Righteous indignation filled many a breast, pity moved many a heart at this sad spectacle of a professed Christian and minister!

On the 7th of April, the Executive Committee of the "Gospel Herald" held a meeting at Dayton. The publisher was present. Two of the five members of said Committee, are Eld. Maple, the editor, and Eld. Reeder, one of the "self-constituted Committee." Eld. N. Summerbell, the chairman of the Executive Committee, was absent in Iowa. Could justice be expected under the circumstances? would not Maple and Reeder rule?

The question was, however, laid before them—viz. Is not my right to reply to the "self-constituted Committee" through the "Herald," to vindicate my character against their charges, to be respected? This the Executive Committee considered in private session, and determined after much discussion, to allow me *three times the space occupied by the "Reports" of the self-constituted Committee.* Two of the Executive Committee insisted that Prof. Allen must not be allowed to reply at all! It would not do! Our people are already tired of controversy! It would injure the circulation of the "Herald!" But Eld. J. Ellis and Bro. Geary finally succeeded in influencing them to allow me as above stated *three times the space of the reports.* Eld. J. Ellis maintained that I ought not to be limited at all. He claimed that the "Self-constituted Committee" had wantonly and unjustly attacked my character in a public journal, and that I ought to have the right to reply through the same paper without limitation. That sweeping charges, occupying but a small space, might require many columns of facts and testimonies to disprove them.

The publisher of the "Herald," John Geary, Esq., who also publishes the "Capital City Fact," (daily,) and "State Capital Fact," (weekly) maintained the same. He said he had never known a case of limiting the first defense or reply of a man whose character had been assailed in any paper, religious or secular; that sometimes, however, when a controversy was likely to become very lengthy and tedious, *both* parties had been limited. But neither logic nor precedents could avail more than *three times the space occupied,* by the "self-constituted Committee's" "Reports!" Maple and Reeder must, of course, have their way. They had a *personal* interest in the matter. They feared to have the *facts* laid before the public!

In the published minutes of this meeting appeared the following resolution in which the reader does not find the "three times the space" clause! Perhaps Maple and Reeder were ashamed of it.

"*Resolved*, That we authorize our editor, Eld. James Maple, to publish a statement or reply of Prof. Ira W. Allen to the so-called 'self-constituted Committee," said statement or reply to be limited in extent and couched in respectful language free from any extraneous matter, and strictly in answer to the charges or specifications contained in the statement of said committee. After the publishing of this statement, further controversy on this matter to be excluded from the 'Herald.' "

Was it not enough for Maple and Reeder to insist that my reply should "be limited," and limited to "three times the space" in the "Herald" occupied by the "self-constituted Committee"? Why must they specify the language that I must use, and the matter which I must introduce, and the manner in which I must answer the charges? Because I had not yet been allowed to reply through the "Herald" to the statements of officious men, did they believe me to be so exasperated as to be incapable of using "respectful language?"

Because my life has hitherto been all sunshine and poetry, and my good name never before been assailed, did they suppose me, therefore, to be so lacking in common sense as to make use of "extraneous matter" rather than the abundant and withering facts which they have placed in my possession? Or was it because they had used *both* "disrespectful language" and "extraneous matter," and feared that I would retort in the same style?

"Be thankful for small favors" is an oft repeated aphorism; and to overlook the impertinent language of weak and inexperienced men is no doubt wise. The combined length of the two reports of the "self-constituted Committee" was one column and two thirds. Three times this amount would give me five columns. This space was far too small to contain all the facts, yet I concluded to occupy it. I prepared a manuscript review of said "Reports," as near five columns' length as I could judge, and dispatched it to Dr. Schenck, with the request that he would submit it to Eld. Maple, etc., so that it might appear in the next week's issue of the "Herald."

A week and more passed by; the "Herald" came to hand, but it did not contain my article! In glancing through the paper, however, my eye caught the following:

A "Review of the Reports of the self-constituted Committee," by Prof. I. W. Allen, arrived too late for insertion in the present number of the "Herald."

"Better late than never," perhaps. It will be out in full next week.

What was my surprise, therefore, two days later, when Eld. S. in-informed me that he happened to be in Columbus when my "Review" reached Bro. Geary. Bro. G. laid the matter before him, told him of the receipt of my "Review," and of instructions from Eld. Maple, to cut it down to a small compass, some three columns. Said, he did not know what to do, whether to cut down the article as well as he could or return it to Maple; and wished the advice of Eld. S. Bro. S. replied, that in his opinion, neither the editor nor the publisher should alter the "Review;" that if it could not be published in its present form, it should be returned to Prof. Allen, with the reasons for so doing. He said, his advice, however, would be, to publish the "Review" in full, that justice demanded it, and he hoped that he (Geary) would insert the article just as it was. On learning the above, I wrote immediately to Bro. Geary (May 3d) saying, that if my article could not be published in full, it must be returned to me. A few hours later and the following note reached me:

"COLUMBUS, O., 30th, April 1858.

"BRO. ALLEN—I received the copy of your "Review" on Tuesday afternoon, then too late to get it into the last "Herald." Several paragraphs were marked by Bro. Maple to be cut out, so as to bring it within three columns. * * * It has been cut with care so as to preserve the points, and still it makes, I think, over five columns. * *

"Very truly yours in haste, GEARY."

The next day a copy of the outside impression of the "Herald" came to hand, but instead of being "cut with care," I found it severely "hacked and hewed." Several very important passages and paragraphs were left out; and the entire section, containing the letters of Maple and Geary showing by what trick or fraud Eld. McWhinney, the chairman of the "self-constituted Committee," got its first report into the "Herald," was entirely omitted! Indeed, the whole article had been clipped of some of its most pointed passages, and now seemed to me to be very tame. I do not, however, lay any blame on Bro. Geary. He followed, doubtless, to the best of his ability, the instructions of the editor. I do not doubt that he meant to do just right. The blame falls where it is richly merited, upon Eld. Maple.

The amount published was just equal to five full columns, the space to which the action of the Executive Committee entitled me; but it was set up in large type and liberally spaced. Had a part of the article been set up in small type, the whole could have gone in; and this they should have done, or returned the "Review" to me for abridgement.

But thinking that this out-side impression, just received, might be intended as a proof copy, I immediately corrected the typographical errors and returned it with a letter of instructions to the publisher; but they reached Columbus too late. The whole edition of the "Herald" was worked off and a large part of it was in the mails.

In the meantime, a letter from Dr. Schenck had reached me, in which he informed me that Maple, although he had objected to quite a number of things in my article, had finally agreed that *it should be published in full,* save some five or six lines which were erased by Dr. S., to whom I had given discretionary power to make any slight changes, not affecting facts which his judgment might suggest or approve. I immediately informed Dr. Schenck (May 5th) of the discrepancy between his letter and the above note from Bro. Geary, to which he replied as follows—viz:

"FRANKLIN, May 10th, 1858.

"PROF. ALLEN—*Dear Sir and Brother:* Your letter of 5th inst. was duly received, and I assure you, I was greatly surprised to learn you had received a proof-copy of the 'Herald' containing your reply to the 'Self-Constituted Committee,' *abridged;* and especially to learn it had been done by Bro. Maple's direction. I could not credit it, but supposed there must be some mistake. Soon after the receipt of your manuscript 'review,' Mr. Maple called at my house, when I handed it to him. He read it over marking it on the margin as he read. After he had finished, I inquired if he had any objection to its insertion in the 'Herald.' He replied a part of it would do. I asked what part he proposed to omit. He named first the copy of his own and Mr. Geary's letters. I said I considered them an important link, showing the duplicity of the committee, and the warmth of the chase, their determination to publish a report which they feared to submit to the censorship of the editor, but which they claimed was an unprompted and impartial defense of the truth.

"He did not wish to involve himself in any way.

"I responded, that if these letters stated the truth, he would not be involved; and its defense called for their publication.

"After some further conversation, he agreed they should go in.

"He made other objections, and said the article was too long. I answered that a reply to the charges could not well occupy a less space, and that I thought you had been unjustly limited; that the committee were doubtless several hours in hearing the testimony on which they founded the charges, certainly if they took the evidence of all the classes and Professors at Antioch; and as they had been published in the 'Herald,' its columns should not be closed against their full and fair review. That simple justice to you and the denomination, a due regard for honesty and plain dealing, demanded this. That the whole of your article ought by all means to go in; that if it could not, my directions were explicit to retain and return it to you.

"After quite a lengthy discussion, he said it should all be published, excepting some half-dozen lines that I erased. He immediately wrote upon its back to this effect—'Bro. Geary, try and get this in the next 'Herald,'—enclosed and mailed it in my presence.

"You may, therefore, imagine my surprise at the receipt of your letter. Feeling there must be some misunderstanding, I immediately wrote about as follows:

"BRO. GEARY:—I have just received a line from Prof. Allen, informing me that he has received a proof-sheet of the 'Herald,' and that a considerable portion of his article in reply to the 'self-constituted committee,' is omitted by Elder Maple's direction. I think there must be some mistake. Please explain. "Yours, &c."

To which I have just received the following reply:

"COLUMBUS, O., 8th May, 1858.

'W. L. SCHENCK, Esq—*Dear Sir:* Yours of the 6th is just at hand. In reply I would say, that, *I had Bro. Maple's instructions to cut Prof. Allen's "reply" to three columns,* but after reading it over carefully two or three times, I found I could not do so without spoiling it entirely. I then thought I should return it to Bro. M., that he might take the responsibility of condensing himself. Fearing its transportation backward and forward might occupy too much time, I undertook the task, but could not get it within the required limits. * * * * Trusting that this explanation willl be satisfactory,

'I am, dear sir, fraternally yours, JOHN GEARY.'

"You may imagine my feelings at the receipt of this letter. It placed Eld. Maple, in whom I have heretofore had the fullest confidence, and for whom I have felt the warmest friendship, in a very unenviable situation. I trust he may yet be able to explain what seems inexplicable.

"To be sure I had not misunderstood the conversation referred to, as it occurred in the presence of my family, I have read that part of this letter referring to it to Mrs. S. We understood and recollect it alike. With much respect, I am yours for truth,

"W. L. SCHENCK."

But the editor is not yet satisfied. His duplicity to Dr. Schenck, one of the leading members of his church, and President of the Franklin Convention, Oct. 28th, 1857; his betrayal of honorable and confidential trust; his desertion of his true and long tried friends; his fulsome puffs of those persons whom he had a few months before styled a "little scheming, selfish, greedy clique"; and his suppression of most important facts from my "review" were not enough!

He must commit another dishonorable act. He must violate the decision of the Executive Committee, which he had a hand in making on the 7th of April, viz: "After the publishing of this statement (my reply) further controversy on this matter to be excluded from the "Herald."

And this decree *he did violate,* by publishing in the "Herald" of

May 13th, both an editorial against my "review," and an article from Eli Fay!

This editorial shows that Mr. Maple either did not understand my article, or that he meant to deceive the readers of the "Herald." It is full of misrepresentation from beginning to end. To consider all of its falsities I have now neither time nor space, nor is it necessary. A notice of one or two will be sufficient.

He endeavors to pit Prof. McKinney against me by saying that Prof. McK. says he left the College voluntarily, and that my "review" maintains that he was removed, and removed by Mr. Mann!

My review states no such thing, as every careful reader of it knows. Besides, I have never made any such statement to any person or on any occasion.

He claims that Miss Shaw "left the College of choice." I have never stated to the contrary; and Mr. Maple knew this, or ought to have known it.

He also says that "Mr. Burlingame is not and never has been a member of the Christian Church, and is in no way a representative of the same."

Does Mr. Maple mean to intimate that the mere putting down of a man's name upon a church book, constitutes him a member? We have some *nominal* members of our Church or Denomination, who are a curse to us every day they live; and simply because their *names* are with us, but not their *hearts*. Mr. Burlingame's relatives are members of our church; and one of his uncles, at least, is one of our ministers; and if his own name has not actually been entered on our church book, he is a Christian, and is heart and hand with us.

Would Mr. Maple also intimate that a man cannot be a "representative" of a church or an association simply because he is not a nominal member of the same? Have not corporations the right to choose any person as their agent or "representative," provided their charters do not restrict them?

If Mr. Burlingame was not a representative of the Christians at Antioch, how will Mr. Maple interpret the following extracts from Mr. Fay's letters?

Mr. Fay says in his letter of March 25th, 1855, speaking of Mr. Burlingame:

"*He must not leave the school.* You see plainly that a crisis is coming, and the Christians will as certainly be victorious in an open war, as God reigns. If he will stand by, he will have a noble place.'

On June 29th, 1855, in reply to a note communicating Mr. Burlingame's intention of resigning, Mr. Fay writes a long letter, the last which he ever wrote me; and from that time to this I have received nothing from his pen save, the note at the head of this introduction. He says:

"NEW YORK, June 29th, 1855.

PROF. ALLEN—*Dear Sir:*—I hasten to reply touching the future connection of Mr. Burlingame with the College. I write to *you* as I have not time to write to both." * * *

"Now, sir, in view of all that has passed between Mr. B. and myself, I am surprised that he should possibly infer that he would not be wanted another year. When I engaged him, I told him distinctly that we hoped he would conclude to spend his days at Antioch. When I was there last winter I assured him, as you know, with all the force of my office, that he should have a better place than he was then filling, as soon as possible. On those conditions, I understood that he agreed to remain. * * *

"I hope and pray that he will not entertain, for one moment, the thought of leaving the school. You and he must see, by the manner in which distinct elements are assuming their own peculiar forms there, that there will be good places for our own men before long, as soon even as Mr. B. will be prepared to take a place, to which a laudable ambition would lead him.

"Antioch will survive all present threatening aspects. It will stand forth in glory. Mr. B. must stay and be glorified with it. * *

"Hoping that Mr. B. will remain with you, and for the prosperity of our pet institution, I am

"Most truly yours, ELI FAY."

Thus the reader sees that Mr. Fay regarded Mr. Burlingame as one of "our own men," a "representative" of the Christians. His election, also, a year later, by a large majority of the Trustees, and in the face of the determined opposition of Mr. Mann, (described in Part I.) to the Principalship of the Preparatory Department of Antioch, with a salary of $1,000, and a seat in the Faculty, proves that he was regarded by the Trustees as true to their interests—to the interests of the Christian Denomination.

It should here be said in explanation of the above letter, that a large part of the inducement for Mr. Burlingame to leave a lucrative position at the East, and accept the post of instructor in the Preparatory Department of Antioch College, was the assurances of those who employed him, that very soon, probably at the beginning of the next year, he should have a more prominent and remunertive position.

But Mr. Maple says: "Mr. Burlingame and Miss Shaw were both invited to continue, but declined."

Why did he not go further and tell the readers of the "Herald" why they declined? The fact is, they would not return to Antioch, because of the doings and influence of Messrs. Mann & Co., because they saw and felt that Antioch was not the College of the Christians in reality, if in name; and because they were fully satisfied that our Churches and friends were being greatly deceived by professions and outside show, and most severely injured by potent influences in the College. I have abundant evidence in my possession to prove this. Had the Christians really controlled and directed Antioch, both Mr. B. and Miss S. would doubtless be teaching here to-day. Of course they left "of choice," as Mr. Maple said. So do many flee yearly from the tyrants and oppressors of Europe "of choice," and brave the hardships of long journeyings and the dangers of the ocean in order to enjoy civil and religious freedom.

Mr. Fay's article in the same number of the "Herald," (May 13th) is headed "AN EXPLANATION," which means, when taken in connection with what follows, *to explain away facts by falsehoods.* Such a foolhardy, reckless, slanderous article never met my eye in any political newspaper. I know not how the most practiced villain, the most venomous defamer could crowd more lies into the same space.

These are plain words, but they are true. His article consists of nine paragraphs, of which only two or three can here be noticed. The main drift is to explain away the letters and facts of my review bearing upon him. He says:—"5th. I did receive letters from two other persons corroborating Mr. Allen's statements," but then tries to weaken their testimony.

Drowning men, it is said, will catch at straws. Let us quote from Mr. Fay's own language. Accompanying his letter of March 25th, 1855, (see part 1st.) he sent me an extract from a letter which he had just penned to Mr. Mann. After giving Mr. M. some advice about the Preparatory Department, he goes on to say:—

> "Your school will probably be smaller next term, and fewer teachers will be needed. I most earnestly advise it, because it will tend to allay a feeling rapidly rising there, and which, if unchecked, will eventuate disastrously to the College and all concerned.
>
> "Since my return, I have been literally flooded with letters, expressing the greatest dissatisfaction with matters and influences there.
>
> "As certainly as we are living men, Antioch is destined to an explosion unless great care is exercised. You shall know the whole, when I know a little more."

I have other written testimony, of later date, showing that Mr. Fay had received many letters "from other individuals corroborating" my statements. Why, then, this attempt to deceive the public? Does he suppose that the readers of the "Hereld" have forgotten the entire past?

He further says:

"It is also true that I wrote a letter to Mr. Allen soon after the last, (June 12, 1855), which he quotes, from which he deemed it prudent to make no extract, in which I strongly intimated my suspicions that he had deceived me, and that he dared not meet Mr. Mann face to face with his complaints, since which I have received no letter from him."

This statement contains three contradictions of facts; three out and out falsehoods, viz.:

1st. "In which I strongly intimated my suspicions that he had deceived me."

2d. "And that he dared not meet Mr. Mann face to face with his complaints;" and

3d. "Since which I have received no letter from him."

1st. Mr. Fay did write me a letter soon after "the last," which I published; but it contains no hint that I had deceived him. Its date is "June 29th, 1855," and from it I have quoted above. I have on file all the letters ever received from Mr. Fay, and have just read them all through from beginning to end, and do not find the slightest intimation or most delicate hint of "suspicion that I had deceived him." If Mr. Fay has any doubts on this point, his letters can all be made public, and speak for themselves.

2d. The letter alluded to does not contain any intimation that I "feared to meet Mr. Mann;" but it does say: "Your intimation that possibly I am under the influence of Mr. Mann can perform no mission. If you had read our correspondence for the last two months, you would not have made it. There is probably no man in the Board of Trustees, upon whom Mr. Mann looks with so much suspicion." This is Mr. Fay's reply, and his own reply, to an allusion in my letter, that some persons in Yellow Springs believed that he was giving himself up unduly to Mr. Mann. Time, however, has shown these persons to be true prophets; for Mr. Fay has gone over religiously, I fear, and otherwise to Mr. Mann, and become his complete tool. His only letter which contains any intimation of "fear" is the one which I did publish. (See part 1st.)

3d. Mr. Fay did receive letters from me after the 29th of June, 1855. From August 6, 1855, to May 10, 1856, I wrote and sent to Mr. F. no less than six letters; and these letters were received, but they were answered by his wife, and accompanied with assurances that Mr. F. was "quite unwell," or "absent from home," but he would write me "soon" or in "a few days," and the wish was expressed that I would *continue to write.*

Mr. F.'s replies, however, never came, and my letter of May 10th, 1856, was the last to him; for it was by that time quite evident that Antioch College, as intended by its founders, and the founders themselves had but little, if any good, to expect from Eli Fay. His vituperative "Incoginto" articles were not very commendatory!

But I have space to notice only one statement more of Mr. F.'s article; nor is it necessary, for those which I have noticed are a very good sample of the others, and quite as consistent and truthful. He says:

"Nor have I the least desire to conceal the fact that to Mr. Allen are largely attributable those fears and suspicions among our own people, which have heretofore prevented us from raising money to pay our debts and greatly diminished the patronage of the College.

"And when I consider the secret, insidious, yet persistent manner in which Mr. Allen has sought to alienate the sympathies of our people from Mr. Mann, as President of the College, I consider it far more wonderful that Mr. Mann has succeeded at all, and has any friends remaining, than that a small and an inveterate faction has been formed against him."

However extensive and potent my influence is, and has been, and whatever little I may have done to save the character and money of our people from the all-devouring vortex prepared and enlarging for them in Antioch College, I do not think I merit so much eulogy. Would Mr. Fay make my influence more effective than that of all the Professors and Teachers who have been mal-treated by Mr. Mann; than the influence of all the students, and of the citizens of the town and vicinity?

The truth is; Mr. Mann has destroyed his own influence. He had hardly set foot in the College, and received the charter and keys of the Institution, before he commenced to sow the seeds of dissention; and these had already sprung up and were bringing forth fruit before I arrived in Ohio. Then followed the expatriation of Prof. Holmes, the unjust dismissal of Mrs. Holmes, the cruel treatment of Miss Chamberlain and others, together with the introduction of influences and changes prejudicial to the interests of the founders of the College. These things, of course, aroused much feeling; and the frequent letters of two or three hundred students, and of many citizens, carried the unpleasant intelligence to their homes and friends, scattered over the States.

Mr. A. S. Dean, too, (a relative of Mr. Mann by marriage) has stood with one hand in the College treasury and the other in his pocket, with his head all full of book-store, town-lot, rich-farming, and house building speculations; while, at intervals, when the College Treasury was low or empty, he has held out both hands, and poured out honied but deceptive words, to the people for their hard earned money.

The all-devouring, ever-increasing whirlpool, at Antioch, has, however, alarmed the people, prevented the influx of money, and cut Mr. Mann and relatives somewhat short of funds.

But this deficit will doubtless be of short continuance, for Fay, McWhinney, A. S. Dean, Mrs. A. S. Dean, and others of that "little, scheming, selfish, greedy clique," have been struggling for subscriptions or loans, and have succeeded to quite an extent in deluding the people. How easy to deceive persons living at a distance from the College!

Some of our ministers and friends, however, hundreds of miles from Antioch, are too wide awake to be caught in such a snare. One of these, Elder ———, of New York, a man of much experience and much beloved, wrote on May 20th, 1858:

"I thought as soon as I read your review, that they (Maple and others) would pay no attention to their own published resolve—that after your reply there should be no more controversy on the subject in the paper. They have the advantage of you altogether. 1st, they have the papers under their control. 2d, there are several of them combined to help each other; and, 3d, they can make resolves and break them at pleasure, to suit their convenience. As things are, you can only be heard in your own defence by their permission, and then they can suppress what they please of an article, and omit words so as to render the sense obscure and make you say what you never designed to say."

That this statement is true, every one who understands the facts well knows. But Maple was not yet satisfied. He must violate the "resolution" of the Executive Committee again, which *he did* by publishing another editorial against my review, in the "Herald" of June 3d, headed with the names of the "self-constituted Committee."

A few months ago he styled these men a "Smelling Committee," and said that "their report was got into the 'Herald' by a trick," and could hardly find words in the English language sufficiently expressive to denote his abhorrence of their course; but now he says: "They are men of pure characters, and we know that they are incapable of being influenced by the base motives ascribed to them." He then incorrectly and unjustly charged me with ascribing "base motives" to these men in my review, when he well knows that I charge the responsibility home upon Eli Fay, and speak simply of the "words and deeds" of his committee-men, without sitting in judgment upon their motives.

To the Great Judge of all the earth I leave their motives; but their "doings and sayings" will be criticised by the public.

I therefore hurl back Mr. Maple's unjust charges, and beg to know what he expects to gain by repeatedly breaking his promises; by his short-sighted attempts to deceive the public; by denouncing his true and long-tried friends; and by prostituting the "Herald" to fulsome eulogies of Horace Mann and his sycophants, whom a few months since he denounced in no measured terms? Does he hope by this course to injure my influence with our Churches and the friends of Antioch at a distance? I have no fear that his dark insinuations and cowardly onslaughts (*cowardly* because he will not allow me to reply through the paper) will affect in the least any of my acquaintances; but it is perhaps my duty to the numerous strangers who read the "Herald," and into whose hands this review may fall, to depart from my usual custom even with strangers, and give a brief extract or two from some of the letters in my possession.

From a somewhat lengthy letter by one of our leading men, and very active in our educational movements, written a few weeks after the assignment of the College property, Sept. 12th, 1857, I extract the following paragraph:

"PROF. ALLEN:—I hope you will not leave educational employments. The Christians will soon have a place for you, and that place second to none in their gift; at least I think so. It may not give you great wealth, but will give you a competency, an honorable place in society, and you will feel the consciousness of being in a useful position, and consequently, happy in the belief that you are answering the end of your being."

Elder J. McKee, of Watertown, N. Y., one of the fathers in the "Christian Church," one of the founders of Antioch College, and of most lovely and noble Christian character, who has been intimately acquainted with our family since my earliest childhood, commences a long letter of Jan'y. 18th, 1858, in the following words, which, although intended only for my eye, I trust he will pardon me for presenting here:

"MY KIND FRIEND:—Yours of the first inst., is received; and I most heartily and cheerfully reciprocate its fraternal and Christian sentiments, good wishes, and every friendly feeling. It is highly pleasureable to be remembered so affectionately by one whose amiable virtues, stern integrity, persevering and undeviating Christian course, have won for him so eminent and enviable a reputation at home and abroad. * * *

Yours with high esteem,

"Prof. I. W. ALLEN. J. MCKEE."

The following letter, sent me several years since by President North, D. D. LL.D., has never been seen, I believe, by any person, not even by my most intimate friends:

"This certifies that Mr. I. W. Allen, was formerly a student in this College, and that having pursued a full and regular course of Collegiate study, he was graduated in connection with the class of 1850.

"The subscriber takes pleasure in adding, that during his connection with the Institution, Mr. Allen was uniformly distinguished by great moral worth and excellence of character, as well as by superior scholarship in every department of study, and that he possessed in a high degree the confidence of the officers of the College.

"Since leaving the College, Mr. Allen has been successfully engaged in the business of instruction as a Classical teacher; and it gives me pleasure to say, that I believe him qualified both by his attainments and experience to act as such in our higher Seminaries of learning.

"SIMEON NORTH,

"President of Hamilton College.

"Hamilton College, Sept. 12, 1852."

REVIEW.

It is a great deal easier to set a story afloat than to stop it. If you want truth to go round the world you must hire an express train to pull it; but if you want a lie to go round the world, it will fly; it is as light as a feather, and a breath will carry it. It is well said in the old Proverb, "A lie will go round the world while truth is pulling its boots on." Nevertheless, it does not injure us; for if light as a feather it travels as fast, its effect is just about as tremendous as the effect of down, when it is blown against the walls of a castle; it produces no damage whatever, on account of its lightness and littleness. Fear not Christian. Let slander fly, let envy send forth its forked tongue, let it hiss at you, your bow shall abide in strength. Oh! shielded warrior, remain quiet, fear no ill; but like the eagle in its lofty eyry, look thou down upon the fowlers in the plain; turn thy bold eye upon them and say, "Shoot ye may, but your shots will not reach half way to the pinnacle where I stand. Waste your powder upon me if ye will; I am beyond your reach." Then clap your wings, mount to Heaven, and there laugh them to scorn, for you have made your refuge God, and shall find a most secure abode.

C. H. SPURGEON.

Was any proper or sufficient notice of the meeting (Oct. 17, '57) of the pretended "self-constituted committee" extended to me? I received a note from the interested and officious Eli Fay, Mr. Mann's instrument; but it gave me no notice of a meeting of a "committee of three," or of a "self-constituted committee." This note is given in the preceding introduction; and the reader will see at a glance, considering its subject matter, its date, and attendant circumstances, that it is a remarkable production, and one to which, in a Republic, only a blind, vile, most bitter partizan feeling could have given birth.

This letter does not invite me to any mutual advantages, to any participation in the selection of the committee, or in the appointment of the time! It does not even give me sufficient notice, in point of time, for an investigation (involving the history of the College), which, if entered upon at all, should be entered upon with the greatest deliberation, wisdom, and Christian candor. Does the letter even intimate, who are to be the members of said "committee of five gentlemen?" No, all is behind the curtain! all is in the dark!

This notice does not allow me *one single privilege*, except to be present and confront his witnesses, if I "desire to do so;" (dare to do so); and in view of the arrogance of the letter and attendant circumstances, does it allow me even this privilege? Was it not virtually a most emphatic hint for me to stay away? So I thought; so others thought; and as the notice was wholly incompetent, and the whole scheme, so far as it could be guessed at, was entirely uncalled for and foolish, if not malicious and deeply wicked; I determined, as stated in the introduction, to take no notice of Mr. Fay's letter. No high-minded, justice-loving man could stoop, save to pity such weakness and foolish officiousness.

2d. Was said committee "self-constituted?" Each member of the committee has acknowledged that he was invited to Yellow Springs by Eli Fay; and the chairman, T. M. McWhinney, says he was not only frequently invited but *urged* to come. Elder H. Simonton, writes as follows:—

"NEW CARLISLE, O., Dec. 26, '57.

"BROTHER ALLEN—*Dear Sir:*—Your line to me came in due time. As I have had but little to do or say either in the prosperous or adverse condition of Antioch, I still feel disposed to say but little, and what I do say, to be for the good of all concerned. As I have no personal feelings to serve, I will in a *cautious* manner, answer your questions.

"1st. Mr. Eli Fay did invite me to visit the Springs.

"2d. He desired me to act as one of *the committee* to hear *his reasons* for not retaining *you* and *Mr. Doherty* in the College.

"3d. You ask me why I did not stay on the 16th of October. 1st. I had business of greater importance at home—that would pay me much better. 2d. I did not think the matter was got up right—a little too much on one side, &c.

"4th. A few days previous to the 16th, Mr. Fay was at my house and mentioned the matter to me. The last words I said to Mr. Fay on the subject were: 'If it is the desire of all persons concerned to have such an investigation, and they desire me to be one of the committee, I will consent; but I would rather they would get some other person.'

"5th. I am not posted in the ——— of those who have the fatherly Care of Antioch. I have my doubts whether all of them are as well posted as the importance of the case demands; if they were, they would tell the *same story*, and *mind* the *same things*.

6th. The committee were desired to publish the result of their investigations, as I learned from Mr. Fay.

I doubt any man will call in question the truth of my statements. Should any one do so, send him to me; and he and myself will settle the matter. Bro. Fay, and all connected with the College, have treated me well; and I wish to do the same to them; and think I can't do it in any better way than by telling them the TRUTH when called on.

"Yours as ever, H. SIMONTON,"

This letter will in part explain that portion of Mr. Fay's note which says: "I shall present to a committee of five gentlemen the reasons &c;" yet Eld. Simonton has given but a part of what he told me about said Fay's ludicrous manœuvres, in constituting or endeavoring to constitute said "committee of five;" how he flattered and hoodwinked McWhinney until the encrustations of soft-solder became so thick that he (McW.) could not see out; how he attempted to varnish him over in the same way, saying now, Simonton, you are just the man to act on this committee, your influence is great and potent with the Christians, and if two such distinguished men as yourself and McWninney come over to the College, and hear my "reasons" and then publish a "Report" with your names appended, it will set College affairs all right with our Churches! &c!

Eld. S., however, gave Mr. Fay to understand, that he had better save his breath; that such fulsome praise could not go down with him; that he had doubts about the propriety of such proceedings. Mr. Fay went to see Eld. S. again, but without much effect as the sequel shows; for although he was in Yellow Springs on the 16th Oct., he could not be prevailed upon to remain and act on the committee; and some of his reasons for refusing he gave to Prof. Doherty. But the insidious influences of Mann, Fay & Co. have, we fear, swerved even Bro. Simonton from the straight way, and blinded even his eyes to the truth. Do not his numerous and lengthy articles in the "Gospel Herald" during the past summer, so far as they have any point, indicate this?

But who was to be the fifth committee-man? Dr. H. C. Foster, of Enon, informed me that he was invited by Mr. Fay to come over to Antioch, with others to see what the moral and religious influences of the Institution are.

No intimation was given him that anything would be said concerning myself or Prof. Doherty, although he was invited only the day before the meeting, and as Dr. F. supposed, to act as a substitute for some member of a committee appointed by a conference or convention.

At first he consented to come, but on further reflection, he asked himself—What can a committee learn about the true moral and religious condition of an institution by walking through its halls, or passing a few hours under its roof, when it is known beforehand by the Professors and Teachers that such a committee is to be present on such a day, on such a mission? He, therefore, concluded, that such a plan was short-sighted and foolish, and determined to have no hand in the affair. But he added, I now regret, on your account, that I was not present on that occasion; for I should have used my influence against such unjust proceedings.

A sixth gentleman was also invited to be present, but declined. How many more persons were consulted and urged in order to make up "a committee of five gentlemen," I am not informed. Only three persons, it seems, were induced to participate in the matter! "Self-constituted(?) Committees" seemed to be obtained with difficulty!

3d. Was this committee disinterested? If they were, as they professed, self-appointed, and only desirous of obtaining the truth; why did they not notify me of the meeting, or at least, some of my friends, who are acquainted with the history of the College? Why did they allow themselves to be led to the College by Mr. Fay, and listen only to his witnesses? Why did they not call on me, when they were no doubt aware that I was at my house, but a few rods from the College buildings? Why did they not call on some of my friends, and take their testimony if they had any regard at all for impartiality and truth? Why did they listen only to the witnesses of an *interested party*, who had *a case to make out?* Why, in fine, did they not imitate Eld. Simonton, and others, who would not yield to the flatteries and seductions of designing men?

4th. Was not this committee wholly *ex parte?* How could an investigation be more partizan and untrustworthy? The committee was brought together, or constituted by Mr. Fay who acted as witness; sergeant-at-arms, a kind of godfather of the whole concern, and seemingly as proprietor of the College itself! His witnesses were persons whom he had been instrumental in placing in office in the present temporary school, with brilliant prospects ahead, if Mr. Mann's great scheme could be carried through; but few or none of them were truly in sympathy with "the Christians." Why should they not keep back a part of the truth, throw out insinuations, and talk to please Mann and Fay; especially since Mr. Mann has Antioch College under *one thumb*, and several of the blustering Christian ministers under *the other!* Besides, Mr. Mann will probably carry the day, and then a $1000 per year and a Professorship for life are worth struggling for!

Why should not the committee, too, magnify the testimony, and by their sweeping reports, make the Christians believe that Antiooh College is now in operation as a school; and that Profs. Doherty and Allen are neither worthy of seats in the same, nor of the sympathy or fellowship of its founders? Why not do a *little* evil that *great* good may come? Why not injure Prof. Allen's influence with the Christians, in order that the College may be wrested from the denomination, and placed in Mr. Mann's hands, through the agency of a "Joint Stock Company!" What conclusions, I ask, would not such a committee come to from the malicious statements of one's enemies, and the private intrigues of designing men?

Suppose Mr. Fay's note had given me the names of his committee, and sufficient time to bring my witnesses together—most of whom are now in New York, New England and Europe—could I have expected justice from a committee packed by him? To suppose me capable of submitting my reputation to such a committee under such circumstances would be to pronounce me not far removed from insanity or idiocy!

EXAMINATION OF THE FIRST REPORT.

The following Report appeared in the "Gospel Herald," of Nov. 12th, and was the first evidence which I received that any such inquisitorial meeting *had been held* concerning myself:

"COMMITTEE'S REPORT.

"Whereas, certain remarks have been made touching the action of the committee (Hon. A. Harlan, Rev. H. W. Bellows, D. D., and Elder E. Fay,) to which was referred the selection of the Faculty of Antioch College for the ensuing year;

"And whereas, these remarks have, as we believe, been *very* prejudical to the best interests of the College—in that they have led, at least some, and perhaps many, of the warm hearted patrons of the College, not only to distrust the committee, but to lose confidence in most, if not *all*, of those who have the supervision of the institution; and this feeling of general distrust having grown out of the fact that this committee refused to re-appoint two of our brethren, Professors Doherty and Allen, men in whom we had *implicit* confidence;

"And whereas, the facts that influenced that committee in its action were to be had by any who sought them, and knowing that for us to believe rumor, when *truth* could be obtained, was not only to do injustice to ourselves and the committee, but the *grossest* wrong to the College;

"Therefore, we, the undersigned, formed ourselves into a committee, for the purpose, not only of satisfying ourselves as to the *surprising* action of that committee, but, furthermore, of presenting, if it were ever deemed proper, the result of our inquiry to others of our friends, that they, too, might know why that committee acted as they did.

"And now, permit us to say, that having gone there to the College on Saturday, the 17th day of this month, and having heard the testimony of the students, class by class, and moreover, having heard the testimony of the Faculty—we say that, having gone to the only place where we supposed the *truth* could be elicited, and having gathered *all* the *facts* that we could, it *is our most deliberate and abiding conviction that that committee could not, in view of the evidence presented them, have appointed either of those two brethren to a Professorship in Antioch College.*

"Had they appointed them, we cannot but believe that their action would have been to gratify a *few* personal friends, rather than to have consulted the *general* interest of our beloved Institution.

"We have but to say in conclusion, that this committee is "self constituted," and this report gratuitous; hence we submit it, with the hope that if you are still not satisfied with the action of that committee, that you will, for the sake of our long cherished College, adopt some plan whereby your conclusion may hereafter be *based* upon facts rather than rumors.

"Franklin,
Oct. 28th, 1857."

T. M. McWhinney,
J. G. Reeder,
O. J. Wait,
} *Committee.*"

This is a remarkable document; and although it may, perhaps, on its face, appear very smooth and ingenuous to persons unacquainted with the facts, yet it is highly deceptive and inaccurate.

It was "conceived in iniquity," and "brought forth" in the "Herald" by fraud, "by a trick," as the reader has seen from the letters of Maple and Geary in the "Introduction." Such "a trick" needs no comment. Even demagogues and politicians would despise the doer. Judge Douglass, in his able December speech before the U. S. Senate, says—"Neither the North nor the South has the right to gain a sectional advantage by trickery or fraud."

But here, at the outset of the examination of this report, let me exonerate Messrs. Harlan and Bellows from any connection with Eli Fay in appointing this "smelling commitete," or in concocting the above "Report." I have no evidence that either of these gentlemen had any participation with Mr. Fay in this wicked scheme. I cannot believe that they would stoop for a moment to such foul business, to such a tricky, dark plot. Let the righteous indignation of the people fall where it is richly merited—upon Eli Fay and his master.

But to the Report. 1st, "Whereas, certain remarks," &c. This refers, doubtless, to the articles of Eld's. Maple, Pike, Summerbell, Millard, Holmes, and others, which appeared a few months since in the "Gospel Herald." (See Part 1st.) Were not those articles true? Did they not carry conviction to the minds of our brethren, and show them that Antioch had been wrested from their embrace, and placed "not upon a denominational basis"? Will McWhinney maintain that the remarks of the above named brethren have "been *very* prejudicial to the best interests of the College" as intended by its founders?

That their remarks have "been very prejudicial" to the selfish interests of Mann, Dean, Fay & Co., and to the College as it now stands monopolized by that clique, is without question true, and I thank God for it; for I cannot believe it right to fundamentally change the character and charter of an institution without the consent of the association or denomination which founded it.

2d. By the expression—"the selection of the Faculty of Antioch College for the ensuing year"—and others which appear in the report, people at a distance are deceived. The school of 1857 and '8, carried on in the College buildings which were rented of the assignee, is not Antioch College, if we can rely upon the statements of Harlan, Pike, Mills, Merrifield, and others It is a temporary school, organized by a few individuals for only one year, during the suspension or assignment of the College. It is under the direction of Mr. Mann, at whose dictation or suggestion the teachers have been selected. The Christian denomination, therefore, is not responsible either for the existence or the character of this school. The "Herald of Gospel Liberty," of Oct. 22d, speaking of the school, says—"The Christians have no legal claim to a single Professorship, as the College now stands." Why then does this committee labor to create the impression that the present school is Antioch College, and that the present teachers constitute "the Faculty of Antioch College?" I am heartily tired of such deception and intrigue. Why not call things by their right names. Why seek to hoodwink the Christians? Why not practice the maxim—"Honesty is the best policy?"

"He who walketh uprightly, walketh surely."—Proverbs.

3d. They speak of a "general distrust," and say it has grown out of the fact that this Committee (Fay and others) refused to re-appoint two of our brethren, Professors Doherty and Allen, men in whom we had *implicit* confidence." Did the simple fact that said Committee did not appoint two Professors as teachers in "Mr. Mann's Select School" cause such a "general distrust?" If so, Professors Doherty and Allen must consider themselves highly complimented by the public. This treasonable act of Mr. Fay to the Christians, without doubt, added new fuel to the flames; but their distrust and indignation were previously at a great height. The reader of the preceding pages, (Part 1st) has seen many evidences of this. Mr. Mann had hardly set foot into the Institution before troubles commenced, and they have been increasing from that day to this. The testimonies substantiating this are ample. Mr. Fay's letters from New York city in the spring of 1855, prove this. He says:

"I sincerely hope you will maintain the independence of your position, and defend your rights at all hazards!" "Antioch College is the property of the *Christians*, and should be under their control." "Submit to no insults for your own sake, and for our sake, and for the sake of Antioch." "You see plainly that a crisis is coming, and the Christians will as certainly be victorious in an open war, as God reigns." "I stated distinctly to (Mr. Mann) that there had been a *general* uneasiness among all the teachers ever sent there by the Christians, and that not more than one—and indeed I knew not that there was one—who was satisfied with the administration of affairs."

Such are some of the statements of Eli Fay, made a little more than three years ago, and they indicate the right spirit. But where is he to-day? The merest tool of Horace Mann; and religously, perhaps, several points below Theodore Parkerism! The Eli Fay of 1850-'5, and the Eli Fay of to-day, are, it is thought, as far removed from each other as the zenith and nadir; almost as different as white and black.

"Had the contest, however, been an open war"; had not Mr. Fay and others deserted the Christians; had they not practised wire-working, trickery and fraud, instead of showing themselves upon the open field, the above prediction would have proved true; "the Christians" would have been "as certainly victorious as God reigns," they would have vindicated their rights and their honor by driving out the money changers, the usurpers, from Antioch.

Let the reader glance over the statements of Maple, Pike, Summerbell, Millard, and others, found in Part 1st, and he cannot fail to see that this "general distrust" is no new thing.

Maple, speaking of Antioch College, says:

"Its whole history has been a round of disaster and disgrace." "The chief Agents are rich, and the College is bankrupt, and an enormous sum, sufficient to build two large Colleges, remains to be paid." "Antioch College is a still more complete and miserable failure in a religious and denominational point of view." "A clean sweep has been made of all the representatives of the Christian denomination." "We can assure Messrs. Dean, Fay & Co, that our people will not be the tame and spiritless tools of their little, scheming, selfish, greedy clique. There is some self respect and denominational honor left in the Christian Church, and the course pursued by the managers of the College will call them out."

"The following gentlemen were chosen with the full approbation of the Christian denomination, as our representatives in the Faculty of Antioch College. They are still available, and have, by the most sedulous culture, been making constant improvement in every qualification necessary for their offices; and now their names are all omitted from the list of the Faculty. Professors Allen, Doherty, and Holmes." "Antioch College is, under its present arrangement, unworthy of the confidence of the Christian Church."

B. F. Carter, says: "New England is in favor of a denominatial College. The plan adopted at Marion is our plan."

D. E. Millard: "Let us rally to the support of *our own* institutions, and strive to make them what we had hoped of the once 'great' but now *fallen* 'Antioch'"

D. P. Pike: "I now wish we were at Marion with our present experience, and about to make a beginning for a College of OUR OWN." "Something is working against us denominationally at Antioch College. No teacher of our denomination can long succeed there."

N. Summerbell. "We have been injured, deeply injured, but it is not too late to recover; yet let none be deceived. Antioch has never been under our control, and now that she is acknowledged dead, let her be buried."

But I need not multiply extracts. The following letter, however, by Prof. H. D. Burlingame, of Albany, N. Y., who was for two years instructor in Antioch, will interest the reader.

"ALBANY, N. Y., Oct. 18th, 1857.

"FRIEND ALLEN:—Your favor of the 13th instant, has been duly received, and read with great pleasure. * * * I am rejoiced to hear from you that the friends of Antioch, *not as it is*, but as it was *designed to be*, and as we hope it may yet be, are not all dead. Let there be a determined and unwavering effort put forth to gain what has been lost, and all may yet be well; but better far for the Denomination, that not one stone of that magnificent structure remain upon another, than that Antioch should remain as it is!

"It is now a 'bone of contention,' distracting the church and diverting its effort from the cause it seeks to build up; and by being held out to the world as the representative of the Christians, the denomination is placed in a false position, which cannot fail to obstruct its progress and narrow its influence. Does any one doubt that Antioch College, under its present administration, does not represent the Christian denomination? I do not doubt it. You do not doubt it. No one who has witnessed the workings of Antioch College for the last four years can doubt it. If the influence of the College at the present time is Christian, what makes it so? Where are its representative men who were elected to seats in its Faculty to watch over the interests of the denomination?

"Where is Prof. Holmes? Sacrified. Where Doherty? Where Allen? Where McKinney? Where the assistant teachers of that denomination? All sacrificed. And who, and who alone, represents the denomination now? A school boy; a student, hardly through his course of study, alone represents the Christian Denomination in 'Great Antioch,' the new College of the Christians of which we have heard so much!

"Surely, no one who is acquainted with the state of things, will make so groundless a charge as to accuse Mr. Mann of representing the Christian Denomination? Or any one introduced into the Institution through his influence? It is unjust to make such a charge against them. They are not guilty.

"If Mr. Mann's sympathies are with the denomination; if he likes their views better than the views of any other denomination with which he ever met, as he has often asserted; if, in short, he has aimed to make Antioch what its founders designed it should be, why the unpleasant collission between him and the representatives of the denomination in the Faculty and Board of Instruction? Why have they, through his means, been dismissed from their posts, or voluntarily left in disgust? Is this likely to be the case with those, who, in good faith, are laboring with heart and hand for the advancement of a common cause? Why is it that the great mass of the denomination have no confidence in the Institution, and feel that they are grossly mis-represented by it? Is it because the entire denomination is so stupid as not to know whether Mr. Mann is laboring for their interest or not, and appreciate him accordingly? I think not. I think the denomination is competent to acknowledge and appreciate *bona fide* co-operation. The truth is, the co operation has been wanting; and we who have inhaled the College atmosphere for two or three years, feel and know that such is the case. We feel and know that particular care has been taken that the sentiment may prevail with students and others, that whatever of excellence there might be in the Institution, emanated from a *certain* source; and whatever talent and aptness to teach there might be, existed in the *elect alone.*

"If the Christian Denomination has been, and is, well represented in Antioch, how is it that every Teacher and Professor who entered within its walls through the influence of the denomination have felt it to be otherwise? Why have all such Teachers felt that to succeed in teaching in the College, was to succeed in withstanding Horace Mann & Co.'s secret opposition? There is but one true answer to these interogations.

"I was much surprised to learn that Weston had commended Mr. Mann's course by accepting a place in the College under existing circumstances, especially as you know he has always, until recently, been most vehement in his denunciations of Mr. Mann's policy, and that he should apologize for the driving of Prof. Holmes, and others, out of doors, seems almost incredible. This is indeed a strange world.

"Your Friend, BURLINGAME."

Are not the above statements sufficient to prove, beyond a doubt, that this "general distrust" is no new or sudden thing? It is of several years' growth. All the representative Professors and Teachers of the Christians came from different parts of the Union. Most of them were strangers to each other. They had a deep interest in Antioch College, and a high opinion of its President. They came to the Institution at different dates, yet a residence of a few weeks or months was sufficient to force them each and all to unpleasant conclusions. They found Antioch *in name,* and perhaps *legally* "the College of the Christians," but not so *in reality,* not so *spiritually.* They found strong controlling influences in the Institution which they believed to be anti-Christian, to be contrary to the wishes and intentions of the founders of the College. They were forced by stern facts, and in direct opposition to their inclinations, to the conclusion, that Horace Mann, on paper, or *theoretically,* and Horace Mann *practically,* are two very different entities.

4th. "And now permit us to say, that having gone there to the College on Saturday, the 17th day of this month and having heard the testimony of the students, class by class, and moreover, having heard the testimony of the Faculty—we say that having gone to the only place where we supposed the *truth* could be elicited, and having gathered *all* the facts that we could, it *is our most deliberate and abiding conviction, that that committee* (Fay & Co.) *could not, in view of the evidence presented them, have appointed either of those brethren* (Doherty and Allen) *to a Professorship in Antioch College.*"

Does not this paragraph simply if not directly state that the students, class by class, as well as the Faculty, gave testimony against me, testimony in view of which I ought not to have been appointed to a Professorship?

Now what are the facts? Immediately after the appearance of the above Report, I conversed with several of the Professors and students, and with two members of the committee, and all, without exception, declared that, to the best of their knowledge, no student was present at said committee meeting, Oct. 17th, P. M., or presented any testimony reflecting on myself, and nearly every one volunteered the statement that he had never heard ought from any student against me, and some said that they had frequently conversed with students about the school and the Professors, and had uniformly heard nothing but commendations of myself, which was what they could not say of any other member of the late Faculty, save one.

And here I feel that justice to the students of Antioch College demands the statement that their bearing towards myself has always been most gentlemanlike and respectful; that our intercourse has been mutually pleasant and of the most satisfactory character, and that after an acquaintance with the students of several Eastern Colleges, I am free to say, that I have never before met a more earnest, studious and orderly class of young ladies and gentlemen.

Soon after the appearance of the Report, the following correction was published in the "Gospel Herald:"

"CORRECTION.

"MR. EDITOR:—In the 'Gospel Herald' of Nov. 12 there is a very *serious* misstatement made by that so-called *self-constituted* Committee, in reference to Prof. Allen, which should not go uncorrected, for it not only reflects upon the character of Prof. Allen, but represents students of Antioch as having done what they never did do.

"That committee says, 'And now, permit us to say, &c.'

(Here supply the above paragraph touching the testimony of the students, class by class, &c.)

"Now we would ask if the above does not *state* that the students, class by class, gave testimony against Profs. Doherty and Allen? It appears so to me and to all the students who have read the report, and who, with myself, wonder how the committee could have made such an evident mistake.

"The facts as we understand them are as follows: We of the College classes, who at the close of last year's session signed a petition for the removal of Prof. Doherty, were solicited by Rev. Mr. Fay to meet on Saturday, the 17th, to state, before a committee, our reasons for signing that petition. A part of the gentlemen students did so, but there were no ladies present.

"But *we did not hear a word said in reference to Prof. Allen, not a single question was asked our class in reference to him*, and members of other classes say the *same*. Moreover, we supposed this committee was selected by both parties concerned, and not self constituted, as it appears from the report. But neither Prof. Doherty nor Prof. Allen was present; the reason of their absence we know not.

"The committee says, 'having gathered *all* the *facts* that we could,' &c. Again it seems to me that they are inconsistent, for how can a committee gather all the facts, when only one of the parties concerned is present?

"In justice to myself and to the students of Antioch College, and to Prof. Allen, whom the students consider as second only to Pres. Mann, and were much surprised to learn that he was not re-elected, we ask for the publication of the above correction in your paper.

"I have written this article through the solicitation of no person and unknown to anybody. Yours for truth, A STUDENT.

The reader will understand that Mr. Fay's committee held two meetings, one at 9 o'clock, A. M., to which some of the students were summoned and questioned concerning Prof. Doherty; and another at 1 o'clock, P. M., in which Mr. Fay and some members of the Faculty vituperated me!

As to the "testimony of the Faculty," I find that, of a Faculty of seven persons, two had nothing to do with the matter; and that three others who told me all the testimony they gave, said nothing it seems to me, which would have influenced any other than an *ex parte* committee determined to make out a case. One of the three said he was present at the meeting only a part of the time, answered only two or three questions, and gave no testimony against me.

The second of the trio said he was present only ten or fifteen minutes, just before the meeting closed; and then only because Mr. Fay came down to his residence, and insisted that he should go up with him to the committee meeting; that he had declared to a Bro. Professor in the morning that he would have nothing to do with the matter, would not go to the meeting even if requested to do so; but that he could not well withstand Mr. Fay's importunity, and finally concluded to go up a few moments. He added, that all he had to say was in answer to the question of the committee, whether there had been harmony and sympathy between Prof. Allen and Pres. Mann? He replied that his own intercourse with Mr. Allen had always been pleasant and satisfactory; but he had thought that there was not perhaps a complete harmony between the President and Prof. Allen.

The third, or last of the trio, said that the only testimony which he gave was a matter of hearsay, an inference which a certain person or persons, had made from some remarks of mine, and which might or might not weigh against me, depending on its correctness or incorrectness.

The facts could have been stated in a moment by myself. The inference was incorrect, a misconstruction.

Thus, of the seven members of the Faculty, two had no connection with the matter, and three others had, according to their own admission, given no testimony which, it appears to me, could have biased the judgment of an impartial committee.

"The testimony of the Faculty," therefore, appears to have been given substantially by two members, Mr. Mann and Mrs. A. S. Dean, and chiefly, perhaps, by the latter. How very influential has woman always been since mother Eve's day in Eden!

In College affairs Mrs. Dean has exercised almost unlimited control over Mr. Mann. I do not now call to mind a single instance in which he has successfully resisted her demands; and after a three years' residence in the Institution, I am by no means surprised that the impression became general during the first collegiate year that "Miss Pennell is virtually President of Antioch College."

It is, no doubt, difficult to oppose a determined woman, especially if she believes herself to be an Aspasia, or Cleopatra; but I say "let truth and justice triumph though the heavens fall."

"Having gone to the only place where we supposed the *truth* could be elicited." Would the committee intimate that the "truth" could only be elicited from Eli Fay and A. S. Dean, both of whom are known to be notorious falsifiers! and from their coadjutors whose veracity is questionable!

"Having gathered all the facts we could." If there is any truth in this expression, it exhibits a very great weakness on the part of the committee! Why *could* they not call on myself and others living near the College? They certainly can not plead a want of time; for two of the committee, McWhinney and Reeder, live within a few miles of Yellow Springs; and from the time of their meeting to the publication of their Report there was nearly a month.

Besides, on Oct. 28th, some fifteen days before their Report appeared in print, and before I knew that they had held any meeting touching myself, we all met in convention at Franklin, O., where, had they so desired, they could have consulted me. The truth is, they had no such desire. They did not wish to be impartial. They had no regard for right and justice, they had been so thoroughly duped as to believe that "all the facts," the whole truth could be obtained from Eli Fay and his informers, my treacherous and only enemies! McWhinney even *falsified his word to me;* for being at his house iu Enon, soon after the appearance of the "Report" and before the Franklin Convention, he promised again and again, that the next time he came over to Yellow Springs *he would surely call on me* and have a consultation.

He has frequently been in Yellow Springs, since that time, on one occasion remaining two days, yet has never called on me. Where can the truth be found?

"Truth is perished, and cut off from their mouth.—JEREMIAH.

"They trust in vanity, and speak lies; they conceive mischief, and bring forth iniquity.—ISAIAH.

"Sanctify them, O Lord, through thy truth; thy word is truth.—ST. JOHN."

5th. "Had they appointed them, we cannot but believe that their action would have been to gratify a *few* personal friends, rather than to have consulted the *general* interest of our beloved Institution."

The exact reverse of this is believed to be the fact. Prof. A. L. McKinney speaks on this point, as follows:

"Setting aside the injury it (the Report) has done, Professors Doherty and Allen, which is enough, in all conscience to condemn it in the estimation of all candid men; I desire to refer to a section of said 'Report' impugning the motives of those who were desirous that Prof.'s Doherty and Allen should be retained in the College Faculty. It is this—'Had they appointed them, (Doherty and Allen), we can but believe that their action would have been to gratify a few personal friends, &c.

"1st. This gives out the impression that but *few*, and these mere personal friends, were desirous that these two gentlemen should be retained as Professors in the College. Well, what are the 'facts in the case?'—Let the petition, signed by a large number of gentlemen of worth and repectability, living at Yellow Springs and elsewhere, and presented to the committee, (Harlan, Bellows and Fay), whose duty it was to appoint the Faculty, asking that Prof. Doherty should be retained; I say let this petition say whether there were a *few* personal friends to be gratified.

"In reference to Prof. Allen, nine-tenths (and I speak within bounds, I think) of the students, and of the friends of the College, were desireous that he should still fill his chair in the Institution. So much for the *few* personal friends to be 'gratified.'

"2d. It calls in question the motives of those who wished these gentlemen retained; that they would see the prosperity of the College sacrificed, its influence limited, its brightness dimmed, its glory obscured; all to gratify a little personal regard; that personal regard limited to a '*few*' was *first*, and the interests of the College *second*.

"We thank this 'self-constituted committee' for the compliment (?) they paid to our candor, and hope they may use another standard of measurement when they again propose estimating the motives of men.

"TROY, O., Jan. 14, '58. A. L. MCKINNEY."

6th. "We have but to say in conclusion, that this committee is 'self-constituted,' and this report gratuitious; hence we submit it, &c."

That this Report is gratuitious, or void of candor, equity and facts, is doubtless true; but that the committee is "self-constituted," is not so clear, especially after Mr. Fay's travels and arduous endeavors to form a "committee of five gentlemen," and after the admissions of the "committee of three," that they were invited to the College by said Fay!

7th. The reader of the Report has noticed that great stress is laid upon the word "facts," yet *not one single fact* is given as a basis of the committee's *"deliberate and abidiug conviction,"* concerning myself and Prof. Doherty.

Why such prating about facts when they are wholly suppressed? Is not this suppression of pretended facts far more injurious than any specific statements could have been? Does not such a report excite the suspicions of many readers who are unacquainted with the history of the College, and give full play to their imagination to fancy any flagrant, immoral act?

But what are the facts? asks the reader of this page. Why this Report? Were not the committee-men sincere? Their motives I leave to the great Judge of "quick and dead." I will not say they were not sincere; for Saul thought he was doing God service when "breathing out threatenings and slaughter against the Christians;" yet in this nineteenth century, in this age of civil and religious light and liberty, I do not understand how persons of good common sense could have been so duped, or done what they have done.

The existence and publication of the report are some of the fruits of Eli Fay's schemes and back of him, doubless, of Horace Mann's intrigues.

As to "the facts;" the careful reader of the preceding pages can not have failed to notice them. They are numerous, but have all, or nearly all grown out of Mr. Mann's administration of affairs; out of the great contest between himself, aided and abetted by A, S. Dean, Eli Fay, T. M. McWhinney, O. J. Wait, who claim to be Christian Ministers, and lately by Austin Craig, James Maple, and others, and by the College debt, on the one side; and the Christian Denomination proper, and its representative Professors and Teachers, on the other; a contest between a centralized "scheming, selfish, greedy clique," and a disgusted, widely-scattered religious denomination; a contest of opinions, and a contest of principles.

To many of Mr. Mann's acts I never have, nor never can subscribe, so long as I have any love for truth and justice. My integrity can not be bartered for office, preferment, or the favors of any man; and these things Mr. Mann well knows from lengthy conversations years since. For differences of opinion I care nothing, so long as men are honest, gentlemanly and christian; but when they descend to schemes, intrigues and wicked plots, my respect vanishes, and I *pity them.* "To err is human," but "live and let live." Let men be honest and charitable, be their opinions what they may.

I believe, and would to God that Mr. Mann might also *believe* and *practice* his own words, published some five years since in the first Circular Catalogue of Antioch College: "Until two men *are* alike in all respects, they can not *believe* alike in all respects; and as no two men ever were alike in all respects, no two men ever believed alike in all respects; however many times they may have signed, rehearsed, or sworn to the same articles of belief."

There is something very ludicrous as well as detestable in Mr. Fay's maneuverings, and in the proceedings of the "self-constituted committee." From the committee's Report, one might think, if unacquainted with Mr. Mann's wire-working clique, that Profs. Doherty and Allen had done something too horrible to be mentioned. All must be shrouded in the dark! just as in the case of Mrs. Holmes three years since!

What one of our oldest and most prominent ministers in Ohio thinks of such sham pretences, may be gathered from the following article which appeared in the "Gospel Herald" of Dec. 17, 1857, soon after the first Report of the pretended "self-constituted committee."

THE REASON WHY?

"I see in the 'Herald' of the 29th ult., that a Brother complains that there is so much darkness shrouded in the Report of 'the self-constituted committee' that he cannot see the reason why Prof.'s Doherty and Allen were not re-appointed as members of the Faculty of Antioch College. Well, as I was once at the College during a term, and being politely invited to hear their classes recite, I gladly embraced the opportunity, and paid strict attention to some of the things I saw and heard, and notwithstanding I did not consider myself 'a committee' at the time, but for the sake of my blind Brother who cannot see any light in the self-constituted committee's Report, I have concluded to constitute myself one now, and report my 'investigations,' in the hope of casting some light on this dark subject.

"First, on entering the hall I saw Prof. Doherty seated at the head of his class with his face shaved so close that it was hard to tell whether it ever had any beard or not. He seemed to be perfectly at home, and well understood his business, spoke with firmness and manifested a little of the temper of an Irish gentleman.

"On entering the apartment of Prof. Allen, I saw a man like Sampson, on whom a razor had never come. He spoke as soft and mild as a mother to a darling child, and represented well the character of a regular down east Yankee, while he seemed to understand perfectly what he was about. Both classes seemed to love and respect their teachers, so you see, my dear Brother, one was not re-appointed because *he shaved every day*, and the other one turned off because *he did not shave at all*—one an Irishman and the other an American. Pshaw, it is easy to see that neither of these men are fit to teach in Antioch College.

"December 12, 1857." IRONICAL."

But in order to give the reader some slight idea of Mr. Fay's labors before the "self-constituted committee" was thought of, I will remark that, in the Spring of 1857, Eld. McWhinney was at the Springs, and invited and strongly urged me to come over to Enon and attend the meeting in his Church. He also invited Bro. Layton to drive over. We accepted his invitation; and on the next Sabbath drove over and listened to a discourse by Eld. McWhinney. Eld. McW. seemed highly pleased to meet us and showed us all the attentions of which he was capable. At the close of the morning service, Dr. Foster invited us to his house to dine, where we had a very pleasant interview; and after the Sabbath school exercises in the afternoon, we returned to the Springs.

Some weeks after, Eli Fay called at Dr. Foster's house, and although personally a stranger to the Dr. he catechised him closely about Prof. Allen's conversation on the Sabbath alluded to above. The Dr. answered all his questions, although he thought them not a little singular. After the lapse of some time, the circumstance of Mr. Fay's call on Dr. Foster was mentioned to me by different persons; and accordingly I dropped Bro. Foster a note, asking him if this rumor was true, to which he replied as follows:

"ENON, Dec. 6th, 1857.

"BRO. ALLEN—Your note is received; and in reply, I have to say that Mr. Fay called on me some time last summer, and asked if Prof. Allen had been at our house, I replied that he had; that Prof. Allen and Mr. Layton were over to attend meeting a few weeks before, and dined at our house.

"Well, did Mr. Allen say anything about having Mr. Mann removed from Antioch College? No, not a word. Did he not say anything about being appointed President of the College himself? No, not a single word. Did not Mr. Layton, during the call, say anything about these things? No sir. There was not a syllable uttered in my house by either of the gentlemen on the subject.

"Mr. Fay appeared much surprised! and said that he had heard from some source that I had intimated as much! What the object of his inquiries was, I was unable to solve at that time; but I suppose it was to hunt up some objections against you, as a sufficient reason why you should not be re-appointed. Yours with much esteem,

"H. C. Foster."

Mr. Fay also tried his hand among the students; but not with so much caution as a man engaged in such vile business should exercise, if he wishes to keep it secret. Passing through the Gentlemen's Hall one day, he accosted a student, and asked him what he thought of Prof. Doherty. The student replied, that he thought very much of Prof. Doherty, that he regarded him as a gentleman, a fine scholar, and an able Professor.

Ah! I did not know what your opinion was! said Mr. Fay and passed along. It so happened that this student was one of our ministers, Eld. ———, a young man of fine promise, well known among our Churches in Central Ohio, and much beloved. Will not Mr. Fay be a little more cautious hereafter when he starts out on such business? Who can refrain from—at least pitying a man who deserts and betrays his friends, and then skulks around behind their back and tracks them here and there, to see if some word has not been dropped in the freedom of friendly conversation which can be twisted and tortured into an accusation?

Whose character is safe, so long as such men are allowed to prowl around in community, and to get up "self-constituted Committees" to do their bidding, and to publish false and defamatory reports? We have great confidence in humanity; and in the general uprightness and integrity of the great masses; and we believe, therefore, that such persons not only merit, but that they will receive the scorn and righteous condemnation of the world.

EXAMINATION OF THE SECOND REPORT.

The preceding "Riview" of tho first Report is substantially a copy of the manuscript which was read to Mr. Maple, Dec. 25th, and which he refused to publish, on Feb'y 2d, as above stated.

In the "Gospel Herald" of March 18th, however, he says:

"SECOND REPORT OF THE SELF-CONSTITUTED COMMITTEE.

"In another column will be found a second report from the "self-constituted Committee." We have had this report in our hands for several weeks, and have hesitated long about publishing it; for there is nothing so painful to our feelings as to be under the necessity of publishing anything of this chaıacter. We should not have permitted this report to have seen the light if circumstances did not seem to demand it. The Executive Committee have authorized its publication."

It appears, therefore, that while he persisted in refusing me the opportunity of replying to the "first Report," he held in his safe keeping the "Smelling Committee's second Report" which he finally determined to publish!

"Painful to our feelings!" so one would suppose, if the editor had any appreciation of justice left; but who placed him "under the necessity of publishing" said second Report?

Why did he not come out immediately after the appearance of said committee's "*first Report*" in Nov. last, and expose the "*trick*" by which it was got into the "Herald," as an honest man and editor would have done? Why did he remain silent so long, and then deliberately publish the committee's despicable "second Report" while he kept the columns of the "Herald" closed against me?

He says "the Executive Committed have authorized its publication," which means, being interpreted, that three of the five members of the Executive Committee—viz, James Maple, editor of the "Gospel Herald;" J. G. Reeder, member of the "Smelling or self-constituted Committee," and C. Winebrener, member of Maple's church, "authorized its publication."

And why not? Maple and Reeder were personally interested in the matter and determined to injure me; and Bro. Winebrener's consent was obtained by Maple through misrepresentation. For this unjust and cowardly transaction, the other two members, Elds. N. Summerbell and J. Ellis, were in no way responsible.

The "second Report" being lengthy, will not be reprinted in full in this place, but the portions which are worthy of notice will be given in order as they are tested by the *touch-stone* of TRUTH.

First comes the lengthy preamble in which they allude to the "first Report" as follows:

"Without *specifying any* of the facts proven, we gave it as our deliberate and abiding conviction, that the committee could not, in view of the evidence presented them, have appointed either of those two men to a Professorship in the College."

The reason why we made a *generic* rather than a *specific* report, was to screen the "illogical moral character" of Mr. Allen. And we would not *now* be willing to make a disclosure of the *facts* were it not for the reason that we have learned, personally and otherwise, that Mr. Allen is taking advantage of that want of *specificness* to the great injury of the cause of truth, and the Christian character of those who made that Report; and hence the *mercy* that we showed him, has been turned against us; and thus the innocent have been made to suffer for the wickedness of the guilty."

These committee-men seem to have a very high opinion of their own "Christian character," and appear to be greatly concerned for "the cause of truth;" and fear that the indignation which good men throughout the country are manifesting towards them, and the condemnation which is being heaped upon their base reports, may forsooth, injure "the cause of truth!" Why did they not honestly say, injure their selfish ambition and prevent the accomplishment of their or Eli Fay's wicked schemes?

They speak of *mercy!* In the "Yellow Springs News Letter," a low scurrilous paper, *called Mr. Mann's organ, and now defunct,* O. J. Wait also, or more probably some one for him, says: "I learn that Mr. Allen is trying to make *capital* out of the mercy shown to him in the report of the Investigating Committee, who visited the College on the 17th of October, 1857."

What a gross misapplication of words! You might with much greater propriety speak of the *mercy* of the "Star Chamber," and the "Spanish Inquisition," for they could *only kill the body.* Indeed, this pretended mercy is infinitely baser and blacker than the mercy of the midnight assassin, who endeavors to plunge his dagger through your heart; for the soul is worth infinitely more than the body; and he who endeavors to destroy your soul, your character, is the most despicable and black-hearted of all villians.

But let the reader pay especial attention to the sentence. "And hence the *mercy* that we showed to him has been turned against us." If the "mercy" of which they speak was really clemency, love, charity, why do they complain that it is now manifested to them, or as they say, "turned against us?" Have these "professed ministers" forgotten the teaching of the good book, "With what measure ye mete, it shall be measured to you again?" Murder will out; and the very language of these committee-men belies their professions. Did they not intend by their "First Report" to make a most deadly thrust at Professors Doherty and Allen? Do not the style and arrangement (which smacks of Horace Mann) show this?

They represent themselves as impartial men, desirous only of the truth; and say "we had implicit confidence" in our brethren, Professors Doherty and Allen, but—"having gathered *all* the *facts* that we could, it is our most deliberate and abiding conviction, that that Committee could not, in view of the evidence presented them, have appointed either of those two brethren to a Professorship in Antioch College."

It is quite doubtful whether these men ever were truly our friends; and yet they pretend to be our "brethren." In no other way could they have thrown out more malicious and injurious insinuations. The very darkness in which they shrouded their pretended facts tended to give additional activity to the natural inquisitiveness of the people. Yet after all this, it is cheering to learn that these "Reports" have had little or no influence with those who are acquainted with College affairs, except to bring down their indignation upon the Committee; and that even those, who live hundreds of miles distant, see through the hollow-heartedness of the transaction.

"We *do* know from notes taken of a speech of his made before the students of Antioch, that he has said that he "would have preferred the facts."

Of course, when anything is said or published about myself, I prefer "facts" to fiction, truths to untruths. But why this allusion? Is it not intended to convey the idea to persons unacquainted with the circumstances, that I had labored to drag the students into the College difficulties?

The facts are briefly as follows: The "self-constituted Committee" had made the students a party in the College troubles by making use of them against Prof. Doherty. They also stated that "the students, class by class," had given testimony against myself. This the students knew to be false; for they gave no such testimony; and they would, no doubt, have corrected the Committee's Report through the press, as they frequently did orally, had they not feared that Mr. Mann would bring his official influence and power to bear against them in their present and future connection with the school. But some time in Jan'y, the 22d I believe, the three highest classes held meetings in their recitation rooms, on permission of their Teachers, and appointed committees to prepare a correction of the Report of the "self-constituted Committee." On learning this, Mr. Mann determined to put an end to the matter by an immediate and decisive blow. Accordingly on the following morning he requested the aforesaid classes to remain after morning prayers, and proceeded to make a speech, in which he eulogized the "self-constituted Committee" and commended their Report, and charged upon me;—"that I had taken measures to have the class meetings called in my behalf," when the fact is, I was not aware that any such meetings were to be held until after they had taken place. But suppose I had known that such meetings were to be held, or had requested them, for the purpose of correcting a false statement which had gone forth to the world in print, where would be the impropriety?

The matter was a very simple one. Either "the students, class by class" had given testimony against me or they had not. If they had given such testimony the statement was correct; if they had not, the the Report was false.

But the students, and all others who are acquainted with the facts, agree in saying that no such testimony was given; hence the desire, and the very proper and praiseworthy desire, of the students to correct the untrue statement of the "self-constituted Committee."

Mr. Mann said many other singular things to the students one of which is:—that "any attack on that Report is an attack on the College!" What would any unbiased mind infer from such a declaration? How could Mr. Mann have more clearly hinted that he had a hand in getting up the Report, or that it had received his sanction?

If to correct false reports and charges is to attack Antioch College, where does Antioch stand? upon truth or upon falsehood? upon justice or upon injustice and oppression? He also went on to say that a report had been circulated in this community that "Mr. Mann put Mr. Maple's name to the report of the Franklin Committee," which he pronounced to be false. Let the reader, however, turn to Part 3d, and examine Mr. Maple's letter to Eld. Lynn, and see if he did not say, on Dec. 6th, 1857, that—"he (Mr. Mann) put my name to it unjustly."

But why should Mr. Mann drag these things in before the students? Why should he desire to make them a party to his troubles? Why should he talk to them about rumors which they doubtless never heard; and strive to prevent them from correcting a false report? Was it not evidently to shield himself from the shafts of truth, and to injure my reputation in the eyes of the students? Did not Mr. Mann also, evidently intend that I should not be present and hear his speech to the students? The only notice which I received of the meeting came from Mr. Mann's own hand, and was brought to our door by his son, only about four or five minutes before the students convened. It so happened that I was at home, and although I could not well leave, yet I determined to go over and hear and take down Mr. Mann's speech, and at the close of his remarks he dismissed the students without giving me any chance, as I understood him, to make a reply. I was afterwards informed that Eli Fay, who was living a mile or more from College, was in reserve that morning in the Lady's Hall; but he did not show his face in the College chapel; for Mr. Weston slipped out during Mr. Mann's speech. I almost regretted that my unexpected presence prevented Mr. Fay from making his speech to the students. What a fine time they would have had, had I not been at home just at the minute when Mr. Mann's note arrived!

Being actively engaged during the following week I had no time to notice Mr. Mann's speech until Saturday, Jan'y 30th, when I sent a note early to Mr. Mann, requesting an opportunity of making a few remarks to the students addressed by him a week previously.

After chapel exercises the students were requested to remain, when I laid before them briefly the facts in the case, showing that Mr. Mann's speech was mostly irrevalent; that the case under consideration was very simple, for they either gave testimony against me, "class by class," or they did not; if not, where was the wrong in correcting the Committee's Report.

Mr. Mann arose immediately, and replied at considerable length. Touching the lateness of the notice sent me the previous Saturday morning, he said :

"Such notice was wholly gratuitous. We might have held that meeting properly without giving any notice. We were under no obligation to give such notice, but on that morning it occurred to me that Mr. Allen might take exceptions to it ; accordingly, I wrote the note in haste and sent it to him."

What a doctrine is this, that Mr. Mann has the right to assail my character before the students, without giving me any notice of the meeting ! He went on again to eulogize the "self-constituted Committee," and said :

"Those who assail their Report attack the College." "That the meaning of their Report is, that the present members of the Faculty should be where they are, and that some others should not be of the Faculty!" "That it was proper in legal matters, in reports of courts, to make general statements as to the testimony, as is done in their Report." &c., &c.

Are not these remarkable sayings for the President of a College? That they who question the "self-constituted Committee's" Report are attacking Mr. Mann's school, built up upon injustice, oppression and falsehood, all rotten at heart and falling in pieces; and that the "self-constituted," or more properly the "persecuting Committee," was brought together to do Mr. Mann's bidding, to inform the public that Horace Mann, his relatives and obsequious friends should be teachers in Antioch, may not perhaps be questioned; but that it is allowable in legal matters, in reports of the courts, to state that certain persons gave such and such testimony against Mr. A. B. or C. D. when, in truth, said "certain persons" were not in court at all, and did not give any testimony against said A. B. or C. D. *will be questioned* by every sane and well informed mind.

I again made a few remarks to the students, when Mr. Mann followed at some length; but I was informed that his attempts to mistify a simple matter did not gain much sympathy for him with those students who are able to think for themselves. Indeed Mr. Mann was informed by one of the students, at the close of his speech, on January 23d, that he (Mr. Mann) had stated some things incorrectly; that Prof. Allen had not requested the class meetings to be held, &c.

But Mr. Mann was not satisfied with public efforts; he must labor in private. One of the leading students told me that Mr. Mann had labored to convince him that Prof. Allen was hostile to the College, and that any thing done to strengthen him was a damage to the Institution, and consequently a damage to the students themselves! that himself (Mr. Mann) and the students were one party seeking the good of the College, and Prof. Allen and others were opposed to the College. What rank deception! What palpable design! But Mr. Mann was not yet satisfied. No relations so friendly; no confidence so sacred, which he must not fathom or destroy, in order, if possible, to fish up some objections or charges against those whom he wishes to injure. To illustrate this I will mention one case, but out of respect for the young lady concerned in it, it shall be made as brief as possible, and her name not mentioned. For convenience, however, we will call her Miss X. and her brother Mr. X. In the winter of 1855–6 Mr. X., with whom I had formerly been acquainted, in New York, wrote me from the most distant county in Ohio, asking some questions about Antioch College, and saying that one, and perhaps two, of his sisters desired to attend some good Institution. I replied to his interrogations, and in a few weeks, early in the spring of 1856, Miss X. arrived in Yellow Springs and came to our house. We received her cordially, told her we did not wish to take any boarders, but as she was a stranger in the place she could stop at our house if she could make herself at home, and it could be mutually agreeable, until she could find a boarding place. From this time on, she continued in our family for about one year and a half, and made herself more at home than I had supposed it possible, for one not related by blood. When in the house she was almost continually with the family, seldom occupying her own room even for an hour, except as a sleeping and toilet apartment. She studied with members of the family, conversed with members of the family, and enjoyed the freedom of the house as much perhaps, as if she had been under her own ancestral roof. We gave her our confidence, and conversed as freely with and before her as we did among ourselves. In fact it was understood that while she remained in our house, she was one with us, and if, in the freedom of familiar home conversation any thing was said not proper to be spoken of abroad, it was to be regarded as strictly confidential.

As is well known, many things have been done at Antioch, which have aroused no little feeling, and occasioned no small amount of talk through the town. Some of the common and well known remarks concerning the College, were mentioned in our family, principally at table, not as new or original with us, nor with a view to bias or prejudice Miss X.'s mind, but as a matter of sociality. Miss X. was a student, it is true, and it may be objected that we ought not to have discussed College affairs in her presence; and with most students such a course would have been followed, but most of our family were students, and Miss X. was a young lady of age and experience, of mature mind, and had a judgment of her own, and knew how to use it. Besides, we had been acquainted with her brother in New York, (he having been our roommate in College,) and also partially acquainted with the family, and we believed them to be persons of integrity and discreetness. Where, under all the circumstances, was there any impropriety in speaking of College matters, especially when we remarked little or nothing but what was known and talked of in town, and which, with much more, Miss X. may have heard from other sources? We can see none; and no person of good judgment, we think, can find any.

After Miss X. had been with us for more than fifteen months, and after the College property had all been assigned, and after Mr. Mann's school for 1857–8 had opened, she boarded in the Ladies' Hall, where she was thrown more under Mr. Mann's influence. She also cherished a warm passion for one of Mr. Mann's clique, Dr. W———, and was much in his and their society. At the close of the school, June 30th, 1858, evening, Mr. X., who had been in town for three or four days, in conversation with myself, took occasion to speak of his sister and the strong influence exercised over her during the last year, and hoped she had said nothing unpleasant or improper concerning myself, adding that she at first declined, and afterwards hesitated and delayed some time before she could make up her mind to give Mr. Mann a statement. I asked him to what he referred. He said to a written statement; that Mr. Mann had urged his sister to state to him on paper what she had heard me say about him; that she declined and thought it would not be right; that he insisted, and told her the matter might come up before court, and then she would be compelled to state what she knew about it; but if she would make out a written statement for him, she probably would not be called upon to appear before court; that his sister still hesitated, and wrote to him on the subject asking his advice, and finally concluded, in order to avoid the necessity of appearing in court, to give Mr. Mann the statement desired. But, said he, I supposed you knew all about it. I told him that this was my first knowledge of the existence of such a statement; yet I had thought that Miss X. might have said something to Dr. W., and he to Mr. Mann, which, perhaps, might be tortured into some objection to myself. Mr. X. said he hoped his sister had said nothing in the statement either improper or unpleasant, for he should always feel very grateful to me for all that I had formerly done for him, and for all my efforts latterly for his sister's advancement; and he presumed that her feelings were the same.

Since Miss X. has given Mr. Mann a written statement concerning myself, I suppose it would not be improper that I should also receive a copy of the same? Certainly not, said Mr. X.; sister would no doubt, have sent you a copy at the time, had she not thought it might be an intrusion. I learned of Mr. X. that they were to leave early the next morning, and as there would be no opportunity for me to see Miss X. in person, I requested her brother to ask her to send me a copy of said statement by mail.

I mention this circumstance simply as one illustration of Mr. Mann's course at Antioch College, that the reader may see whether or not there is anything so dishonorable, anything so unchristian, to which Mr. Mann will not stoop to carry out his purposes? Who, even among Mr. Mann's own relatives, does not blush for shame at his dark plots and underhanded schemes to hunt up some charge against those who honestly differ from him? Why did not Mr. Mann leave his love of wire-working and intrigue behind him in the political arena, or at Washington, and come up to Antioch with the determination to "do justice and love mercy"? Why is Mr. Mann so morbidly sensitive about his reputation? Rev. C. H. Spurgeon, of London, says:—"Some men are so very particular about reputation. They think — Surely, surely, surely they shall lose their character. Well, well, if we do not lose them through our own fault, we never need care about any body else." If Mr. Mann will look well to his own acts, his own character, need he have any fears about his reputation?

To those who are acquainted with his unjust transactions in connection with our College, Daniel Webster's remark on the 15th May, 1850, touching a letter of Mr. Mann attacking him, will hardly be deemed inappropriate:—

"This personal vituperation does not annoy me; but I lament to see a public man of Massachusetts so crude and confused in his legal apprehensions, and so little acquainted with the constitution of his country as these opinions evince Mr. Mann to be;" and they will find more truth than poetry in the following remark of Webster, made about a month later, in relation to another letter of Mr. Mann, viz:—

"One hardly knows which most to contemn, the nonsense or the dishonesty of such commentaries on another's words. I know no passion more appropriate to devils than the passion for gross misrepresentation and slander."

Is not this effort of Mr. Mann to extort a statement from a young lady, somewhat similar to Mr. Fay's effort with Dr. Foster, at Enon, mentioned on a preceding page, and with his trials with persons in this town to manufacture something out of nothing? Who can sufficiently contemn such low cunning?

A few weeks later, the statement of Miss X. came to hand. It is quite brief, and one half of it or more consists of apologies for stating the remaining portion. It is quite inaccurate, but this, I have charity to believe, arose more from misunderstanding than a desire on the part of Miss X. to willfully misrepresent. Who will be surprised that a young lady, even of good judgment, could be filled with prejudice, and prevailed upon to make a brief and inaccurate statement, when such men as Eld's. Maple and Weston, in whom we had so much confidence, have been caused to "right about face!" But suppose this statement to be true, it is then no more severe than the remarks of our leading men to me; no more pointed than the statement of others in this work; indeed, no plainer or more forcible than I have spoken to Mr. Mann himself. I should be pleased to present the statement of Miss X., and numerous other circumstances connected with it in these pages, but as before remarked, my regard for the lady shall reserve both her name and her statement, and other attendant circumstances, unless future transactions shall make it my duty to place them in print.

"Now, however much we may have desired to cover Mr. Allen's 'multitude of sins,' we now feel, in view of the course he is taking, that it is our duty—a duty that we owe to ourselves, to the world, and to God, to state in plain Anglo-Saxon terms the reasons why the Committee did not re-appoint Mr. Allen to a Professorship in the College."

"Multitude of sins." I challenge these committee-men, or any other persons, to go wherever I have lived previous to my arrival in Yellow Springs, and find aught against my character from any respectable person; or even from any person *in* Yellow Springs, except from my enemies, the members of that "little scheming, selfish, greedy clique," Dean, Fay & Co.

We do not, however, claim perfection, although we strive towards that state. We confess that we come far short of that which we desire to attain; yet let him who is without sin cast the first stone. "Duty that we owe to ourselves." It is highly doubtful, whether these men owed either their first report or their second to themselves, their own selfishness, or even to Eli Incognito, to screen him from the shafts of truth.

Is not the prophecy of Eld. John Ellis, one of the Executive Committee of the "Herald," to Fay, Craig and Weston, being fulfilled? After these persons had zealously labored with Eld. Ellis one day last winter, and importuned him for permission to publish statements which were substantially the same as those which have since appeared in the "second report;" he told them that he verily believed, even if said statements were true, that their publication would injure President Mann far more than Professor Allen; and for two reasons, viz:—

1st. That it is now quite generally believed that Mr. Mann is domineering and tyrannical; and that if any man crosses his path, he is sure to put his foot, if possible, upon his neck.

2d. It is also quite generally believed that Mr. Mann is a wiley, scheming wire-worker; and that he accomplishes his subtle purposes through others, while he stands and looks on with apparent unconcern. Now, if you publish these statements, the public will at once say that it is the work of Mr. Mann; that he is persecuting Mr. Allen; and is using you as his tools for that purpose! Finally, Craig and Weston acknowleged that they thought it might be an injudicious step; but Fay persisted with dogged obstinacy. Elder Ellis, however, did not give his consent, and did not even know that the "second report" was to be published until he saw it in the Herald!

Whether these committee-men owed the publication of their "reports," as a duty "to the world," I presume the world is competent to judge. Do civilized communities usually commend officious busy-bodies?

"To God!" Was it really the duty of these men to high Heaven to publish to the world deeply colored exparte statements and absolute falsehoods! Is not this the heighth of presumption, if not blasphemy? How very sanctimonious the committee! They would make it appear to be their religious duty, although appointed by no conference or convention, although brought together by the mendacious Eli, to publish to the world charges against one whom they call Brother, and that, too without calling on him or consulting him in the matter! charges, which, if true, ought to banish him from civilized society.

Here it is again, "In view of the course he is taking." What a subterfuge! Can they prove that I am taking any other than a straightforward manly course? Because they find good men every where frowning indignantly upon their officious, unchristian course, would they make me ubiquitous? the animating spirit of all these just retributions?

One of our ablest and most successful clergymen of a distant State, said to me a few weeks since, speaking of the "self-constituted Committee" and their "Second Report"—

"I know nothing about the facts in the case, but even were the charges true, they had no right to publish them; and when I see men come forward and voluntarily engage in such business, I regard them as near like the devil himself, as any persons well can be."

Let the reader clearly understand that Antioch College is a public Institution; that I have been one of its officers, and that its founders, if not its patrons, have a right to know how I have administered the department placed under my direction. Indeed, I am both willing and highly desirous that not only *they*, but the *whole world* also should know how I have discharged my duties to Antioch. I may have erred in my judgment; and perhaps often; yet I have the consciousness of pure motives and upright intentions; and for any injury which I have done to Antioch, or to any of its officers, I am not only ready and willing to suffer, but to make the most ample restitution within my power.

"But before we state these facts, we wish to say that we *shall not* enter into a 'newspaper fight' with Mr. Allen."

On this point I need spend no time, except to transcribe a line or two from a letter of an able and considerate Clergyman, viz.: "They do not want a 'newspaper war' with you. Indeed! Why then begin the attack in that very direction? It is an unmitigated, shallow, shameless, naked dodge."

In the "Yellow Springs' News Letter," "Mr. Mann's organ," (defunct), O. J. Wait, says: "On learning that Mr. Allen took exceptions to our Report, we offered him a new hearing." "He has not accepted it. We think HE DARES NOT."

In the "second report," "a *thorough* re-hearing" is offered before a new committee, two-fifths of which (two out of five persons) I may myself choose!

Very nice on the surface! Fair-faced, perhaps, and plausible to persons at a distance; yet to those who know the circumstances, the *merest subterfuge!* Gracious offers, indeed! a "new hearing!" a "re-hearing!" when they very well know that I have not yet had a *first* hearing; that I have not even received any notice, from any person, or in any way, to appear before "a committee of three persons;" and that it is impossible for me, under the circumstances, to accept any such offer (setting aside its nature and form of presentation) however much I might desire a fair investigation! It is known that all the departments of the present school are filled and controlled by Mr. Mann, his relatives and friends, and that they can be called together at short notice, to attend a "self-constituted Committee" meeting. It is also well known that most of the persons whom I could call as witnesses, are scattered over the world. One is in Europe; four or five are in New England; some in New York, and others in different Western States. These are persons who have been connected with the Institution as Profeseors, Teachers, or otherwise; who know the facts in the case; who have been driven away by the unwholesome influence of Mr. Mann and relatives, or have resigned and left in disgust, on account of such influence. Now it would be impossible to bring these persons together at any one time and place; and even could it be done, the expense would not be less than some $2,000, which would, in my opinion, be better expended in paying the creditors of the College; for I have no desire to prop up my character by *ex parte* or any other kind of committees. If my character has not strength sufficient to stand, and stand firmly without such props, then let it fall, the sooner the better.

But it may be asked, can you not obtain the written testimony of your witnesses, and lay their statements before an impartial committee? To this I would reply:—

1st. That it would be quite impossible to obtain an impartial committee. It might be prejudiced in my favor, and this I should exceedingly regret, for my only desire is for truth and the strictest justice.

2d. Written statements would not go far in an examination when pitted against the smooth cunning, and plausible sophistries of persons who are present to sustain their own cause by side issues, wiley questions and underhanded influences. Justice could not be thus obtained.

In the trial of A. S. Dean, a few months since, in this place, before a committee of the "New York Central Christian Conference," written testimony was thrown aside, and the oral testimony of unimpeachable witnesses was treated with about the same indifference.

3d. I could not engage in an *ex parte* investigation; nor have I a desire for an investigation of any kind before a committee; not from any fear of the strength and purity of my cause, for I am willing that the whole world should know it, and put it to the severest test; but because I wish my character to stand upon the *firm basis,* and the only firm basis, of *intrinsic merit alone.*

"We think HE DARES NOT." I have no fear of truth, of honesty and charity, or of any manly or Christian virtues. I have no fear of an honorable opponent, or of any enemy, so long as he has an appreciation of justice; but I do confess to an entire distrust of base wiley intriguers, of men, who *openly* claim to be friends, aye, *brethren,* but lie in wait *secretly,* and skulk behind "self-constituted Committees" to hurl poisoned javilins at one's character. I have an *entire distrust* of the devil and of all his servants, whether men or angels; and hope that I may always be able, under the severest trials, in the midst of the most alluring temptations, to say: "Get ye behind me."

The following brief but pertinent letter from Eld. Seever, was addressed to me just after the "Second Report" appeared in print:

"ENON, Clark County, O.,
March 26th, 1858.

"BRO. ALLEN:—I am very sorry to see the publication of the operations of a 'self-constituted Committee' in the 'Herald,' so detrimental to your character, or so intended to be. Such committees to me look like a dagger in the dark from which the wounded can have no redress or no power to vindicate his cause. These committees are a strange innovation among us, and the most dangerous precedent that could be made. If this plan is adopted among us, whose character is safe? Should one, two, or three brethren form some objection or conceive some antipathy against any person, all they have to do is to form themselves into a "self-constituted Committee" and summon the enemies of their victim, and down his character goes. I must say that I give my most decided opposition to such a precedent among us, regarding it as an unsafe rule of action, and dangerous in its tendency, and to be despised and spurned by all good men.

"BENJAMIN SEEVER."

After the preamble come the charges. The Committee says:

"But to the facts—having formed ourselves into a committee, and met in the College, on Saturday, the 17th day of October last, in the presence of the Faculty and others, it was proved to us—

"1st. That Mr. Allen, though very friendly to Mr. Mann's face, and often visiting him and sharing his hospitalities, and the pleasures of his social parties, had for a long time secretly used his utmost influence to create a prejudice against Mr. Mann, and that, too, where such prejudice would prove most fatal to Mann's usefulness as President of the College."

"The Faculty and others." Some members of "the Faculty" had nothing to do with the investigation, as shown in a preceding page. The word "others" includes, perhaps, Eli Fay, S. G. Fessenden and Miss Wilmarth, who, of course, would do all they could for Mr. Mann and "his dear Rebecca!"

"It was proved to us." What a delightful time the committee must have had! The witnesses were few in number, and all on one side! Of course they were not under the necessity of comparing and reconciling conflicting statements, or of sifting out and summing up the truth from a large mass of testimonies, by the formula or doctrine of probabilities. How they must have congratulated themselves, in reflecting on the arduous task of the clerical committee of the N. Y. Central Christian Conference, in clearing A. S. Dean, a few months previous, of some forty charges!

1st. Said clerical committee was appointed by an ecclesiastical body. It was, therefore, legitimate.

2d. Said committee received volumnous testimony, embracing some forty charges against Mr. Dean, and presented by some twelve or more citizens of Yellow Springs, most, if not all, of whom were men of high respectability and unimpeachable integrity. "The general charges were *falsehood, misrepresentation and deception.*"

3d. In the face of all these witnesses, said committee cleared A. S. Dean! and (in the words of another) on testimony "simply his own, except in a single item among forty." Yes they "permitted him to prove himself clear by his own testimony!"

Not so with the "self-constituted Committee."

1st. They were appointed, not by any civil convention, nor doubtless by any ecclesiastical body, save "Eli Fay." Of course they were, therefore, directly responsible for the *official* discharge of their appointed duties, only to said "Eli" or to his superior Horace Mann!

2d. The witnesses at their investigation were all on one side, brought together by Mr. Fay, of whom O. J. Wait wrote me—"He and we did regard him, (Fay), not you, under trial."

3d. How easily, therefore. and without doing violence to their conscience, could they clear Mr. Fay, and accuse absent persons! How easily can *ex parte* "self-constituted Committees" slander good people!

Eld. M. Cummings says, in a late number of the "Messenger," "Men or companies of sterling integrity are often made the subjects of hate by those of opposite principles."

But to the charges. "1st. That Mr. Allen, though very friendly to Mr. Mann's face, and often visiting him," &c. I have always been "friendly" enough to transact *necessary* business with Mr. Mann." "Often visiting him." This sounds very much like one of Mr. Mann's principal charges against a lady student, who called on him more than a year since to obtain an honorable dismission, to attend another institution. He could not give her such a dismission, it is said, because "she had attended one of his Saturday evening parties, (for students) without an invitation!" when the invitation had been given out publicly in the chapel, as usual, to all the students! Mr. Mann well knows, or ought to remember, that he has frequently and specially invited myself and Prof. Burlingame to meet guests at his house, or to soirees, and because we did not, on some occasions, find it convenient to attend, he has unmistakeably expressed his displeasure on account of our absence. But now the cry is "often visiting him!" I do not remember ever entering his house without an invitation, except on business.

As to "hospitalities," I have never experienced them very frequently (not at all since Mrs. Mann published her "religious cook-book!") nor extensively, and if he has ever laid himself out in that direction, I would refer the inquisitive reader to Eli Fay and the "self-constituted Committee."

"Used his utmost influence to create a prejudice against Mr. Mann."

This is incorrect. Previous to the development of Mr. Mann's plot a year since, I said but little about his unjust acts, and that chiefly, as before stated, to Eli Fay and two other persons, whose right and duty it was to know them, I wrote at their request.

During the past few months I have freely answered questions; and am now writing out the facts for the perusal and consideration of all interested. Mr. Mann's *own acts* have proved "most fatal" to his usefulness.

"It was proved to us—

"2nd. That when Mr. Allen had brought an accusation against one of the subordinate teachers, and had failed to sustain it, he then *positively* falsified the record to screen himself. This was when Mr. Allen was acting as Secretary of the faculty."

That this charge is decidedly untrue, the simple facts will show. The third Collegiate year of Antioch closed July 1st, 1856, and was followed by our long vacation of ten weeks. Having heard frequently, during the year, and from different sources, that Miss Wilmarth was accustomed to speak to the students and others in terms disrespectful of, and prejudicial to myself, I thought best to mention it to the "Committee on Instruction," whose duty it was to appoint assistant teachers. Accordingly, on the 8th of July, I called on Mr. Mann, the Chairman of said Committee; told him in brief what I had heard, although I presumed he was, to some extent, knowing to it; and that I had good reasons for believing the statement true. He denied, most pointedly and in toto, of having ever heard any such remarks from Miss Wilmarth, or of having any knowledge of the matter! He expressed great surprise; could not believe that Miss W. would, or had said such things; that it was not her nature, &c.; and all this, notwithstanding Miss Wilmarth had spent her evenings in Mr. Mann's family for weeks at a time! and when Mrs. Mann, it is said, was accustomed to hear, from different sources, of nearly every occurence in the College!

He thought the charge a very grave one; and said, if any teacher had done such a thing, he would exert his whole influence to have her removed from the institution. Mr. Mann thought she ought to be spoken to on the subject *that she might not do so again;* and if I would not call and see her, he would.

I replied, that it was doubtful whether speaking to her would do much good; for it was evident, from numerous witnesses and abundant testimony, that her *disposition was unpleasant;* and that when a woman of her years and inclinations had pursued such a course, a few moments' conversation would hardly restrain her; but that, if either of us called on her, it was perhaps most fitting that I should do so; and that *I would see her that afternoon.* Told him that I deemed it my duty to mention the matter to him, the Chairman of the "Committee on Instruction." I called on her, stated my object, and asked—if she had ever spoken disrespectfully of me to the students? She would not reply; but evaded the question; quibbling on the word "disrespectful;" did not know what people would consider "disrespectful," &c., &c. I arose to leave. She then seemed to relent somewhat, advanced towards me and said, she was certain that she had never said anything against my moral character, or aught against me as a gentleman; but did not know but she had said some things in jest to students which they had considered disrespectful.

Next day, July 9th, I was notified that there would be a special meeting of the Faculty in the afternoon, to transact some items of business. I was present; and after the aforesaid matters of business were attended to, Mr. Mann, to my surprise, brought up the case of Miss Wilmarth, and wished to know if the Faculty had not better examine into the matter. Several assented. I objected, and protested against any such proceeeding for two reasons—1st. That all the Professors and Teachers were appointed by, and held responsible to, the same power, the "Board of Trustees;" the only difference being that the Professors were elected directly by the Board, while the assistant Teachers were generally appointed by the "Committee on Instruction," composed of Trustees, and appointed and empowered by the Board of Trustees in their regular annual meetings to act during the interval, or the year; and therefore, that the trial of a teacher did not fall within the jurisdiction of the Faculty, but within the powers and duties of the appointing power, the "Committee on Instruction."

2d. That no examination of the case could now be made, even if the Faculty should assume the right to investigate; for nearly all the persons, whom I could call as witnesses, were absent on visits to their homes or relatives; and some of the most important had left, not to return.

Notwithstanding my protest, a majority of the Faculty decided to investigate.

(QUERY.—When has not Mr. Mann managed, by hook or crook, to have a majority of votes in the Faculty? Certainly, ever since Prof. Holmes left for Europe.)

On learning that none of my witnesses were in town except Mr. and Mrs. Salsbury, they sent for them. Mr. and Mrs. S. not only stated that they had heard several students use improper expressions, the same which they had heard from Miss Wilmarth herself, concerning Prof. Allen; but they also brought other charges of a very serious nature against Miss W. But Mr. Mann, lawyer or politician like, would have every thing his own way; he must have definite names, and the *exact* statements of each; and because Mr and Mrs. S. had not taken down the statements of the students on paper, and would not put exact sentences into the mouths of each of them, the most of their testimony was set aside as incompetent!

Miss Wilmarth, on the other hand, was allowed to make her own statements in her own way, which were, of course, accepted by Mr. Mann! He thought the charges not sustained!

Mrs. Salsbury's statements, however, touching Miss McArdle, a lady student, with whom Miss Wilmarth was generally known to be quite intimate, could not be so easily set aside. But who ever knew Mr. or Mrs. Dean to be so snugly cornered that he or she could not slip out in some way? It was maintained that Miss McArdle's statement concerning Miss Wilmarth, could not be depended on, for she had on some previous occasion told a falsehood!

How could the charges be substantiated in the absence of nearly all witnesses, or indeed, if all were present, so long as the testimony of the accused is taken as indubitable proof? Besides, it is quite evident that Mr. Mann was determined to clear "his dear Rebecca the Second." He must not wait until the next term. The case must be rushed through immediately, during the absence of my witnesses! That this was the determination seems evident from the fact that Mr. Mann, immediately after our conversation the day previous, went straight to the house of Mr. Dean, where Miss Wilmarth lived; called three times at the same place in the afternoon of that day, and several times the next day (July 9th) before the hour for the Faculty meeting arrived! His calls would certainly seem to be numerous enough to plan for an investigation when nearly all my witnesses were absent; and when Miss Wilmarth had, or at least, called none for herself!

Regarding the investigation as very superficial, and unfinished, I made the following record—"Miss Wilmarth, before the Faculty, to answer to some charges preferred by a member of the Faculty."

Some three months later, viz., after the fall session had opened, Mr. Mann and relatives insisted that "the minutes" should be amended; whereupon, after considerable talk, Mr. Doherty moved an amendment, which was itself amended by Mr. Mann, by the insertion of the word "trivial." To this amendment I was opposed for several reasons, two of which are: 1st. The charges were not "trivial," but, as Mr. Mann said to me in July, when the matter was first mentioned to him, they were "grave." 2d. That the investigation was incomplete, unfinished, and the minutes as they stood, so represented it. The amendment, *amended*, however, passed; and I was required, against my protest, to record it as an integral part of the former minutes, as follows: "But on examination the charges were found to be trivial, and were not sustained;" instead of in the form of a resolution, with the date of its passage! Is this parliamentary? Thus, for all the *falsification* of the record there is, they are responsible, who ordered the change.

At my request, the following words were also added: "Witnesses examined, Mr. and Mrs. Salsbury, only."

Believing the amendment to he highly injudicious, if not incorrect, I resigned my office, as Secretary, being determined never again to be used as an instrument for such a purpose.

Soon after the appearance of the "Second Report" of the "self-constituted Committee," Prof. Doherty, who was present at the investigation above mentioned, handed me the following statement:—

"Yellow Springs, O., April 13, 1858.

"Prof. Ira W. Allen—*Dear Sir:*—You request me to state what is my recollection of a certain transaction which occurred in the Faculty of Antioch College during the time you held the office of clerk, and which is prominently set forward in the following paragraph of the 'Second Report' of a 'self-constituted Committee,' published in the 'Gospel Herald' of March 18th ult. 'It was proved to us, 2nd, that when Mr. Allen had brought an accusation against one of the subordinate teachers, and had failed to sustain it, he then *positively* falsified the record to screen himself.'

"I feel bound in conscience to give my recollection of this affair, although I well know the bitter, revengeful spirit of those who are persecuting you, and the danger of incurring their enmity.

"1st. First, then, I observe, that by an honorable understanding and a positive vote, passed at one of our earliest meetings of Faculty, it was agreed that the transactions of Faculty should be regarded as strictly confidential; but now we see that when malice has a prospect of being gratified, all such resolutions are trampled under foot, and the most dishonorable breach of trust and the basest violation of positive law committed without shame and without scruple. This alone will show the true nature of that reckless persecution which has been exercised in your case.

"2d. The transaction referred to was as follows: Some charges were made by you against one of our young lady teachers, of having spoken disrespectfully of you to the students, and the Steward of the College and his lady were called as witnesses.

"They also charged the same teacher with having been out of doors at a late hour of the night in company with a young man. The young lady teacher was then heard in her own defence, and to the majority of the Faculty, including myself, she seemed to have satisfactorily accounted for her absence at the time referred to; but as the investigation took place during the Summer vacation, when some of your witnesses were absent, including the young man implicated, you expressed dissent, and considered the trial as not yet concluded.

"Acting then as clerk, you made the following entry on the record of the Faculty, viz.: 'Special meeting, July 9th, 1856. Present: Pres't. Mann, Prof.'s Doherty, Allen, Pennel and Mrs. Dean.' * * * * 'Miss Wilmarth before the Faculty to answer to some charges preferred against her by a member of the Faculty.'

"At a subsequent meeting of the Faculty, when the record was read, I, fearing that some injustice might be done to the character of the young lady teacher, moved that the following additional clause be added—'But, on examination, the charges were found to be trivial, and were not sustained.'

"Against this you protested, on the plea of the unfinished state of the trial and the necessary absence of important witnesses; but all the other members of the Faculty voted for my amendment, and you, at our dictation, entered the additional clause on the book, and then, feeling aggrieved, resigned your office as clerk.

"Now I dictated the clause which gave you offence, just on the principle I now put in practice in writing this letter—viz: an honest love of justice and a determination to vindicate the cause of the oppressed; a principle which I know my fellow-citizens will sustain.

"There was, therefore, as any one may see at a glance, no attempt whatever on your part to *'positively* falsify the record,' as this rash 'self-constituted Committee' has affirmed, and I deeply grieve to see the names of three ministers of the Christian Denomination attached to so erroneous and so injurious a statement. I have confidence, however, in the assertion, that while error is temporary, truth is eternal.

"Yours, &c., W. H. Doherty."

George L. Salsbury, Esq., who was Steward at the time referred to, writes me as follows:—

"Cardington, O., Aug. 3d, 1858.

"Prof, Ira W. Allen—*My Dear Sir:*—Yours of the 30th July was received by due course of mail. * * * * In answer to your inquiry about Miss Wilmarth's conduct at the College while I was there, I am thoroughly satisfied, from what I saw and heard, that there was a settled purpose on her part to prejudice the students and others against you, both by word and sneers, for which she is perfectly qualified. As to miss Wilmarth's conduct in having parties in the Hall contrary to our orders on Sunday evenings, &c.; I will refer you to a statement drawn up by myself at the time, at the suggestion of Mr. Mann, who requested me to draw it up and submit it to his inspection and let him forward it to Messrs. Pike, Devore, Phillips and Palmer, who had made (as Mr. Mann said) some remarks about the matter in the meeting of the Trustees. Said statement is herein enclosed. (We omit the statement for want of room.)

"I wrote it out and showed it to Mr. Mann, and after fruitless attempts on his part to get me to alter it, and so garble it as to misrepresent the facts in the case, he then requested me not to send it because it would, as he thought, do Miss Wilmarth more harm than good.

"Soon after that occurrence, Miss Wilmarth had a room fitted up on the second floor of the Ladies' Hall, on the West side of the stairs, as a parlor or sitting room where she received her company, frequently entertaining young men there by day and evening. As to her being out evenings, I can say that she was very frequently out at evening with young men from 9 o'clock until 10 and 11 o'clock, and on one occasion, I recollect until about 1 o'clock at night. She would very frequently get the key of the front door of me (there being two) so that she could get in when she returned. Some times she requested me to leave the back door of the Hall unlocked so that she could get in; and on other occasions, after a pane of glass had been broken out, they would run their arms through the sash and unbolt the door and get in that way. Her course of conduct with one young man was such as to give occasion for many remarks by a large number of those who boarded in the Hall and were conversant with the facts.

"As to her course of conduct towards the Christian Denomination, I frequently heard her speak of them, but never except with a sneer and to ridicule them; and she always sneered at the idea of the Institution's being a Christian College, saying they had never done much towards building it, and always speaking diminutively of the Christians as though they were a poor, ignorant set, beneath her notice, touching the words off with that peculiar flirt of her head which you know flies back quite easily when she wishes to be very wise and consequential.

"I do not desire to be understood as wishing to convey the idea that Miss Wilmarth was of bad character; but what I do mean is, that as a Teacher in the Institution where the rules were as strict as they were there, and at they ought to be where so many of both sexes are thrown together, her example was bad in those respects of which I have spoken, other young ladies seeing such examples set by one of the Teachers, felt that they had just as good a right to break over the rules as she had, yet I know of no one who carried the thing to such an extent as she did. There are many other things connected about the Boarding Hall while I was there, which, at this time, I do not feel disposed to mention, and which were a sufficient reason why she should not have been retained there as a Teacher; and I am free to say, that I think she would not have held her situation had she not been a relaiive of Mr. Mann. Just trace her course as Teacher before she came to the College and then answer the question—where were her claims to the Teachership in the College? and also, whether she would have been placed there had it nor been for the disposition to get the whole flock of family relatives and friends into the College so as to make it a kind of family receptacle. Was there not one connected with the Christians who was at least as well qualified to fill that place as was Miss Wilmarth? Let the record speak. Where is Mrs. Holmes, Miss Shaw and Miss Chamberlain? And where are Prof's Doherty, Allen, Holmes, McKinney, Burlingame and many others who might be named? Let Mr. Mann answer if he chooses, or any one else. Let any one tell me why it was or is that there can be no others to fill that place and other places. Ah! you and I know full well; and so do Prof. Doherty, Prof. Burlingame, Prof. McKinney, Eld's Ladley and Lynn and others who have lived there long enough to become acquainted with the wire-working of a certain clique which has governed the College: We know, and some of us to our sorrow.

"I do not pretend to be qualified to be a Teacher, but one thing I will venture to say without fear of successful contradiction, that there are more than one, whose heads have been cut off, and they turned away, as well qualified to take charge of that College in an educational point of view, at least, as the present head of it is, and much better in many other respects; and their only crime has been, that they have been denominational in their feelings and conduct towards the Christians, and have possessed too much independence to be made tools of to serve selfish and sinister purposes.

"But I have already extended this letter to a greater length than I at first intended, and must close by subscribing myself,

"Your Brother in Christ, G. L. SALSBURY."

Prof. H. D. Burlingame, now Principal of the Albany Female Seminary, Albany, N. Y., is well acquainted with Miss Wilmarth's course at

Antioch, and in his letter on a preceding page he embraces her as well as others when he says:

"Surely, no one who is acquainted with the state of things will make so groundless a charge as to accuse Mr. Mann of representing the Christian Denomination? or any one introduced into the Institution through his influence. It is unjust to make such charge against them. They are not guilty."

Abundant evidence against Miss Wilmarth, from other sources, might be presented; but we fear that we have already taken too much notice of her and of the malicious and unfounded charge of the "self-constituted Committee." We have given the above statements, however, that the reader may have a pretty good specimen of the impartiality(?) with which investigations at Yellow Springs are conducted; excepting of course "self-constituted," *ex parte* Committees and their proceedings, which in point of "*mercy*" surpass everything heretofore discovered!

As an instance of the former class, Mr. A. S. Dean was cleared by a clerical committee, about a year since, of some forty grave charges made against him by several of our most candid and respectable citizens; and cleared substantially on his own testimony!

Instances of the "self-constituted" class are yet rare; but the invention is "great," the offspring of a "rare genius!" Great light has dawned! "The *great experiment* is successful!" "Antioch is safe!"

"3d. It was proved to us that in the Faculty meetings he would cast his vote in a given way, and then go to the students, and preparingly to keeping on friendly terms with them, would insinuate that he voted differently; and in some instances positively denying his vote."

If there was any proof favoring this charge, it was a *reductio ad absurdum* statement; for the accusation is untrue. Indeed, the charge is so evidently absurd and silly, that I should take no notice of it, were it not found in company with others of a graver nature. If it was my desire to please the students; what object could I have had in voting so as to displease them, contrary to their known or supposed wishes, and thus give myself the trouble and disgrace of insinuating to them that I had voted differently? The idea is too preposterous for men of common sense to swallow; and I challenge the world to prove the accusation other than false.

Prof. Warriner, Mrs. Dean's right hand man, it is true, acknowledged to me, that he had informed the "self-constituted Committee" on being questioned by them for testimony, that, in a conversation with a couple of lady students during the previous vacation, he learned that they supposed, from a conversation with me, that I had voted for a certain measure; when he himself was the only man who voted for it.

You say, they *supposed* that I voted in the affirmative? Yes; but did they say that I had told them that I had voted thus? No, they only *inferred* so.

Well, Mr. Warriner, I wish you to understand that I have never told any person whomsoever, that I voted differently from what I did on that question or any other question or occasion, political or otherwise; and furthermore, that I do not consider myself responsible for all the *suppositions* and *inferences* of people.

"4th. It was proved to us that Mr. Allen did tell several positive falsehoods to Mr. Fessenden concerning Mr. Mann; and when Mr. Fessenden, as his only means of self-defence, told Mr. Mann what Mr. Allen had told him, he was severely censured by Mr. Allen. Mr. Allen said to Mr. Fessenden 'you ought to have denied to Mr. Mann you ever heard me say anything about it, for it was not designed for other men's ears.' Mr. Fessenden inquired: 'Do I understand you, Mr. Allen, to say that I should have denied the facts?' Mr. Allen replied: 'It is morally right for you to say to Mr. Mann that you did not know, and that I never told you.' This *enormous* charge was sustained by the testimony of Professors Fessenden and J. B. Weston. Who in the Christian Denomination will think any the less of Antioch because she *spears* such men from her halls?'

This is the only charge of the "self-constituted Committee" for which they give any names as authority. To strangers, and all persons unacquainted with the circumstances and facts in the case, this accusation of two so-called "Professors" against me, may appear weighty and severe; but when tested by the touchstone of truth, its apparent force will, it is believed, *vanish away*.

The *apparent* weight of any charge depends, of course, upon the reputation of the accusers; and reputation is often at, and sometimes above par, at a distance, when at home it is in low esteem. The *real* value of a charge, however, depends upon the intrinsic character of its maker for intelligence, good judgment, and unyielding integrity. To enable the reader to judge intelligently of this accusation, we shall be under the necessity of entering somewhat minutely into the matter, and of stating the facts at considerable length.

Soon after my arrival in this place, in Sept. 1854, Mr. Fessenden was introduced to me as the teacher of music in the College. He appeared very deferential, almost obsequious; but this I attributed, as our acquaintance increased, to his very limited attainments in all departments of knowledge, except in music. He was, however, enthusiastic in his chosen profession, and, as I believed, in most respects, an excellent instructor in music. He was also extremely nervous and excitable, and a great talker; yet, at that time, I had no evidence that he was dishonest. Indeed, being a great friend of musical culture everywhere, and especially desirous to see this noble humanizing art patronized and cherished in Antioch College, I was willing to do what I could for Mr. Fessenden and his department. I also found him often in the society of Prof. Holmes, and enjoying his confidence; and accordingly I gave him my friendship, and, to some extent, my trust. He made himself quite free, spoke in the highest terms of Mr. and Mrs. Holmes and others; volunteered a history of his unpleasant acquaintance with A. S. Dean, and did not seem to be satisfied as to Mr. Mann's feelings towards him. He said that soon after he came to this place he endeavored to effect an arrangement with Mr. Dean, who was in the book-trade, and his clerk, Mr. Blake, to furnish him with sheet music, &c., but that their terms were altogether too exorbitant. He therefore stepped across the street to the store of Messrs Lawrence and Winchell, with whom he effected an arrangement on reasonable terms. As soon as Mr. Dean got news of this, he swore vengance on Mr. Fessenden, and told him to his face, if I mistake not, that he would injure his influence. Mr. Blake's tongue was not silent, for he represented Mr. F. as a tyro in his art, and said that he could not play "Old Hundred" through without committing several mistakes! Mr. Fessenden's conversation exhibited a feeling of fear and insecurity. He told me that he had been informed that Mr. Mann was not his friend. I remarked that I knew nothing about the matter, that I had been in Yellow Springs but a short time, was actively engaged in my own department; and if that was the case, others had a much better opportunity to know it than myself. After the mal-treatment of Bro. Holmes, and his departure for Europe, Mr. Fessenden was told that his head would come off next, which of course did not tend to quiet his fears, or allay his apprehensions.

The Antioch Musical Association having elected me their President, Mr. Fessenden was occasionally at my room on business, and he still exhibited, at times, a feeling of insecurity. He told me that he should spend the coming vacation of ten weeks principally in Boston, and his reasons for going, the principal of which was that he might perfect himself still more in his art, and thus bring a stronger influence to bear against Dean and others who desired his removal; said that he had learned that Mr. Dean had in his possession, applications from persons in Boston for the Music Chair, &c.; and seemed to fear that Mr. Mann was not his friend. I listened to his statements; told him that I knew nothing about the facts in the case; but that I was much pleased with his plan of passing the vacation in the East for still higher acquisitions in music.

He hoped that if any sayings or doings touching himself should come to my knowledge, that I would communicate them to him; for, said he, I shall not wait to be turned out or have my head chopped off; before the blow comes I shall resign and leave. I replied, that if anything of importance came to my knowledge he should be informed of it.

Some months later, and during the absence of the President, there was a party for students and others at his (Mr. Mann's) house, and during the evening, I was introduced to a Mrs. Coe. She informed me that she had just come on to live in Yellow Springs and educate her daughter, and made many inquiries about the school, said she wished her daughter to give considerable time to music, and enquired if we had a good instructor in that department. I told her I thought we had; that Mr. Fessenden was quite enthusiastic, very much devoted to his business, and I presumed an excellent instructor in his chosen art. Why, said she, I met Mr. Mann in Western New York, as I was coming on, and he told me that the teacher of music was quite moderate, but, that he had recently spent some time in Boston to advance himself, and that he was perhaps a fair or average instructor! Her tone of remark, as well as her words, gave me to understand that she had come to the place with no very favorable ideas of Mr. Fessenden's ability.

It may be that Mr. Mann was not wholly responsible for Mrs. Coe's impressions or statements. Perhaps she had heard much more from Mrs. Mann, A. S. Dean, or Mr. Blake, than from Mr. Mann; yet in her conversation with me, she used Mr. Mann's name only, and stated what she professed to have heard from him in New York. A few months later the Trustees met, when King and Dean, members of the Board, and Blake, Assistant Treasurer, brought the subject of the Music Department before the meeting, and commenced a fierce attack on Mr. Fessenden. They made very incorrect and extravagant statements about Mr. F., the amount of money he was receiving, &c., and both the nature of the resolution before the Board, and the fierceness of his adversaries exhibited a determination to remove Mr. Fessenden from the College. On leaving the meeting to go down town, I met Mr. F. coming up near Mr. Mann's house, and told him what was going on in the meeting of the Board, remarking that it was surprising to me that Mr. Mann should sit and allow Dean and Blake (his relatives by marriage) to go on in that style against him, (Mr. F.) when a word from his (Mann's) mouth would make them whist; that if Mr. Mann was truly his friend he would, I thought, defend him; and advising him to be on his guard, I passed on. The conversation alluded to, did not probably exceed two minutes, was prompted by the best of motives, and was made in compliance with my promise before mentioned. I was again in the meeting of the Board, and defended Mr. F. against Dean, Blake, and King; and when the vote was taken, Mr. Fessenden was almost unanimously sustained.

Soon after my brief conversation with Mr. F. near the President's house, Mr. Mann pounced upon him and wished to know if Prof. Allen had ever intimated to him that he (Mann) was not his friend, &c. Mr. F. was taken wholly by surprise, and after some hesitation on his own part, and considerable forcible persuasion from Mr. Mann, he acknowledged that I had, stating what I had told him, and doubtless much more, both in matter and manner, for others have said much more than myself to Mr. F. concerning Mr. Mann. Mr. Fessenden was extremely unhappy after this, and could not sleep, he said, for several nights. He therefore laid the matter before Mr. Weston, then a student, whom he knew to be my friend, and asked his advice in the matter. Mr. W. made known the case to me in brief. I remarked to him I hoped Mr. Fessenden would not feel so wretched about it, and that he had better come to me and talk it over. Shortly after, Mr. F., in company with Mr. Weston, called on me in my study. Mr. F. appeared much dejected. I asked him to tell me the circumstances of the case. He then related them, and hoped that I could overlook the matter and pardon him. I told him that I cared but little about the affair so far as he was concerned, could overlook it, and hoped that he would give himself no further uneasiness about it; but that I regarded it as very small business for the President of a College to be prying into the private intercourse of friends; that no gentleman would be guilty of such an act.

The matter of right to withhold things communicated by a friend in confidence, was then spoken of at some length. I told them that it was quite surprising that Mr. Mann and other politicians should deny point blank having any knowledge of certain affairs, when there was good reason to believe that they had knowledge on these points; that I could explain it in but one way, *viz*:—That what was committed to them in confidence by a friend, they regarded as not for the public, nor for any third person; and hence, when questioned on such points, they replied they had no knowledge of the matter, *i. e.*, for any third person. But, I remarked, be this as it may, and be the morality of such a course what it may, had Horace Mann asked me any question touching a matter of confidence between myself and yourself, or any other friend, I should have informed him that I did not consider myself at liberty to answer any such question; or that I regarded the question as wholly improper, and that the matter was "none of his business." But, Mr. Fessenden, you doubtless did the best you knew how under the circumstances. I therefore overlook the transaction so far as you are concerned. Set your mind entirely at rest. Mr. Weston said but little; and the interview passed off, so far as I knew, to the entire satisfaction of all three present; and nothing to the contrary reached me until the "Second Report" of the "Persecuting Committee" came out in the "Gospel Herald." My relations with Mr. F. continued pleasant, and I regarded Mr. Weston as one of my most intimate friends. He was a student, it is true, but several years my senior; had been for some time one of our New England ministers; and was considered as a denominational man. I saw that his firmness was small, and hence, that he was easily influenced; but I regarded him as strictly honest, and from the circumstances of his education thus far, believed that he would make an able advocate of our interests as a people. I knew him to be an intimate friend of Prof. Holmes. He called frequently at my study. I gave him my confidence. We talked often and freely about College affairs, and the religious and educational interests of our denomination. I was hardly more intimate with any friend. Mr. Weston graduated one year since, just as the College property was assigned, and the Institution severed from its denominational control by Mr. Mann and friends. The College was no longer to be what its founders had intended it should be. It was to be placed on what Mr. Mann calls a "thoroughly liberal basis," in the hands of "new friends." Many of our leading men, some of whom live in New York, New England, and states distant from Ohio. now regarded Antioch as lost to us as a people forever, unless we could raise money, buy back, and then control the College. Indeed, some of our most prominent ministers told me that this would be impossible so long as Horace Mann remained; but if he, his relatives and pets would leave the Institution, our churches would very quickly raise money sufficient to pay off every cent of the indebtedness.

Thus matters stood when Mr. Weston was invited to act as an instructor in Mr. Mann's temporary school for one year; and when he had good reason, we think, to believe that Prof. Doherty, Holmes, McKinney, Burlingame, nor Allen would have anything to do with said school. But he yielded and accepted (contrary to the strong written advice of at least one of our most influential ministers,) and since that time has advocated what he before denounced! There are persons in this place and State, and in other States, who can testify that Mr. Weston has heretofore disapproved of Mr. Mann's acts and influence in the College. No wonder that Prof. Burlingame wrote in October last:

"I was much surprised to learn that Weston has countenanced Mr. Mann's course, by accepting a place in the College under existing circumstances, especially as you know he has always, until recently, been most vehement in his denunciations of Mr. Mann's policy; and that he should apologize for the driving of Prof. Holmes and others out of doors, seems almost incredible."

The following letter is from Mrs. Salsbury, an intelligent and energetic lady, who was Matron of the Ladies' Hall during the year 1855–6, and had excellent opportunities for becoming acquainted with the influences exerted in, and over the College :—

"CARDINGTON, O., Aug. 4, 1858.

"BRO. ALLEN:—When I think of Antioch College, I do not think of it as a Christian Institution, or College, and I will tell you some of my reasons for such thoughts and feelings. I spent one year at Yellow Springs, in the Ladies' Hall. The position which I occupied is known to yourself. I soon saw that Antioch was not under the influence under which I had fondly hoped she was, and that was Christian. There were two elements at work there, one for the Christian Denomination, and the other opposed to it; and this latter was felt by many others as well as myself. I know full well that had I not been denominational in feelings and views, I should not have received the treatment which I did at the hands of the present managers of the College. I am frank to confess that I did take a decided stand for the Christians, when I saw an effort making to wrong them out of their undoubted rights.

"Bro. Weston always manifested, when talking to me (and that was not unfrequently) his disapprobation of the course of Mr. Mann, in many ways. Many times has he said, if he were free, i. e. if he were through with his studies, were graduated, he would speak out and let the denomination know some of the iniquity which was practiced against the Christian Teachers at the College. There was no one who was more indignant in regard to the treatment of Mrs. Holmes than was Bro. Weston, and I verily believe he felt all he said at that time. I hope not, but I very much fear from what I have seen from the pen of Brother Weston, that he has sold his birth-right for a mess of pottage.

"I was not at all surprised when I learned that your services and Bro. Doherty's were not needed at Antioch any longer. I saw the spirit that was manifested towards you both, as well as towards Miss Chamberlain. She told me herself that she was never so shamefully treated by any persons or in any place, as she was during her stay at Antioch College. Well, Bro. Allen, they have driven out all the intruders, for as such have the Christians been regarded by the party in power. Need I say more? Respectfully yours,

"NANCY R. SALSBURY."

In Bro. Merrifield's letter on another page, dated "Yellow Springs, O., Aug. 6th, 1858," he says:—

"It is equally significant that there is but one person in the whole teaching force who was a member of the Christian Connection many days before his or her appointment. The single exception alluded to above is reported to have said that his religious views have undergone a change since he came here."

But let these evidences, touching Mr. Weston's former and present course in relation to College matters, suffice; yet we deeply regret that Mr. W. has deceived or labored to deceive our people through the "Gospel Herald" and other channels. His article concerning Prof. Holmes' refusal to fill the Greek Chair, during the past year, is very deceptive! I have testimony over Prof. Holmes' own name to prove this; and there are in existence other strong statements on this very point.—We hope for Mr. W.'s sake that it may never be necessary to give them to the public.

More than a year since Mr. Fessenden was stoutly opposed to Mr. Fay's becoming pastor of the Christian Church of this place. He was quite excited about the matter, and took occasion to inform me that he had found out a plot laid by A. S. Dean and others for getting Mr. Fay into the Pastorate of the Christian Church of this place, at a salary of $800 per year, and of ousting Eld. J. C. Burghdurf from the Treasurer's office in the College, and putting Mr. Fay also in there, at a salary of from $700 to $800 per annum; that both offices would pay some $1,500 to $1,600, an amount sufficient, they thought, to bring Mr. Fay to the Springs to labor for the interests of A. S. Dean & Co. Whether all of Mr. Fessenden's information was correct, we are not able to say; but a part of it was soon corroborated by the action of Mr. Mann, a member of the Church, and of A. S. Dean and others, not members, for they succeeded (see history of the Christian Church, &c.) in saddling Mr. Fay upon the Church for three months on trial. If they attempted to place him in the Treasurer's office they failed, for Eld. Burghdurf discharged the duties of that station with ability until the College property was all assigned. Mr. Fessenden said he could not speak out on this subject, for it might damage his business.

He told my brother, A. L. Allen, not long after the assignment of the College property, and only a few weeks before the Franklin Convention, in October last, in a conversation about the divisions and collisions that had taken place, the dubious state of College affairs and its future, that he hardly knew what to do with himself; that he had worked hard in his department for nearly four years, and now, just as he was in a fair way to realize something for his labors, and had a pleasant home, he feared that he might not be retained, for it would depend upon what Mr. Mann and party might do; that his case was rather peculiar, it was for his interest to keep in the favor of all parties as much as possible; that he could not and should not take sides with any party on College matters, as it would operate against his business, and he would very likely lose some students thereby. On taking the cars for the Convention, however, my brother found Mr. Fessenden in company with Mann, Fay and others, bound for the same place; and, in conversation that passed between them, brother alluded to the neutrality of his (Fessenden's) position. Mr. F. replied that he had intended to take no sides on the College question, and had told him so; but he now found that he could hold out no longer, that he was compelled to take sides! A few hours later and Mr. Fessenden's action at the Convention in lobbying, voting, &c., afforded proof sure that he had now pledged himself to Horace Mann & Co.!

He not only exerted himself in the Convention; but since that time, in families and public places, has he labored zealously for Fay, A. S. Dean, Horace Mann and favorites; and denounced his old and well tried friends, through whose influence he was more than once saved from being kicked out of the College by some of the very persons whom he is now serving! He said in a store, in this town, in the presence of several persons, that *he should not dare to oppose Horace Mann, for his bread and butter depended on him!*

What would not such a man say or do? When a man does not do an act because it is right; and refrains from a course not because it is wrong, but from a mercenary motive, *where is his integrity?* This subject is not yet exhausted; but, perhaps, sufficient evidence has been given to show the reader the utter flimsiness of the above startling accusation, made, as it was, by men who had belied their own former statements and professions.

"Several positive falsehoods." Mr. Fessenden doubtless told his story to the "Persecuting Committee," when Mr. Mann denied point blank, as is his custom, that he had said any such thing, *ergo*, the committee say that "Mr. Allen did tell several positive falsehoods to Mr. F. concerning Mr. Mann." Now this matter is very simple:—

1st. I told Mr. F., simply what Mrs. Coe told me that Mr. Mann told her in New York. The truth or falsity of those statements rests either with Mrs. Coe or Mr. Mann.

2d. I informed Mr. Fessenden, as a friend, of the attack of Dean, King and Blake, on him, in the meeting of the Trustees; and cautioned him, touching Mr. Mann's silence, as Jefferson cautioned Madison against trusting Aaron Burr, with this difference, however, that Jefferson did it "habitually." Jefferson says:—

"I had never seen Colonel Burr till he came as a member of the Senate. His conduct very soon inspired me with distrust. I habitually cautioned Mr. Madison against trusting him too much."

Where is the impropriety of my caution? I challenge any man to make affidavit, that I ever told Mr. Fessenden a falsehood, without perjuring himself.

"His only means of self-defense!" Defense against what? Against Mr. Mann's base quizzing, and crafty wire-working?

"Severely censured by Mr. Allen." I did not censure Mr. F., unless he took my statement of what I would have done under such circumstances, as censure. The quotations which the committee, through Mr. F., puts into my mouth, I never uttered on any occasion, never thought them, never saw them, until the "Persecuting Committee's" "Second Report" reached me; and I do not understand how Messrs. Fessenden and Weston, looking back through the mists of twenty months, and from their new stand-point, could have concluded that I ever uttered such abominable statements, unless they are a hundred per cent. weaker than I supposed them to be. I will not, however, sit in judgment on their motives, yet I do not understand how they could have drawn any such inferences even from our conversation on politicians, for by speaking of the dishonest course of some politicians, I by no means subscribed to it, or commended it as moral and right. I will not charge them with deep-seated malice and crafty designs in making the above statements, if, indeed, they ever did make them as given by the Committee; but I do say that I cannot see how they *honestly* came by such statements, or could *conscientiously* make them. I knew, it is true, that these gentlemen had not much firmness and decision of character, and that they were very easily influenced by others, yet I did not think that they would sell themselves for the honors and emoluments of office!

"Professors Fessenden and Weston." Mr. Fessenden is simply the instructor in music. He is not a member of the Faculty, and has no seat or vote in that body.

Mr. Weston only graduated a year ago, and since that time he has been simply an instructor in the temporary school, *viz*: Principal of the Preparatory Department. If he is Professor at all, he is one of Mr. Mann's creation!

"Antioch because she *spears* such men from her halls." Antioch College, as established and intended by the Christians, has never done this. Horace Mann and his clique, who have seized the College, have done this, and *they alone*.

"This *enormous* charge," therefore, I most boldly and emphatically pronounce to be unfounded in truth.

"5th. It was proved to us that Mr. Allen himself instigated the removal of Professor Holmes, and afterwards tried to convince Holmes, and others, that it was an insult to him and a great indignity to the Christian Church."

The falsity of this accusation is so perfectly barefaced to those even partially acquainted with Antioch, that this alone must cast a deep suspicion over all portions of the Committee's report.

"The removal of Professor Holmes." When did this "removal" take place? In the Spring of 1855, when Prof. H. left for Europe? If so; why was his name continued in the College catalogues up to the close of last year? The truth is, that Mr. Holmes requested the Trustees to grant him a leave of absence; or rather Mr. Mann asked it for him; and he was not removed from the Institution until the 27th day of June, 1857, when the Trustees, after assigning all the College property,—

Resolved, "That the President of the College, Professors, Teachers, Officers, Employees of the College, now receiving compensation for services, be and they are hereby discharged from further service."

To prove that Prof. Holmes was not previously removed, it will only be necessary to state—

1st. That he received, during his absence of over two years, a part of the salary paid to the Greek Department (although, owing to Mr. Mann's course, the balance, after paying his substitute, was unfortunately very small); and

2d. That his name was continued in the College catalogues as the regular Professor of the Greek Department up to the close of the last collegiate year, July 1, 1857. It was believed, however, by some persons that Mr. Mann intended from the first to make this "leave of absence" virtually a "removal"; to prevent Prof. Holmes, if possible, from ever again entering upon the duties of his office. But now it comes out in print! Why was not the writer of the Report, why were not these committee-men more guarded? Why, in their eagerness to injure me, did they make a back-thrust through Mr. Mann's very heart!

"That Mr. Allen himself instigated the removal." The truth is—I was not aware that there was a petition in existence against Bro. Holmes until near the close of the Spring term of 1855; and until after the Trustees had assembled for their March meeting, when I was informed of it by Prof. Pennell, Mr. Mann's nephew. He asked me what course Prof. Holmes had better take. I told him I did not know; that the matter was wholly new to me. He wished to know if it would not be best for Prof. H. to go to Europe? Told him I could not say, that I was unacquainted with the circumstances of the case, (they had taken good care that I should not see the petition!) but asked him if this movement among the students, which in my opinion could not be very extensive, could not be suppressed, *promptly put down*, by the Faculty? Is it necessary that Prof. Holmes leave the College at all? He thought it would be quite impossible to suppress the movement, and that Mr. Holmes would be under the necessity of leaving the Institution for one year or more; and thought his best course would be to go to Europe. I said, if Bro. Holmes must leave the College at all, that might perhaps be the pleasantest and most profitable course for him to pursue; adding, that I was by far the youngest member of the Faculty; had been on the ground but a few months; and that I should leave the matter to others; indeed, that, *in my opinion*, the Faculty had no right to entertain such a case, but should discharge their duty promptly by bringing the movers and signers of the petition to punishment; that the Trustees, even, could not listen to, or entertain for a moment such a petition from the students; and that young men, in any Eastern College worthy the name, would be expelled, or otherwise severely punished for such an act.

Late in the evening of the same day, there was a meeting of several members of the Faculty in Mr. Mann's house, at the close of which, he informed me that Mr. Badger (Henry Clay Badger, a student) was waiting in another room to see him about the petition; and requested me to go in with him. I asked to be excused, stating that he was President of the College, and if it was at all proper for any member of the Faculty to listen to a student on such a subject, he was that member. He then urged and finally insisted that I should go in, saying he desired my advice in the case. I finally yielded, and accompanied him.

Mr. Mann opened the conversation, and continued it for some time with Mr. Badger, touching the case tenderly, and handling him with the "softest kids," not even chiding him for his prominent part in the transaction! He then requested me to say something. I addressed Mr. Badger, and said that I regretted exceedingly to find him in his present position; and believed that he would never have pursued such a course, had he taken time to reflect. He replied that he had not entered upon this matter hastily or unadvisedly; that he was laboring for the best interests of Antioch College.

I then reprimanded him severely; stating my belief that he was engaged in a very unwise movement; that the students of a College had no right to get up a petition against a member of the Faculty; that by so doing they were meddling with the rights and prerogatives of the Trustees, the appointing and controlling power; and that the Board could not, in my opinion, countenance such a course for a moment.

With an additional caress or two from the President, Mr. Badger withdrew. Mr. Mann then remarked, "you take very strong and extreme ground, Prof. Allen, against the right of students to petition; far more so than I should dare to take!" To which I replied, that I had only briefly expressed my convictions of right on the subject, and as it was near 12 o'clock, I bade him good night.

Does this look like "instigating the removal of Prof. Holmes?"

QUERY—Would not my doctrine have been very palatable to Mr. Mann, and rigidly excuted, had a petition appeared against his relatives or favorites? No doubt of it.

But what object could I have had in desiring the absence of Bro. Holmes? Let the reader think of this. I had been in Yellow Springs only about six months; and could not have been induced to exchange my depratment for any other within the gift of the Trustees. I was much better acquainted with Bro. Holmes than with any other member of the Faculty. I knew him to be thoroughly in sympathy with the religious denomination of which I was a member, and to which my parents and friends belonged. I admired his wisdom and zeal in sustaining prayer meetings in the College, and the spirit of his searching discourses in the College chapel. I knew him to be untiring in his efforts to instruct and benefit the classes under his charge; and I also believed that his highest ambition, next to that of being a pure and upright man, was to advance and guard in the highest interests of the College and of its founders, the Christians. What motive, what object, I therefore ask again, could I have had for the removal of my best friend from the institution? The charge is too preposterous to be believed for one moment!

"Afterwards tried to convince Holmes, &c."

On this accusation, I would simply remark, that no efforts have been put forth by me in that direction, and for the very obvious reason that I believed Bro. Holmes had no doubts on that point. He felt the insult, perhaps, far more keenly than any other person; and if he was not fully satisfied before he left for Europe, that Mr. Mann was no real friend of his or of the Christians, the dismissal of Mrs. Holmes, shortly after, by Mr. Mann from her position as instructor in Latin, and from the Institution, and that too after he had assured Prof. Holmes that Mrs. H. should be continued as Teacher during his absence, must have removed all doubt.

"A great indignity to the Christian Church."

If the mal-treatment of Prof. and Mrs. Holmes, of Mr. Burlingame, of Miss Shaw, and of Prof. Doherty and other Professors and Teachers sent to the Institution by the Christians, is not "a great indignity to the Christian Church," then I know not what could be. The wresting the College from under their control, can scarcely be any addition to the offence.

But on this point Prof. Holmes himself, spoke at length (as stated on a preceding page) before the Miami Christian Conference (Ohio,) at its last session, (1857,) charging home upon Mr. Mann and to his face, the cause or the responsibility of his absence from the College. He related the circumstances of the case, described Mr. Mann's interviews with him, and his determined persistency in forcing him to consent to go to Europe, until the sympathies of the large audience were wrought up to a very high pitch.

Mr. Mann *could* not, at least *did not* reply. Ask the persons who were present on that occasion, if Prof. Holmes charged Mr. Allen with "instigating his removal," or reflected on him in any way.

"6th. It was proven to us, from his own letters, that Mr. Allen had circulated false reports touching the general administration of the College."

Whatever I have written or said as my own, "touching the general administration of the College," I have believed, and do believe, to be true. It is possible that in writing to intimate friends, I may have mentioned some of the current statements in Yellow Springs touching College transactions, not altogether free from error; yet of this, even I, am by no means certain. My intention has been to say but little on such points, even of what I have seen and heard, and then only to persons who have a right to know them; and I am not yet aware that I have failed to carry out such intention. I have no fear of Messrs. Mann, Fay, McWhinney, Reeder and Wait, publishing all the letters which I have ever addressed to them "touching the general administration of the College," and I hereby give them full permission to make such letters public. During our whole connection with Antioch College, it has been our aim to labor for its highest interests, for the interests of its founders, for the great cause of *truth* and *justice;* and as before stated, if we have wronged any man, we will cheerfully make the most ample restitution in our power.

We have now presented the leading facts touching the formation of the "self-constituted Committee," and their action which, have come to our knowledge; many of these facts came to us without our solicitation; the others have been cheerfully given on inquiry; and had we pursued this subject with anything like the zeal and pertinacity with which Messrs. Mann, Fay & Co. have falsely accused and persecuted us, many more deeds of darkness might doubtless have been brought to light. But we are satisfied. We have no desire to know more; and we presume that facts sufficient have been presented to enable the reader to judge intelligently of this matter. The reader has seen that this affair was "conceived in iniquity;" and the first Report, at least, "was got into the 'Herald' by a trick;" that for a short time, thereafter James Maple, the editor, seemed somewhat desirous to have justice done, then *"wheeled right about face"* and went over to his enemies. That while he denied me the right to reply to the *first* Report of the "self-constituted Committee," he published their *Second* Report; that he persistently refused to give me a hearing in the "Herald" until the Executive Committee voted me a limited space, and even then "hacked and hewed" my Review in such a way as to destroy its force; and to cap the climax, he violated the decision of the Executive Committee by publishing two editorials against my Review, and also a defamatory article by Eli Fay! Thus for months past has the "Gospel Herald," our Western Denominational organ, been controlled by Mr. Mann's clique.

We believe in the main with Mr. Spurgeon, as expressed at the head of this review, that the Christian need not fear slander or lies ; that lies touching a true man's character, produce just about as tremendous an effect, as does thistle-down when it impinges the walls of an impregnable castle. Reputation may dissolve and disappear, for it is often fictitious, but true character is impregnable. We have presented the above review, therefore, from no mere personal interest, but for the benefit of all concerned and especially of the Christian Connection. We have endeavored to write in an impartial and charitable spirit, and we now bring the subject to a close, as we hope forever, by selecting two brief letters from the numerous communications in our possession:

LETTER OF A. M. MERRIFIELD, ESQ.

Mr. Merrifield is one of the most enterprising and influential laymen of the Christian Connection. During the years of 1849 and 1850 he visited several of our leading clergymen in the States of New York, Massachusetts, Rhode Island, Maine and New Hampshire, for the purpose of arousing them to the importance and especially to the practicability of establishing a first class " Institution of Learning." He was largely influential in the first General U. S. (quadrennial) Convention, held in Marion, N. Y., in 1850, and in making the preliminary arrangements in that meeting for the establishment of Antioch College. He was a member of nearly all the important College Committees for the four following years, was architect, building agent, and first

Treasurer of the College, and has been one of the Board of Trustees down to the present time. No man perhaps, has a more intimate acquaintance with the history of the Institution.

"WORCESTER, Mass.,
April 8th, 1858.

"DEAR SIR:—I have read two articles that have appeared in the 'Gospel Herald' over the signatures of certain Christian Ministers of Ohio who style themselves a 'self-constituted Committee.'

"By the way they handle you and Prof. Doherty, I should think they came nearer a trio of conspirators met to rob men of their good name, than a band of brothers intent on doing as they would be done by.

"In regard to yourself, I am happy to be able to say that I have heard many students in Antioch speak of you and I cannot call to mind a single instance in which any one of them, in my hearing, has spoken of you, either as a man or as a teacher, but in terms of high praise.

"I see no reason to hope that any one, who is true to the idea the Christians had in building Antioch College, can teach for any considerable length of time in it, until it ceases to be governed upon principles so fundamentally different from those expressed at the Marion Convention, as are those which have obtained ascendency over it.

"So far as you are concerned, it makes but little difference what wires were pulled to effect your removal or rather your non-re-appointment. The result is the same with you that it has been with every teacher who has had an opinion on College matters, different from Prof. Mann's, and independence enough to maintain it. The idea that every one who opposes a measure of the President is of necessity his personal enemy and to be treated as such, may do for a political party but it has worked badly in Antioch.

"May we not, on the principle that a little leaven leaveneth the whole lump, hope for a salutary change in the policy of the College.

"I have alluded to what I believe to be a fact, that every man in the Christian Church of any considerable influence, who has resided long in Yellow Springs, is dissatisfied with the policy which has been pursued, believing it to be prejudicial to the interest of the College and to the Christian Connection.

"Should the College be redeemed by the Christians let us hope that they will so manage it, that it will be a good institution in which to educate their children, rather than a convenient Family Hack.

"Yours truly,
"A. M. MERRIFIELD."

LETTER OF HON. WILLIAM MILLS.

Judge Mills is a man of great activity and energy of character. Few persons have done more for any town than has Mr. Mills for Yellow Springs, building it up mostly on his own estate. He was chiefly instrumental in obtaining the location of Antioch College for this place, for which purpose he gave twenty acres of land for the College Park, and raised $30,000 cash, two-thirds or more of which he himself paid› He was one of the corporators, and second Treasurer of the College. and since 1854 has been one of the Board of Trustees:

"YELLOW SPRINGS, O.,
August 21st, 1858.

"*To whom it may concern*:—This is to certify that I have been acquainted with Prof. Allen, the bearer, for some five years, and that during the whole period of his connection with Antioch College as Professor of Mathematics, Astronomy and Civil Engineering, his competency and faithfulness as an iustructor were never called in question, he having qualified himself for that position by much previous preparation, and by a sojourn for a considerable time at one of the best Universities in Europe.

"WILLIAM MILLS."

PART THIRD.

Redemption of Antioch College to the Christians.

As malicious insinuations and false statements are being thrown out concerning Indiana's plan, and the author of said plan, I deem it my duty to my brethren of the Christian Connection to present a statement of the facts. Returning from the East early in October, to pass the winter quietly, yet actively, with my books in Yellow Springs, I hoped the College problem would be solved in favor of its founders and their original design. In a short time, however, the Western Convention, which assembled at Franklin, O., Oct. 28, called me away to aid in realizing the wishes and accomplishing the designs of the Christians concerning the Institution; but before we speak of said Convention, let us turn our attention for a few moments to some very important preliminaries.

The reader of the preceding pages has seen that the dedicatory exercises of the College had hardly passed before trouble arose touching the administration of the Institution, and, that, during the second year of the College, discontent and distrust had increased to a wide extent. Numerous testimonies, and especially Mr. Fay's letters, conclusively prove this. Elder Maple's pointed and withering editorials of August 13th and September 3d, had gone forth to the world, carrying conviction wherever they went. In August, also, a letter of one of our lay-brethren, E. W. Devore, to Dr. Bellows, of New York city, was published in the "Christian Inquirer," and, among other statements, contained the following:

"If Antioch fails, the fate of Meadville is sealed; consequently, all that has been expended both on Antioch and Meadville, will be entirely lost."

This is sharply reviewed by "O. S." of Meadville, in which review he says:

"The statement that, 'If Antioch fails, the fate of Meadville is sealed,' is not sustained by the facts of the past or present in relation to the Theological School. When it is said that, 'If Antioch succeeds, scores of young men will go to Meadville,' it is a part of that extravagant talk about the rapid propogation of Unitarianism, of which there is too much, and which does more harm than good. If Antioch College succeeds, as we desire it may, it may through its very success beget a love of secular science more than of Divinity, and a desire of distinction and success in secular pursuits rather than a willingness to spend life in a profession in which there is a prospect more obvious to young men of self-denials than of speedy and considerable wordly rewards. Whether the present plans in regard to Antioch succeed or fail, the school of Meadville, which has already done something, will continue, probably, to do a fair proportion of work to supply the wants of Christ's Church."

Bro. Devore in his reply to the article of "O. S." says:

"I presume I am as anxious for the success of Meadville as the gentleman is for that of Antioch; but I wish them to be mutually helpmeets to each other. I am also anxious that a greater intimacy should be induced between the Unitarians and the Christians, believing as I do, that there are elements in each, that if possessed to a greater degree by the other, would be a great benefit."

"I still cling to the position that nothing has, or probably ever will transpire that would be more effectual in the dissemination of Liberal Christianity than the success of Antioch College; and hence my exertions; for I assure you that I am unsectarian, spirit, soul, body, and I have never been in a Unitarian church, and have never heard but one Unitarian preach, viz: Dr. Bellows; yet I love Unitarians because they are Liberal—they do not wish to bind men's consciences—they do not wish to enforce creeds; but the Bible is their motto—advance, and not stand still, their theory."

Bro. Devore seems to be almost as much charmed with the Meadville Theological School and Unitarianism as is Rev. Eli Incognito!

In the "Gospel Herald" of Oct. 1st, appears a lengthy editorial from the pen of Eld. J. Maple, from which I extract the following:

"ANTIOCH COLLEGE.

"The great question now before the Christian denomination is Antioch College. It is *the question with us*, and it embraces interests vast and far reaching to us as a denomination; but the Christian Church is not dependent upon Antioch College for its existence. It has a firmer foundation than this, and if we are only faithful to her interests she will stand firm though Antioch College, and a thousand like her, were swept out of existence. But we do not undervalue the importance of Antioch to us as a religious denomination. We know that it can be made a mighty instrument in advancing the pure Heaven-born principles of the Christian Church; but to make it such an agency as this in advancing our cause it must be *our College, under our government, and denominational in its character*. Such it was designed to be, and such it should ever have remained. This is all that we ask, and for this we shall contend as long as we have the use of our tongue or pen. Make it such and it shall have our hearty support, and we know that it will have the support of all our friends in the West.

"Antioch College has occupied our thoughts for months, almost to the exclusion of everything else. It is constantly in our mind during our waking hours, has visited our midnight dreams, and wet our pillow with tears. We are willing and ready to do all in our power to redeem Antioch and make it what it should be. We have no other desire; but wish our people to understand the true state of affairs, financially and denominationally, so that they may act understandingly and guard against breakers in the future. In what we have written we have not been governed by sectional or personal feeling, for we have none on this subject. We have acted from a sense of duty and an earnest desire to promote the interests of the Christian Church, believing them to be identical with those of the kingdom of Christ. We knew that our articles on Antioch College would awaken deep feelings and call down on our head much abuse. We have not been disappointed. Many hard things have been said about us, but we care not for all this. We have a higher object in view than personal care or fame, and we know that thunderstorms are sometimes necessary—they purify the atmos phere and promote the general health. Such, we hope will be the result of the present storm. It will purify the moral atmosphere and promote the spiritual health of our denomination."

God grant that such may be the result. May the fierce storm which is now raging, and which threatens by its thunders to force a part of the Christians into the temples of false prophets; and by its furious hail to drive the whole denomination over into the glittering plains of charming "isms," so-called reforms, but reforms which appear not in the divine teachings of Christ; or otherwise to sever into fragments the Christian Connection, which for the last fifty years has been quietly advancing, yet successfully and nobly to a commanding position: may the fierce storm now raging, I repeat, "purify the moral atmosphere, and promote the spiritual health of our denomination," exhibit to the world the "bow of God's peace," and leave behind, the serene deep blue heavens of His eternal love.

To some taunts thrown out by the "Christian Messenger," Elder Maple goes on to say:

"Brother Cummings, we are neither *sick nor dying*, nor are we 'denominationally discouraged.' We have only spoken the words of truth and soberness; and what we have said will 'eventuate in some good.' It has done good already. * * * We know that there has been years ago, much boasting about what Ohio could and would do; but the editor of the 'Gospel Herald' had no share in this boasting. He did none of it. He then believed it to be the most impalpable of all gasses, and he now knows it to be the intangible shadow of a ghost; but we know that there are thousands of good and true hearted friends of Antioch College in Ohio who, are willing to help to bear the heavy burden under which it is groaning. They have done nobly, and are ready to do more; but they are *Christians, and must know that their money goes to sustain a Christian College before they pay any more.* Give them this assurance, and we believe that Ohio will do her duty."

"It has not been our object to discourage the members of the Christian Denomination from doing their duty, and we do not think that we have said anything calculated to produce this unfortunate result. We only wish our people in the West to be true to themselves; to their principles and sentiments; to their God and religion. We published what we believed to be the truth in regard to the College, so that our people might know their duty and act understandingly. If the College is not now a denominational institution, our people should know it, so that they may redeem it and make it ours emphatically. We say now, and ever have said to 'Ohio, face the storm;' do your duty; pay promptly your share of the $60,000, and more, too, if necessary. We believe that she is willing to do it on the condition that it is made a denominational College, and reconsecrated anew to the interests of the Christian Church. We know two men in Ohio who have pledged themselves to pay $1,000 each to redeem it, and we believe that there are a 'few more of the same sort.'

"We are most emphatically in favor of a Convention, and will go any distance to attend it. We have not thrown 'cold water' on this plan.— We have not said a word against it. We have only stated facts, believing them to be of vital interest to us as a people. We are prepared 'to act in concert with our constituents in saying what shall be done— if anything—when and how;' but we are not yet prepared to 'put on sackcloth for the past,' for we have not seen that we have done anything to repent of. We do not regret standing up for the interests and honor of the Christian denomination, and we hope we never shall. We spoke out in plain earnest language, because the College had passed from us, was no longer denominational, and we most earnestly desired to see it redeemed and made what it was intended to be—*a Christian Institution under the government of those with whom it originated.* 'There is nerve in Ohio,' and we think that she will do her duty towards redeeming Antioch, and also in defending the interests of the Christian denomination."

Brother Cummings, (Editor of the Christian Messenger,) says again—

"One thing is certain: if Ohio has nothing to do but howl a wail over the calamities which have, through their bad management, befallen us, the Central and Eastern States will pour no more treasures into her bosom. Much depends upon what is done in the West; if other sections could see that they are making a worthy struggle for life, we doubt not but that they would cheerfully do their part towards blotting out past follies and misfortunes."

"We think Brother C. takes a wrong view of the subject in the above extract. He intimates that the money paid by 'the Central and Eastern States' was simply to benefit Ohio. We have never looked at it in this light, but have ever supposed that the College was intended for the good of the whole denomination, East and West, North and South. It belongs to the Christian Church, and so far as we are concerned we know no East or West. The Christian people are our brethren whereever they may live, and their interests are ours. The brethren in New England have decided what they will do, and if we understand their position, it is the same we occupy, *they will help redeem Antioch if it can be made what the Marion Convention designed that it should be, a denominational College;* but if this cannot be done, they will 'let her drive.' This is what our people say in the West. To deliver Antioch College from debt, and let it remain what it now is, and under the government of the influence that has brought it to its present state we will not give one cent, but to redeem and restore it to the hands of the Christian denomination, we will pay all that our circumstances will justify, and more too. *Can this be done?* This is now the great practical question before us. We believe that this glorious end can be accomplished, if we are only faithful to our principles. There is money enough in our denomination to redeem Antioch and build half a score more just like it if it can only be made available. We belive it can by pursuing the right course. A Convention has been called to meet in Franklin, Ohio, on 28th of this month. Delegates have been appointed from the most of the Conferences in Ohio; but the Convention should not be made up of these alone. ALL the scholarship holders and friends of education and the Christian Denomination should attend it. Brethren, now there is an opportunity to redeem Antioch and make it what we all desire it to be. It is for you to decide this great question, and on you rests the responsibility. What will you do? Come up to the Convention and 'let us reason together,' and see what can be done. In our last there was an earnest appeal from the pen of Brother Simonton. Read it and catch his spirit. The College is worth redeeming. Shall we let the golden moment pass unimproved? No, *never*. Let us take hold in earnest, redeem it, and restore it to its original basis."

L. D. F., of Rochester, N. Y., presents in the 'Messenger,' of Oct. 1st, the following pointed and pertinent remarks. He alludes to the plan proposed by Bro. Palmer, and exhorts the ministers and brethren to take hold of it with promptness and energy.

"BRO. CUMMINGS—A few weeks since, I noticed in your journal a very simple proposition by our friend, Mr. Palmer, of the Broadway Bank, New York, for the relief of the College. I have been waiting with solicitude to see some response to that suggestion; but seeing none, I have thought best to allude to it. His plan was, for the members of the denomination—*all*—to unite in paying *one* dollar per annum, for five years, which would put the Institution entirely out of debt, and endow it with a good fund. This could be done and no one feel burdened; and it would insure the success of the enterprise.

"Who, let me ask, is not willing to be taxed so little, for so great an object? But many will say, enough has been done already to have placed the College out of all embarrassment and we are tired of doing and sick of the concern!! And shall we, therefore, stop short and lose all that has been done? This would be too much like the man who should decide to put out both of his own eyes, for the sake of putting out one of his antagonist's!! We feel fully the distress and mortification accruing from the state of finances of the College, and its financial management; but shall we seek redress by injustice to ourselves? Shall we sullenly court disgrace and denominational defeat by culpable neglect in the duty before us? Let us arise as one man and fly to the rescue. Are there none to be found with whom the College finances can be confided? Then we deserve defeat! But that we should act like children in a pet, and abuse ourselves because others have abused us—be reckless of this Institution because others have outraged its financial interests—is intolerable. We hope for manliness in the denomination.

"Now let every minister take hold and put into practice among his people this plan. Or, as you suggest, let there be a Convention immediately to devise and concert measures to accomplish this great work. Brethren, be indignant, as you deserve to be, at the wrongs done you; but don't for humanity's sake play the child in your anger, and inflict deeper wrongs on yourselves. L. D. F."

"ROCHESTER, N. Y., Sept. 23, 1857."

QUERY—Who are they who have done us wrong? Are they Unitarians or Trinitarians? or are they not those who stand nominally with us, "Wolves in sheep's clothing?"

In the "Herald of Gospel Liberty," (Newburyport, Mass.,) Eld. N. Summerbell says:

"The less said about Antioch College *in our paper* the *better*. This I discovered near two years ago, which accounts for my silence upon that subject

"New England does right to turn her resources over to Andover. I hope New York will patronize her own school also, and that the *West* will soon commence the work."

In an article from the "Salem Gazette," and republished in the "Christian Inquirer," (Unitarian,) among some false statements appears the following farcical one—viz: "The Faculty is now a unit, and highly satisfactory to the students!!"

QUERY—Do the students control the College, and dictate, who shall and who shall not be Professors in it? or is it not Horace Mann under pretence of unity and of pleasing the students?

The "Herald of Gospel Liberty" of Oct. 22d, in an editorial on Antioch, says:

"Of the seven Professors, five are members of Christian Churches, in good standing. Yet the *Christians* have no legal claim to a single Professorship, as the College now stands."

About the first part of this extract there may be doubts; but the last period is a fact. The reader of the preceding pages has noticed that the school at present in operation is not Antioch College; and for its glory or shame, the Christian Denomination, doubtless, is not legally if morally responsible.

In the same paper, Eld. A. G. Morton, of Providence, commences an article on the College with the following questions: "How is it with Antioch?" "How are the College matters getting along?" and after referring to some of the past acts says:

"Now leaving all the past to take care of itself, like the dead burying the dead; we are told that the College can be redeemed by the denomination for $60,000, such a statement is made and is probably correct. The redemption should be whole and complete, bringing the whole property free from all incumbrances and endowments whatever, into the possession and under the exclusive control and direction of the Christians. This, or nothing, should be done." * * *

"Meeting the enquiries stated at the beginning of this article, and learning more and more every day of the dissatisfaction with the course being pursued among us in relation to the present condition of affairs, it seems to me that if a spirited and intelligent effort could be made, the College might very easily be recovered and secured to the Christian Denomination. Let the subject be considered."

From the above extracts, and the preceding Reviews, the reader will gather a pretty good idea of public opinion (especially among the Christians) concerning the College, previous to the 28th of October, 1857. On that day, "the Convention to devise means for the redemption of Antioch College from her present embarrassments, met at the Christian Church, Franklin, Warren Co., Ohio," and it was hoped that said convention would devise and adopt such a plan as would at once restore the confidence of the Christians to the Institution, and be the means of placing the College upon a firm financial and denominational basis, of making it emphatically *the College* of *the Christians.*

It was a delegated Convention. Delegates from most of our large Conferences, especially in the West, were present. It was expected that it would be strictly a *Christian,* a denominational Convention, as was the Marion Convention, Oct. 1850, at which the College sprang into existence. In this expectation, however, we were to be disappointed; for Horace Mann came down to Franklin with a company of men, few or none of whom were delegates to said Convention, and some were not even members of the Christian Church nor had they any special interest in the Christian Connection! The Convention was organized at 10 o'clock, A. M.; the usual preliminaries resulting in the appointment of Dr. W. L. Schenck for President, and Prof. McKinney for Secretary. Prof. Doherty moved that a committee of five be appointed to report a plan to carry out the object of the Convention, which motion, after some remarks from Mr. Mann and others, passed, and was adopted. "Prof. Doherty, Elds. Maple, Long and Jacobs and Prof. Allen were appointed said committee."

On the question of voting, the President "decided that delegates only had a right to vote," when a determined and obstinate opposition manifested itself, which was led by Mr. Fay, who labored to show among other things, that delegates should not vote "as representatives of their Conferences, but in their individual capacity," &c. The discussion went on spiritedly for some time, when—

"Eld. Reeder moved that the Convention resolve itself into a mass Convention, and that all persons present be invited to speak and participate in the proceedings."

This resolution, after an animated and protracted discussion passed (the delegates voting as individuals) and the mass meeting adjourned to 2 o'clock, P. M.

"AFTERNOON SESSION.

"Eld. Lynn gave notice of his intention to protest against the abrogation of the rights of delegates in the representation of their respective bodies.

"The President explained his understanding of the effect of Eld. Reeder's resolution to be that it gave visitors the privilege to participate and vote, and that delegates still maintained their rights as before.

"Eld. Lynn concurred with the President, and said that no delegated body could change its character.

"Eld. Reeder said that he agreed with the explanation given by the President, and he was certain that the Convention so understood it."

To this construction of Eld. Reeder's resolution, Messrs. Mann, Fay & Co. objected, and a spirited debate followed. Mr. Mann offered a resolution to the effect that each person cast but one vote. "Prof. McKinney contended that the Convention had no right to take delegated power from the meeting."

"The question being called for on Mr. Mann's resolution, a vote was taken, which resulted in the affirmative." And thus, after nearly a whole day's pointed discussion the "delegated Convention" was declared to be a "mass meeting!" and hence, any visitor could now offset the action of a whole Conference through its delegate, although said Conference might have fifty ordained ministers, and ought, according to usage, to have fifty votes!

EVENING SESSION.

Prof. Doherty, Chairman of the Committee on Plan, reported in part which on motion was ordered to be taken up in sections for discussion.

"Prof. Doherty read the preamble.

"Eld. Fay objected to that part which stated that the College was not now under the control of the Christian Denomination. He knew that to be false. Two thirds of the present Faculty were members of the Christian Church.

"Eld. Wait made a statement with regard to the present Faculty of Antioch. He said it was strictly in accordance with the plan laid down by the Marion Convention. He pronounced the statement in the preamble untrue.

"Eld. Long said that as soon as the College was assigned to Mr. Palmer it was no longer the property of the Christians, and that the officers now could not be under the control of the denomination, neither was the school which was now held there.

"Eld. Wait looked on the matter differently. He believed that the corporation still existed, and will continue to do so until Mr. Palmer closes up the entire business. The assignment of the building did not dishonor the school, nor did it forfeit its denominational character.

"Eld. McKinney said that it was now the general opinion that the school was carried on by private individuals. From a communication which he saw published in the 'Gospel Herald' this point was conceded. He was therefore astonished at the remarks of the former speaker."

Many others were also astonished at the reckless and defiant manner in which Eld's Fay and Wait spoke. They seemed to be almost wholly regardless of facts! And thus the debate went on the whole evening, the advocates of the preamble standing firm and repelling the fierce onsets of Mann, Fay & Co. It was really amusing to see Mr. Mann surrounded by persons always ready to vote for him, and continually on the alert to make speeches at the suggestion of their chief!

SECOND DAY.

"The Convention met at 9, A. M.

"After a brief discussion, the preamble was amended and adopted.

"The first resolution was then read.

"A question being asked if the resolution was intended to carry out the spirit of the Marion Convention, was answered by one of the committee in the affirmative.

"Mr. Mann moved to amend so as to read the College shall be used and conducted hereafter according to the Marion plan.

"Professor Doherty contended for the passage of the resolution in its original shape. He was opposed to any further copartnership with any denomination. The people of the New England States, and others, were in favor of the Christians owning it, and no other.

"Eld. Long requested to be informed as to the nature of the Marion plan.

"Eld. Wait replied, and moved to further amend so as to read according to the Marion plan, scholarships excepted."

These amendments were objected to by myself and others, for the very obvious reason, that the Marion plan was not intended to be more than a general outline. The Marion Convention expected that the Provisional Committee and their successors in office, would guide and control the College in accordance with the original design; and that they would pass such laws and regulations as they might find necessary for the execution of said design. Besides the spirit and the letter, of the Marion plan had been violated, and who could assure us that it would not again be thus violated?

"Elder Maple moved that the words of the College charter should be substituted" viz:

"To be under the direction, control and management of the religous denomination called "CHRISTIANS," professing no creed but the BIBLE, and having no test of fellowship but CHRISTAIN CHARACTER, which originated as an organized body in the United States about the beginning of the nineteenth century, under the labors of Abner Jones of New England; David Purviance, of Kentucky; James O'Kelly, and F. Williamson of North Carolina; Bremville Barret, of Virgina; Nathan Warley, of Ohio; and others whose sentiments have been advocated in the 'Herald of Gospel Liberty' of New England; 'Christian Palladium' of N. York; 'Christian Sun' of North Carolina; and 'Gospel Herald' of Ohio."

Eld. Maple's amendment or substitute was not, however, satisfactory to that clique of persons, several of whom were not members of the Christian Church; and who seemed determined to rule or ruin the Convention. And why should they not prefer the general Marion Plan? With this watchword they could perhaps conciliate enough of the Christians to aid them through with their plans; and besides it was more distant, more general, and but few in the community knew what it was. "Distance lends enchantment to the view," and darkness and ignorance are often necessary in the execution of a plot.

The debate continued for some time when,

"Brother Winebrenner moved to lay the resolution and amendments on the table, which was carried.

A motion was made to recommit the report to the committee for revision with instructions to report only on the financial affairs ot the College in future.

Prof. Warriner, contended that the Convention had nothing to do with the future control of the College. If it was to be redeemed by a joint stock company, the holders of the stock would settle that question. The race was now to the swift. If the Christians subscribed the largest amount of capital to the stock they would control it; if not, they could not, and need not expect it.

Prof. Allen was opposed to committing the resolutions again to the committee to report only on the finances of the College. The people would not pay out their money for its redemption unless they were satisfied how, and by whom it was to be conducted in the future. It is a duty we owe to ourselves, to the denomination, and to our Creator, to educate our sons and daughters. It was on this broad platform that we and every liberal Christian stood: it was not sectarian. The Christians had a right to control their own institutions, otherwise the churches East and West would not respond.

"Prof. Doherty was in favor of some plan for the redemption of Antioch College. If he was certain that the people would be satisfied with a mere financial report, he would agree to it, but they would not. He came to the Convention with the determination to agree with any man or any proposition that was liberal. From his knowledge of the country, he was satisfied, that unless the College became more denominational, it could not and would not succeed. A denominational basis must, therefore, be laid down. The pubilc demands it to restore confidence".

Adjourned untill 2, P. M.

AFTERNOON SESSION.

"Brother Jacobs was opposed to the recommital of the report. He was sorry to see on the part of some a disposition to put down any effort made to place the College on denominational principles, which the Conferences restricted them to. He did not cherish any sectarian spirit; he did not object to other denominations having their Colleges, and he thought the Christians should have theirs. Why should we not be allowed to control our own matters? If we could not, the Christian denomination was not worth contending for.

"Mr. Mann said the object of the Convention was to raise money to pay the debts of the College, which money will be handed to the creditors, and the property will then revert to its original owners. Mr. Palmer will then deed back to the corporation all he has received, and then it will be conducted on the same principles as heretore. We want no new charter or constitution which the resolution anticipates. Mr. M. could produce letters showing that the people were satisfied with the former conduct and management of the College. He (Mr. M.) then read an article from the 'Herald of Gospel Liberty,' stating the sentiment of the public mind East on that subject. He looked on the resolution as reported as not suitable to their wants. He feared it would fail in enabling them to raise the money, and he believed the amount might be procured on some other financial plan.

"Elder Lynn adverted to the same article read by Mr. Mann from the 'Herald of Gospel Liberty,' in which the Editor stated 'that as the College now stands the Christians have no legal right to claim a single Professorship in the institution.'

Elder Reeder then moved the following as a substitute for the resolution on recommitment, and the proposed amendments, viz:

"Whereas, Antioch College is now to be sold: Therefore,

Resolved, That we recommend to the friends of the College to form themselves into a company to purchase the same, on the principle of joint stock."

Two days and an evening had now been spent in a fruitless discussion, and the first resolution of the committee's report had not yet been passed. Caucuses, or private meetings, had been held in the hotel where Mr. Mann and some of his clique had rooms; and they had resorted, also, to malicious insinuations and base misrepresentations and wire-workings, to gain votes; and as they had succeeded in turning the "delegeted convention" into a *mass* meeting, there seemed to be no prospect of adopting any plan to make the College a "Denominational Institution," which is so forcibly advocated by Maple and others in the above extracts. It was, therefore, thought best to pass Eld. Reeder's resolution and then adjourn *sine die*, and thus throw the question of Antioch's redemption, untramelled, before the whole Christian Denomination. The Denomination could then call a general convention, or take such other action as might be thought proper. Eld. Reeder's resolution, therefore, passed unanimously; but the resolution to adjourn *sine die* was lost by a majority of one.

"Elder Wait then offered a resolution that a committee be appointed to draft an address to the people on the subject.

"An amendment was proposed, that the chair nominate said committee.

"The amendment was discussed by Elders Reeder, Long and others.

"A second motion to adjourn *sine die* resulted—yeas 16, nays 18.

"The question being called for on the resolution for the committee to draft an address with the amendment, was carried.

"President Mann, Elders Maple and Reeder, were appointed said committee.

"*Resolved*, That a committee of three be appointed to draft rules and regulations to govern a stock company and to proceed to organize, was carried.

"The committee to draft the address, with the addition of Brothers Harless and Heath, were appointed.

"Adjourned *sine die*."

Thus the Convention ended by rushing in two committees, of both of which Mr. Mann was chairman; and although the committees contained some good brethren, yet the friends of a *free, denominational*, CHRISTIAN COLLEGE, had little or nothing to hope for, from their future reports. A wiley, determined man was at the helm, and however assiduously the Christians might labor at the oars, would he not guide the ship?

Let us now turn for a moment to the " Christian General Convention assembled at Marion, N. Y., Oct. 2d, 1850," before which was offered the following resolution, viz :

"6th. *Resolved*, That our responsibility to the community, and the advancement of our interests as a denomination, demand of us the establishing of a college."

A protracted, animated, and most interesting discussion followed, in which Eld's Pike, Brown, Chadwick, Case, Phillips, Crosby, Holland, Ladley, Devore, Seever, Knight, Wait, Marvin, Elliot, Brown, Kimball, Wellons, Freese, Doherty, and Sweet, and A. M. Merrifield, Esq., took part, "*agreeing upon the undoubted necessity of a Collegiate Institution among us, and upon our readiness, willingness, and ability to erect and endow such an Institution;*" when the question was put by the President, and the resolution passed *unanimously*, by yeas 521.

Here was a General Convention, composed of 82 delegates, representing 26 conferences, 521 ordained ministers, and as many votes; and all these votes, without exception, were cast for a *denominational* College. The College then voted into existence upon a *denominational* basis, has been alienated from that *denomination*, and wrested from its control; and why, I ask, would not, did not, the Franklin Convention adopt a plan by which said College might have been redeemed to the Christians, and *fully restored to their control?* Why was such a fierce opposition made by Mann, Fay, and others, to the report of the Committee? Was there any thing in the preamble and first resolution of said report which could militate against the interests of the Christians, and which merited such a determined onset? The reader may wish to be introduced to this notorious preamble and resolution. Here they are:

PREAMBLE.

"WHEREAS, It appears that Antioch College has, by a series of unfortunate circumstances, which it would be tedious and unprofitable to mention, become bankrupt, and the property been assigned by the late Board of Trustees into the hands of F. A. Palmer, Esq., of N. Y. City, to be sold for the benefit of its creditors; and is now carried on as a private enterprise by a few individuals not under the control of the Christian Denomination—and whereas, it seems very desirable to secure the possession of the College to the religious body by whom it was erected, in order that it may be managed, in future, in accordance with the intention of its founders: Therefore,

Resolved, That this Convention recommend, and *do hereby initiate* the formation of a 'Joint Stock Company,' for the purpose of raising funds and purchasing, at the lowest possible rate, the College Buildings, Furniture, Instruments, Library and Apparatus, the same to be secured for the use of the Christian Denomination alone, without the interferance, supervision or control of any religious body whatever."

Is there any thing in this preamble and the resolution, hostile to making Antioch College a Christian Institution, a *denominational* College, for which Eld's Pike, Morton, Ross, Maple, N. Summerbell; Messrs. Merrifield, Geary and Kearns, and numerous others of our leading ministers and laymen have so earnestly and eloquently contended? Are not both the spirit and the letter of these articles in entire harmony with the Marion Plan, and the spirit of that noble convention? Why then, and whence the opposition they met at Franklin? Comes it not from that foreign element or influence which has taken shelter under the wing of the Christian body, from that vulture which is eating out the very vitals of our denomination? God grant that we may look well after the interests of our own household, that we may not deny the faith and become worse than infidels.

The reader will notice from the above resolution from the Committee's report, made to the convention, that the formation of a "Joint Stock Company" was recommended, but it was to be almost wholly different from the one now before the public. Said Company was to be composed of several Branch Companies; one in New England, one in the Central States, and one or two in the Western States; each Branch Company to have its own officers, and to manage its own affairs; but all working together harmoniously in buying, endowing and controlling the College.

The shares were to be placed at $200 each, a sum within the reach of a large number of our brethren; and any minister who would secure and pay into the treasury five shares, or $1000, was to have a share for himself, and all the rights and privileges of a regular shareholder. This arrangement would, doubtless, have interested a large number of our ministers, and given them a voice in controlling the College.

But it may be objected that this is too great an inducement to hold out to our ministers. We think not, for many reasons, some of which are:

1st. Our ministers are not as well paid as they ought to be for their services.

2d. This proposition would create a more general and *practical* co-operation on the part of the ministry, and secure large amounts of money.

3d. It would lay a broader and more permanent basis for College patronage, for our ministers are, or should be, influential in the sections of country where they live. Just look at this a moment. What a plan for successful action! We have, it is said, from 1,200 to 1,500 ministers and about the same number of churches; say 1,200. Now suppose only one-half of this minimum number should fully comply with the plan, we should have received $600,000, *i. e.* 600 ministers each raising $1,000, would obtain together, $600,000; more than half a million of dollars!

Provisions were also embodied in the plan, in which the Scholarship holders would be interested, and which would secure the management and control of the Institution *forever* to the *Christian denomination.* What a grand basis for successful action would such a plan, interesting more than 2,000 ministers and Scholarship holders, scattered over the whole country, have been! Could failure be possible with such a plan?

Had this plan, or one essentially like it, been adopted by the Franklin Convention, and published to our brethren of the whole country, it is believed that confidence would have been restored, and that money sufficient to sweep away all the debts, and endow the College, would before this day have been secured. The Convention, however, resulted otherwise; for in the words of an able writer—"A united minority always prevails against a divided majority," and, as Elder Pike says, in an article published in the "Herald of Gospel Liberty," Oct. 29th, while the Convention was in session :

"Nothing but a close co-operation will be succesful in this hour of necessity. If we ever rise as a people, we must have union of effort and piety of heart."

From the same excellent and timely article, I extract the following :

"The *Christians* are a body of people who profess no denominational name, and reject creeds, taking the Bible as their rule of faith and practice. They number not far from 150,000 communicants, and from 1,000 to 1,500 ministers. They are too liberal for their own interest, and need a better system of united co-operation to succeed denominationally. * * * Education, and missions must be encouraged as our denominational intention. Education, generally, among our members, and high biblical and classical attainments in our ministry will not be detrimental to true godliness and holy zeal for the salvation of sinners.

"Our churches should know each other, and each other's interest. The laity should be better acquainted, and a united system of operations will tend in such a direction. If the Christians are a people worthy of having an existence, then they must be strictly denominational. I have for years been contending for this point. I am opposed to any amalgamation in any of our interests with the denominations of the country. I would cultivate friendly feelings with all, but unite with none as such. We are suffering to-day in New England, because of our liberality. Had we been more careful to maintain a more decided distinctiveness, we should have had twice the influence we now have in New England. This may be called sectarian. Be it so; our church relations resemble our family relations. He that provides not for his *own household* is not worthy to have a family of his own. He who looks not after his own particular church and those churches that associate with him, will soon be without either.

"I am for a decided arrangement to complete our denominational existence upon a firm and permanent union. * * * When we begin an operation we appear unwilling to trust our own strength, but must begin to think of soliciting aid, by which we become entangled and often fail. Every such failure depresses and sinks our influence, and thus like Samson, we lose our strength; and in this divided state, if continued, we shall sooner or later die out, crumble to pieces, or be swallowed up by others. The way to secure the permanency of the Christians, especially in New England, is to consolidate their strength, rally around the Christian Institute at Andover, open a Biblical department, pray earnestly; live consistently for the salvation of souls."

Finally, on the 19th of November, the reports from Mr. Mann's pen, but nominally from the Committees of which he was Chairman, made their appearance in the "Gospel Herald." The reception, however, which they met, seemed to be very cool; for they did not appear in the

"Christian Messenger" until December 24th, and still later, and apparently with great reluctance in the "Herald of Gospel Liberty." These reports were not, therefore, adopted by the Franklin Convention, as has been falsely stated during the last few weeks by Elder Maple, and others. They were never submitted to that Convention; and had they been, they would, doubtless, have been rejected by an overwhelming majority. Indeed, just after the appearance of the reports in the "Herald," Eld. Maple wrote me the following note, which shows, at least, that he would not have voted for such a plan and circular had they been laid before that Convention; especially when this note is interpreted by his letter of Dec. 6th, to Elder Lynn.

"FRANKLIN, Ohio, Nov. 21st, 1857.

"MY DEAR BRO. ALLEN:—Yours of the 14th inst., has just been received." * * * "Mr. Mann has treated me very unjustly and dishonorably in regard to the report of the Committee on the redemption of Antioch; and I have written a protest against the unlawful use he has made of my name. It will be out next week. I have many things to say, but must close for want of time to add more.

"Yours in love, JAMES MAPLE."

Elder Maple's letter to Elder J. T. Lynn:

"FRANKLIN, O., Dec. 6th, 1857.

"BRO. LYNN:—I have received two letters from you, and the reason why I have not answered them before is, that I have been sick and unable to write." * * * "There are some things in the Committee's report on the College to which I objected, and told Mr. Mann that they must be left out, or he must not put my name to it; but notwithstanding this, he put my name to it unjustly. I had prepared a reply to him for the 'Herald,' in which I exposed his unjust use of my name, but I finally concluded to write to him and tell him that I would have nothing more to do with him or the College, and let the whole thing go.

"I have done so, and the College may go by the board for me; for I shall have nothing more to do with it. Mr. Mann has shaken my confidence in his integrity. Yours in love,

"J. MAPLE."

The Franklin Convention was considered as sectional. On this point Elder P. Roberts, of N. Y., speaks out in the "Messenger" of Dec. 3d, and desires a general Convention, to be held in New York. He says:

"First, give the whole denomination a chance to redeem it, and then if they do not do it, localities and limited districts can take their chance." * * * "The N. Y. Eastern Conference and New Jersey have paid in $10,000 since the Convention in New York city, Jan. 30th, 1856. We feel, therefore, that we have rights which the action of the Trustees, in assigning the property, has not wholly deprived us of."

In the "Gospel Herald" of Dec. 10th, the Northern Illinois Christian Conference speaks through our able Brother, Goff, and recommends, 1st; the immediate purchase of the College, in trust for the churches:

"I do beleive that there are 20, or 60, or 120 men among the Christians who will at once assume the $60,000 in trust, and engineer the College through its difficulty."

"2d. For its ultimate purchase and ownership by the Christians, that it may not be diverted from its original purpose and design." Substantially the plan suggested by F. A. Palmer, Esq., of New York city. "That every member of the Christian Church pay one dollar per year, for the next three or four years, which would produce a fund sufficiently large not only to relieve, but also to amply endow the College."

In the "Gospel Herald" of December 17th, Elder A. Bradfield, of Ohio, says:—

"It is certain that the College is greatly embarrassed in its financial relation; and distrust hangs over the educational department, which has not been a little augmented by the late discussions in the Herald. Fears and dark forebodings of the future hang gloomy over the minds of the friends of the College, &c."

To save the College he recommends:

"The assuming of the whole debt of the Institution, including the amount of the scholarship funds used in payment of debts other than educational. To take advantage of the circumstances and compel the scholarship-holders to donate the amount of their scholarships (provided it could be done) to the payment of the debts made by the building of the College, &c., would be no less honorable than high-way robbery. Salaried agents need not try any more; the people have lost confidence, and it must be regained by some more feasible plan."

He further says:—

"For the government of the College; let it be under the control of the Christian Denomination. Let Trustees be elected by delegates from each conference in the denomination; each conference having as many votes as there are ordained ministers in the same."

Bro. Phillips, writing to the "Messenger" on Antioch College, says, that the confidence of our people should be restored by an investigation of "the whole matter," by a statement of "its true indebtedness," and by the assurance that if said indebtedness is cancelled, the College will be "placed on a sure basis." He further remarks:—

"Not much wonder that our people become discouraged and refuse to give their money; for at one time a report would be published that our great Antioch was so much in debt, and if that amount was raised it would liquidate the debt, and our people would pour out their money like water. The next news would be that the debt was twice as much. Our people began to think that it was not known how much the College was in debt, and that if they would give all the money they could raise, the beloved Institution might still be lost to the denomination. I am satisfied that if a true statement of the indebtedness would be made, and our people assured that that amount would pay the whole debt, and the Institution be placed on a solid basis, and the benefit secured to those that have paid their scholarships, that our people will fly to the rescue. I like Bro. Palmer's plan, viz.: each member of the denomination pay one dollar a year for five years. He said that this would pay the whole debt, and endow the professorships. If that will do it, it can be done. * * * * D. PHILLIPS."

"December 8, 1857."

From the above extracts, and other articles which appeared in our papers, suggesting important ideas which the "Joint Stock Co." plan could not meet; from the general silence on that plan, and the lack of confidence in some of its chief leaders and advocates; as well as from communications from different sections of the country, and the statements of persons whom I met, it appeared evident, to my mind, that said "Joint Stock Plan" could not permanently meet the views and satisfy the feeling of our people. Besides, some of our brethren in the East, regarding the Franklin Convention as sectional, (general, in truth, it was not, nor denominational after its *delegated* power was destroyed,) were desirous of calling a general College Convention, to be held somewhere in New York. To this I wás opposed for various reasons; some of which were:—

1st. The United States Quadrennial Christian Convention is close at hand.

2d. Such a College Convention must necessarily be sectional, for but few of the brethren would come from a great distance.

3d. The expense of such a Convention should be saved; for the times are hard, money scarce, and Antioch deeply in debt.

4th. I thought a plan could be presented which, if adopted by our editors and laid before our people in the papers, would obviate any necessity for a general convention.

While looking over the broad field of the Christian Church, and considering the views of her leading men on the College question, the following letter from Eld. Maple reached me, viz.:

"FRANKLIN, O., Dec. 21st, 1857.

"MY DEAR BRO. ALLEN:—I suppose you begin to think that I have forgotten you entirely; but I assure you that this is not the case. Your very interesting letter was on my table some two weeks before I saw it; for I was flat on my back, sick, unable to attend to anything. * * * I have no hope for Antioch, and have made up my mind to have nothing more to do with it. Mr. Mann treated me very unjustly in making out the Report of the Committee. There are some things in it to which I objected, and told him that he must strike them out, or leave out my name.

"He changed the language, but not the sentiment, and sent it out with my name to it. I prepared a review of his conduct, and it was in the hands of the printer; but I concluded to let the whole thing go, and have nothing to do with it. I wrote to Mr. Mann to this effect in a private letter. * * * If you have anything to say, the paper is at your service. Yours, in love, JAMES MAPLE."

Now in view of all the above letters, extracts and statements, the failure of the Franklin Convention to adopt any plan for the redemption of the College; the cool reception of Mr. Mann's "plan," and the almost total silence of our papers thereon; the general distrust in the management of College affairs, and the lack of confidence in the present school; and especially, in view of the numerous, earnest and repeated demands that Antioch College be placed upon a *denominational basis*, made emphatically a CHRISTIAN INSTITUTION; what, I ask, would a true friend of the College naturally do? Would he not examine the whole ground, and see if a plan could not be devised on which the Christians might unite in the great and noble work of redeeming Antioch College from its present unhappy alienated condition? To this subject I turned my attention, and endeavored to weave together in one comprehensive plan, the excellency of the plans proposed by Palmer, Goff, Bradfield and others, and to incorporate therein provisions satisfactory to the scholarship holders and other able brethren.

Accordingly, being on a visit at Franklin, on Christmas day, and although I had not committed my plan to paper, I stated its leading features to Eld. Maple. He said he had no faith in the proposed "Joint Stock Plan," would not lift a finger to aid it in any way, and did not believe it could succeed. He had fully made up his mind to have nothing more to do with it, or with the College. He thought my plan an excellent one, just the thing, if the friends would only take hold; but he feared that our churches and brethren were so dishartened on account of the mis-management of the College, that they would not work on any plan. He believed that, if any plan could succeed, it would be such an one as I had proposed; and said, if I would write it out and send it to him he would published it.

I returned the next day, wrote out the plan, and forwarded it to him on 29th December. The article was hastily prepared, and the plan was presented more as a suggestion to be improved upon than as a perfect basis of action.

I withheld my name for the time being, not from any fear of endorsing every thing which I had written; but simply that my friends might not take the plan for more than it was worth, nor my enemies for less than its value, but that it might pass for *its intrinsic merit alone.*

The notorious, mercurial Rev. Eli Incognito, and another excentric gentleman (H. C. Badger) seem to be greatly exercised on this point (judging from their late malicious efforts in the "Messenger,") but I have yet to learn, that I have not the right to use 'Indiana' or any other "*non deplume*," so long as I do not take the known signature of any other person or writer. I hold myself responsible for all that I have written over the signature "Indiana," but not for the typographical errors, of which there are several in the printed article.

I may have erred, perhaps, in the presentation of the plan, but I thought it would do good. My motives were pure. My object was in a humble way, to aid in rescuing Autioch College from its present unhappy condition and in restoring it to its founders. The insinuation of selfish interests is malicious and unchristian. I have never asked for a position in Antioch College, and never shall. Indeed, on receiving the notice of my election as one of the Faculty of the Institution, in the Autumn of 1852, I reluctantly, and after a debate in my own mind of several days, accepted the appointment; and more than once during the last three years have I thought seriously of resigning my Professorship, as some of the principal Trustees well know, for they have insisted on my remaining.

Whatever faults I may have, I have never been accused of a selfish ambition except by the small but determined clique which is now struggling to obtain complete ascendancy over the College.

By page 20th the reader will find that, in addition to the duties of my own extensive Department, I had taken charge of the class in the dramas of Schiller and Gœthe, and was consequently doing more than two men ought to have done, and *simply to save the College expense.* (Does Mr. Fay find evidence of selfishness here?)

Notwithstanding all this, Mr. Mann treated me with great injustice in reference to the German Department, and I then made up my mind that that term would end my gratuitous teachiug in Antioch College. This decision I mentioned in a note to Bro. Walter, and from his lengthy letter in reply I give the following extract:

"SPRINGFIELD, Ohio, Nov. 2d, 1855.

"Prof. IRA W. ALLEN.

"MY DEAR BROTHER:— Yours came to hand on the 30th, ult., and would have been answered immediately but in consequence of my continued affliction." * * * "I am glad to hear you say that you are determined not to take so much on yourself the next term. Now stick to that. For the more you do and the more sacrifices you make, the less will you be thanked in the end, and the more curses will be heaped upon your head. I know this by experience. For thirty years I have labored hard and perseveringly, by night and by day, have sacrificed my health, property and the comforts of being at home with my family; and yet, in many instances, I have been abused, slandered, misrepresented, and my name cast out as evil; and the worst enemies I ever had were those for whom I did the most and befriended in time of need." * * *

"Yours Respectfully, ISAAC N. WALTER."

This is no doubt the experience of many in this world of prejudice and sin. But who would have believed a year since that Eld. Maple would desert his best friends, and that J. B. Weston would go over to the embraces of Horace Mann and A. S. Dean!

Mr. Mann's clique may perhaps succeed for the time heing, and fill the offices of the Institution with relatives and obsequious friends; it may perhaps succeed in completly wresting the College from the hands and the hopes of its founders, from our brethren who have paid their money and given their influence and their earnest prayers to this noble cause; yet the day of retribution will surely come. The Christians shall yet know who have been true to their interests; and who have been laboring to undermine and destroy. This designing clique shall yet know and feel that a God of justiec reigns in Heaven, and that the wicked shall not always "flourish like a green bay tree." We live in hope. We have faith in truth. We believe the Christians will yet rejoice in educational prosperity, and if Antioch College can be placed under the government and control of the Christian Churches or Conferences, we shall then rejoice, and so far be satisfied, and not till then. To aid in the accomplishment of this noble object we presented the following plan:

"PLAN FOR REDEEMING ANTIOCH COLLEGE TO THE CHRISTIANS

"1st. The Christian Churches of the United States and the Canadas will assume the whole College debt.

2d. That the said Churches will raise *twice as many dollars as they have members* for the year 1858, and as early in the year as possible, for the purpose of buying the College property of the assignee, F. A. Palmer, Esq., of N. Y. City.

3d. That the said Churches will raise as *many dollars as they hove members*, for 1859, for the purpose of refunding in full or in part, the $40,000, borrowed or taken from the "Scholarship fund."

4th. That the said Churches will raise as *many dollars as they have members*, for 1860, and the same sum for each subsequent year, or untill they shall have obtained sufficient money to purchase and endow the College.

5th. That all the Christian Churches which shall comply with the foregoing provisions, shall have authority and power to manage and control the Collage.

6th. That each of said Churches, which has 100 members or less, shall have one vote; each which has more than 100 members and less than 200, shall be entitled to two votes; and each which has 200 or more members, shall have three votes.

7th. That said Churches may cast their votes by their own delegates, or by proxy on written permits, signed by the proper officers of the Churches.

8th. That said churches shall manage and control the Institution by a "body corporate" of at least thirty-five Trustees, who shall have such powers and be elected at such times as may be determined on by the aforesaid Churches, or by their delegates, in meeting assembled.

9th. That said Churches shall give *the right to free tuition in Antioch College* for life or for a term of years, to all holders of scholarships who have paid or shall soon pay their notes.

10th. That all moneys raised according to articles 2d, 3d, and 4th shall be used in purchasing and endowing Antioch College, but in case the said churches fail to secure said College, then shall their delegates, in their assembled wisdom, determine whether such moneys shall be refunded to the several Churches, or be so applied as to advance the educational interests of the Christians, by establishing one or more new Institutions.

11th. That the subscriptions shall be in force when the sum of twenty thousand dollars is reached, and that the first meeting of the delegates of said churches shall be held at such time and place as may be designated by a majority of them, or by any other satisfactory appointment.

It is hoped that the above plan will commend itself to the Christians and all their friends, by its conciseness, clearness and comprehensiveness.

INDIANA.

PLEDGE.

"We, the undersigned persons and churches, adopt the above 'plan of Indiana,' and do most heartily recommend it to our sister churches, our brethren and friends throughout the United States and the Canadas; and we do hereby pledge ourselves to pay the sums placed opposite our names, should a sufficient amount be pledged to render said plan binding."

But how was this plan received?

The article containing it was forwarded to Eld. Maple, December 29th, but for some reason unknown to me did not appear in the "Herald" until January 14th, and then accompanied by an editorial, from which it was quite evident that he had materially changed his views within a few days, and had either gone over, or was toppling over to the interest of the advocates of the "Joint Stock Company."

How Bro. Maple could turn such a short corner, desert the educational interests of the denomination, and go over to "Messrs. Dean, Fay & Co.," whom he has published to the world as a "little scheming, selfish, greedy clique," and declared that "our people will not be their tame and spiritless tools," I can not divine, unless the following statement meets the case:

1st. That the organ of firmness is but partially developed in Eld. Maple's cranium, and

2d. That the "little, scheming, selfish, greedy clique" has intrigued him from his former position, or, as has been hinted, bought him off with promises of future emoluments and honors.

Should this "scheming clique" succeed in pushing the "Joint Stock Company" through and purchasing the College; and in the mean time, should not Eld. Maple turn another "short corner" and desert them, he may stand a chance, perhaps, of receiving a "D. D." as has Austin Craig.

A part of Maple's editorial of January 14th is, however, excellent. He commences by saying: "Antioch still has its claims on the Christians, and they are not heedless of them. A deep and abiding interest is felt by our people, in all sections of our beloved Zion, in Antioch College, and there is a universal desire to redeem it from its present unfortunate condition."

The following lines are also worthy of repetition, and no doubt, came from his heart rather than his head, viz:

"The debts must be paid without delay, and every dollar of it should be paid by the Christians alone. We should not think of looking to a foreign source for one moment. There is no need of looking to others for help, and self-respect and denominational honor should forbid it. We say this with the kindest feelings towards our religious neighbours. Our great reasons, for desiring to have the College redeemed by the Christians alone, are, the good that such an effort would do us as a body in a spiritual point of view. We are not as liberal and as much devoted to the cause of Christ as we should be. We have been too sectional in all our enterprises. We need some great work, like the one now before us, to develop to ourselves our own resources, to cultivate our benevolence, to teach us self-reliance, and bring us into more harmonious action as a body. These are our reasons for advocating the redemption of Antioch, by our people alone, and we cannot see that there is anything selfish or ungenerous in this desire. Of course we do not desire to, nor will we reject the kind offers of any friend, or friends of the Christians, come from what source they may; but we do most earnestly desire that its claims should first be brought home to the hearts of the Christians, and that they do the work themselves, on account of the great good that it would do to them as a body."

In the same number of the "Herald," also, appeared a brief article from the vigorous pen of Bro. Goff, from which I clip the following:

"Bro. Maple—On the 27th inst., at our monthly fellowship meeting, the Church, in Blackberry, resolved, unanimously and cheerfully to pay for the purchase, or endowment of Antioch College, one dollar for each of its members for the next four years from the 1st of January 1858." * * * "Is there one Church among us that will not resolve, as we have done, and then pay their vows? I do not believe it." * * * "*Will not every Christian Church throughout the West give this matter their immediate attention, and report through the 'Gospel Herald?' Brethren! you cannot do less, and this you cannot do too soon.* Isaac C. Goff."

"December, 1857."

A little later and Brother Church, of Pa., wrote for the "Messenger" opposing the holding of a General Convention for Antioch, as a waste of time and money, and advocating a "thrilling appeal to the friends through our papers."

"I would like to have each of our periodicals send out such an appeal in their columns, and ask each Minister without delay, to send in for publication, the amount he and his congregations will pay towards the redemption of Antioch, when the whole amount is secured.

"Notwishstanding I have done all that I thought was my duty in that direction, as sixty thousand dollars is said to be sufficient to free the College from all pecuniary liabilities, I will hereby pledge myself and the Christian Church, in Spring, for one hundred and twenty-five of it—($125.) J. E. Church."

"Spring, Crawford Co., Pa., Jan. 11, 1858."

The "Messenger" of Februaay 4th says: "We give it (Indiana's plan) to our readers with the hope or desire that the churches will think well of it and act accordingly." * * *

"We will cheerfully announce any churches who comply with the plan as proposed by Indiana, if they will take action, and will send us their names, and we most earnestly hope they will. The plan proposed by the late Western Convention has its difficulties which we thought might be overcome, but the experiment already made makes it doubtful of success. It worked well for a season, but it is not easy to find so large a number of men who will pay $500 each, as is necessary to accomplish the work; and if they could be found, others might be found able and crafty enough to pay a premium for their stock and take it out of the hands of the denomination, even if they were to purchase it under that arrangement. Anything that can be done to restore confidence in the churches and inspire action on their part, would certainly be omnious of good. Could they feel that they should and could control the institution, we doubt not that a response would be forthcoming."

The "Christian Sun," of Virginia, of February 5th, says: "The plan proposed some time since to raise an amount sufficient to liquidate the debt, by the formation of a 'Joint Stock Company' is not likely to succeed, the shares being put at $500 each, an amount too large for most men. Various plans for its redemption have been proposed and discussed through the 'Gospel Herald' and 'Christian Messenger' and other papers, until, to an outsider, every thing looks like 'most glorious confusion.'"

We give, by requst, the last and most feasible plan (Indiana's) for its redemption which has yet appeared.

An able friend and Bro. communicated an excellent article to the "Gospel Herald," of Feb'y. 11th, from which I extract the following:

"As far as I have been able to learn from our papers and from individuals, one spirit seems to pervade the entire denomination—that of redeeming Antioch College, 'to be under the direction, control and management of the religious denomination called Christians,' as was designed by the Marion Convention, and as has been desired by all subsequent conventions. However individuals may have differed in their plans, their professons have been one, their aims one. If some plan could be proposed which all could clearly see would secure to the denomination the control of the College, and allay the feelings that have been created by failure of the Scholarship system, it must succeed. From numerous articles that have appeared in your paper, it is evident a suspicion may and does exist in reference to the proposed 'Joint Stock Company.' All institutions founded upon a joint stock basis, as Banks, Manufacturing Companies, Rail Roads, Schools, &c., frequently change hands, and *are always liable to such changes.* Hence, many suppose such a plan will not answer if we desire Antioch *to be and remain ours.* They will not take hold. They feel it is insecure. It likewise has been, and may be, objected to this 'Joint Stock Company' that even if it secures the sixty thousand dollars proposed, we have no assurance that it will succeed. This amount is based upon the collection of the Scholarship notes; upon the ability of the assignee of the College to make a good deed at private sale; and upon the presumption that no injunction will be laid upon the sale being effected or proposed—all of which are exceedingly uncertain. The Scholarship-holders have been cut off from the consideration for which they subscribed their money, that which has been paid has been diverted from the purpose for which it was given, and now they are sued for the balance. Enraged at such a course, they may enter suit against the Trustees for spending, as they suppose, in violation of faith and trust, the forty thousand dollars received, and thus, if the Joint Stock plan is pursued, we have the sad prospect in view of years of litigation and trouble. And the success of that plan, even then, secures only the bare College grounds and walls, which without the means to carry on the institution—a competent endowment, are but so much useless lumber.

"There has been a plan recently proposed in the columns of your paper, which, with slight modifications, must meet the entire approbation of every member of the Church. It is simple, comprehensive and practical. It appeals directly to every church, and every member of the denomination, securing to the churches the governing powers, and to the College a patronage large and sure. It makes agents, without pay, of every minister and every well wisher of the College in the Church. It gives every brother and sister of every church that adopts it a voice in the control of the College. With a slight modification, it conciliates the Scholarship-holders, and restores and enlarges the endowment fund. It gives the College to the denomination, to be under its influence and direction *forever*. It resuscitates and breathes into it a vitality—a vigorous vitality, that shall be co-existent with the church. Such is the plan of Indiana. What more can we ask? If any make excuses under this plan, we must attribute them to their miserly spirit, to their want of interest in the Church's noblest enterprize, or to some dishonest purpose. It may be objected that it is too late in making its appearance. 'Better late than never.' It contains nothing that should prevent the plan of the Joint Stock Company merging into it. I presume there is not a single subscriber to that, who would not willingly be transferred to this, and there is not a church in the denomination, that is not abundantly able to adopt it Suppose, however, that only a thousand of our churches, with an average of sixty members, act upon it. This will secure one hundred and twenty thousand dollars ($120,000) the first year, at the very light tax of an average of two dollars per member; and in five years more, by an average tax of one dollar per member, will secure an endowment of three hundred thousand dollars, ($300,000.)

"Brethren of the Christian Denomination, what more can we desire? Here is a plan which proposes, by a tax so light the poorest may not feel it, to purchase and munificently endow Antioch College, to be, *now, and forever*, under the guidance and control of the Christian Church. Awake then! arise to action! Let every minister and every member in the denomination see to it, that *his church* holds a meeting at the earliest possible hour, and that they take *immediate* and *effectual* action to carry out the plan of Indiana."

Numerous were the verbal testimonials in favor of this plan. Elder John Wm. Brown, of Gallia Co., O., being in Yellow Springs at about this date, told me that he had traveled more than 1,000 miles since the Franklin Convention, preaching to our churches; and that he had not yet found one church member who was in favor of the "Joint Stock Company;" but, he added, that nearly all with whom he conversed were decidedly in favor of the "Plan of Indiana." He further stated that, in his opinion, it would be safe to say that not one in one hundred of the members of our churches, would be in favor of the proposed "Joint Stock Company." And this feeling, if I am correctly informed, was quite general among the Christian brethren in various sections of the country. In the "Gospel Herald" of Feb'y. 25th, appeared the following excellent article by Dr. W. L. Schenck, President of the Franklin Convention, Oct. 28th 1857:—

"LET THE CHRISTIANS REDEEM ANTIOCH COLLEGE.

"Antioch College can and must be redeemed to the Christian Denomination. Let that truth be enstamped upon every Christian chapel and every Christian heart.

"The age is past when illiterate ministers can satisfactorily advance the cause of Christ, and Christ no longer endows them by the miraculous administration of his spirit with the 'gift of tongues.' Whatever scientific or literary knowledge they obtain now is secured by labor—study. The first great consideration then is a College, where we may develop the intellectual resources of the rising generation, and teach them how to study diligently, successfully. The world is ready to receive the glorious teachings of our church—the Gospel, untrameled by party prejudices and party lines—the love of God shed abroad in the heart, and causing all in whom it shines to recognize in every Christian the image of his Redeemer. All we need is efficient laborers; but, unfortunately, from the want of educational advantages, many of our brethren would fail to attract audiences from the more intelligent and refined classes of society, and should they be attracted, no matter how precious the jewel presented, it would be done so imperfectly, and be wrapped in such uncouth garments, they would fail to perceive or appreciate it. This difficulty can only be removed by awakening an educational interest among our people, and building up a College whose merits shall not fail to secure them patronage.

"We must first awake an educational interest. Can this be done by a few wealthy individuals taking stock in a company? We fear not. But rather by some plan that shall bring the subject home to the heart of every church, and each member of every church; teaching them the importance of having a College in which to educate their children, and making them feel *the College is theirs; theirs to control, theirs to support, theirs to patronize*. Thus we may most effectually bring this great question home to every hearthstone in the church.

"We have no suspicion of foul play, or bitterness of feeling towards our Unitarian brethren. *They deserve none.* We have no preference for plans any further than they carry out the great considerations desired. We have tried a *Joint Stock Plan.* It created distrust, division, failure. If, by such a plan we should raise every penny required within the bosom of the church, we can not have an assurance that it will remain there; it will always be open to suspicion. Distrust will soon follow it. The stock is a donus gift. The giver may live so distant from the College as never to be able to enjoy its immunities—the privilege of voting for Trustees, etc. Designing individuals may, in a few years, for a mere pittance, purchase enough of such shares to enable them to control the College. At best, death, which comes sooner or later to us all, may transfer our stock into the hands of those who have no interest in the College or denomination. We must adopt a plan which all will feel is safe, which is above and beyond suspicion—in which no distrust or division can arise.

"*But what is done, must be done quickly.* It is contended that dollar subscriptions won't do, that that process is too slow. As a general rule, dollar subscriptions are beneath the dignity of the enterprise, and ought to be beneath the dignity of our people. Yet we want some plan by which the widow's mite, with her prayers, shall not be refused, nor the rich man's thousands—some plan where all may give as God has blessed them—some by which those who cannot give five hundred dollars, may give what they can—a plan comprehensive, yet speedy and practical in its operation.

"But we must not only have the College, and *have it now*, but we must take immediate measures to secure the means for its support. The carcass is worth nothing to us unless we place within it a soul, and supply the nutriment that shall keep that soul alive. It must be endowed. How shall this be done? By adopting the stock plan, and issuing new stock? This will engender new distrust, by calling upon the churches to furnish the endowment? They will not do this if it is to be governed by—they know not whom. But it must be done, or the enterprise fails.

"We say, then, and every reflecting mind in the denomination feels that we must establish a College, redeem Antioch upon a basis free from all suspicion and distrust, that it must be properly endowed, and that an interest in this College, and in education, must be awakened and kept alive throughout the whole denomination. By what plan can this best be done? *Undoubtedly, that proposed by 'Indiana.'* But we are told 'we want no more plans in the field.' That may be true. But *we want the best plan in the field.* Let others merge into this. This has been done in part, and it was doubtless this partial merging that suggested the plan to which we have referred. The agent for 'the Joint Stock plan,' when here, proposed and sought subscriptions under the proposal that they should be given to the church, and that the church should control them. Such a course has also been most ably and eloquently advocated in recent editorials in the 'Gospel Herald' and 'Messenger.' Then, let not a part only, but *all* subscriptions be given to the churches. Let all the churches adopt and comply with the plan proposed, and within six months the desired end will be accomplished, to stand a glad memorial of the educational interest of the Christian Denomination *whilst a Christian Church exists.* Let every minister and every member of the church make himself a self-constituted agent for the redemption of Antioch College, and let him work diligently and faithfully to the end. Let each excite the other to good works by precept and practice. Let them pour into the treasury their dollars, and tens and hundreds of dollars, *and let the individual and collective prayer of the Church go forth for the redemption and guidance of our beloved institution. Thus God will soon reveal to us all things done speedily and in order.*"

"The 'Messenger' of Feb' 25th, also speaking on the subject of plans, makes the following admission: If 'Indiana's' plan could have been put in motion months ago when the way was clear, and the friends of the College hardly knew what to do, it might have succeeded."

Just a week later and the accompanying clear, high-toned communication from the pen of Prof. McKinney was published:

PLANS FOR THE REDEMPTION OF ANTIOCH COLLEGE.

"Several plans for the purchase of Antioch College have recently appeared in our different periodicals, accompanied with arguments and appeals. All of these have their good points; and yet none are free from exceptions. In this case, it is wisdom to adopt the one against which the fewer objections lie. I am in favor of any one by which the College can be *purchased* and *secured* to the *Christian Church.* I believe it is the desire of all who are now working to redeem the College, to place it under the control of the denomination. We hear it said: 'There is just where it should be; and there is where it must be, if it succeeds in its liberal Christian intentions. We would not place it elsewhere if we could.' These sentiments suit me; and I presume meet the approbation of our brotherhood everywhere.

"But let me be understood clearly; I am in favor of the College, if purchased by us, being under our control in the fullest and broadest sense of the term. And further still: I am in favor of this, if it is announced to the world that our people have purchased it, although means to accomplish this may have been secured elsewhere than in our churches. I am, therefore, opposed to any partnership arrangement whatever, unless it be frankly, undisguisedly proclaimed to the world, that all may know it. It may be said as a certain *squib* did once say, that this is a desire to make the Institution *'intensely denominational.'* It is simply to have it what it is, where it is, and controlled by whom it is declared to be. This is what I ask; and the demand is surely reasonable.

"But to the plans: To the 'Joint Stock Company' I have two prominent objections. 1st. The shares are too large; each being $500. This places them beyond the reach of more than nineteen twentieths of the friends of the College. This objection may be met by saying, 'that if one cannot take a share, then let a church, as such, take a share.' It must be remembered, that by far the largest proportion of our congregations are not able to take even one share; and especially is this true, under the present pressure of the money market; and also since the entire amount of the stock must be paid within a few months. My 2d objection is, it leaves the question of the future control of the College altogether contingent: 1st. A majority of the capital stock will rule the minority; and takers of shares have no warrant who will own the majority. 2d. Admit that the stock is taken, at least a majority, by the Christian Church, it is contemplated as transferable property, and hence may be bought up by any one. And 3d. The number of shares may be increased to double or triple that mentioned as the basis of the company contemplated: therefore the forces to control may be constantly shifting. These are my candid objections, stated without argument.

"'Indiana's' plan meets more fully my views than any that has been suggested or presented. To it there is but one objection in my mind; and that is this, time to carry it into effect; and it is possible that even that will be removed; for we are not sure that Antioch will be sold at as early a day as some intimate. There are too many interested in consequence of heavy claims they hold on it, to permit a hasty sale. But to the plan—I am in favor of it, because it obviates the very objections lying against the 'Joint Stock Company.' 1st. Its conditions are such that nineteen twentieths of our congregations can secure a share, and hence very nearly all our members will feel themselves interested, because partners in the institution. And 2d, it will place the College under the control of the Christians; just where we all say it should be. These are my reasons, at least my main ones, why I—by far—prefer Indiana's plan. If the College should not, in the final efforts now being made for its redemption, come under the influence and management of the Christian Church, without the intervention of any other denomination, then I shall stand toward it in the same relation I do toward other well conducted Colleges in the West. As I before said, I am utterly opposed to any partnership, with any other denomination, I care not what. For this I have my reasons, not convenient to be mentioned now.

"But to carry out Indiana's plan, or any plan, promptness and concert of action are imperative. Delay in this enterprize is positively inadmissible. Let us have a Convention of all the Conferences in the Union, to meet early in the coming spring at some central point, to take such steps as may be thought best to secure the purchase of the College and place it where it ought to be. A. L. McKinney."

"Troy, Ohio."

In the same No. of the "Herald" also came the following card:

"PLAN OF INDIANA.

"This is just the plan on which to build up a large institution, and create a general interest in education among the Christians. *The 9th article will interest the holders of scholarships.* Come friends one and all, let us take hold of the work of *redeeming Antioch to the Christians* in right good earnest. You may put down my name for the Second Christian Church of this place, on the '*Plan of Indiana*' for $125.

"Yours, for Antioch, John A. Layton".

"Yellow Springs, O., March 1st, 1858."

For more than a month had the "Herald" been closed to articles which did not chime in with Mann and Fay, and the "Joint Stock Company," with the exception of those above referred to, which for some personal or other reason Mr. Maple did not dare to shut out.

For several weeks had Maple put forth strenuous exertions, and written lengthy editorials, in order to bring the "Joint Stock Plan" into favor with our Churches and people. In the "Herald" of January 14, he says:—

"We can see no light in any direction, but in the plan for a Stock Company;" and in the issue of February 4th, he states: "The plan proposed by the Committee, we believe to be the best, in every respect, that could have been devised." "There is nothing objectionable in it to any candid, unprejudiced mind. It places the government of the College just where it should be, in the hands of those who purchase it."

How do these statements compare with Mr. Maple's letters a few weeks before, two or three of which are on preceding pages? Dec. 21 he wrote me:—

"I have no hope for Antioch, and have made up my mind to have nothing more to do with it. Mr. Mann treated me very unjustly in making out the Report of the Committee. There were some things in it which I objected, and told him that he must strike them out, or leave out my name. He changed the language but not the sentiment, and sent it out with my name to it. I prepared a review of his conduct and it was in the hands of the printer; but I concluded to let the whole thing go and have nothing to do with it."

In a letter of Dec. 6th, to Eld. Lyon, he wrote the same in substance, and added:—

"I finally concluded to write to him (Mann) and tell him that I would have nothing more to do with him or the College, and let the whole thing go. I have done so, and the College may go by the board for me; for I shall have nothing more to do with it. Mr. Mann has shaken my confidence in his integrity."

On Dec. 25th also, he told me in person that *he had no faith in the proposed "Joint Stock Plan,"* and *would not lift a finger to aid it any way*, and *did not believe it could succeed*, that *he should have nothing more to do with it, or with the College;* and yet in a few days he sits down and writes an editorial in which he commends the Stock Plan! Are not the above statements directly at variance? In the "Herald" of February 4th, Maple also says:—

"The way is open, and our people may come forward and take every cent of the stock, and thus make the College theirs forever. * * * Our people have the money and the disposition, and now that they have a feasible and common sense plan before them, they are taking hold in earnest."

A week later, he says:—

"The (our Churches) may take every cent of the stock if they will, and we believe that they will do it."

A week latter still, February 18th, he says:—

"We believe that our Churches will take every cent of the stock, if our friends, who are so denominational and love the Christian Church so well, will only quit throwing dust in the air to blind the people."

How do these published statements sound when compared with his emphatic declarations, that he would have nothing more to do with the Joint Stock Plan, or with the College, or with Mr. Mann! Do they harmonize, or do they not rather grate harsh thunder one against the other! Besides, how could Mr. Maple say: "*We believe that our Churches will take every cent of the stock,*" when some weeks, if not months, previously, about $10,000 of stock was subscribed in this town (Yellow Springs) to start the lists, the most of which was put down by persons who were not members of the Christian Church. Did not Mr. Maple know this? or did Mr. Fay who had been at his house so often, and labored with him so zealously, deceive him? We fear that Mr. Maple was aware of it. But be this as it may, *he did know* that the Joint Stock Plan was general and open, and that Christian or Infidel, Unitarian or Spiritualist, might take just as much of the stock as he pleased. He also knew that the agents for this plan, in Ohio, were not over scrupulous of right, or particularly denominational in their feelings, for touching one of them, (McWhinney) he says: "The Report of the Smelling Committee was got into the "Herald" by a trick;" and touching the other: "Our people will not be the spiritless tools of their little selfish, scheming, greedy clique." Would not these agents, therefore, receive stock subscriptions from whomsoever they could obtain them? In view of all these things, did Maple *really* believe *"that our Churches will take every cent of the stock?"* Or did he not intend to "throw dust" into the eyes of our people, and thus aid that "little scheming, selfish greedy clique" in rushing the Joint Stock Plan through, and scheming the College into their own hands?

But further, in the "Herald" of February 4th, Maple says:—

"We have heard from the agents now in the field, and they have succeeded beyond our most sanguine expectations. * * * Those Churches which have been visited by the agents have responded nobly, and we believe that all others will do the same. Bro. McWhinney says: '*If the College is redeemed, we expect, &c.*' This seems to imply a doubt about its redemption; but we have no doubts on this point. The great heart of the people is in this work, and it will be accomplished."

What has dispelled Mr. Maple's "many doubts?" He said a few weeks before, that he did not believe the Stock Plan could succeed; did not believe that our Churches would adopt it; and as for himself he would not aid it in any way whatever. To this many can testify, Dr. Schenck, Prof.'s Doherty and McKinney, Eld. Lynn, and others. Why has Maple so much more sanguine than McWhinney? A week later, February 11, he writes:—

"Wherever the agents have gone, they have been met with open hearts and liberal hands."

A week later still, he says:—

"There is but little opposition to the Stock Company among our brethren in the West. We have corresponded with all our leading ministers and lay-brethren, and we find the feeling to be the same everywhere. * * * We know of but three ministers and some half a dozen lay members who are opposed to it (the plan). They are good brethren, but we think that they have allowed their feelings and prejudices to run away with their reason. * * * The Agents have succeeded beyond the most sanguine anticipations of our most ardent friends. * * * The work will be accomplished, notwithstanding the gloomy prognostications of dyspeptic prophets."

And in another part of the same article, he says:—

"Our agents report that on the presentation of their 'plan,' they are met with a different one. An individual professes his willingness to give, but he has a better way. 'Adopt my scheme,' says he, 'and I will subscribe liberally.' It is very important to meet this objection—to remove this obstacle from the way of our agents."

He then goes on to argue the impropriety of this opposition, at considerable length, and closes with these italicised words:

"But any one who assumes to block up the way of the Committee, or seeks to anticipate their efforts by soliciting subscriptions in a manner hostile to theirs, must be an enemy to the College."

Why could not the editor wait one week to contradict himself! Many of the readers of the "Herald" might perhaps forget what they had read in one number of the paper by the time the next issue had arrived; but this contradicting one's self in a single number of the "Herald" and in a single article is a *little too barefaced*, even for forgetful people!

A week latter still, February 25th, Maple states:—

"The Stock Plan meets with almost universal acceptation. Wherever the agents go they meet with a hearty response. There are but few opposed to it, and these are confined to one locality. We mention this because we learn that our brethren in the East have received the impression that this plan meets with much opposition in Ohio. This we are happy to state is a mistake, &c. * * * The West is united, and why cannot the East unite with this section of our Zion in this plan."

What do these extracts from the editorials of four consecutive numbers of the "Herald" signify? What does Maple mean by such sweeping assertions? Does he suppose that our people will shut their eyes and swallow them down, asking no questions; without the data, the facts and figures to substantiate them? If the agents would come forward and tell the truth, and the *whole truth*, touching the opposition to the Joint Stock Plan, and their success, we believe that a very different case would appear. If this is not so, where are the facts and figures?

If "the agents have succeedod beyond the most sanguine anticipations of our most ardent friends," why have they not published the large amounts of money secured in the "Herald," and put their names to them? Why keep their splendid successes so much in the dark!

That Mr. Maple has "corresponded with all our leading ministers and lay-brethren," and found "the feeling to be the same everywhere" in regard to the Joint Stock Plan, I have never believed for a single moment; and that, "there are but few opposed to it, and these are confined to one locality"—"but three ministers and some half a dozen lay-members who are opposed to it," *we know* to be very, *very* wide of the truth. We can count up ministers in different parts of the State who are not and never have been in favor of said "Joint Stock Plan," and as to lay members, we believe, if the question was laid before them, even now, after the "Herald" has advocated the said Stock Plan, for some nine months, to the exclusion of nearly every article opposed to it, that it would be voted down by an overwhelming majority.

In his editorial of Feb'y 25th, Mr. Maple says:

"Our brethren in the West are voting, almost to a man, in favor of making the College ours, and their votes are all genuine, for they are in the form of one hundred dollar bills, and from this denomination, up to three thousand dollars."

Pretty liberal for these hard times. The Christians must have improved some since Rev. Eli Incognito figured out $12,000, as the amount donated by them to the great Antioch! But let us look at this statement a moment. On another page of this review, Eld. D. P. Pike says: "The Christians number not far from 150,000 communicants, and from 1,000 to 1,500 ministers." Now, of the 150,000 members, it will doubtless be readily granted that at least 70,000 reside West of the meridian for the Eastern boundary of Ohio. But Maple says—"are voting, almost to a man." For this qualification let us make the liberal allowance of one in seven or 10,000, then there will be left 60,000 paying members. Suppose now that these 60,000 brethren pay each the lowest sum mentioned, viz: $100, and the aggregate amount of their donations, or stock subscriptions, would be ($6,000,000) six millions of dollars! But this is a low estimate, for some, it seems, pay as high as $3,000 each. Let us take then the medium number between $100 and $3,000, viz: $1,550; and this multiplied by the 60,000 paying members, gives us ($93,000,000) Ninety-three Millions of Dollars! Quite a snug little amount for these brazen times. Enough to endow Antioch pretty well! Wonder why the friends had such a sore struggle last July to raise $21,500, to pay off Mr. Reyburn!

In the "Messenger" of Feb'y 4th, the editor makes some objections to the Joint Stock Plan, on account of the size of the shares, and the liability of the stock's changing hands. To this Maple replies: "This is all a dream of a distempered imagination." If to make the above objections against the Stock Plan is a proof of a distempered imagination, a large number of our people must be distempered, and among them Prof. McKinney and Dr. Scheuck, whose articles appear on preceding pages. We had supposed that *doctors* at least keep themselves free from distempers!

But this is not all. Mr. Maple says:

"The idea of appointing a committee to hunt up the true amount of the indebtedness of the College, strikes us as foolish and absurd. Mr.

Palmer offers to sell us the College for $60,000, and it makes no difference to us if the College debt is $60,000,000. We can get it for $60,-000, which is less than one-half its real valve. The amount of indebtedness is nothing to us. We have *now* nothing to do with that question."

This doctrine appears strange to us. We had supposed that men or associations were responsible for their debts, whether contracted by themselves or their agents. We had supposed that a man should not repudiate his debts so long as he has abundant property at his command to pay them in full. Is the amount of Antioch's indebtedness nothing to the Christian connection? If a denomination, or a portion of a denomination establish a College, and some of their agents and officers are reckless and involve the institution heavily in debt, is not said denomination, or portion of the same, responsible? Now, what are the facts relative to Antioch College? If I mistake not, they are briefly as follows: The Christian conferences or connection, through their delegates in general convention at Marion, N. Y., 1850, voted to establish a College, and appointed a Provisional Committee of 34 persons, of whom 13 were designated as a sub-committee, to carry out their designs. This committee chartered and erected Antioch College, and had full charge (or should have had) of its affairs for about four years, or until Sept., 1854, when the institution was delivered up to the Board of Trustees chosen by the Scholarship holders. During those four years a large part of the present indebtedness of the College was contracted in erecting the buildings, &c., and for which the connection is undoubtedly responsible, whatever may be thought of the transactions of the last four and succeeding years. Under these circumstances, is it right for the denomination or its agents to repudiate the College debts, or at least their just share of them? We think not; and we admire the spirit exhibited by Eld. A. Bradfield, and others, who have recommended that our Churches or Conferences assume and pay the *whole* College debt, and then endow and control the institution, and make it all that the Marion Convention designed it should be. Is it right, therefore, to say: "The amount of indebtedness is nothing to us. We have *now* nothing to do with that question"?

But near the close of his lengthy editorial in the "Herald" of Feb. 25th, Maple says:

"The College must be sold on the 2d day of June next. This fact sinks deep into our soul. Antioch, our beloved College, to be sold so soon; and shall we be ready to purchase it?" * * * "Brethren, our heart bleeds, our hand trembles, and our eyes are filled with tears, as we write; for interests, dearer to us than our own life, are involved in this work. Every minister should go to work at once to collect stock for the company, for there is no time to be lost."

"Every minister should," &c. If this is so, a large majority of our ministers have been very remiss! But why has Maple fallen so desperately in love with the so-called "Joint Stock Company," the plan for the formation of which, with its drafter, he denounced so vehemently a few weeks before? Did the advocates of said plan offer him some shares in the proposed company, a "D. D.," or a future chaplaincy in the College, if he would lend his services and the columns of the "Herald" *to drive the plan through?* Or did they rather circumvent him with insinuating schemes, long-faced cunning and sanctimonious chicanery, and lead his common sense and better judgment submissive captives, and put the eyes of reason out? We hope that no such advances were made; and if made, we trust that they were not accepted. But why this sudden transition from hate to love—from detestation to admiration strong?

"Our eyes are filled with tears." Perhaps they were, for Mr. Maple seems to be very impressible; yet some persons would be more inclined to believe the statement, had he not said, in his description of Commencement Exercises and Mr. Mann's Baccalaureate discourse:—"He closed with a pathetic address to the graduating class, which drew tears to the eyes of all present." We were present on that occasion, and saw no persons shed tears except Messrs. James Maple and J. B. Weston!

"Our heart bleeds." How his heart could bleed for fear of the non-success of the "Joint Stock Company," when he had styled its leading advocates a "little, scheming, selfish, greedy clique," we can not well explain. But should he now look back over his zig-zag course for the past year, over his broken vows and dishonored resolutions, and exclaim, "*our heart bleeds,*" community would probably put some confidence in the sentiment.

But we have probably taken sufficient notice of Mr. Maple's remarkable February editorials. We deeply regret that he ever wrote such articles, and especially that he closed the columns of the "Herald" against nearly every communication which did not chime in with the Joint Stock Plan and Mr. Mann's clique. Many (may I not say multitudes?) were waiting for our editors to come out in favor of the plan for placing the College under the control of our Churches or Conferences, and especially for the columns of our papers to be opened to articles on that subject; and had Eld. Maple not gone over to the advocates and interests of the "Joint Stock Company;" had he only come out in favor of "Indiana's" plan, and hence in favor of the interests of the Scholarship holders, and of the control of the College by the Churches or Conferences, the other papers would doubtless have followed, and this denominational plan would, we think, have swept the country of doubts and distrust, and have placed the institution upon a firm financial and educational basis. But our brethren have thus far waited in vain. The columns of our papers, and especially of the "Gospel Herald," have remained closed, and strenuous exertions have been put forth, not only in Ohio and the West, but also in New York and the East, (as the reader will presently see,) by Mr. Mann's coadjutors, to rule the Christian Connection and direct its action; and although they are, as we believe, greatly in the minority, yet being closely banded together, and determined and persistent in their efforts, they have to some extent succeeded in accomplishing their designs; for, as before stated, "a united minority always prevails against a divided majority." How, under all these influences, under such arbitrary power, could the best of plans succeed? We trust that the majority of our people will no longer remain divided and discordant, but oppose a united and invincible front to all encroachments upon their rights and prerogatives.

CALL FOR THE STAFFORD CONVENTION.

The reader, doubtless has a vivid recollection of a very gaseous announcement which appeared in our papers in the latter part of February, reminding him of *Theater play cards* and *Barnum puffs*. Here is the exclamatory heading of the article:

"THE GENERAL CONVENTION FOR ANTIOCH!
THE TIME AND PLACE SETTLED!
DENOMINATIONAL HONOR IS NOW AT STAKE!
THE TIME IS COME FOR FINAL ACTION!
DON'T FORGET THE THIRD AND FOURTH OF MARCH!
HASTEN TO THE RESCUE!!"

Among the startling statements of the announcement are the following:

"VISITORS EXPECTED.—The astounding fact that the fate of Antioch College may, within the next three months, be decided adversly to the Connection, is the reason why all the prominent ministers, teachers, editors and men of standing, in the States and Canada, should meet in Convention, for counsel and co-operation. The College Faculty, Trustees and Assignee should he directly represented. Let us have two-thirds of the ministers in Central and Western New York, and as many more as posssible from East, West, North and South. * * *

"TO THOSE WHO CANNOT COME.—Write!—*Write!* At an expense of three cents, you can thrill the heart of the Convention. Write your honest views about the best way to redeem the College! *Do not fail to write, if you cannot come!"* * * *

"The object of the Convention is not to meddle with the past affairs of the College but to work for its present redemption &c."

The close of the whole magnificent (?) notice is simply:

"J. R. HOAG,
"In behalf of the friends of Antioch College.'
"Morganville, N. Y. Feb. 10, 1858."

Such was the notice for a pretended *General* or *United States* Convention for Antioch College. The meeting took place on the 3d and 4th of March, and its minutes filled column after column of our papers with a gilded tissue into which were woven malicious insinuations and base falsehoods. Who is so stupid or ignorant of College history, that he can not, at a glance, see through the whole farcical scheme?

A notice for a General Convention, and yet it was not written until Feb. 10, and did not appear in any of our papers until Feb. 18th, hardly two weeks before the day appointed; and in the "Gospel Herald," which has the widest circulation of any of our denominational journals, not until Feb. 25th, only six days before the Convention was to open! and then signed by only one man! Was such an announcement sufficient? Of course, very few persons even in Western New York, where the meeting was held, took sufficient notice of the call to attend.

I have examined the minutes of the meeting carefully from beginning to end, but find only the names of *ten* persons reported as present! and of these *ten* the five most active, or at least the most worthy, were from Yellow Springs and vicinity! viz: Fay, Dean, Craig and Weston of Yellow Springs; and McWhinney, of Enon! How *general*!

Doubtless some of the neighbors at Stafford, with their children, came in to see the Elephant, and after the exhibition retired, thinking it a wonderful animal, and thankful for their escape from the monster! The grand divertisement however would have been still more magnificent, had *His Serene Highness* condecended to be present! but, as it turned out, *his Marshals* were adequate to the occasion!

It further appears from the minutes, that a few persons addressed letters to the meeting. The extracts from which form about the only sensible portions of the report. Here are some of them:

F. A. Palmer of New York City, "As I cannot attend, and the question may be asked—what the Assignee will do with the property, and when it will be sold?—I thought best to stay, that unless money is raised in some quarter to pay the most pressing debts of the College before the 2d of June next, it must be sold."

Eld. D. E. Pike, of Mass.: "I am in favor of any plan, any feasible plan, that will make it a *denominational* school, emphatically a *Christian College*. * ° I am utterally and forever opposed to *co-partnership*; I dislike the ship; it leads to discord and discontent. I will not sail in that ship." * * *

Why did they not publish Eld. Pike's letter in full? Were they afraid of its influence?

Eld. John Ross, of New York, "I see that the Joint Stock Plan, with shares of $500 each, appears to be popular in the West, and will probably succeed if any does; but I am not favorable to that plan for several reasons. * * I wish to save the College to our people, and shall enter warmly and heartily into any plan that our people may adopt that presents to my mind any chance of succes."

"But I am not favorable to the plan for several reasons." Why were not these "several reasons" published? Why do we find such brief extracts from the letters of Eld's. Pike, Ross, Millard and others of our leading clergymen! and much more lengthy ones from Snow Richardson and Alvin Coburn, and Mr. Mann's letter in full? There was no design in this, was there? Eld. Ross it seems did not see "any chance of success" in the "Joint Stock Plan." Why did they not give his letter in full?

Eld. D. Millard, of New York, "I hope Antioch will be saved to our people."

Eld. J. E. Church, of Pennsylvania, "Let the College be cleared of its enormous debts, and become the property of the Connection, and then we can devise means to conduct it and make it an efficient instrumentality of good to the Church of God and the world."

Eld. J. H. Currier, of New York, "I wish it to be redeemed by the Christians, and forever secured to their control. If we cannot redeem *that*, we cannot build another.',

Eld. M. Cummings, of New Jersey, "I have anxiously desired, for a long time, that the denomination, as such, might, in its assembled wisdom, decide this College question; and that individual responsibility might be swallowed up in that of the body."

"* * * In common with the gentlemen above named, and others, Ira W. Allen wrote in favor of redeeming the College to the Christians, and recommended the reimbursement of the old stock-holders and the securing of a large endowment fund." * * * "Prof. E. Chadwick had noticed from the letters of G. N. Kelton, I. W. Allen, M. Cummings, that it was desirable that the old Scholarship holders, whose notes had been or would be paid, should have the same rights with the stockholders in the new company, which might be done by enlarging the amount of the capital stock, as the intention of the new company was not to declare a dividend. In this way the feelings of the scholarship holders would be conciliated."

To these suggestions of Prof. Chadwick, Eli Fay and A. S. Dean made direct and decided opposiion. Of course, it would never do to let in so many members to the right and pivileges of the "new Company."

Such a step would degrade the "Company" from an *Oligarchy* to a

Democracy, trom a *Centralized Aristocratic power* to a *Republican board of control*, from the *divine right* of the *few* to the *healthy government of the many*, of the *great masses of our Church members.*

Mr. Fay declares among other things: "We can not blend the interests of the two, as they are seperate organizations. I stand prepared to refute the slander that the Trustees squandered the moneys of the College, and precipitated the failure, and to prove that these very men have done more for Antioch than any other thirty men in the Connection."

This sounds very much like "Incognito." What can he not prove in his own estimation! A. S. Dean follows Mr. Fay, giving vent to a lengthy tirade, and heaps abuse upon the Scholarship holders. And why should he not be brave boyond the bounds of Ohio, and in a Convention of his coadjutors? Why should not Fay and Dean go in for the "Joint Stock Company," and for the reputation of the rights of the Scholarship holders, and of the $40,000, due to the Scholarship Fund? They had perhaps forgotten the voice of the Mt. Vernon (Ohio) Christian Conference in 1856. According to the minutes of said Conference for that year, it appears that the forenoon of Aug. 28th was spent in discussing Antioch affairs.

EXTRACTS FROM THE MINUTES.

"The subject of the proceeding of the managers of Antioch College, was discussed at considerable length; whereupon a committee consisting of Elds. J. W. Marvin, A. C. Hanger and A. Bradfield, was appointed to draft resolutions expressive of the sense of this Conference, with regard to the course pursued by the managers of Antioch College as expressed in their circulars. Adjourned to 2 o'clock P. M."

In the afternoon the Committee on the College affairs reported the following:

"*Resolved*, That it is the sense, and belief of this Conference, that all religious enterprizes should be conducted with prudence, in honor, justice and truth. And further be it

"*Resolved*, That it is the belief of this Conference, that the course pursued by the managers of Antioch College, in procuring, and now in collecting the scholarship notes, and in the appropriation of the *Scholarship Fund*, is a violation of faith, imprudent, dishonorable and unjust, and should be denounced, and repudiated by all true Christians.

"The report was unanimously adopted and the committee discharged.

"It was then, on motion,

"*Resolved*, That the opinion of this Conference, the Board of Trustees of Antioch College, should remove Mr. Dean from his present station as Treasurer and Clerk of Antioch College."

But were not the letters of Messrs. Kelton and Allen misapprehended by Bro. Chadwick? Did they recommend that the scholarship holders "should have the same rights with the stockholders in the new company, &c.?" Mr. Kelton speaks out on this point through the "Herald of Gospel Liberty," in these words:

"MEDWAY, N. Y., April 5, 1858.

"BRO. CARTER:—To the call for letters from those who could not attend the late Antioch Convention at Morganville, I responded frankly. In the published reports of the sayings and doings of said Convention, I am, unhappily, and probably, unintentionally exhibited in a false light. I have never proposed nor advocated an expansion of the nominal value of Antioch, so as to include scholarship interest in the new stock company. But in my letter to said Convention I did propose to increase the nominal value or indebtedness so as to cover the amount that has been paid for the redemption of Antioch since January, 1856, and did propose to allow all those persons or societies that have paid $100 or more, since January 1856, to become members of the new company by paying the balance of $500, and those who have paid over $500 to possess two shares by making the amount of $1000, interest not included. This proposition was made to restore confidence, and to revive an Antioch interest in those societies that have already and promptly paid from $200 to $700 on the strength and faith of the bondsigner's pledges. By amount paid since Jannary, 1856, I of course do *not* mean scholarship notes or pledges made prior to 1855. I did say that my proposition was but common justice to Eastern New York, New Jersey, &c. The Convention could of course ignore the proposition, but it is not quite pleasant to be made to say what was not written. * * *

"GEO. N. KELTON."

Neither in the plan which I presented some ten months since, and which is given on a preceding page, nor in the following brief letter which I addressed to the meeting at Stafford, did I intend to convey the ideas which Bro. Chadwick laid before the Convention. Both the plan and the letter will speak for themselves.

"TO THE PRESIDENT AND DELEGATES OF THE CONVENTION FOR ANTIOCH COLLEGE, STAFFORD, N. Y.

"DEAR BRETHREN—However much I am opposed, for important reasons, to a General Convention for Antioch College at the present time, and especially on account of the unprecedented short and insufficient notice for the same, yet, being deeply interested in everything which pertains to the real prosperity of Antioch College and of the Christian Connection, and in the promulgation of their free and noble principles, I shall rejoice in any action of the Convention, be said Convention small or large, sectional or general, which shall tend in any way to re-establish said College upon a firm and wise basis.

"I would, therefore, respectfully recommend to the delegates and brethren in Convention assembled, that the plan, which may be adopted and ratified by them, embrace the three following propositions, viz.

"1st. *That the scholarship holders be interested* by guaranteeing to them the rights and privileges in the Institution, which shall be a full equivalent for the money which they have paid, or may pay on their notes.

"No argument is necessary on this subject. The wisdom, aye, the necessity, of this step must be apparent to all.

"There are from 1,000 to 1,200 holders of scholarships scattered over the whole country, most of whom are men of influence. A large majority of these gentlemen are also members of the Christian Church; and to cut off all their rights and title in the College, which they hold by virtue of their scholarship-deeds, and to force the collection of their notes by law (even were it possible,) must be prejudicial, if not fatal, to the future prosperity of the Institution.

"2d. *That the College be placed under the patronage and control of the Christian Churches or Conferences.*

"It is well known that the confidence of many of our churches and brethren has been destroyed, and with abundant reason. How then can their confidence be regained, and munificent donations from them be secured, unless the institution is placed under their direction and concontrol? The plea of sectarianism is wholly pointless. The Christian Connection is a non-sectarian body. The Christian Churches stand with open hearts and out-stretched arms to receive and fellowship all who are truly "born again," and who take the Bible as an all-sufficient rule of religious faith and practice.

"Sectarianism, however, does not necessarily attach to any body or denomination of Christians as such, but has especial reference to the spirit and motive manifested in its acted life, in its measures, and in the administration of its institutions.

"And yet under present circumstances, under present national customs and precedents, the College can be non-sectarian and retained such, only under the direction and control of the Christians; and under such government only can the Institution be of permanent benefit to us as a great, free Christian body.

"3d. *That a large "Endowment Fund" be provided for.*

"All persons well acquainted with Colleges and Universities are fully aware that such institutions cannot long flourish without ample endowments, unless indeed they are under government patronage, and receive large annual appropriations.

"The wisest provisions for an ample endowment fund should, therefore, be incorporated into the plan adopted by the Convention; and such provisions, it seems to me, must be founded upon, or embrace, the first two propositions of this letter.

"There are other important points more or less intimately connected with the above leading propositions, and any successful plan for the redemption of Antioch College, but I need not allude to them.

"They will readily suggest themselves to the Convention.

"I shall heartily acquiesce in any plan which will fully restore the Institution to its founders and place it upon a wise, liberal and permanent basis.

"Hoping that the noble spirit which breathed through the Marion Convention and still lives in the hearts of our veteran ministers and our people, may fill old Stafford to overflowing; and praying that the love and wisdom of our Heavenly Father may pervade and guide all the deliberations of the present Convention.

"I am yours, most truly in Christian love, IRA W. ALLEN.

"Yellow Springs, O., Feb. 25, 1858."

But what rights are our churches and church members to have? What privileges are the scholarship-holders to enjoy? Be patient dear friends. The August Stafford General (?) Convention has provided ample rights and honors for you! It has adopted Mr. Mann's plan for a "Joint Stock Co." and in case this company succeeds (which is very doubtful, unless its tactics are changed,) it accords three distinguished privileges to you all—viz:

1st. *The right* to send your children to the College if they are sufficiently bright, and if you will pay a *good tuition fee.*

2d. *The right* to raise and pay into the College treasury *several thousand dollars each year,* to meet the annual expenses of the Institution.

3d. *The right* to raise and pay over to the "Joint Stock Company" a *large endowment fund,* say from $200,000 to $500,000.

And if you observe these three rights well and faithfully, I presume you will be allowed an additional right, viz :

4th. *The right* for a few years to call the College *Christian,* although it may really be governed by foreign influence and power!

In proof of which accorded rights please read the following resolutions and statements from the minutes of said Convention :

"*Provisions for the College Expenses while the work of Redemption goes on, and for its permanent Endowment.*

"Resolved, That if the College be purchased on the Joint-Stock Plan, we recommend also the immediate and hearty adoption of the plan suggested by F. A. Palmer, Esq., of New York city, for the purpose of defraying the current expenses of the College, and of endowing the same. Said plan recommends that the churches respectively pay into the treasury of the College, annually, a sum equal to the amount of one dollar per member.

"Resolved, That measures be adopted by this Convention, to have this subject presented with all its momentous importance, to our Conferences at their next sessions." * * *

"Prof. Chadwick thought the second resolution would frighten the people by asking too much at this time.

"Mr. Fay asked how we could, without this plan, carry on the school after it is paid for. The plan, requiring each member to annually give $1, was proposed some time since by Mr. Palmer, (the assignee) and accords with 'Indiana's,' and obtains much favor with the people.

"Prof. Chadwick thought the resolution would embarrass the agents and suggested a reduction in the *teachers'* wages at the College to help the thing through.

" Prof. Craig said Mr. Mann could command double the salary he now gets, in another place, were he is disposed to go.

"Mr. McWhinney said the resolution looks to the future of the College, and the friends are demanding provisions of this kind. The College cannot live an hour without a revenue. Eld. Goff's congregation had voted for it cheerfully; and it ought to be the basis of the Endowment Fund." * * *

" The Chairman said his church, (the best in Western New York) had expressed a willingness to adopt this plan, although their town had recently raised $15,000 for a local institution.

" Mr. Hoag said that while the 'stock plan was prefereble for redeeming the College, the 'dollar plan' might be the best for endowing it; but that the resoluion did not furnish the details for carrying it out.

" Mr. Fay thought it would be time enough to arrange the details after the College is redeemed.

" The question was then called for, and the resolutions were adopted UNANIMOUSLY !"

Of course they passed *unanimously* ! What " Joint Stock Company," or what agent of a " Joint Stock Company," whether Banking Railroad, or Manufacturing, would not gladly pass such resolutions, if they could only obtain the money ? What a fine thing it would be for any such Company to receive dollar donations yearly from all the members of the *Christian* Denomination, or any other body or society of persons ! Would not such a corporation get on gloriously !

Suppose, for instance, that a number of men should form themselves into a " Joint Stock Manufacturing Company," some of them being Christians, others Unitarians, and others still Spiritualists and Infidels, but a majority Christians; and further, that they should expend their entire stock in putting up large buildings, and should then appeal to the Christian Denomination to pay in at the rate of a dollar per member yearly for several years for the purpose of filling the buildings with machinery, defraying the current expenses, and forming a large revenue fund; and for the purpose of strengthening this appeal, suppose the company's agents should call, through some willing instrument, a general convention of the Christians, then go on and control the meeting, make magnificent speeches and pass valient resolutions, and assure the Christians that they will manufacture many things useful to every family, in their great Factory, but that the Christians shall have the distinguished privilege, in consideration of their money, of purchasing their manufactures at the same, or about the same price put upon such articles by other establishments ! and further, that they may call the manufactory a " Christian Institution."

Would the Christians not consider such an offer as an insult to their common sense? especially if, after paying in their money, and buying the products at the market price, they should find them only gilded and varnished articles without strengeh or durability?

Would not such an offer be spurned, and with right?

And yet, my friends, was not the Stafford Convention a greater farce, and their proceedings a far greater insult to the Christian church than the above supposed case could be?

In the *manufacturing* enterprise the Christians would only lose their money, while in the *educational* movement, in a College owned and controlled by a Joint Stock Company, they would not only lose their money, but, perhaps, also, their sons and daughters, young immortal minds, whose worth is infinitely above rubies. By as much then as the mind is more valuable than gold, we pray our brethren to be careful how they pay out their money to *Joint Stock Educational enterprises* over which they may have no control.

But why speak further of Fay, Dean, Weston & Co., and their maneuverings at Stafford? Do not their proceedings on the afternoon of the second day show conclusively the weakness of their cause, and the hollow-heartedness of their professions? The published call says: "The object of the Convention is not to meddle with the past affairs of the College, but to work for its present redemption."

Yet no sooner do they find themselves sole masters of the meeting, than they conjure up phantoms which they declare to be College history, and publish to the world the grossest falsehoods concerning the Christian Church of this place. Of course Mr. McWhinney, who, perhaps has bowed with greater humility to kiss Horace Mann's great toe, than did ever priest before the Roman Pontiff's, must needs drag in before his boon companions and the spectators, a preamble and resolution eulogizing "the past and present educational administration of Antioch College" and the *Christian character* of Mr. Mann!

What is the present educational administration of the College, as stated on a preceding page, Antioch College is not now in operation as a school. Mr. Palmer's council declared publicly in a Court in this place, a few weeks since, that Antioch College is neither in operation nor in existence; and yet Mr. Mann's heroes at Stafford declare that Antioch College is in operarion as a school. Who are correct, the lawyers, or Mr. Mann's puppets? Besides, who is not moved to pity at the spectacle of a "Christian character" which requires to be propped up by the fulsome flatteries of servile friends and the foolish resolutions of pretended conventions! We regret to see that the character of both Mr. Mann and Eld. Fay require so many resolutions and endorsements to keep them afloat. We would recommend to them the following lines by Bro. Pen Point, which we clip from the "Messenger:"

PUFF-UP VERSUS BLOW-UP.

"Some men are so light, and puff-ball like, that having friends who are good at generating gas, they make it an easy matter to obtain a high heave into the air, by the breath only of fulsome flattery. Thistle-down floats very high, upon a breath of air, because it is so very light. Ministers who float high on very the flatteries of inconsiderate friends, perhaps church resolutions, are safe from a fearful fall only if they are light. Men of true Christian love, or charity, 'are not puffed up.' To them the flatteries of inconsiderate friends are disgusting. Slander is the *powder* of flatteries, with which they blow up such as do not bow to their behests, or tickle them, to be tickled in return. PEN POINT."

And here let me ask, why Mann and Fay and their "persecuting committee" have been trying for the last twelve months to blow me up with their "*slander powder?*" It is simply because I would "not bow to their behests," neither "tickle them," nor be tickled by them. Of course they will burn their *powder* after me; but let it burn. Let them fire their pop-guns. I shall not get up "self-constituted Committees" to shield me from their squibs, nor scheme for the *resolutions* of Conferences and the *endorsements* of Conventions to prop up my character. If I can not become popular only by trickery and fraud. Let my name rest in everlasting forgetfulness.

J. R. Hoag, Secretary, writes, March 8th, to the "Gospel Herald" as follows:—

"BRO. MAPLE—The Stafford Convention was harmonious in spirit, united upon the 'Joint Stock Plan,' and determined to push the work through and save the College. Sir, it was a profitable time. Never have I heard such speeches, and witnessed such self-devotion to a single purpose. Ohio may well be proud of her two agents, (E. Fay and T. McWhinney), who, thus far have succeeded so nobly. Glory to God for the prospect! Hallelujah to the Lamb! * * * The plot against the administrations of Hon. Horace Mann was exposed and denounced; the slanders against the Board of Trustees confuted and repelled; and the integrity of the principle agents defended with the amplest testimony. The 'Joint Stock Plan' was unanimously adopted for redeeming the College, and the 'Dollar Plan' for creating an Endowment Fund."

What a glorious time these devotees to the "single purpose" of building up a mighty "Joint Stock Company," and swindling an "Endowment Fund" out of the Christians on the "Dollar," or "Indiana's" plan must have had! And then the defending *the integrity* of A. S. Dean, "with the amplest testimony" must have been a magnificent affair! What a pity it is that Eld. Hoag did not invite some artists from Paris to catch the splendors of the scene and transfer them imperishably to the silvered plate, or to the canvass!

What did Mr. Hoag know about "the plot"? Did he ever see it? Does he swallow all that Eli Fay and A. S. Dean tell him? We know nothing about the "plot" mentioned in the minutes of the so-called Stafford Convention, and do not believe that there has been any such thing; but that Mann, Fay & Co., have been plotting and scheming in a way most damaging to the interest of the Christian Connection, we do believe.

But in the "Herald" of March 11th, Mr. Maple comes out with an editorial on "the Stafford Convention" which he commences in these words:—

"We have several times given our readers notice that a general Convention of the friends of Antioch College would be held in Stafford, N. Y., on the 3d and 4th inst., for the purpose of adopting a plan for its redemption."

The truth is that the notice, or call for the Convention, did not appear in the "Gospel Herald" until the 25th of February, and before the next number of the paper was published the Convention had adjourned, or was near its adjournment. Does *once* mean "several times?" We have heard constant readers of the "Herald," persons of great candor and excellent judgment, say that this statement is false. This is one illustration of the loose and reckless style in which Mr. Maple has talked and written during the last several months. He also says:—

"There was astonishing unanimity of thought and feeling. The redemption of the College was the absorbing theme. To accomplish this great work there was but one plan thought of for a moment. All saw at a glance that our only hope is in the plan for a 'Joint Stock Company,' adopted by the Franklin Convention, and that plan was adopted without a dissenting voice."

"Adoped by the Franklin Convention?" It is well known that "*the plan* for a Joint Stock Company," so much talked about was not adopted by the Franklin Convention, nor even submitted to it. It was not made public until about the 20th of November, some three weeks after the Convention, and *then* and for several weeks thereafter Mr. Maple was not satisfied with it as numerous persons can testify. He felt very indignant at the course pursued by Mr. Mann, and wrote an article to expose him to the public, as stated by himself on a preceding page. At the close of one of his letters he says:—"*Mr. Mann has shaken my confidence in his integrity.*" Mr. Maple very well knows, that if said plan had been submitted to the Franklin Convention, it *would not have been adopted*; and that for two months thereafter he himself *would not sanction it.* Why then his announcements through the "Herald," that said plan was adopted by said Convention!

"There was astonishing unanimity of thought and feeling." How could it have been otherwise? There were hardly persons enough present to disagree. The minutes speak the names of only ten persons, and they were all or nearly all members of Mr. Mann's clique. Selfish considerations therefore, if nothing else, would harmonize them. A. S. Dean, of course, had more than $1,000 per annum at stake! J. B. Weston, E. Fay, T. M. McWhinney, A. Craig, and H. C. Badger had also much in jeopardy! and the other four members of the Convention, either sided with Mr. Mann's clique, or did not dare to resist and expose the plots of his supple instruments. The "unanimity" was not therefore a thousandth part so "astonishing" as the call for the size and character of the Convention! We also clip from the same article:—

"The Convention also adopted very strong resolutions endorsing Mr. Mann and his administration of the College, and expressing the utmost contempt for that little, miserable, sectarian clique which has been whining and snapping at his heels for some time past. New York will give her money with the express understanding that Mr. Mann is to remain at the head of the College."

"Of course, these persons who are hanging to Mr. Mann's coat-tails would not let such a fine opportunity pass. They must endorse their chief and his whimsical administration!

I know of no "*little, miserable, sectarian clique*" at Antioch, or interested in Antioch, save *Mr. Mann's clique.* And that his clique is most bitterly sectarian and partizan I do know. I am acquainted with several prominent Colleges in this country, and with some of the leading Universities of Europe, and I have never heard so much of sectarianism, or seen it so thoroughly practiced and exemplified, as by Horace Mann and his clique in Yellow Springs. If any man under Heaven puts forth strenuous exertions to carry out his notions and execute his whims; if any man upon the face of the earth rides his hobbies with an iron vengance, than does Horace Mann. His ingenuity fails to devise terms sufficiently strong to express his contempt of what he calls *sectarian*, or to denote his administration of "*liberal* Christianity." But what does "liberal Christianity" mean? What does "sectarian," or "intensely denominational" signify? We can perhaps give no better definitions of these terms, as they have been used in our papers for a year or more past, than the following by Bro. Summerbell, which we clip from the "Herald of Gospel Liberty:"—

" 'LIBERAL' VS. 'INTESELY DENOMINATIONAL.'

"The true version of these words in the connection in which they have been used of late, is as follows:

"Liberal—Unitarian, stringent and exclusive.

"Intensely Denominational—Liberal, Christian opposition to tyranny and exclusiveness, open, free, fraternal and kind.

"N. Summerbell."

By the term "sectarian clique" Mr. Maple probably means the large majority of the Christian Connection which is highly displeased with matters and influences at Antioch, and will not aid *the* Joint Stock Company which *he* so blindly and devotedly puffs. His low, cowardly flings will not trouble them. They are not to be disheartened by contumely, nor intimidated by threats; and of this they will presently con vince him and his adopted clique.

On what conditions "New York will give her money" we will not say; but we hope she will give *intelligently* and for a *Christian object.* We think she can expend her money to better advantage nearer home, than to throw it into the bottomless vortex at Antioch. We see no reason why she should not have a College of her own. But Mr. Maple continues:

"The way is now clear. One 'plan' only is in the field. On that all will work. It will not only be useless, but absolute madness, to talk about other plans longer. Indeed, we will publish nothing more touching other 'plans,' as their adoption is now an impossibility. If any of our friends had other plans, they should have been presented at our Conventions, whose business it was to consider them."

"One 'plan' only in the field?" According to the minutes of the so-called Stafford Convention, two plans were adopted, viz: 1st: The "Joint Stock Plan" for the formation of a Company which shall control the College; and 2d: "Indiana's Plan," or the "Dollar Plan," "for the purpose of defraying the current expenses of the College, and of endowing the same," or, in other words, *to pay the current expenses of the "Joint Stock Company" and to enrich the same!*

What a fine thing it would be to have Horace Mann, A. S. Dean, Eli Fay, T. M. McWhinney, James Maple, and a few more such persons, with a sprinkling of Universalits, Spiritualits and Infidels, formed into a "Joint Stock Company," to direct and control the educational enterprises of the Christians! Will not our Churches take hold at once and carry out the magnificent scheme! If our people will only adopt the "Dollar Plan" and pay in $100,000 annually to such a company, they can, of course, be excused from having any control of said company or of the College!

"On that (plan) all will work." This is another of Mr. Maple's reckless expressions. We are confident that *all* will not work on *that plan.* We presume that nine-tenths, if not nineteen-twentieths of our brethren will not aid in forming or sustaining such a latitudinarian

"Joint Stock Company;" and we are not sure but that the opinion of Elder John Wm. Brown, of Gallia Co., Ohio, is nearer the fact, viz: "That not one in one hundred of the members of our Churches are in favor of the proposed Joint Stock Company."

We do not see why the adoption of any other good plan should be an "impracticability," unless Mr. Maple intends to keep the "Gospel Herald" under the exclusive control of Mr. Mann's clique for the future, as he has during the last ten months. We believe there are *impartial journals* and *honest editors* in the world; and if it should be necessary, we doubt not that the Christians of the West are able to establish and sustain an independent and impartial Christian Herald. "If any of our friends had other plans, they should have been presented at our Conventions, &c." Why did Mr. Maple attempt to equivocate and deceive our people, the readers of the "Herald?" Did he mean by "our Conventions" the Conventions of Mr. Mann's clique? If so, why did he not so express himself that the readers of the paper would not understand him to mean the Conventions of the Christian Connection or Churches? Mr. Maple well knows that the *delegated Convention* at Franklin was changed into a "Mass Meeting" by a desperate struggle on the part of Mr. Mann and his accomplices; and that the so-called Stafford Convention was controlled by, if not mostly made up of Mr. Mann's adherents! Does Mr. Maple mean to say that our friends *should have presented* their plans *at such Conventions?*

Elder Maple was a member of the Committee appointed at the opening of the Franklin *delegated* Convention, to draft a plan for the redemption of Antioch College to the Christians; and he well knows that said Committee was not allowed to make its report; for after a hard day's struggle, said Convention was changed into a "Mass Meeting"; and when in the evening the Committee on Redemption attempted to make a report, it was met by a most determined opposition from Mr. Mann's clique, Fay, McWhinney, Wait, &c. The result was, that the whole evening, and the next day, were spent in battling over the *preamble* and *first resolution,* and then two committees were hastily appointed and the "Mass Meeting" adjourned *sine die!*

Should our friends *have presented* their plans at such a Convention, or at the little *mass meeting* in Stafford, of which only three or four day's notice was given in the West? We submit this question to any candid, sensible individual.

But what is this "Joint Stock Plan" of which we have all heard so much; and which, it is falsely averred, was adopted by the Franklin Convention, and will reedeem Antioch College to the sole control of the Christian Denomination? Here it is entire. Let us examine it:

"PLAN OF ARTICLES OF AGREEMENT

"For the formation of a Company for the purchase of the property, lately belonging to Antioch College :

"1. The Capital stock of said Company shall be Sixty Thousand Dollars, at least, to be divided into shares of Five Hundred Dollars each.

"2. Each share shall entitle its owner to one vote, except that no person, in his own right, shall cast more than ten votes; societies or different individuals may unite to subscribe, in which case they may elect or depute some person to cast the vote or votes to which they may be entitled.

"3. Shareholders may vote in person or by written proxy.

"4. The shares shall be payable in two equal instalments, the first on or before the first day of May, 1858; the second, on or before the first day of the ensuing September. Said instalments shall be paid at the Broadway Bank, New York, to F. A. Palmer, Esq., who shall have the power, and our signatures invest him with the power of collecting the same from us, for the purpose specified.

"5. Should the amount of the subscriptions hereto exceed the sum of sixty thousand dollars, or exceed the sum necessary for the purchase of the College property, (exclusive of the scholarship notes,) the residue shall constitute an Endowment Fund, to be paid over to the Treasurer, hereafter to be appointed, for the use of the College.

"6. The subscriptions shall not be binding unless a sum sufficient for the purchase of all the College property transferred to Mr. Palmer, (exclusive of the scholarship notes,) shall be subscribed, on or before the first day of May, 1858.

"7. The shareholders shall meet at the College on the last Monday of June, 1858, for the purpose of organization, the adoption of a charter, the choice of officers, and such other business as they may choose to transact, and this shall be held due notice of said meeting.

"8. Any person with the assent of two members of the committee may constitute himself an agent for procuring subscriptions, and when the subscriptions obtained by him shall be paid to Mr. Palmer, and not before, he shall be entitled to receive three per cent. thereon if obtained in a city, and five per cent. if obtained in the country. Places containing a population exceeding 20,000 shall, under this article, be called CITIES, and all other places COUNTRY.

"JAMES MAPLE, THOMAS HARLES,
"HORACE MANN, ALFRED HEATH,"
"J. G. REEDER.

"Franklin, Nov. 10th, 1857."

Now, dear reader, will you read this plan again and again, carefully, and see if it presents a safe and sure basis for redeeming Antioch College to the government and control of the Christian Denomination ; for making it a *Christian Institution?*

1st. Is it an *honest* plan? Does it assume or propose to pay the whole College debt, which, on the 27th of June last, the Trustees declared to be "not less than $130,000," of which $40,000 is due to the

Scholarship Fund? No, not at all, but on the contrary, it is based upon the supposition, that all the College assets, (exclusive of the scholarship notes) can be purchased for $60,000, or less. Thus the proposed "Joint Stock Company" would repudiate $70,000 of the debt, or what is perhaps still more culpable, would pay it by repudiating the scholarship claim of $40,000, and forcing the collection of the unpaid scholarship notes!

How can such a dishonest plan gain the confidence of any civilized community? In the autumn of 1855, Bro. I. N. Walter wrote to me as follows:

"Dr. Stebbins writes me, since his return home, from the Trustee meeting: 'If the money for Antioch can be raised, well, if not, we fail legally, but not educationally, for we shall take the College back, and go right on with our work.'"

"That is, we shall let the College be sold for a debt of $120,000, and buy it back for fifty thousand ($50,000) and then go on with our enterprise. But what a moral disgrace that will be. It will be almost as bad as repudiating the debts at once, though I may be mistaken in my view of the subject."

Now put this statement of Dr. Stebbins, in 1855, in connection with the report of Dr. Bellows and others, made to the Trustees in 1857, and with other circumstances mentioned in this volume concerning Horace Mann and his accomplices, and who will ask if there has not been scheming behind the curtain?

We think that Bro. Walter was not mistaken in his view of the "moral disgrace" of such a transaction. Any man, be his standing and views what they may, can take any amount of stock in the Company and use as many as 10 votes; and if he wishes to take more than 10 shares, he can give the additional ones to some person who will use the votes as he may desire. Thus he can make every share exercise a vote. It is said that if the Joint Stock Company succeeds, four men stand ready to endow the Presidency. If this is true, these four men would be entitled to at least 40 votes, and if they should be Unitarians, the College would, no doubt, henceforth be Unitarian; for so large a balance of power, as forty votes, would control the College.

But suppose that two-thirds or three-fourths of the stock is taken by the Christians, how soon might the capital stock be enlarged so as to take in large endowment donations and bequests from Unitarians or from Infidels, and they thus lose the control of the Institution.

I see no permanent safety in such a plan. We have suffered enough already on account of our loose views of freedom and liberality. Our people seem to have a horror of the cry "sectarian," and many of them do not seem to distinguish between the pleasant and unpleasant signification of the term.

3d. Does this plan interest the scholarship holders, or propose to render them an equivalent for their notes paid or soon to be paid?

No; far from this. It seeks rather to repudiate all their claims; to pay out all the Endowment Fund on the debts, or to use the balance for its own purposes. It cuts off all their rights in the College. It then brings suits against them to force the collection of notes for which no consideration appears. Can such a course gain the favor and patronage of the twelve hundred holders of scholarships scattered over the Northern States?

Who can blame the said holders of scholarship deeds for resisting to the last the payment of their notes which were set apart as an inviolable Endowment Fund, when they know that if paid, the money will be used in payment of debts—a violation of a sacred trust? Or who will chide in the least those scholarship holders who have paid their notes for the amount of $40,000, if they bring a suit for recovery against those Trustees who paid it out on debts in violation of the College charter.

In the "Messenger" of January 14th appeared a lengthy editorial on the *difficulties* and *debts* of Antioch College, in which Bro. Cummings says:

"It seems hard, very hard, for men, perhaps with limited means, with dependent families, and strongly desirous of using their money to educate their sons and daughters, to be driven to make payments when they may regard all as lost."

4th. Does it contain any practical provisions for raising a good Endowment Fund. We find none. It is true "Fay, Dean & Co," passed some resolutions at the so-called Stafford Convention adopting "Indiana's" or the dollar plan for the purpose of paying the current expenses of, and raising an Endowment Fund for, the "Joint Stock Company;" but who will show themselves so superlatively foolish as to adopt said resolutions or act upon them?

5th. In case said company fails to purchase the College property, what then? What use will be made of the stock? Will the company found a new College? or will the stock revert to the subscribers again?

Would not the framers of this plan have exhibited their good sense in making provisions for such a contingency? Or was their zeal so great in the prosecution of their schemes as to overshadow their judgment?

Let the reader now turn back to page — and read "Indiana's" plan again, and see if it is not every way greatly superior to the joint stock plan which we have been considering. Its provisions are broad and ample, such as to interest many if not the most of our brethren and churches. Its advantages, in brief, are the following:

1st. It assumes the whole College debt, which is both honorable and honest.

It interests all the churches by calling on them to pay for and then control the institution. This is wise.

3d. It interests the holders of scholaships by giving them more than an equivalent for their money. This is prudent.

4th. It provides for an Endowment Fund, without which no large institution can long succeed. This is necessary.

5th. It provides for new institutions in case the churches and friends do not succeed in securing Antioch College.

The reader will notice that this plan comes within the reach of all, even the poorest, and at the same time does not prevent the rich from giving their hundreds and thousands. This plan interests, or may interest, every member of the denomination, by receiving his or her money and granting him or her a voice, thrugh the Church, in governing the College.

It is, therefore, broad, free and democratic, placing the controlling power in the hands of the sovereign people, but the joint stock plan would form an oligarchy, an aristocracy, for it calls on the rich for shares of five hundred dollars each, and places the entire control of the College into their hands. Those who are in favor of tyrannical oligarchies will of course accept the latter plan; but all those who accept the sentiment "*vox populi, vox Dei,*" who believe in the divine right of the people, will adopt the former; for only on "Indiana's" plan, or one containing essentially the same principles, can the College be made a *permanent* blessing to the Christians.

Mr. Mann's joint stock plan is weighed in the balance and found wanting.

CONCLUSION.

In glancing back over eight years, we find a body of Christians taking no *creed* or *confession of faith* but the *Bible;* requiring no *test* for Christian fellowship but *Christian character;* calling themselves by no name save *that* first *given to the disciples* of Christ at Antioch; and numbering from 1,200 to 1,500 ministers, and as many churches, engaged in establishing a great College. Their purposes were noble: to do their part in educating rising generations, to offer the same advantages to females as to males, to lay a broad and sure foundation upon the free and glorious principles of God's revealed Word, and to rear thereon a Temple of Science from whose consecrated halls no narrow, bigoted or poisonous influences should go forth. To carry out these purposes they erected extensive and commodious buildings, and called to the Presidency Horace Mann, L. L. D., whom they knew only by reputation, yet supposed him to be not a man of ability, only, but of *integrity*. He asked for the privilege of appointing two of the Professors himself, which was granted, and accordingly the Christians could appoint but four of their own men.

Mr. Mann came to Antioch in the autumn of 1853, bringing his nephew and neice, as Professors, and almost from that very day down to the present time has the College gone deeper and deeper into trouble. Mr. Mann was not only President of the Faculty, but also a member of the Board of Trustees, Chairman of the Committee on Instruction, and for a while a member of the Executive Committee of the College; and most, if not all, of these offices he has used, we think, to the great disadvantage of the Institution. He set himself against all, or nearly all, the Professors and Teachers sent to Antioch as the representatives of the Christian Connection, and as they left the College he filled their places with his or Mrs. Dean's relatives or especial friends; until, in the present school, only two of the original Faculty are found, viz., Mr. Mann and Mrs. Dean. Whose school, therefore, is the one now in operation, the school of the Christian Connection or of Horace Mann and Mrs. A. S. Dean? The Faculty of the past year was known among the students and citizens by the expressive title of *"milk and water;"* and in the Faculty for the present year, the students say there is but *"little milk left."*

Now, why has the great Antioch come to this? Why has Horace Mann administered the offices which he has filled in such an arbitrary and unjust manner? Why has he violated the plainest principles of truth and justice, and thus forfeited and lost the confidence of many or nearly all the citizens of Yellow Springs and vicinity? That Mr. Mann has done these things, is certain; but *why* he has done them, we leave for the reader to determine.

The preceding pages will throw much light upon these questions, and perhaps sufficient; yet, for the benefit of those who may still have a lingering doubt, should there be any such, we will give two or three additional illustrations.

1st. Among the "Laws and Regulations" of Antioch College is the following:

"Before any student will be permitted to board in the village, the person with whom such student proposes to board, must date, sign, and send to the President, a paper in substance like the following:—

"I propose to take the following named persons, as boarders, ———, and I hereby promise to exercise parental supervision over them, and to report to the President, or some member of the Faculty, any violation of the rules of the College, which any of them may commit."

To see that this law was complied with, was the duty of the President; and during the terms previous to the spring of 1857, he had reported to the Faculty that all persons taking boarders had complied with the above requisition. Early in the spring term of 1857, however, it seems that Mr. Mann was a little wider awake, or more honest, for he found two persons who declined to subscribe to the above requirement, of whom one was Bro. John A. Layton, in whose family and under whose supervision, Bro. Kearns, of Indiana, had placed his son and daughter. Mr Mann tried for several weeks, both personally and through others, to influence Mr. Layton, and then Mrs. Layton, to sign the required certificate, but without success.

Several papers have been placed in our hands, touching this matter, which we give as fully as our limits will allow. From Mr. Mann's lengthy letter to Bro. Kearns, we extract as follows:

"ANTIOCH COLLEGE, June 5th, 1857.

"THOMAS KEARNS, Esq.—*Dear Sir:* About a week ago I wrote you a long letter, giving you a full account of the matter to which you refer in yours of June 4th, just received. I stated what our rules are and have been for three years, and the reasons for them." * * * "We have for three years required that the keeper of the household promise to look after them, (students,) while on his premises, in the same manner that we would if they remained on ours. This rule has been almost universally complied with, and without, so far as I know, a single instance of complaint, until this term." * * * "Every other boarding-house keeper (except Mr. Layton) in the village, but one, has done it—I think as many as twenty. We offered to take the certificate of his wife." * * * "You can not find half-a-dozen among all our 300 and more students, who do not approve the rule. But Mr. Layton has some strange notions about it, and refuses.

"Now, the rule is reasonable, nay, indispensable. It has been in operation three years, unless, here and there, there may have been a case of accidental omission.

"Yours, &c., HORACE MANN."

The following protest is by thirty-three promanent citizens of Yellow Springs, and heads of families, many of whom are now of extensive influence:

"YELLOW SPRINGS, O., June 3d, 1857.

"TO THE FACULTY OF ANTIOCH COLLEGE—*Gentlemen:* We whose names are hereunto subscribed, respectfully present our protest against the 37th rule of the "Laws and Regulations" of Antioch College, touching pupils boarding in private families, especially when parents and guardians have made arrangements themselves for the care of their children, as we regard it an infraction of our domestic privileges, since it imposes upon us the obligation of informing some member of the Faculty of any violation of the rules of the Institution, however small or trifling it may be; and, moreover, we regard this rule as injurious to the College, as any attempt to enforce it must produce more or less alienation of feeling between the citizens of the village and the governors of the College.

(Signed,)	J. A. Layton,	Dr. W. H. Grimes,
	H. Davis,	J. D. Hawken,
	E. Lawrence,	Eld. A. T. Tullis,
	Dr. A. Cheney,	S. W. Kershner,
	Benjah Wilson,	Dr. A. H. Platt,
	S. W. Goe,	A. H. Cooper,
	Eld. Jesse Jacobs,	Prof. A. L. McKinney,
	Joel Wilder,	E. Rice,
	W. B. Huffman,	Eld. J. T. Lynn,
	Isaac Kershner, P. M.,	A. W. Sroufe,
	William Jackson,	J. W. Hamilton, J. P.,
	F. D. Leonard,	L. Wilson,
	Joseph McIntosh,	Jacob Sheller,
	M. Haight,	Dr. E. Thorn,
	E. Sipe,	F. Hafner,
	J. C. Kershner,	Chas. W. Hill,
	F. Applegate.	

YELLOW SPRINGS, O., June, 1857.

"Names of persons who have not complied with the 37th rule of the 'Laws and Regulations' of Antioch College before this term:

(Signed)	E. Lawrence,	Judge Wm. Mills,
	J. A Layton,	E. Tulleys,
	F. Applegate,	H. Davis,
	E. Rice,	Eld. Snow Richardson,
	Wm. Brown,	Mrs. Bradshaw,
	Dr. W. H. Grimes,	J. Sloan,
	Mrs. Bowers,	Eld. C. A. Morse,
	J. Kershner, P. M.,	Mrs. Blaisdell,
	M. McKinney,	Dr. A. H. Platt,
	Dr. Jas. DeNormandie,	R. Edmunds,
	Eli Fay,	Miss Marrott,
	H. P. Hurst.	

Except one term:—Mrs. Chesebro, W. Gowe.

Most of the above twenty-five persons have been permanent citizens of Yellow Springs for several years, and have boarded, it is thought, nearly all the students who have boarded out in private families.

How will the reader reconcile these documents with Mr. Mann's statements to Bro. Kearns? Shall we believe Mr. Mann, or these twenty-five reliable citizens?

2d. In the "Gospel Herald" of Nov. 12th, 1857, a miserable pettifogging article of several columns length, by Horace Mann, was published, in which he makes most grave charges against the Miami Christian Conference, and Eld's. Ladley and Maple. From this article, it appears that on the 17th Sept., 1857, Mr. Mann addressed a letter to Eld. Ladley, in which were several false statements. Eld. Ladley, therefore, took no notice of it. On the 5th of Oct., Mr. Mann takes J. B. Weston under his wing, proceeds to the residence of Eld. Ladley, and after troubling him about an hour with pettifogging questions and remarks, requests that he return his (Mr. Mann's) letter. This Bro. Ladley declined to do.

Mr. Mann then desired said letter long enough to take a copy of it. This Bro. Ladley regarded merely as a make-shift on the part of Mr. Mann in order to obtain the letter, and therefore again declined to give it up.

Mr. Mann then returned home, and prepared an article for the "Gospel Herald," containing a verbatim copy of his letter to Eld. Ladley (!) and also a statement by his own accomplice, Mr. Weston. He says:—

"Luckily, I found the rough draft from which my letter to him was written, so that, with the aid of memory, I have reproduced it substantially, if not verbally, correct."

A very lucky thing indeed, to find a copy of a letter which has been carefully preserved! Who cannot see through such pretences? The Editor of the "Herald" declined to publish the article, and returned it to Mr. Mann, accompanied by a letter specifying several false statements in the said article, and concluding in these words:—

"I should much prefer to have these corrections made before publishing the communication. If you desire to have it published as it now is, I will do it; but I shall take the liberty to correct the mistakes in it. Yours, very truly, JAMES MAPLE."

Mr. Mann then sent said article again to Mr. Maple, and insisted that it should be published, together with additional statements which exhibit, it seems to me, any thing but a spirit of truth and Christian candor. This article, aimed so pointedly at one of our leading ministers in Ohio, who is a resident of Yellow Springs, and has numerous friends scattered over the States, and is known only to be loved and respected for his unassuming yet noble and undeviating Christian character, has done much, we think, to unmask Mr. Mann's real character to the Christian connection.

Mr. Maple published Mr. Mann's communication in the "Herald" of Nov. 12th, as above stated, and accompanied it with a lengthly editorial correcting some of its false statements; from which editorial we extract briefly as follows:—

"When we wrote a short notice for the last issue of the 'Herald,' stating that the controversy on the subject of the College must be closed, we fondly hoped that this very unpleasant matter would not be brought up again. The *Executive Committee* have decided that no more shall be published on this controvert subject; but we take the responsibility on ourself to publish a communication from Mr. Mann, as he earnestly desires that it should appear. We regret that he demands this, for we think it will have a tendency to injure the great work of redeeming Antioch College, which all so much desire. It will give rise to unpleasant differences of opinion. There are several mistakes in Mr. Mann's communication that we must, in justice to ourself, take the liberty of correcting.

"1st. Mr. Mann affirms that he was refused a hearing before the Conference. This is a most unfortunate mistake. The true facts in the case are the the following: Brother E. Fay offered a resolution appointing a committee to call on the Editor of the 'Gospel Herald' to demand of him his reasons for certain statements in the 'Herald' about Antioch College. The Conference refused to pass this, from the consideration that it was a matter over which they had no control, as the 'Herald' does not belong to the Miami Conference, and the Editor is responsible to the Western Christian Book Association alone. This, as all must see, was a correct decision. After this, Brother Simonton offered the following: "Resolved, That this Conference *suspend* business at 3 o'clock this afternoon to hear Messrs. Harlan, Mills and Mann in relation to the financial condition and the religious and educational character of Antioch College." This passed without a dissenting voice.

"Mr. Mann says that *"the Conference was induced to adjourn an hour earlier than usual."* There is not one word said about adjournment in the resolution, and it did not adjourn the Conference. It only *suspended* the business of the Conference. It is true the chairman left his seat, but this was a voluntary act on his part. The Conference did not instruct him to do so, and we think he did wrong in vacating his chair. This act of the President did not dissolve the Conference. The clerk still retained his seat, and just as soon as the chairman left his seat the Conference appointed another person to fill his place. Thus all must see that Mr. Mann has made a mistake, and charged the Conference unjustly with refusing to hear him. There was no disposition to do anything of this kind. The vote to hear him was unanimous. *Not one voted against it.* We think that Mr. Mann has done a body of honorable Christian men great injustice in making the very serious charge of unfairness against them." * * *

"2d. Mr. Mann says: 'As we had been denied a hearing before the Conference, it could not by any possibility occur to us that one would be granted, in our absence, to our assailants.' This is a still more unfortunate mistake than the first, for we know that he was invited to stay, and was assured that the matter would be brought up again in the morning. We heard Mr. Lynn request him to stay." * *

"We are not alone in this matter. Others heard the same. Elders A. L. McKinney, Rush and C. A. Morse; Messrs. W. T. Hawthorn, G. McCullough, C. Winebrenner, and many others heard the same."

"These brethren are not 'implicated in the fabrications against the

College.' They have not, with the exception of Mr. McKinney, so far as we know, taken any part in the controversy. Even if they had, could they not tell the truth? My dear brother, this is an unkind thrust at brethren." * * *

"3d. Mr. Mann seems to think that there is a contradiction between Mr. Ladley and myself, but we are not able to see that this is the case. We stated in our first article on the College just what Mr. Ladley told us. In the Conference he said, 'that he had good reasons to know that some students had been turned aside from the religion of their parents, &c.' In our reply to Mr. King in the 'Herald,' of September the 10th, we said: 'Brother Ladley stated publicly that he knew this to be the case.' We did not say that he knew this from personal observation, for he did not say how he knew it. He only said that he had 'good reasons to know' it. There are two ways in which we know a thing to be true: 1st. By *personal observation.* 2nd. *By satisfactory evidence.*" * * *

"Mr. Mann's language implies that we said that Mr. Ladley knew this from personal observation, when we have never said any such thing. Mr. Mann should take our language just as it is, and not put words into our mouth that we never uttered. Mr. J. T. Lynn said to us in a recent conversation that he knew from personal observation that what Mr. Ladley said was true. He is a responsible man, and we presume is ready to give the facts in the case.

"In our article in the 'Herald' of Aug. 13th, we stated what we had reason to believe to be true. We had the testimony of reliable men, who are responsible for their statements." * *

"4th. Mr. Mann's language in reply to our letter of October 20th, seems to imply that our not replying to his note of the 7th inst. was intentional, and that we had some wrong motive in it. This we regard as very unkind and unjust in him; for we stated our reasons for not replying at an earlier date. Does he suppose that we would lie about this matter? If not, why such unjust insinuations and back-handed thrusts as this? In all this controversy we have tried to deal justly by all. We may have erred in some things; but it has been an error of the head, and not of the heart." * * * "'After we had made our remarks, Mr. Maple came forward and made an apologetic speech, and acknowledge that it would have been better if he had not done as he had in publishing his articles about the College.' This is a mistake. While Mr. Mann was speaking we wrote down just what we wished to say then, and just what we did say. The following is a correct copy of it:

"'Mr. Chairman—There are a few things that I wish to say now. 1st. When we wrote the article on Antioch College, now under consideration, we believed the statements in it to be as true as the Bible that lies there on the sacred desk. We had not the least doubt of its truth. They were made to me by respectable men.'" * *

"'I have many other things to say, but have not time, as it is now more than an hour past the regular time for adjournment.' This is just what we said, word for word. We did not say that 'it would have been better if we had not done as we had in publishing our article about the College.'"

In the "Gospel Herald," of Nov. 26th, Bro C. Winebrenner published a communication in relation to Mr. Mann's article, and a brief card which it contained. The card was signed by Mr. Mann, and Messrs. Harlam and Mills; and what deception Mr. Mann practiced on these gentlemen in order to induce them to sign said card, we do not know. From Bro. Winebrenner's article, we extract a few lines:

* * * "I am astonished to see great men make such mistakes. They say they were refused a hearing before the Conference. If that was not a hearing I do not know what is. A resolution was offered, that this Conference suspend business at three o'clock this afternoon to give Mr. Harlam, Judge Mills and President Mann, an opportunity to speak and say what they wished, and after they had a hearing in all they wished to say, Conference adjourned till next morning. (If Conference was not in session, how could it adjourn?) This resolution was unanimously agreed to; and I am certain there was much more attention paid by all the members of Conference than what there was at our regular Conference business. I do not believe that any one left the house unless necessity required him to do so, as all were anxious to hear them." * * * "Conference did hear them, and gave away their time to them which they so much needed themselves.

"Now as matters and scenes, which we have seen with our eyes and heared with our ears, are so perverted as they are in the statements of those three great men, what may we not think of what is said of that which we did not see or hear with our own eyes and ears?

"Elder Maple's remarks on their statements are correct. * * * "Now if what I have written is not true, it is not true that Conference was held at the People's House. Now let all decide for themselves; I see no other way. As Elder Maple has taken the responsibility on himself to publish these communications, I hope he will now take the responsibility also to have this published, as I *thought it my duty to the members of the Miami Christian* Conference to do so, and also to inform others who were not there to hear and see for themselves." * * * CHRISTIAN WINEBRENNER".

"Miamisburg, O., Nov. 16th, 1857."

The following brief statement is by Eld. J. T. Lynn, who was at that time the standing or permanet officer of the Miami Christian Conference:

"HORACE MANN'S STATEMENTS IN THE PUBLIC PRINTS CONCERNING THE MIAMI CHRISTIAN CONFERENCE.

"Mr. Mann has published in the 'Gospel Herald,' and other periodicals, that the Miami Conference at its sitting in Plattsburgh, Ohio, on the first of Sept. 1857, refused him a hearing in regard to Antioch College.

"We will give *the resolution* offered by Rev. H. Simonton, and unanimously adopted by the Conference which reads substantially as follows:

"*Resolvd*, That the Conference suspend business at three o'clock, P. M. to hear Messrs. Harlam, Mills, and Mann make a satemeut of the financial and religious condition of Antioch College."

"These gentlemen did enjoy that privilege at the precise hour stated in the resolution. Mr. Mann made some statements in regard to the religious condition of the College, prefacing his remarks by saying: *He was exceedingly gratified in the privilege the Conference had granted him, for which they had his sincere thanks.*"

"After these three gentlemen were done speaking, the Conference adjourned in regular order."

"We give this much to show that Mr. Mann's statement in regard to this matter, in the papers, are without foundation in truth.

"The subscriber was Clerk of the Conference at the time.

"Yellow Springs, Ohio." J. T. LYNN."

The statement of many other influential men might be given on these points, but our limits will not admit them. Proof sufficient, we think, has already been given, to convince every reader that *Mr. Mann stated what was not true.*

Now why did Mr. Mann take such a course? Why did he bring such false accusations against the Miami Conference? Why did he make such a fierce attack upon an invalid clergyman who was not able to write or talk much in his own defence? Did he suppose that his base insinuations would destroy the confidence of our brethren in Eld. Ladley, and that he could thus the more easily execute his dark purposes? The javelin which he hurled at Bro. Ladley, has glanced back and pierced through his own heart!

But Mr. Mann was not the only person who was engaged at that time in the effort to injure Eld. Ladley and others. Every person opposed to his clique was a marked man, and at him were their poisoned darts discharged.

A most bitter, unchristian article also appeared in the "Messenger," signed "Q," which was generally believed to be the work of Eli Fay. Eld. Maple reviewed this article sharply in the "Herald" of Oct. 22d. He says:

"This article has the unmistakeble ring of the base coin so liberally dealt out in the 'Messenger' by Mr. "Incognito."

"This is true. It did have the ring of Eli Incognoto's "base coin," but perhaps T. M. McWhinney, with whom he associated so much and so intimately, used the quill.

Touching Mr. Q.'s statement: "D. F. Ladley, *now one of the most bitter opponents of the College,*" &c.

Mr. Maple said: This is emphatically untrue, and Mr. Q. knew it when he wrote it. All throughout his article he takes every oppotunity to degrade Elder Ladley in the estimation of the Christian Denomination; but it will only disgrace the writer. Eld. Ladley ever has been and still is a warm and unflinching friend of the College; but he is, and we hope ever will be, opposed to wresting it from the hands of the Christian Denomination, and making it what it was never designed to be. All who are acquainted with Elder Ladley know him to be one of the purest minded and most honorable men of the age, and none are more ardently devoted to the interest of pure Christianity."

That Mr. Mann has also made false statements on other occasions and on other subjects, can be proved by citizens, of Yellow Springs. Indeed many persons have no confidence in his integrity. Mr. Salsbury's opinion of his veracity can be found on Page 27th, of this volume. From two letters received from Eld. Walter, early in 1856, I extract briefly :

"SPRINGFIELD, O., Jan. 2d, 1856.

"Prof. IRA W. ALLEN :— *My Dear Brother* :— * * * What is the prospect ? Do you suppse that the money will be raised ? If not, do you think that the College will go out of our hands ? President Mann said when he was in Philadelphia a short time ago, that it would have to go ; that he had done all he could to save it, but it must go. When I see you, I shall want you to tell me what great things he has done to save it." * * *

"Accept the kindest regards of

"Yours Respectfully, ISAAC N. WALTERS."

I think it will be very difficult for any one to find out what Mr. Mann has done to save the College.

I am not aware that he did any thing, even as much as to deliver a lecture, to save the Institution before its assignment ; or that he has put forth any effort since that event for the redemption of the College to the Christian Denomination. I am however fully convinced that he has done much to destroy the confidence of the Christians both in himself and in the College, and to prevent the inflow of money into the College treasury. I believe that it has been his aim and study to take the Institution from under the control of the Christian Donomination ; and I am not surprised therefore that he should say in Philadelphia that the "*College would have to go*," that "*it must go*." These statements were made only about a year and one half before the College was thrown from its denominational basis and its property assigned. I fully believe also that it has been Mr. Manns purpose and study to so control and manage the Institution as to aggrandize himself, his relatives and favorits. Numerous evidences of these things will be found on the preceeding pages.

"SPRINGFIELD, O., April 2d, 1856.

"Prof. IRA W. ALLEN : — *My Dear Brother :* — I think upon the whole, I am a good deal better than I was the 1st. of December last. I have gained in strength and flesh, and my friends say that I look better than I have for a great many years; and if I could only get clear of my cough and hoarseness, I should be quite well." * * * "How do you get along in the College? Are the wire-workers operating to get Salsbury out? I want you to be wide awake and see how things move.

"The 1st. of April is here, and is the debt of Antioch paid? I think that but little has been paid, and near all subscribed, I think the hardest struggle is yet to come; and I am fearful that Antioch will have to wade through deep waters before she gets safe to land.

"This is the third letter I have written you without receiving any answer, I do not complain, for I know yon are buisey and have but little time to write; but I would be glad to receive a letter from you at any time, when you have leisure to write.

"Give my Christian regards to Elizabeth and your brother"s.

"With affection I remain, Yours Respectfully."

ISAAC N. WALTER."

"P. S. Remember me to your farther when you write to him."

Here is faintly pictured the views and fears of one of our most sagacious, best known, and best beloved ministers. No wonder that he and others should ask after the wire-workers when Prof. Holmes had been expatriated, Mrs. Holmes dismissed, and various other schemes attempted, and some of them executed! No wonder that, after all the dark and unjust transactions at the College, Elder Walter should request me "to be wide awake and see how things move," and should predict that "Antioch will have to wade through deep waters before she gets safe to land." This distrust existed not only in the vicinity of the College, but in many distant portions of the country; and yet, after the lapse of two years, and by the strenuous exertions of Eli Fay and McWhinney, and others, interested in the Joint Stock Company, in traveling the country and attending our Conferences, some of them have passed resolutions endorsing Mr. Mann. It is to hoped that the thing was not managed with all of them as it was in the recent session of the Miami Conference, at Enon, Ohio, viz: to keep *the matter back until near the close of the session*, or until those members who would probably oppose it, had left for their homes, and *then* rush the endorsement, or the *endowment scheme* on the Dollar Plan, through!

In the "Herald of Gospel Liberty" of 21st January, 1858, appeared an article endorsing Mr. Mann, by Bro. Edmonds, of Boston. Among other things, he says:

"Mr. Mann, himself, opens the College with prayer a large part of the time; and I am told, also prays sometimes with students before administering reproof."

Had Bro. Edmunds known much about the true or interior history of Antioch for the last four years, he would not have written such an article, such a statement as the above, in Yellow Springs or vicinity, would only excite laughter and ridicule! Mrs. Dean said, if we have been rightly informed, that she never heard her uncle (Horace Mann) "pray," or even "ask a blessing at table," until they come to Antioch, at which time Mr. Mann was nearly 60 years old. He seems to find it quite a tax *to read a prayer* occasionally in the *College Chapel!*

Mr. A. S. Dean, (Mr. Mann's nephew by marriage) has also been largely influential in bringing Antioch into her present unfortunate and miserable condition. No man, probably, has done so much, save his uncle Horace, to bring a Unitarian influence into Antioch affairs—and thus displease many, if not a large majority of the Christians—than A. S. Dean. His careless and dishonest handling of the College moneys has also done much, we think, to prevent the donation of large sums to the Institution, and to destroy the confidence of the Christians in their first great College. His struggles too, to get into various offices in the College, his casting some forty proxy votes which he had secured in 1854, to make himself a Trustee, and failing in the attempt, &c., &c., have not elevated him in the estimation of sensible men. But, the reader asks, "Why has Mr. Dean been retained in connection with the College so long?" It has been said that if Mr. Dean removes from Yellow Springs, Mrs. Dean will not remain in Antioch; and if Mrs. Dean leaves, that Mr. Mann will not remain; and if Mr. Mann leaves, that the College will go down, so, of course, Mr. Dean *must remain!* Would the reader wonder if they should all go down into the deepest mire together, if, indeed, they are not already there? But why speak of these things, or many others which might be mentioned? Is not Mr. Dean's spotted character already widely known through the country, and to the everlasting disgrace of Antioch. We would gladly have passed him by in silence could we thus have given an impartial history of the College, for there is nothing, perhaps, that gives us more unpleasant feelings than to have anything to do, by word or deed, with such men; but a sense of stern duty has compelled us to say what we have, and we now pass him by, and we hope, forever, with the following brief quotations.

Rev. Mr. "Q." says in his article above referred to:

"The fact cannot be gainsayed that near all of the disaffection in the Christian Denomination towards the College, is traceable to a half a dozen Ishmaels residing within the sound of its bell!"

On this statement Mr. Maple makes the following pertinent remarks:

"There is more truth than poetry in the above quotation when we look at the true facts in the case. 1st: There is Mr. A. S. Dean, who resides 'within the sound' of the College bell, and has done as much as any other man to create this dissatisfaction 'in the Christian Denomination towards the College.' The insulting manner in which he has been allowed to treat the Scholarship holders has given mortal offence to hundreds of once warm friends of the College. We speak what we know when we make this assertion, for within the last eighteen months we have received package after package of communications from all parts of the country, expressing the utmost indignation at the manner in which the writers had been treated by him. We did not publish these communications, for we did not wish to create any more excitement, but waited, hoping that the evil would be remedied.

"2d. Another cause of this excitement and 'disaffection in the Christian Denomination towards the College' was the course pursued by the committee appointed to select a Faculty, the business of which was done by those 'residing within the sound' of the College bell."

Elder Eli Fay has also been influential in bringing Antioch into her present disgraceful position. Perhaps no man has labored more untiringly for the past two years to bring the whole concern under Mr. Mann's thumb, than Eli "Incognitio." Indeed, I know of no man, with as much *common* sense, who has done the Christian Denomination so much injury.

Mr. Maple says of him in the "Gospel Herald" of Oct. 22d, 1857, "*It is well known that he is a minister of the liberal school.*"

For our part, we prefer to listen to Theodore Parker himself, and to Dr. H. W. Bellows, the advocate of Theaters, for we do not think that their views and doctrines are much improved in coming through Mr. Fay's sensorium. His "too sanguine, fiery and headstrong" temperament frequently leads him into excesses. The reader will find by perusing the accompanying "history of the Christian Church, of Yellow Springs," that he has not gained for himself much credit in that community, or done the cause much honor. He has several times been detected in telling falsehoods, some of which have been charged home upon him, and proved by unanswerable documents and statements to his very face. There are responsible citizens of Yellow Springs, who stand ready to prove that Eli Fay is, or has been, a falsifier. We would refer the reader, on this point, to Elders Isaac C. Goff, D. F. Ladley and J. T. Lynn, and to Brother John A. Layton. A responsible and influential man told me a few days since, that "he believed that *Eli Fay was as black hearted a man as ever breathed.*"

We believe that Mr. Fay was brought to Yellow Springs in the spring of 1857, and saddled upon the Christian Church, in order that he might aid Mr. Mann and A. S. Dean through with their College and Church schemes, and that he has been a most supple and willing tool, we presume they will not deny, for the facts are too palpaple. We believe that our brethren throughout the country cannot be too much on their guard against believing the statements of Mr. Fay, especially concerning those things in which he has a personal and pecuniary interest, viz: College and Church matters, &c. We might write a volume on Mr. Fay's career, but we will pass him by for this time with the following brief extract from an article by Eld Jacobs:

"I have said that Elder Fay has no sympathy for the donomination. I will relate a few facts that prove the same.

"He was employed on trial, for the term of three months, as Pastor of the church in this place. When that time expired he invited the whole congregation to participate in settling a Pastor, thus ignoring the existence of a church, where a church has been organized over five years, and now numbers over 120 members.

"The standing Clerk, by the influence of Mr. Mann, who presided at this meeting, was not permitted to act as Clerk of the meeting until acknowledged by a vote from the congregation. This move caused the Clerk to withdraw from the church, not willing that Pontifical domination should exist in a church to which he belonged. Besides this we all know that Elder Fay has been at open war with our most sacred principles, and endeavoring to introduce a creed among us under the modest name of *a constitution*, which he has proposed to give to this church.

"I attended his ministration for three months and have not heard the word *repent, regeneration or new birth, fall from his lips*; but those who sided with Wm. Denton (a Spiritualist) last winter, in discarding the Bible, say, 'his is the doctrine for me.'

"So we may see what we may expect in the Faculty. The Christians have no representative in the committee, (Harlan, Bellows and Fay,) and we cannot expect any sympathy shown in the selection of a Faculty, JESSE JACOBS."

"Yellow Springs, Ohio, Aug. 22d, 1857."

That Elder James Maple went over a few months since to the embrace of that clique which he previously represented as "*little scheming, selfish, greedg*," and declared that "our people will not be their tame and spiritless tools," must be clearly understood, we think, by every reader of the "Herald." We do not remember to have known any light headed, venal polititian to turn such a short corner. What a disgrace, not only to our denomination, but to the whole clerical profession. Who can look back over his course for the last fifteen months without first a shudder of horror, and then a deep feeling of pity? His course has been more winding, if possible, than that of a serpent. He has made statements one day and belied them on another. He has made promises and falsified them. He has made the most positive engagements, the most inviolable vows, and then broken them! Instances of these things are numerous, but I need not enumerate them here. The careful readers of the "Gospel Herald" are acquainted with them. Indeed, reliable people have told me things concerning Mr. Maple's former character and course of life which I could hardly believe, even after the transactions of the past twelve months. At these late zig-zag, tortuous and dark transactions they did not seem surprised! They could hardly expect better things, said they, of Mr. James Maple. Far be it from me to allude to the past unfortunate course of any reformed man, so long as he walks in the path of truth and integrity, but when he goes back like "a sow to her wallowing in the mire," and does it *deliberately*, people can hardly refrain, nor need they, from taking a look at his antecedents. We deeply regret that Eld. Maple had not stamina sufficient to keep him erect, not only on his own account but on account of the tarnished honor of the connection.

We could write at great length on Mr. Maple's course for the past year, but the limits of this work will not permit it. We have already said something on preceding pages; made some comparisons of his public statements, and can now add but a very few illustrations more. Now, it is, we think, necessary, for his base partizan course is too well known, especially to the readers of the "Herald." In the "Gospel Herald," of November 5th, 1857, Mr. Maple says, touching Antioch College:

"We have a number of communications on hand, but we think that enough has been said. The facts are all before the people, and we think that the controversy had better be brought to a close."

In the "Herald" of the next week, Nov. 12th, in which Mr. Mann's false charges against the Miami Conference were published, Mr. Maple says:

"We will publish two articles in reply to Mr. Jacobs, one from the pen of J. B. Weston and the other from A. Craig; then we shall abide by the decision of the Executive Committee, and publish nothing more of a controversial character."

Need I give other instances? I will give one more from the "Herald" of Jan'y 14th, 1858, clipped from the closing portion of a lengthy editorial on Antioch, viz:

"We have calmly and deliberately made up our mind to put a stop to all controversy about the past, and we hope that our brethren will not write anything more on these unpleasant questions; *for we positively will not publish them.* This is the law of the Medes and Persians."

But this positive law, the decisive, solemn promise, *"calmly and deliberately made."* Mr. Maple did violate, *did break again and again* during the next few weeks; and on the 7th of April the Executive Committee passed a special and positive resolution which he also *violated again and again* during the two or three following months. These violations were most gross and palpable, as any person can see by turning to the back numbers of the "Herald."

On Dec. 6th, 1857, Mr. Maple wrote touching Mr. Mann:

"I finally concluded to write to him and tell him that I would have nothing more to do with him or with the College;" "Mr. Mann has shaken my confidence in his integrity;" and in the "Herald" of Feb'y 18th, 1858, he says: "We believe that he is just the man for the place he occupies, and that a more competent person could not be found in America, or Europe." "His creed is as pure as an angel's thought!"

Possible his creed may be as pure as an angel's thought; but *his practice is not*, unless by the term "angel" Mr. Maple means one of the "*angels of darkness*."

In the Summer and Autumn of 1857, Mr. Maple spoke in terms of very high praise of Prof. Doherty. In Nov. he says:

"In our article in the 'Herald' of Aug. 13th, we stated what we had reason to believe to be true. We had the testimony of reliable men, who are responsible for their statements." "We believe the statements in it to be as true as the Bible that lies there on the sacred desk. We had not the least doubt of their truth. They were made to me by respectable men."

In Feb'y, he says:

"None are better qualified, or have had a better opportunity to form a correct opinion of Mr. Mann's capacity and qualifications for his office than Prof. Doherty, and his opinion will have great weight with our people," and in the 'Herald' of July 8th, he says:

"In our issue of the 13th of August, 1857, we stated that some malignant influence had operated in Antioch College to prevent any revivals of religion, and to turn many students away from the religion of their fathers and lead them into skepticism, if not into infidelity. We have been so situated that we have but seldom visited the College since its dedication, and we knew but little about it from personal observation. The statements made in the issue above mentioned were made on the authority of Prof. H. W. Doherty."

No other name is given in this article as his authority but that of Prof. Doherty, thus saying, as clearly as he well could speak, that he had no other authority! How will this harmonize with his statements above.

"We had the testimony of reliable men," &c. Within the last eighteen months we have received package after package of communications from all parts of the country expressing the utmost indignation at the manner in which the writers had been treated by A. S. Dean."

In Aug. 1857, Maple said:

"We can assure Messrs. Dean, Fay & Co., that our people will not be the tame and spiritless tools of their little scheming, selfish, greedy clique. There is some self-respect and denominational honor left in the Christian Church, and the course pursued by the managers of the College will call them out."

He also says, that McWhinney got the *First Report* of the "self-constituted Committee," into the "Herald" by a trick. And yet in Feb'y 1858, he says, speaking of Fay and McWhinney as agents for the "Joint Stock Plan:"—"They are commended to our churches as brethren worthy of entire confidence." Who can sufficiently despise such vacillation, if not downright dishonesty!

In the "Herald" of July 8th, 1858, Mr. Maple published a lengthy article, containing the most fulsome and grossly exaggerated accounts of the closing exercises of what he calls Antioch College." We do not know how even the easy consciences of Mr. Mann and Mrs. A. S. Dean can bear up under such flattering and disgusting untruths. We will mention but two of them. Speaking of Mr. Mann's Baccalaureate Address, he says:

"He closed with a pathetic address to the graduating class which drew tears to the eyes of all present."

And near the close of his article he remarks:

"We do not believe that as moral and well behaved a class of students can be found in any institution of learning in the world as in Antioch College; and this is all owing to the wonderful influence of its venerable President."

That the students are a well disposed class of young persons we presume is true; at least we know that such was the case prior to the Summer of 1857; but that their morality and good behavior are "*all owing to the wonderful influence*" of Horace Mann, is not very complimentary to their parents, their former instructors, or to the other Teachers in Mr. Mann's school. Indeed the statement is not only untrue, but ridiculously so; and we presume that even Mr. Mann would prefer to have Mr. Maple keep near enough to the truth to be believed by some portion of the Christian Connection.

That the "pathetic address" "drew tears to the eyes of all present," is just about as far from the truth as other statements in the same article. We were present on the occasion referred to, but did not see any signs of tears, except in the countenances of Mr. Mann, Mr. Maple and Mr. Weston! and others who were present saw few, if any, other signs of tears! Mr. Maple's *tears in the eyes of all present* are like the astronomer's *elephant in the moon*, which, on close inspection, was found to be a *small fly* on one of the lenses of his telescope!

Over numerous other statements and acts of Mr. Maple, we pass in silence, for the present, and we hope forever. We regret exceedingly that he has made it our duty to say even the little we have concerning him. Had he pursued a straight forward, manly course, all would have been well, at least so far as he is concerned; and our sincere and earnest desire is, that he may repent bitterly, as did Peter, return to the path of truth and wisdom, and yet be a great blessing to the world.

Concerning Mr. J. B. Weston's surprising, if not venal course, for the last fifteen months, we might write much, but we have no time or space to give him now, other than to refer the reader to preceding letters and statements, and to the following letter of Bro. Merrifield.

We have spoken plainly of some of the doings and sayings of Mr. Mann and his accomplices; yet we are not unmindful of their good qualities. Mr. Mann has done much in former years for common schools and education, and we trust in other departments of practical life. His present coadjutors, too, have some excellent qualities, and a few of them much that is good; yet they all, in our opinion, have great weaknesses, and we exceedingly regret that they should have allowed these weaknesses to serve as approaches to the citadels of their strength, and thus fall easy captives to the enemy of truth and justice. We sadly regret that they, in an unhappy moment, threw themselves overboard, (if indeed they ever were really on board,) into an angry and treacherous sea, and that they are so rapidly drifting away from the staunch and commodious old ship of the Christians. We throw over *this life-boat*, with the hope that it may bring them all safely back to the ship, or, at least, aid them in reaching some secure harbor.

The "Messenger" of April 5th, 1855, in a lengthy circular on Antioch College, to the "Brethren and friends of the Christian Church,' says:

"Four years ago last October, the project and plan of that noble institution was introduced to the General Convention, by Prof. D. Millard, A. M. Merrifield, and others. The plan was ennobling and the scheme grand."

We have already spoken of Bro. Merrifield and his connection with Antioch, on page 164, and we regret that his services could not have been retained. Had he continued to fill the offices of Treasurer and Superintendant of the College, and been ably seconded by men interested in the Christian Connection, we believe that, instead of being in the hands of an Assignee, the Institution would now be free from debt, and on a firm financial and educational basis. During the present summer, Mr. Merrifield spent some two weeks in Yellow Springs, and took especial pains to look into the present state of affairs, by conversing with persons of different views and parties, and he sums up, giving the results of his investigations in these words:

"YELLOW SPRINGS, O., August 6th, 1858.

"FRIEND CARTER—On my informing you at the late meeting of the New England Christian Convention that I intended to visit this place, you requested me to write you my impressions of Antioch College as at present managed.

"The question you ask is, 'Is the College entitled to the confidence and support of the Christian Connection?'

"I answer, I think not. The charter, you will remember, requires that a majority of the Board of Instruction shall be members of the Christian connection.

"At the first election, a President and six Professors were chosen.

"The Trustees believed that in placing Messrs. Doharty, Holmes, Allen and McKinney in the Faculty, that they had well guarded the religious element of the College; and that denominationally the Faculty would be satisfactory. It is a significant fact that *these gentlemen* are all among the 'outs!' It is equally significant that there is but one person in the whole teaching force who was a member of the Christian Connection many days before his or her appointment.

"The single exception alluded to above is reported to have said that his religious views have undergone a change since he came here.

"Let us hope, if we can, that the change is for the better. In an educational point of view, it will not be claimed that there is more than one member of the Faculty who is possessed of marked ability; and that one I think shows more tact in laying pipes and drawing wires than sound discretion in managing the affairs of the College.

"For these and many other reasons I cannot advise any one to send a son or daughter here to be educated until a radical change is made, for I fully believe that better instruction and under far better influences can be had elsewhere.

"Yours, truly, A. M. MERRIFIELD."

The truth is, that Antioch College has gone from us as a denomination. This, no one can successfully contradict, however many statements to the contrary Mr. Mann and his accomplices may publish in the papers. They may deceive the public for a while, but the stern facts will by and by come to light, and what may they then expect from ignorant and exasperated people? Honesty is the best policy, in the long run, and they will yet experience the truth of this aphorism.

O. J. Wait says in the "Herald of Gospel Liberty" of July 15th, 1858:

"Antioch College clears her brow of debt and anguish in August next. The money is *pledged*. Her debts are covered. Her anguish is over and her enemies are foiled. Let the friends of the College rejoice. Let the shout go up and give God the glory. Let those who have toiled and prayed and sacrificed for her redemption be glad."

We saw *then* and see *now* no good reason for such exultation. Money *pledged* is not money *in the treasury*. Strenuous exertions were put forth by Mann & Co. from the 1st of July to the 3d of August, and even then it was with the greatest effort, I am informed, that some seventeen or eighteen thousand dollars, cash in hand, was obtained, and the balance of the twenty-one thousand five hundred dollars arranged for; and a considerable part of this was paid by persons whose property was under execution for from twenty-five to fifty thousand dollars of the College debt, for they hoped thus to get their property released. Mr. Reyburn has been paid, it is true, but Hon. Messrs. Harlan and Mills, and others, inform me that his note is still held against them by some person or persons! The Hartford *mortgage* of some twenty-six thousand dollars is not yet cancelled, and when will it be?

But suppose the above two claims of nearly fifty-thousand dollars *to be fully liquidated* by out and out donations, (which, judging by the past, is a dangerous supposition,) even then the Institution or the "Joint Stock Company" will be more than thirty thousand dollars in debt! Can an institution in such a condition be properly said to be redeemed, even in a financial point of view? We cannot see any good reason, therefore, for the puffs which have been going the rounds of the papers, to the effect that "Antioch is *redeemed*," Antioch *is now safe*," Antioch *is going on under better auspices than ever before*." We believe that such deceptive statements will do even Horace Mann and the "Joint Stock Company" more harm than good.

But even if paid for, could Antioch be redeemed to the Christian Denomination? We have very serious doubts on this point. One of our best known and most influential ministers, writing a few months since on this snbject, said: "*Satan could as soon be redeemed!*"

Of one thing, however, we are confident, viz.: That if Antioch is ever paid for by our brethren, it must be done chiefly by those residing in Ohio. They have abundant means to do it twice over. Even the Miami Christian Conference, numbering some sixty ministers and as many churches, could easily do it, if the members would only work together. We should most sincerely hope that our Ohio brethren would pay for the College, if *then* they *could* and *would* so control and direct it as to make it an honor and a blessing to our people. Can they do this? Will they do this? Certainly not under the lead of such men as Eli Fay, A. S. Dean, and the "self-constituted Committee."

But the reader asks, will not Mr. Mann's schems for a "Joint Stock Company" be endorsed by the next General Convention of the Christians, which is near at hand? We presume it will be, for the present managers of the Institution, on July 1st, 1858, appointed the following persons delegates, viz: Horace Mann, John Phillips, E. Fay, T. M. McWhinney. F. A. Palmer, Dr. H. W. Bellows, to represent the "Joint Stock Company," or the College in its unfortunate assigned condition, in said Convention. But suppose the Convention does endorse the institution represented by these delegates, what of it? Are not the resolutions and endorsements of Conventions often a dead letter as soon as the ink dries upon the page where they are recorded?

One of our writers said a few months since:—

"There is one great reason why we earnestly desire the redemption of the College by the Christian Church, which we have never yet seen urged in any of our papers. It is this: If we suffer the College to pass from our hands, it will be impossible ever to unite all our churches in one great enterprise again."

The day has gone by, if indeed it ever did exist, when our whole Denomination might have been united in any one institution. Our Southern Conferences are laboring gratiously and harmoniously in building up institutions of their own. Our conferences or churches in New England, if true to their own best interests, will do the same on a much larger scale than they have ever done before; and our brethren in the rich and fertile States of the North-West will soon begin the work in right good earnest. Before ten years pass by, we shall have several more good Institutes and Seminaries and at least two Colleges. It is in vain already, and will be hereafter, to talk of uniting all our forces in any one enterprise. Nearly all precedents and usages in our broad land are against it. Paris may be France, and London may energize and govern the whole British Empire, but Washington is not the United States. The very genius of our government, all our civil institutions, is opposed to centralization. So it is with the Christian Connection which is composed of from 1,200 to 1,500 independent churches. Each church is a little democracy or republic, supreme to transact and control its entire business. Our Conferences and Conventions are therefore simply advisory bodies, and have no coercive power over any member of the sisterhood of churches. Hence we say, that if the day ever existed when all our churches might have united in paying for and endowing Antioch College, Horace Mann and others have caused *that day to pass by forever!*

But should the loss of Antioch discourage our people? No, never. Perhaps this apparent loss is a rich blessing in disguise. This case may be like the *rupture* in the old University of Prague, where forty thousand students were in attendance; which was followed by the establishment of several other Universities in different parts of Germany, which Universities soon outstripped and overshadowed the mother institution in the Bohemian Capitol.

Let our brethren, therefore, in each principal section of the country, look well after their own educational interests. May they labor with a commendable zeal and an unconquerable purpose to establish institutions which shall not only be a great blessing to their sons and daughters, but a priceless legacy to further generations.

The following card, by Eld. Summerbell, appeared in the "Gospel Herald" of September 24th, 1857:

"CHRISTIAN SCHOOLS.

"The Christians of N. E., N. Y., and the South have in each section flourishing schools under their control. I propose to the various Conferences in the *West* that measures be taken to establish a school in the '*West*.' We have as good Professors as the United States knows, and they should be employed. N. SUMMERBELL."

In the "Herald of Gospel Liberty," of October 1st, also, the same writer published a brief article, a part of which is as follows:

"THE PROFESSORS.

"By the late developments the 'Christians' now find several of the best teachers in our country unemployed. Among these, Professors Holmes, Allen and Doherty rank among the most learned men of the age." * * *

"Let these men not be neglected. They are tried men and true.
"N. SUMMERBELL."

May our brethren not only look well to their educational interests, but also be very vigilent of their religious rights and immunities. May they not, on the one hand, be narrow minded, nor cling with a blind tenacity to rites and doctrines simply because they are hoary with age; nor on the other, may they be charmed by new "isms" simply because they are new and spicious, nor be led astray by such recent Antioch renovations as the substitution of *reading circles* for Sabbath evening prayer meetings, and the *liberalistic theology* for Christianity; but may they rather pursue the *golden mean*, the path of heavenly wisdom, the *narrow way* that leadeth unto life eternal.

APPENDIX.

REPORT OF COMMITTEE ON THE PLAN FOR A COLLEGE.

Your Committee, to whom were referred the plans submitted, together with the report of the Informal Committee, with instructions to report a plan for the contemplated College, would respectfully submit the following resolutions for the action of the Convention:

1st. *Resolved*, That measures be immediately taken for the founding and erecting of a College.

2d. *Resolved*, That a Provisional Committee of thirty-four be appointed for the accomplishment of this object; of this committee, thirteen shall be designated by the Convention, as a sub-committee—five of whom shall form a quorum for the transaction of business.

3d. *Resolved*, That the College we propose, shall be located in such State and place as the provisional committee shall designate. That, in finally settling the precise place of location, the following be carefully consulted, viz., heathfulness, accessibility by travel, cheapness of living, and the amount offered by the citizens of the place to secure the location of our College.

4th. *Resolved*, That at least the sum of *fifty thousand dollars* must be raised as a permanent endowment. No part of this sum is ever to be expended, but to be kept at interest, on good bond and mortgage securities. The interest thus accruing is to pay the educational expenses of every student sent there by owners of scholarships in the institution.

5th. *Resolved*, That the sum above stated be raised by the disposal of scholarships at *one hundred dollars* each, which schola shaps shall be negotiable. Whoever, then, subscribes and pays one hundred dollars, will own a scholarship, giving such person the right to keep one student in the College *continually, free from educational charges.* Whoever subscribes and pays *fifty dollars*, will have a like privilege half the time.

6th. *Resolved*, That in relation to the site, edifice, and other necessary fixtures, the expense can be met in part, by subscriptions of less denomination than fifty dollars, of which we expect many. The liberality of the citizens in the place of location will also be applied mainly to this branch of expenditure; and in addition to all, we hope the Legislature of the State, in which it shall be located, will make a liberal donation for the same purpose.

7th. *Resolved*, That at least two-thirds of the board of trustees, and a majority of the board of instruction, shall, at all times, belong to the Christian Connection.

8th. *Resolved*, That no person shall be a voter in the affairs of the said College except he own a full scholarship in it. That each scholarship shall entitle the holder thereof to one vote, provided, however, that no owner of scholarships shall be entitled to cast over ten votes.

9th. *Resolved,* That this College shall afford *equal* privileges to students of BOTH SEXES.

10th. *Resolved,* That the foregoing rules may be altered or amended by a majority of two-thirds of the provisional committee, provided that the original design and intentions of the institution be not departed from.

All of which is respectfully submitted by

JOHN ROSS,
DAVID MILLARD,
A. M. MERRIFIELD,
JOHN PHILLIPS,
JASPER HAZEN,
} Committee.

PROCEEDINGS OF THE SUB-COMMITTEE ON THE CONSTRUCTION OF A COLLEGE FOR THE CHRISTIANS.

The sub-committee on the construction of a College for the Christians, appointed by the Christian General Convention held in Marion, New York, October 2d, 1850, met in Marion, New York, October 5th, 1850, and appointed officers pro tem. Eld. D. Millard, President; Eld. E. Fay, Secretary.

2d. Proceeded to elect permanent officers for the committee. Eld. D. Millard, was elected President; Eld. W. R. Stowe, Vice President; Eld. E. Fay, Secretary; and A. M. Merrifield, Treasurer.

1st. *Resolved,* That it shall be the duty of the President to preside in all the meetings of the sub-committee, and to call meetings with the concurrence of two other members of said committee, when they may deem it necessary, and in case of his absence or sickness, the like duties shall devolve upon the Vice President.

2d. *Resolved,* That it shall be the duty of the Secretary, to keep a faithful record of all the proceedings of the sub-committee, in a book provided for that purpose, and to be ready to report to said committee at all of its meetings, and that he be the Corresponding Secretary to said committee.

3d. *Resolved,* That it shall be the duty of the Treasurer, to keep a faithful account of all moneys and securities which may come into his hands, and disburse the same to orders drawn upon the Treasury, and signed by the President and Secretary. And that he shall cause to be published in at least one of our periodicals, a paithful account of the returns of our soliciting agents. And it shall be his duty, when deemed necessary by the sub-commitee, to give sufficient bond and security for the faithful performance of his duty.

4th. *Resolved,* That the portion of the sub-committee residing in Ohio be authorized to employ immediately one agent to solicit funds in the States of Ohio and Kentucky, for the contemplated College; and one for Indiana for the same purpose.

5th. *Resolved*, That Bro. A. M. Merrifield be authorized to employ one agent for the same purpose for the New England States.

6th. *Resolved*, That Eld. Millard, Eld. Fay, and Dr. Joseph Hall be a committee to employ soliciting agents for such portions of the country as are not included in the above Resolutions.

7th. *Resolved*, That each soliciting agent be required to provide himself with, and carry three blank books, in one of which he shall cause to be inserted all the subscriptions for scholarships, and half-scholarships, and in another all unpaid donations, and in the other all cash donations.—And that he be required to report to the Treasurer, every three months in tabular form, the name of every donor and subscriber for the College, with the amount that each individual may have donated or subscribed.

8th. *Resolved*, That D. Millard, E. Fay, and C. C. Davidson, Esq., be a committee to provide printed blanks for notes and bonds, to be used by the soliciting agents.

9th. *Resolved*, That our proposed College be known by the name of the ANTIOCH COLLEGE.

E. FAY, Secretary. D. MILLARD, President.
Marion, Oct. 5th, 1850.

PROCEEDINGS OF THE COMMITTEE APPOINTED TO EMPLOY SOLICITING AGENTS FOR ANTIOCH COLLEGE.

The committee appointed by the sub-committee at Marion, to employ soliciting agents for territories not included in Resolutions No. 6 and 7 of the proceedings of the sub-committee, met at West Bloomfield, Nov. 1st, 1850.

Present, D. Millard, J. Hall, and E. Fay.

1. Appointed Eld. C. L. F. Havens, a solicining agent for the States of N. Y. and Canada West.

2. Eld. J. E. Church, for the States of Penn. and N. J., and that portion of Va., lying West of the Blue Ridge.

3. Eld. W. B. Wellons, for Eastern Va. and N. C.

4. Eld. J. S. White, for Mich.

5. Eld. O. Barr, for Ill., Wisc. and Io.

As Elds. Barr, White and Wellons, live in sections of the country not accessible to the committee, if either of them cannot serve they are authorized to employ a man who will, and report the same to the Secretary.

The blank notes and bonds specified in Resolution 8, in the proceedings of the sub-committee, will be ready for the agents by the time orders can be received.

All orders or letters desiring information, addressed to E. Fay, Honeoye Falls, N. Y., will receive immediate attention.

E. FAY, Cor. Sec'ry. D. MILLARD, Pres't.

MEETING OF THE OHIO SUB-COMMITTEE.

The sub-committee appointed by the Educational Convention, held at Marion, Wayne County, N. Y., in October last, consisting of D. F. Ladley, John Phillips, E. W. Devore, Christian Winebrenner, and Josiah Knight, met agreeably to previous appointment at the Christian Chapel, Fourth Street, Cincinnati, Ohio, Nov. 4th, 1850.

The throne of grace was addressed by H. Simonton. A number of visiting brethren being present, were invited to participate. The meeting was duly organized by appointing Eld. J Phillips, President, and Eld. J. Knight, Secretary.

After carefully deliberating upon the qualifications of an agent to solicit funds for the contemplated ANTIOCH COLLEGE, Eld. John Phillips was unanimously chosen to be the agent.

Articles of agreement were then drawn, and the contract concluded in due form between the committee and their agent, in which it becomes the duty of the agent to canvass the state of Ohio, and as much of Kentucky as it is thought profitable, for the express purpose of raising and collecting funds for the said College, and to report quarterly, or oftener, to the Clerk the whole amount raised on subscription, together with the amount collected—on which report a record shall be given of all names for one dollar and over—all of which will hereafter be made public. It is also the duty of the agent to make remittances to the Treasurer of all moneys collected as often as once in three months.

JOSIAH KNIGHT, Clerk.

Mason, Warren Co., Ohio, Nov. 7th, 1850.

Articles of Incorporation of Antioch College, located at Yellow Springs, in the County of Greene, and State of Ohio.

The undersigned, and their associates, having determined, by the permission of Divine Providence, to erect and establish an Institution of Learning, at the place above mentioned, to be under the direction, control, and management of the religious denomination called "CHRISTIANS," professing no creed but the BIBLE, and having no test of fellowship but CHRISTIAN CHARACTER, which originated as an organized body in the United States, about the beginning of the nineteenth century, under the labors of Abner Janes, of New England; David Purveance, of Kentucky; James O'Kelly and Francis Williamson, of North Carolina; Bremvill Barret, of Va.; Nathan Warley, of Ohio, and others, whose sentiments have been advocated in the "Herald of Gospel Liberty," of New England; "Christian Palladium," of New York; "Christian Sun," of North Carolina, and "Gospel Herald," of Ohio, do hereby agree to adopt the following articles for the government of said Institution:

ART. 1. This Institution shall be known and designated by the name and style of "Antioch College."

ART. 2. The object of this College is to afford instruction in the liberal arts and sciences usually taught in the Colleges, and shall be allowed to establish any department for the instruction of students in the various branches of academical education, moral and theological sciences, and general knowledge not included in the usual collegiate courses; and shall afford equal privileges to students of both sexes.

Art. 3. This Institution shall be under the management of a Board of thirty-four Trustees, who shall be elected for the term of three years, and shall continue in office until their successors shall be chosen and qualified, unless removed for a cause by a vote of two-thirds of the Board present at any meeting thereof.

Art. 4. Vacancies in the Board of Trustees, caused by death, resignation, or removal of any member thereof, may be filled by a vote of a majority of the Trustees present at any meeting of the Board; but persons so appointed shall hold their office only until the regularelection of Trustees.

Art. 5. The Board of Trustees shall meet annually, on the first Monday of September, at Yellow Springs, but special meetings shall be held at such other times as may be deemed necessary, by the request of five of the Trustees, signed by the President of the Board.

Art. 6. The Board of Trustees, so to be appointed, shall be a body politic and corporate, with perpetual succession, having power to sue and be sued; to plead and be impleaded; to acquire, hold and convey property, real, personal or mixed; to have and use a common seal, and to alter, and renew the same at pleasure, and to make and alter from time to time all such by-laws as shall be deemed necessary for the government of said Institution, and shall keep a record of their proceedings.

Art. 7. The Board of Trustees shall appoint from their own number a President, Vice President, Secretary and Treasurer, who shall perform the duties usually performed by such officers, and the Treasurer shall give bonds and security in such amount as may be required by the Trustees.

Art. 8. At any meeting of the Trustees, twelve members shall be necessary to form a quorum for the transaction of business.

Art. 9. Until a Board of Trustees shall be chosen for the government of the Institution, pursuant to the foregoing provisions, the powers and duties hereby conferred upon the Board of Trustees shall remain with, and be exercised by the sub-Committee appointed at a Convention of the Christian Conferences held at Marion, New York, in 1850, whose acts, rules and contracts shall be binding on the corporation until altered or recinded by due authority; but no act of said Board of Trustees shall be so construed as to impair any obligation or contract entered into by said committee.

Art. 10. The Trustees shall be elected by the owners of scholarships, but no person shall be a voter unless he owns a full scholarship, and each scholarship shall entitle the owner thereof to one vote, provided however, that no owner of scholarships shall be entitled to cast over ten votes, and votes may be cast either in person or by proxy.

Art. 11. Two-thirds of the Board of Trustees, and a majority of the Board of Instruction shall at all times be regular members of the Christian denomination.

Art. 12. The Board of Trustees shall appoint the President, Professors, Teachers and Assistants and all such officers and agents as the interests of the Institution demands, and the Faculty so to be appointed, shall have authority to prescribe rules for the reception, punishment or expulsion of any pupil or pupils, to prescribe the course of study to be pursued in the College or any department thereof, to prescribe books, charts, chemical, philosophical and other scientific apparatus, and they shall also have authority to confer such honors and degrees as are usually conferred by Colleges.

ART. 13. The Board of Trustees shall have authority to remove for just cause any member of the College Faculty, or any of the teachers or instructors, officers or agents of the Institution, whenever in their opinion the prosperity and usefulness of the Institution may require it.

ART. 14. No part of the funds which now are or hereafter may be raised, by gift, grant or otherwise, as permanent endowment of this Institution, shall ever be expended, but shall be kept at interest on good bond and security, and the interest thus accruing shall be appropriated to the educational expenses of every student sent to it by the owners of scholarships.

ART. 15. This Constitution may be altered or amended by a vote of two-thirds of the members present at any annual meeting of the Board of Trustees, and any alteration shall be subject to the approval or disapproval of a majority of the electors present at the succeeding triennial meeting of the electors, but shall be binding until so disapproved.

DAVID MILLARD, WM. MILLS,
OLIVER BARR, D. F. LADLEY,
JOHN PHILLIPS, C. WINEBRENNER,
JOSIAH KNIGHT, EBENEEZER WHEELER,
E. W. DEVORE.

Yellow Springs, May 14, 1852.

ERRATA.

On page 20, between 3d and 4th, put in Sophomore Class.

" 228, eighth line, and on 229, fourth line, read Mr. Solsbury, instead of Salsbury.

" 228, read Isaac N. Walter, instead of Isaac N. Walters.

" 213, ten lines from bottom, read admiration instead of administration.

" 183, line fifteen, read feelings instead feeling.

" 196, line ninth, read Lynn, instead of Lyon.

" 196, The (our churches,) read They (our churches.)

" 196, A week latter, read, A week later.

HISTORY

OF

The Christian Church

OF

YELLOW SPRINGS, OHIO.

E. LAWRENCE & SON, YELLOW SPRINGS.

COLUMBUS:

PUBLISHED BY JOHN GEARY & SON, BROAD STREET.

1858.

PREFACE.

No book should be published without good and sufficient reasons. The causes which have led to the following volume are—

1st. The circulation of incorrect and malicious statements concerning the Christian Church of this place.

2d. The publication of the most pointed and false charges against said church in the "Christian Messenger" and "Gospel Herald," both of which have refused to publish a brief contradictory statement from the undersigned.

For these and other reasons we deem it our duty to present the following history of the said Christian Church, compiled chiefly from official records, as a true statement of the facts.

August, 1858.

JOHN KERSHNER,
A. G. KILER,
BENAJAH WILSON, } Trustees of the late First Christian Church.

Signed,

THOMAS KERSHNER,
JOHN KERSHNER,
A. G. KILER, } Building Committee of the late First Christian Church.

D. F. LADLEY, Clerk of said late First Ch. Church.

The above persons were members of the First Christian Church from the day of its organization, January 19th, 1852, to its dissolution, February 9th, 1858, and were in office most of the time.

JOHN A. LAYTON,
IRA W. ALLEN,
THEO. W. DAWSON, } Trustees* of the Second Christian Church.

JESSE JACOBS, Clerk of Second Ch. Church.

E. LAWRENCE, Treasurer of Second Ch. Church.

*The Trustees of the Second Christian Church never belonged to the First Christian Church, and are not personally acquainted with its entire history, yet to the best of their belief the following is a true statement.

History of the Christian Church.

The Church is a divine institution, of which Christ, the Son of God, is head. It is called, in Holy Writ, the "Church of God," and its members have, of course, powers, prerogatives and duties peculiarly and exclusively their own. Their powers they should use; their prerogatives exercise and defend; and faithfully discharge their duties. They, and they alone, can do this, and in the exercise of their rights and the fulfillment of their obligations, they should receive no let or hindrance in any civilized community.

The first Christian Church of Yellow Springs, Green county, Ohio, was organized Jan. 19th, 1852, by Eld. D. F. Ladley, assisted by Eld. J. Knight, and consisted at first of eighteen members. In their first business meeting they passed a resolution, inviting Eld. Ladley to the pastoral charge of the church, and appointing B. Wilson and Jonathan C. Kershner a committee to wait on Eld. Ladley, inform him of his election, learn whether he will accept or not, and report at our next meeting. At their next meeting, March 27, said committee reported that they had fulfilled their instructions, and "that Eld. Ladley was present and would speak for himself with regard to becoming our pastor."

"Eld. Ladley then observed that he would accept the invitation to become pastor of this church for an indefinite period of time, with the understanding that if, at any time, he should think best to change his connection with the church, he would give in writing three months' notice; and that the church should give the same timely notice in writing, in the event that they should wish such a change, which conditions were agreed to by both parties."

June 26.—"Voted, That Eld. D. F. Ladley, A. G. Kiler and John Kershner, be a committee to confer with Wm. Mills with reference to procuring a lot on which to erect a church edifice."

The church made application to the Miami Christian Conference for Christian Conference Fellowship, at its annual meeting (1852,) and was received as a member.

Dec. 18, 1852.—John Kershner, Charles Ohlwine and B. Wilson were elected Trustees of the church.

Jan. 14, 1853.—A lot was selected upon which to build a chapel;

and on the 17th a form of subscription was proposed by Eld. Ladley and adopted, by which to raise money for the erection of said chapel.

FORM.

"We whose names are hereunto subscribed do promise to pay to the Trustees of the Christian Church at Yellow Springs, the sums annexed to our respective names in installments of twenty per cent every sixty days for the purpose of erecting a church edifice in said village: the first installment to be paid the 1st of January, 1854.

At the meeting on the 20th ,three days later, $1,260 were reported as pledged; and $120 more were subscribed on the spot—and on Feb'y. 3d, $16,00 were reported.

Jan'y 27, 1853.—A Building Committee was appointed, consisting of Thomas Kershner, S. Richardson and Charles Ohlwine, and two others to be appointed at the next meeting.

Feb. 7th.—"Voted that Bros. John and Isaac Kershner be the additional members of the Building Committee."

The Trustees were instructed by the church to purchase 20 feet of ground on the south side of the church lot; and the Building Committee as follows:

"*Resolved*, That the Building Committee be and that they are hereby instructed to make all necessary arrangements for and proceed with the chapel immediately, irrespective of any previous arrangements made by the church."

The preparatory work was now prosecuted with considerable vigor. Church edifices in the vicinity were visited and examined, and plans for the chapel were received. Arrangements were made for procuring stone for the basement story, and preparations were made for burning the bricks for the superstructure. The corner stone was laid June 23d; and on July 16th the Building Committee was authorized to borrow $1,000, to put up and enclose the chapel.

Aug. 20*th*.—The Trustees were instructed to receive the lot offered to the church by Eld. Richardson for sheds and hitching ground, at $3,94 per foot; and to obtain a deed for the same.

Eld. Ladley had preached to the church but a part of the time, yet there was a healthy state of religious feeling, and a revival interest manifested.

The church had increased in numbers, from 18 members up to sixty-five, and a still more prosperous future seemed to beckon them onward.

Horace Mann and wife, and Miss Pennell, united with the church Nov. 6th, making 68 members in all.

Nov. 7*th*.—Eld. Ladley's services were engaged for the whole time, or four Sabbaths each month; and his labors were acceptable to the church, and successful in building up the cause of Christ.

Feb. 19th, 1854.—The Building Committee was authorized to borrow $400 more to prosecute the work on the chapel.

Thus the church continued to prosper. Its affairs were conducted in quietness and order, and love and union and Christian fellowship were manifested in a high degree.

During the winter and spring there were 43 additions to the church, making 111 communicants in all.

Among the members admitted to the church were some from the East and other sections of the Union, and during the spring, Eld. Ladley thought he saw discordant elements in the brotherhood, and although a good religious interest continued, he feared that there might be some trouble in the future.

His health likewise began to fail, and all things considered, he determined to resign, and tendered "his resignation of the pastoral office" on the 20th May, 1854, to take effect three months after date according to agreement.

Objections were made, however, to accepting it, and an effort put forth to induce Eld. Ladley to withdraw his resignation, yet he declined to do so; and accordingly the following preamble and resolution were adopted:

"*Whereas*, Eld. D. F. Ladley has this day presented his resignation as pastor of this church, therefore be it

Resolved, That the said resignation be accepted, and that the thanks of this church be presented to Eld. Ladley for the efficient manner in which he has discharged the duties enjoined upon him by the important office he held as our pastor."

Also—"Instructed the Building Committee to borrow money to finish our chapel and if necessary to liquidate the present debt." Also,

"*Resolved*, That each member of this church agrees to be taxed in proportion to the value of his or her property for the purpose of finishing the chapel and liquidating the debt now due on the church."

"John Kershner, S. O. Calvin and Wm. R. King (not a member,) were appointed a committee to correspond with ministers with a view of getting a pastor."

July 17.—"*Resolved*, That the past action of the church providing for finishing the chapel and liquidating the indebtedness of the church by assessment be rescinded, and that a subscription be started immediately for finishing the church as soon as possible."

Aug. 9th, '54.—The Auditing Committee reported.

"The committee have examined the accounts of the Building Committee and find—

Paid on subscriptions - - - - - -	$865 96
Raised by loans - - - - - - - -	2,275 00
Total -	$3,140 96

Amount collectable on subscriptions - - -	$1,336 50
The debt of the church exceed, the amount pledged and collectable on subscriptions - - - - -	1,000 00
The amount expended on the chapel - - -	3,287 49

Accepted as a report of progress."

During the three months following his resignation, Eld. Ladley, according to agreement, performed the pastoral duties; and a revival interest continued. Three persons united with the church in August, and on the first Sabbath in September, the last of his pastoral labors with this society, there was a baptismal season.

It is true, that a very few persons had privately whispered, even before the resignation of Eld. Ladley, that the church ought to have a more learned and eloquent minister; but these things came mostly from persons who did not belong to the church.

Austin Craig being now at Mr. Mann's, "the Committee on Pastor" had an interview with him, but for some reason, no engagement was made.

Dec. 16*th*, '54.—Professor Thomas Holmes was unanimously elected pastor of the church for one year, and commenced immediately to discharge the duties of his office.

A number of persons not belonging to the church desired to have a society formed in connection with the church, of which they could be members and thus have a voice in the election of the pastor and in the transaction of other business. They pretended however that they did not desire to take away from the church her rights; but wished to aid in paying the debt on the chapel, and would do so, if a society could be formed to which they could belong. Perhaps there were some few members of the church who favored these views. Be that as it may, the subject was presented to the church, and on Jan'y. 20th Professor Holmes, S. Winans, S. O. Calvin, J. F. Crist and John Wharton were chosen "a committee to inquire whether it would be expedient or not to organize a Christian association or society in connection with this church; and if so, by what means."

On February 17, 1855, the committee made a report through their chairman, Prof. Holmes, which was accepted, and which we would give in full, did our limits allow. We extract briefly:

"After prayerfully and thoroughly considering the subject, 'they say that they have unanimously agreed upon their report.' They speak of the great interests involved in the subject, and then——. 'While, on the one hand, it is desirable to use every means that the Great Head of the Church will approve, to interest the minds of all, both in their own salvation and in the support and advancement of Christianity on the earth, it is also the opinion of the committee that the church should never become so linked with the world, either as individuals or as a body, as to be limited in the freedom of her action, biased in her judgment, or clipped in her energies by such union."

"Our aim, in the discharge of the duties assigned us, has been to ascertain, if possible, whether any union at all is desirable, and if so, on what principles it can be effected, so that it may be advantageous to both parties and injurious to neither. The result of our deliberations is embodied in the following recommendations—viz.:

I. "That a society be formed in connection with this church, to be called the First Christian Society in Yellow Springs, Ohio.

II. "That the following principles be regarded as fundamental and unalterable in the organization:

1st. "That the members of the church be members of the Society.

2d. "That any person who is not a member of the church may become a member of the society by making arrangements with the proper officers for a seat in the Meeting House.

3d. "That each member of the society have the privilege of casting one vote on all questions of general interest to the society, except in making choice of a pastor, which shall be done by vote of the church only."

The committee then goes on at considerable length to speak of the various considerations which have influenced them to the above conclusions, mentioning the various advantages which will result from such a society to those who are not members of the church, and also those which will doubtless accrue to the church herself; and in conclusion says:

"The committee would further add—It has been thought by some (principally, no doubt, by A. S. Dean and others not members,) that the members of the society should have some voice in the selection of a pastor. On this point, without discussing the question at length, we will simply state that, in our opinion, that step is of doubtful expediency at any time, and that this church at least is not prepared to take it.

"All of which is respectfully submitted, by

Committee, { "THOMAS HOLMES and others."

March 3d, 1855.—"*Resolved*, To authorize the Building Committee to borrow money to meet the liabilities of the church the present year."

"*Resolved*, That each member of the church be requested to present his tax receipt or receipts for the past year to the church clerk, who shall enter the several amounts on the church book, which amounts shall form a basis on which we severally agree to be assessed to raise a sum of money, which, in connection with subscriptions already pledged, shall be sufficient to complete the Christian Meeting House in this place."

March 17.—"Took up the report of the Committee on forming a Christian society in connection with this church, when, after mature deliberation, it was adopted."

"Appointed Prof. Holmes, Prof. McKinney and Eld. Ladley, a committee to prepare a constitution for the society."

"Prof. Holmes, in consequence of his being about to depart for Europe, offered his resignation as pastor, which was accepted, to take effect at the time of his departure from the place."

March 19.—J. F. Crist and F. Applegate were appointed to see Eld. N. Summerbell on the subject of becoming our pastor. R. Edmunds was also appointed to see Eld. J. B. Weston on same subject.

March 24.—"R. Edmunds reported that he had seen Eld. J. B. Weston; that he would, after the next Sabbath, preach for us until the next fellowship meeting; and then, if the church desired it, he would become pastor for $240 per annum, $20 to be paid him monthly." Accepted.

The following preamble and resolution were adopted:

"*Whereas*, The present Building Committee are inefficient in taking that interest in prosecuting the work on our new chapel that we would have them do; therefore be it

"*Resolved*, That we appoint D. Jewell, W. R. King and A. S. Dean as an addition to the present Building Committee, and that those members of said committee who will not act, be respectfully requested to resign. And be it further

"*Resolved*, That said Building Committee be and that they hereby are respectfully, but as earnestly, requested to borrow, on the most favorable terms, all the money necessary, and to vigorously prosecute the work of our new chapel to completion."

"Appointed J. B. Weston, Horace Mann and E. Lawrence to ascertain whether our previous committee have made a draft of a constitution for our proposed Christian society; if they have, to obtain it; if not, to make one; and, in either case, to report at an adjourned meeting, to be held on the 7th proximo, at half-past 2 o'clock P. M."

Mr. Lawrence had, however, decidedly opposed the formation of any such society at a previous meeting, and would not serve upon the committee.

The meeting at which the above resolutions were passed was, no doubt, composed chiefly of persons not belonging to the church; at least, it was controlled by them.

The Building Committee originally consisted of five members of the church, and as it was appointed soon after the church was organized, it was composed of Western men. Since that time quite a number of persons from a distance, and especially from the East, have removed to this place, and a part of them become connected with the church. Two of the five members of the Building Committee had resigned some time previously; and it would appear, from the above preamble, that some individuals now regarded the committee as "inefficient," and were determined to effect a reform by making an addition to said committee of three individuals who were not members of the church. (Two of the three, Messrs. Jewell and King, joined said church afterwards.) These reformers also seemed to be in favor of "*borrowing money*," the very thing which has so troubled the church and cursed Antioch College! Is it not always easier to raise money from the public for the purpose of completing a church or college edifice than, after its completion, to raise funds to replace borrowed capital?

Having thus "doctored up" the Building Committee, they turn their attention immediately to the "Committee to Prepare a Constitution for the Christian Society," which was appointed only seven days before; and before said committee had time to draft a constitution or make a report it is superseded by a new one, composed of Messrs. Weston, Mann and Lawrence.

Thus summarily are two important committees "cared for;" the one placed under the generalship of A. S. Dean, the other under the guidance of Horace Mann! Is any one, therefore, surprised that some feeling should have arisen between Western and Eastern people?

Officiousness in any individual is *unpleasant*, in whatever part of the world he may have been born and educated.

Some of the Building Committee thus enlarged, and others, held an informal meeting on the evening of the 3d of April, and, after a lengthy discussion on the propriety of selling "the pews in our chapel," they passed the following:

"*Resolved*, That we sell the pews of the First Christian Church at Yellow Springs, O., to raise means to complete the edifice and liquidate the present debt; and that a committee be appointed to appraise the value of said slips and take means to raise funds immediately."

"A. S. Dean, F. Applegate and John Layton were appointed said committee."

Of this committee Messrs. Dean and Layton were not members of the church, and, on this account, Mr. Layton declined serving, but they would not excuse him. His objections were overruled.

Four days later, April 7, the church held a meeting, J. B. Weston presiding.

"The Committee on Constitution for Christian Society asked further time in which to report. Granted."

"The minutes of the informal meeting above spoken of were now read, and the action of said meeting was approved and adopted."

"Voted to rescind the resolution passed on the 3d ult., on assessment by tax-receipts, and discharge the committee acting under it."

Two days later, April 9, the church held another meeting, J. B.

Weston presiding ; and, after the minutes had been read and approved, a protest against selling the pews was presented, signed by 32 persons, most of whom were members of the church, and all of them of the Christian denomination.

They considered the recent action of the church on this subject "as an infringement of their rights and liberties as members of the Christian Church and Denomination," and based their protest on various reasons, one of which was that such a sale would be "a wrong to those who have already subscribed to the building, under the impression that it was to be a free house," and ended in these words : "For these and other reasons which might be named, we do hereby, in the name of God, enter our solemn protest against the said resolution, and earnestly request the church to rescind the same, or, in case of refusal to do so, to enter this, our protest, on the records of the church."

"The church refused to reconsider the resolution to sell our pews," and several of the members withdrew immediately from the organization. The protest, with names of the signers, was, according to request, entered on church records.

Two days later still, April 11, the church took up the resolution offered by D. C. Orr at the previous meeting and laid upon the table, and, after amending it to read as follows, adopted it—viz. :

"*Resolved*, That, in selling our pews, our deeds for the same shall secure to the purchaser only the right to occupy the seat for purposes of worship, but no right to remove, to close it, or to prohibit others from occupying it in his absence or that of his family, and that, in choosing a pastor for this church, each pew-holder or lessee, and each church member, shall be allowed to cast one vote and but one, provided always that the person voted for shall be a regularly ordained minister in good standing in the Christian denomination."

"*Resolved*, That a proviso, embracing the principles of the above resolution, be incorporated in the deeds for the pews ; and also a proviso that the pew shall be liable to assessment for all the expenses of the church, in proportion to its valuation."

"*Resolved*, That the pews of our chapel be sold at public auction, at a price not less than their appraised value."

"Adjourned to 7 o'clock P. M. of the 14th inst., for the selling of pews." "D. C. ORR, Cl'k."

April 14, 1855.—The church met according to adjournment.

"The Committee on Appraisement reported that they had discharged their duty, the value of the seats being, in the aggregate, $5,690, every fifth pew being reserved for public use." Approved.

"Voted that the payment for pews be made in five monthly instalments, beginning with the 1st of May. If the money be not paid when due, to bear 10 per cent. interest ; if paid before due, to be discounted at the rate of 10 per cent. per annum."

"*Resolved*, That each pew-holder and lessee shall have a right to vote on the question of settling a minister, and on all questions respecting the assessment of taxes, and that no tax shall be levied on any person who has not had a right to vote on assessing it, except such person may have forfeited his right by some neglect of his own."

Proceeded, after passing several other resolutions, to sell pews.

It should be noticed that the leading advocates of selling and deeding away the pews, Horace Mann, A. S. Dean, Wm. R. King, D. Jewell, &c., were not then members of the church, except Mr. Mann!

Would any other business corporation, whether manufacturing, railroad, or banking, have allowed outsiders to meddle with its affairs, to draft resolutions, and then vote for them? We think not; and are also of the opinion that a church should manage her own business.

On April 21st the sale of pews was continued; and at the church meeting April 28th "the Committee on Sale of Pews" reported; and were instructed to continue their labors.

"The Committee to draft a Constitution for the proposed Christian Society made a report of progress and asked further time." Granted.

A resolution was now passed rescinding "the resolution making the pew-holders and lessees of pews liable to taxation to defray the expenses of worship in the Christian Church;" "and that those who have heretofore contributed or subscribed for building the house be allowed to take no more than one pew each on said contribution or subscription; and that the balance of said contribution or subscription be left in the hands of, or paid to, the Building Committee to assist in finishing the house."

"A sub-committee was appointed by the Building Committee, consisting of A. G. Kiler, John Kershner, Wm. R. King, also David Jewell, to push on the work on our new chapel."

"Horace Mann and John A. Layton were added to the Building Committee." Mr. Layton not being a member of the church and believing that church *members* should transact their own business, refused to serve.

"The Committee to draft a Constitution for the proposed Christian Society" has made no further report down to the present day! and wyh? Had not the advocates of said "society" obtained all they desired, and in another direction?

They had succeeded in carrying through resolutions authorizing a sale of the church pews, and in disposing of some $3,600 worth; they had obtained the right also of voting for the pastor, a privilege which would have doubtless been denied them as members of the proposed "society;" and finally they had succeeded in rescinding the former resolutions making their "pews liable to taxation to defray the expenses of worship in the Christian Church!"

Of course they did not now desire "a Christian society."

The church, June 16th, instructed the "Trustees to give the Building Committee such security against loss in completing our chapel as shall be required by them," also instructed the Corresponding Committee to write to Eld. Summerbell and endeavor to obtain his services as pastor.

Aug. 18*th.*—"The Committee on Procuring a Pastor reported that Eld. Summerbell had been employed to serve as pastor for *nine* months at least, at a salary of $600 per annum."

Nov. 13*th,* 1855.—Mrs. Summerbell reported to the church, $27,25 paid on a subscription to purchase a "communion service," &c., and $26,93 expended, as per bills, for said articles, and the balance of 32 cents transferred to "the subscription for furnishing the pulpit up stairs," all of which is respectfully submitted to the church by

Nov. 8th, 1855. Mrs. SUMMERBELL.

On Nov. 19th the church "voted that Bro. A. G. Kiler, with Wm. M. King, as his assistant proceed immediately to collect the moneys due on the sale of the pews."

"Voted that the Building Committee continue the sale of the pews."

On examination, it was found that only about $1,000 out of the sale of the pews was available; about $500 worth having been taken by irresponsible persons, and the remainder on the contributions of persons who had subscribed and paid considerable amounts towards the building; and of the $1,000 available funds, Messrs. Kiler and King could not collect one dollar!

Such was the practical end of the magnificent (?) plan for selling and deeding away the church pews!

April 5th, 1856.—Mrs. Summerbell reported that $146,75 had been raised for a furnace for the chapel, and $145,71 paid out, as per bills, for said furnace and fixtures; also that $50,07 cash had been raised for furnishing the pulpit, which, with the balance of the subscription for furnace paid and unpaid, left considerably over $50 cash for furnishing the pulpit, which—"I now hereby deliver to the church and desire that a committee be appointed to procure furniture for the pulpit as designed by the subscription. Respectfully submitted,

Mrs. E. J. SUMMERBELL."

Mrs. S.'s report was heard, and received by the unanimous vote of the members present.

"*Resolved,* That a vote of thanks be tendered to Mrs. Summerbell for the faithful and efficient manner in which she has performed her duties as per reports." Adopted.

"*Resolved,* That a committee of three be appointed to furnish the pulpit, &c."

Committee appointed—Mrs. Summerbell, Mrs. Applegate, Mrs. Crist.

The business before the house now being in reference to procuring a future pastor, Eld. Summerbell "made some very appropriate remarks" touching his connection with the church, and giving the members excellent advice in reference to their future action.

It was then moved that—

"*Whereas*, The pulpit of the Christian Church of Yellow Springs will be vacated on the first day of May next; therefore be it

Resolved, That we cordially invite "Eld. Austin Craig" to become our pastor, and that a committee of three be appointed to inform him of this request.

Vote was taken—Aff. 20—Neg. 2.

Committee appointed—Horace Mann, John Kershner, J. F. Crist.

"It was then moved by A. S. Dean that the following resolution be adopted—

Resolved, That this church is greatly indebted to Eld. Summerbell for its present prosperity, and that we hereby tender to him our sincere thanks for his faithful labors while among us, and that we believe any church will be exceedingly fortunate and greatly blessed that procures his labors as a pastor. And we will ever pray for his welfare and prosperity wherever in God's providence his lot may be cast."

The resolution was unanimously adopted.

It may not be improper to state here that some two months before Eld. Summerbell's time expired, a secret meeting of a few individuals was held to make arrangements for procuring another pastor; and Wm. M. King took around a subscription paper to a few families to raise a salary for Austin Craig!

These transactions were conducted so privately that Eld. Summerbell knew nothing of them until Eld. Craig himself called on him and revealed them.

Of course Eld. S. could not then consent to a re-engagement with the church however much his services might have been desired; for he remarked that he never had preached and never could preach to a church where a single vote of any influential member was against him.

Accordingly he began to make preparations for his departure as soon as his nine months should expire. Eld. S. had, it is true, intended to make a tour through the West in the summer of 1856, yet as he came to Yellow Springs, partly on account of the educational advantages of the place, he would doubtless have been pleased to remain had church and college affairs moved along pleasantly and prosperously.

Eld. S. however saw clearly that Antioch College was far from what the Christians had intended it should be; and this was the principal reason why he had so often refused to act as an agent of the College to secure moneys and subscriptions. He was offered a large salary if he would act as an agent, but he could not conscientiously labor in such a capacity. He did not wish to be instrumental in obtaining large sums of money from our churches for Antioch and then see the institution wrested totally and forever from their control.

Some months after the departure of Eld. S., in a hastily-called meeting of the church, Jan'y 19th, 1857, during the debate on the question of engaging Eli Fay as pastor, a gentleman remarked that the church had greatly missed it in allowing Eld. S. to leave Yellow Springs, when Wm. M. King somewhat excited jumped up and said—"We did not keep Eld. Summerbell because he set himself against Antioch College, and we want a pastor who will co-operate with it!" But A. S. Dean immediately checked him and thus the further revelations of a wire-working faction were suppressed! It is true that on one occasion in church meeting, when Mr. Mann declared that Antioch is no more the college of the Christians than of any other denomination, Eld. Summerbell arose immediately and said that that statement was not correct; that the Christian denomination, in their general U. S. Convention at Marion, N. Y., in 1850, had founded Antioch College; and although the institution is not what the Christians intended it should be, yet it is theirs *in name*, and should be theirs *in verity*.

Mr. Mann then arose, and with that adroitness in helping himself out of a bad position for which he is so celebrated, blandly remarked that he must have been misunderstood; that all he meant by his former remarks was that the views and doctrines of the Christians were not taught in the college, any more than those of other religious denominations!

Thus fox-ily was that corner turned; yet some could penetrate beneath the surface!

Was Eld. Summerbell's correction of an inaccurate statement "setting himself against Antioch College?" Because Eld. S. did not say amen to all the transactions and influences at the college, was he, therefore, opposed to Antioch as intended by the Christians at the Marion Convention? Who believes that Eld. Summerbell has not at heart the highest educational interests of the Christians?

May 16, 1856.—A committee was chosen "to fix the time of dedication of our new chapel, and make the necessary arrangements for the same.."

Committee,	Horace Mann,	J. Kershner,
	J. F. Crist,	A. G. Kiler,
	Wm. R. King,	A. S. Dean.

Mr. Crist said that the object of this meeting was not only to make some arrangements for dedicating the chapel, but to see how funds can be raised. Mr. Mann remarked that the pews were sold ; that he had one ; and that it could not be taken from him except by process of law. Mr. Kiler said that the pew was not his (Mann's,) for he had *not taken possession* of it. They did not agree on arrangements to raise money. Mr. Kiler declined serving on the committee ; said he should be absent during the summer. Mr. Crist, however, told Mr. Kiler before he left town that a collection should be taken up on dedication day ; but when the time came he sided with Mr. Mann, and no collection was allowed to be taken.

Six days later this committee reported that they had fixed on the second Sabbath in June for the dedication, and that they had invited the Rev. Austin Craig to preach the dedication sermon.

Horace Mann and Prof. Doherty were appointed to assist in the services of the occasion.

Prof. Doherty declined taking any part in the matter.

On account of engagements to visit churches and friends in Ohio, and preparations for his journey, Eld. Summerbell had not yet left Yellow Springs for the far West ; and, although he had labored zealously and successfully for the church during the previous nine months, and received forty members into the church, although Mrs. Summerbell, of her own good will and unappointed, had raised more than $200 towards furnishing the chapel comfortably and elegantly ; and although they both had labored night and day to edify, instruct and build up the church, yet now another man was engaged to preach the dedication sermon and Horace Mann his assistant !

Yet a large majority of the church, it is thought, were highly pleased with the ministrations of Eld. S., and were, without doubt, desirous that he should not only be re-engaged but preach the dedication sermon.

Why, then, asks the reader was he not engaged ? We answer, for the very practical (if not good) reason that in our churches and all other democratic bodies a few men, and often a very few, take the lead and control the transactions. Where these few are men of sound practical sense and stern integrity as well as of intelligence it is well, but when they are time-serving and designing, then woe to majorities as well as to minorities !

Just as Eld. Summerbell was finally leaving town Mr. Mann sends him a letter saying, that if any storm or unpleasant result had followed from anything which he had said or done he was sorry for it, &c.

Thus Eld. S., one of our most reliable and successful ministers, was allowed to leave our community, and many were the hearts made sad by his departure, many the regrets and prayers that followed him.

Had the above resolution, offered by A. S. Dean and voted for by him and his co-workers—"That we believe the church will be exceedingly fortunate and greatly blessed that procures his labors as a pastor," been *really* the sentiment of their hearts, Eld. S. might doubtless be with us to day.

We trust that the concluding portion of said resolution—"And we will ever pray for his welfare and prosperity," &c., is not wholly a mockery with those who held that "secret meeting," and desired the absence of Eld. Summerbell because "he set himself against Antioch College."

Why must the residence of our true and reliable ministers in Yellow Springs be so brief? Is it on account of worldly ambition and irreligion?

In the church meeting of May 16th—

"The motion to rescind all former acts in relation to the sale of pews was laid upon the table."

J. F. Crist was appointed a committee to call on all pew-holders and learn their wishes concerning the pews.

A committee of three was appointed to present a plan for the reduction of the present debt.

Committee, { Wm. R. King, J. Wharton, Jesse Jacobs.

May 22d.—Mr. Crist reported that he had seen a majority of the pew-holders and that "all felt willing to acquiesce in whatever the church saw fit to do in the premises." Adopted.

The Committee on "Plan for the Reduction of Present Debt" reported that if "a majority of those who had purchased pews be in favor of surrendering their claims to said pews the balance be respectfully invited to do so; but in case any refuse to surrender their claims to their pews, that they be allowed to hold them on the former sale, and that they be subject to all the rules and regulations that have been heretofore made in reference to the taxing of the pews." They also recommend "that all the pews, excepting those reserved as above, be leased for one year, and that the lessees be taxed on the amount of rent they pay, in the same manner and for the same purposes that pew-owners are taxed, and that they have the same privileges in all respects as pew-owners." * * *

"Your committee would recommend the leasing of the pews for one year at least, as many of the students would like to rent a pew who would not, under any circumstances, purchase one." * * * Adopted.

Mr. Jacobs had no hand in getting up the above report, and when it was presented he opposed it.

"It was then *Resolved*, That W. R. King, John Wharton and J. C. Burghdurf be a committee to request all those who have purchased pews in this church to relinquish the same, and likewise to fix the price for which each pew ought to be rented, and report at the next meeting of this church." Carried.

May 31*st*.—The Committee on Renting the Church Pews reported that they had appraised the value of the slips for leasing, having laid the highest priced ones at $30, and the lowest at $15.

Adopted, { 11 Yeas, 1 Nay.

The same committee was instructed to superintend the renting of the pews.

On the second Sabbath in June the Dedicatory Services were held, Eld. Walter being present and assisting. Mr. Mann read portions of scripture; Prof. A. L. McKinney made the dedication prayer; and Eld. Craig delivered the discourse; and, strange to relate, the only allusion to the great subject of the occasion was made in the dedicating prayer. The discourse seemed to be very ill chosen for such an occasion, and deeply injured the feelings of some. Eld. Walter was sorely grieved, not only on account of the sermon, but because no collection was taken towards paying the debt on the house. When Eld. Walter arrived in the morning, just before the exercises were to commence, and learned that the Committee of Arrangements had decided not to have a collection taken up, he was on the point of returning to Springfield immediately, but was finally prevailed on to remain. As it was well known that the chapel was not paid for, many men came from a distance with considerable sums of money in their pockets to aid in making up a large contribution for the church. Some would have given $100 each, some $50 each, and others smaller sums; and it was found, by an after estimate, that some $1,500 (enough to cancel at that time one half of the debt,) might have been realized on that occasion had an opportunity been given.

But the reader asks why was not such opportunity given and the money received? Simply because Horace Mann, A. S. Dean and W. R. King opposed it. John Kershner was very urgent that a collection should be taken up, and so was Mr. Kiler, but he was absent, and, of course, could not vote. He, however, sent over some men of means, from the section of country where he was, to aid in making up a liberal donation for the liquidation of the church debt.

Why were their gifts not received?

The only reason known why Mr. Mann opposed the taking of a collection is the one which he then assigned—viz: "That it would not do to speak of money matters on that occasion, for it would hurt Eld. Craig's feelings (?)" and yet, on the next morning, Mr. Craig desired $50 for his services!

Perhaps it is not generally known that it is customary, in many parts of the West, to take up collections on dedication days; and, had the money been received at this time, the chapel would long since have been freed from debt.

July 12th.—Mr. Mann, Chairman of "the Committee on Pastor," reported that he had received letters both from Eld. A. Craig and from his church, but they were not considered favorable to his coming immediately.

"Report received and committee discharged."

A proposition from Prof. A. L. McKinney was laid before the church, when it was—

Resolved, That we accept the proposition of Eld. McKinney to supply our pulpit to the 1st of September next ensuing.

Jesse Jacobs, D. F. Ladley and J. C. Burghdurf were appointed a committee "to correspond with such ministers as the church shall designate" for the purpose of obtaining a permanent pastor.

Resolved, That the Building Committee make a full and complete report of all the dues and outstanding debts of the church one week from to-day."

July 19th.—"*Resolved,* That the Committee on Renting the Pews be discharged."

In the latter part of July another effort was made by subscription to liquidate the church debt; but, as several of the men of property only subscribed $1,250, the matter was abandoned.

The statistics of the church, as furnished to Conference, Aug., 1856:

Delegates, { R. Edmunds, A. L. McKinney.

Whole number of members	129
Additions the past year by letter	16
On confession of faith in Christ	23
Removed by death	1
" by commendation	11

Prof. McKinney's temporary engagement with the church closed on the 1st of Sept., after which the pulpit was vacant for some Sabbaths.

Prof. Doherty regretting this state of affairs gave out an appointment early in October, and preached a very pointed sermon, sharply rebuking the church for her follies, for her lack of stability and commercial integrity, and exhorting her to a more zealous, consistent and complete life in the future.

After the discourse he made a proposition to the church, the substance of which was that he would supply the pulpit for one year, two sermons each Sabbath, if at least $400 could be raised and paid quarterly in advance; that his engagements were such at the College that he could not perform all the duties of regular pastor; that he should regard the arrangement as temporary, and would, consequently, give way at any time during the year when the church might obtain a good, permanent pastor.

Professor Doherty's proposition was accepted, and a committee, consisting of Prof. Allen, J. C. Burghdurf, and A. G. Kiler, appointed to carry out the arrangement.

About $300 was subscribed on the spot, and the amount of pledges very quickly ran up to $516, which the committee thought sufficient and accordingly made no further solicitations.

The church and friends appeared to be highly pleased with the ministrations of Bro. Doherty, and all things moved quietly on and in order. The audiences were large, the chapel being sometimes filled to its utmost capacity.

A social "Tea Party" was given in the church by the choir, at which sweet music was discoursed and speeches made, for the purpose of raising funds to pay the chorister, sexton and other church expenses. It was largely attended by nearly all the leading citizens of the place with their families, and was highly successful.

The Committee on Pastorate, above mentioned, had been in correspondence with several of our ministers to procure a permanent pastor, and reported Jan'y. 3d, 1857. The report was accepted and the committee instructed to write to certain other ministers, which was immediately attended to.

But a few days later Mr. A. S. Dean brought on Eld. E. Fay from N. Y. City, and took him around calling on some members of the church and others hinting that his services could be had as pastor, &c. Some four years previous Mr. Fay had preached for a time to the First Christian Church of N. Y. city, and then became interested in a Water Cure establishment up town, listened to discourses by Bellows, Chapin and other liberal divines, and engaged in writing his "Incognito" articles.

Thus after driving "water cure," "sermon listening" and the "Incognito quill" for considerable time he concludes to sell out his city interests, comes to Yellow Springs under the wing of A. S. Dean, and after some days labor, it is said, in making calls, and buying or attempting to buy some votes, they finally succeed in obtaining a call for a church meeting.

Wm. R. King was deeply interested in securing Eld. Fay as pastor, and on Sunday, Jan'y 11th, endeavored to have a church meeting called for Monday evening, the 12th inst.; but the Standing Committee on Pastor sent a notice to Prof. Doherty that they were not ready to report, and he accordingly did not comply with Mr. King's request.

Another week passed by, during which Mr. Fay and friends were busy in electioneering.

On Sabbath evening, Jan'y 18th, before church service commenced, Mr. King was on hand zealous for Mr. Fay.

Two notices were handed to Eld. Doherty to be read, one by King requesting a church meeting on the following evening, Jan'y 19th; the other stating that the Committee on Pastor was not ready to make a report, but would be, a few days later, at the regular monthly meeting of the church. Prof. Doherty remarked that the notices conflicted. Mr. King then arose and said that there would be a meeting the following evening, and that it was necessary that the Committee on Pastor be present and report.

On Monday evening, 16 members of the church and several outsiders came together.

The Committee on Pastorate was called on for a report. They said they could now only report that they had written to all the ministers with whom the church had directed them to correspond, that some whom they had lately addressed had not yet replied, but they were expecting letters from them in a very few days; and further that none had refused to come, who had replied. Notwithstanding this report the committee was discharged!

Wm. R. King then presented Eld. Fay's proposition to become pastor of the church, which was as follows:

"That he would take the pastoral charge of the church for one year, for the sum of $800, and in the event the pews should be sold, he would buy a pew for the 'pastor's pew;' and if the pews should not be sold he would donate $100 to the church."

An objection was made to taking any vote on such a question that evening, for many members of the church were not aware of the meeting. Mr. A. S. Dean replied that he had attended a great many meetings of the church, and there were as many members present that evening as he had ever seen at a business meeting; that they might have been there if they would, that they did know of the meeting for he had seen as many as 40 of them that day, and if they were not present it was their own fault!

The question then arose as to who should vote, church members only or all persons present? Some insisted that only members of the church should vote.

Mr. A. S. Dean said he was not a member of this church, but he was a member of the denomination, and he should claim the right to vote; said he had always taken a deep interest in this church, done a great deal (?) for it, and he ought not to be denied the right of voting! Still objections were made.

Eld. A. Coburn (then connected with the College) said he was not a member of the church, but he desired a vote, and thought he should have that right.

The debate continued for some time, but was finally ended by passing a resolution—"That all present be permitted to vote on this question at this time."

It was then desired that Mr. Fay should enter upon the pastoral office immediately, as Prof. Doherty had only just commenced his second quarter of three months, and that the money raised for Mr. Doherty go towards making up Eld. Fay's salary. This met with decided opposition. It was said, that the ministrations of Prof. Doherty are highly satisfactory, that he has already entered upon his second quarter, and that Mr. Fay, if elected at all, could not commence before the 1st of April.

In order, therefore, to avoid a total defeat, Mr. Mann moved an amendment—that we employ Mr. Fay for three months on trial, to commence the 1st of April, and at the rate of $800 per annum.

It was urged, that three months are a very short time; and at its expiration, if you do not like Eld. Fay, you need not re-appoint him! But even this was objected to. The friends of Mr. Fay then said that it is highly desirable to clear the church of the heavy debt resting upon it, and recommended Eld. F. as an excellent hand to raise money, saying that if he should be elected pastor the debt could easily be paid off!

A. S. Dean said that Eld. Bryant was accustomed to write his sermons and consequently would not suit the Western people; that Eld. Fay on the contrary always spoke extemporaneously! that he was also an adept in raising money, and was just the man for the place.

The payment of the debt was certainly very much desired, and if Eld.

Fay is so skilled in obtaining money, some of the church members thought that they had better perhaps try him for three months.

The amendment or second proposition was therefore put, and the result was

For Mr. Fay or the amendment,

1st - - - - the outsiders,
2d - - - - 10 church members.

Against Mr. Fay or the amendment, 6 church members.

"*Resolved*, That Messrs. Mann and Dean be a committee to wait on Eld. Fay and report the proceedings of the church." Meeting adjourned.

And thus it was asserted that "the church" had elected Mr. Fay pastor, when only a part of the members were advised of the meeting; and when out of more than 100 members only 16 were present, and when of these 16 (the portion of the church most favorable to Mr. Fay) only 10 voted for him!

The whole proceedings were hasty, if not ungenerous and unchristian; for only one day's notice was given, and this not general; and the meeting called on an evening, of all the week, perhaps the most unsuitable for a gathering of church members, many of whom live two or three miles in the country! Who could not obtain an election under such circumstances?

Jan. 31, 1857.—"The church met in its monthly meeting."

"Two letters, one from Eld. Goff and one from Eld. Fanton, were presented and read." "The clerk was directed to write in answer to these letters and inform them (the writers) that we have obtained a pastor."

"The committee to wait on Eld. Fay and inform him of the action of the previous meeting—Reported *that he gladly received the appointment!*"

Mr. Fay knowing that Eld. I. Goff of New Jersey had been written to on the subject of the pastorate of the church, goes out and calls on him at Irvington, and after some conversation on the subject, tells him that he (Fay) has concluded not to go to Yellow Springs as pastor of the church on account of the strong opposition to him.

Eld. Goff then writes to Eld. Ladley saying that if desired he will be at Yellow Springs and preach on the first and second Sabbaths in April.

Eld. Ladley replies recommending him not to come in April, for Eld. Fay has been elected three months on trial, to commence with April; but that the brethren and friends will be happy to receive a visit from him if he can come before Professor Doherty's engagement closes.

March 5th, 1857.—On motion of A. S. Dean—

"*Resolved,* That the church proceed forthwith to a sale of its pews; but in no case for less than the former appraisement."

"*Resolved,* That every pew-holder or lessee of a pew for a term if not less than one year, be entitled to vote in the choice of a pastor, provided no person shall be voted for who is not in good standing in the Christian Church."

"*Resolved,* That the Building Committee sell the pews."

"*Resolved,* That the first Saturday in April, at 2 o'clock, be appointed to sell the pews!"

Notwithstanding Mr. Fay's statements to Eld. Goff, he came to Yellow Springs and commenced his labors on the first Sabbath in April; and soon the church members began to disappear, and the chapel to fill up with new classes of people.

He started out with two subscription papers, on one of which persons favorable to selling the pews were to sign, and on the other those who desired a free house.

On June 28th, Sabbath, Mr. Fay announced to the audience that the term for which he had been appointed as pastor expired that day, and his name could go before them for re-election only on one condition—viz., that all persons who attend worship here, whether members of the church or not, have the right to vote!

After the discourse the audience was requested to remain, Mr. Mann was called to the chair, and suggested the propriety of appointing a Secretary. A. S. Dean moved that a Secretary be appointed; but as the regular church clerk was present, Mr. W. R. King moved an amendment—that the church clerk act as clerk.

The following resolutions were then passed:

"*Resolved,* That we are satisfied with the labors of Eld. E. Fay."

"*Resolved,* That we appoint Eld. E. Fay as pastor for an indefinite time according to his former proposition, with the understanding that if either the church or Eld. Fay desires a change the one party shall notify the other at least three months before the change shall take place."

What insincerity! what double-dealing is here manifested!

These resolutions were passed by the audience or congregation under the direction of Messrs. Mann, Dean and King, and yet there are only two parties, "the church" and "Eli Fay!"

Mr. Fay would not allow his name to be used by the church for re-election, but only by the congregation, and yet the church, and the church *only,* is made responsible to Mr. Fay!

Two questions at least naturally suggest themselves here—

1st. Did not Mr. Fay fear to trust his name with the church for re-election?

2d. Did not Mr. Fay desire to make a corporate body responsible for his salary ?

But few church members were present at this church meeting ; for Mr. Fay had "lectured" them nearly all away, and most of those present on this occasion left after the discourse, offended at Mr. Fay's singular proposition! Some had heard him lecture but once, others twice or three times; yet that was enough to convince them that his so-called sermons contained something other than Bible doctrine. Some went to the Presbyterian church, others to the Methodist service and others still to the Ebenezar Christian Church, three miles out of town.

Still a few attended Mr. Fay's meetings occasionally, and were present on this occasion ; but they were sorely offended by the extraordinary proceedings, by his ignoring the church, and committing everything into the hands of the congregation, and after all that, by making the church, and the church alone, responsible to the congregation's preacher.

The church clerk resigned and requested a letter of dismission from the church, and others either remained at home or attended other meetings.

July 4th.—Eld. D. F. Ladley was appointed church clerk in place of Jesse Jacobs resigned.

Voted, to furnish a letter of dismission and commendation to Bro. Jacobs according to his request.

Thus things moved on! and why not ? Those who failed in Jan. to look behind the unnaturally eager countenance of certain individuals, and penetrate beneath the surface of things, were now led to ask themselves some questions, when it was known that Mr. Fay had loaned considerable sums of money to Messrs. Dean and King, and that Antioch College had been wrested from the Christian Denomination, and all the College property assigned.

Eli Fay seemed to be one of Mr. Mann's principal instruments in college transactions ; and why should he not be in church affairs ?

Why should not the Christian Church be reformed as well as Antioch College. Why should not the Christian Church be merged into the audience or congregation, no matter how wicked and profane, as well as "the College of the Christians" into the latitudinarean or infidelic element ?

The Christian Church (it is asserted) is behind the age; is old-fogy-ish! She believes "the Bible to be an inspired book," "the sacred scriptures of the Old and New Testaments to be a sufficient rule of faith and practice," "Christian character to be the true test of Christian Fellowship ?"

"The Bible an inspired book?" What stupidity! So are "Campbell's Rhetoric," "Theodore Parker's Sermons," and "Comb's Constitution of Man," inspired works.

"The Bible a sufficient rule of faith and practice?" What madness! Do we not believe many things, in this enlightened age, not taught us in the Bible? and practice many things, too, for which that book gives us no direction?

We believe it our duty, therefore, to lift the church up out of this heathenish darkness, this sectarian bigotry, into the broad sun-light! and how can this be effected except by legislating for church members through the enlightened masses?

How long shall sordid interests and worldly ambition distract the church?

How long shall wolves in sheeps' clothing be permitted to scatter the flock?

Aug. 1*st.*—Appointed delegates to Conference, viz—Horace Mann, A. L. McKinney and E. Fay.

About this time Mr. Fay asked for a vacation of a few weeks, that he might rest and recruit. He said it was now fashionable in our cities for churches to grant their pastors vacations, and close their chapels during the hot season; and further that his health was giving away quite rapidly, and if he was not allowed a furlough of a few weeks, he might be under the necessity of giving up preaching altogether. He deemed it necessary to go up the lakes where he could enjoy quiet, and a bracing atmosphere!

This request appeared not a little ludicrous; for Mr. Fay had given but one discourse per week since he came to Yellow Springs; besides Yellow Springs itself is a cool and favorite summer resort for city people, and the summer months are just the season when a church edifice should be kept open!

Of course Mr. Fay's request was granted! and off he starts for Mackinac to meet Mr. Mann to complete arrangements, perhaps, for the temporary school next year, or during the suspension of the College.

Mr. Fay returned in a few weeks, refreshed and strengthened no doubt by his Northern trip, and resumed his ministerial labors again.

His audiences were made up, as before, principally of liberalists.

The spiritualists and infidels averred that Mr. Fay preached their views to their satisfaction. One man (a trustee of Antioch College) said, "I have been called an infidel for the last 12 years; but, if I am an infidel, Fay is, for he preaches just what I believe."

Mr. Fay occasionally quoted the Bible to sustain his views, and sometimes used the word "church," especially when he desired to misrepresent and defame the different denominations of Christians.

He neglected the ordinances, "Baptism" and the "Lord's Supper," and received no members into the church!

His great effort seemed to be to vilify the leading Evangelical Churches including our own; to tear down rather than build up; to say something new and startling to the audience, in fine to preach up "the development theory" or "rationalism."

Will such preaching save souls from everlasting perdition?

Oct. 3d—After the monthly meeting the Building Committee met Mr. Fay in Mr. Crist's store to consider the Church Finances.

Eld. Fay was asked how much he had, subscribed for the payment of the church debt.

He said between $3,000 and $4,000. This report was highly encouraging, and although time was passing and the debt increasing at 10 per cent. interest per annum, yet they concluded to give Eld. Fay more time.

About the last of Nov., however, Mr. Kiler seeing no stir to obtain more money called on Mr. Fay to learn the amount already pledged and to see the papers himself. Mr. Fay was not at home; but Thomas Kershner obtained the papers a day or two later.

Mr. Kiler was much surprised on seeing the subscription papers, for they did not tell the same story as Mr. Fay!

As previously stated, Mr. Fay had carried around two papers, one for a free house, the other for the sale of pews. The members of the Building Committee signed $2,000 on each paper to start it. Eld. Fay had possession of said papers for more than six months, and it was now found that not a dollar had been subscribed since the preceding spring, soon after Eld. Fay started out! And further, that only $1,000 had been subscribed, outside the Building Committee, on the paper for a free house! and on the other only $400, and the price of two pews conditionally.

Thus, instead of $3,000 to $4,000 Mr. Fay had only obtained $1,000 available subscriptions, and counting the $2,000 of the Building Committee, there was only $3,000 all told! And it may here be added that Eld. Fay could not have obtained even the $1,000 of subscriptions had he not been aided by Mr. Kiler and others. The committee at once saw that the chapel would never be paid for at this rate, for the interest was accumulating at the rate of $600 per year.

On the next and last Sabbath morning in November, Mr. Kiler was met at the chapel door by W. M. King, and requested to subscribe towards the expense of printing Mr. Fay's thanksgiving sermon.

Mr. Kiler asked King what Eld. Fay was doing to raise money for the liquidation of the church debt, adding that *that* was the *first thing* to be attended to, and if Eld. Fay would raise money enough to clear the chapel of debt he would then subscribe handsomely for said sermon.

Mr. Kiler immediately stepped into the vestry and dictated to Mr. King a notice for a meeting of the Building Committee on Finance, to be held on Saturday next, December 5th, and sent it to Eld. Fay to be read after the discourse.

After service, however, Mr. Fay gave notice to the congregation that there would be a church meeting on next Saturday, and requested a full attendance of the friends, for he would then state on what terms he would continue to preach, and incidentally added that the Building Committee would also be present.

After meeting was dismissed, Messrs. Kiler and Thos. Kershner stepped into the vestry to talk a moment about church matters, and soon Eld. Fay came in. Mr. Kiler asked him how he was succeeding in obtaining subscriptions for the church. Eld. Fay replied that he could now do nothing, for the Building Committee had taken away the papers and his authority! and yet Mr. Fay had not obtained a single subscription for more than five months!

Dec. 5th, 2 o'clock P. M.—The church meeting was organized by appointing Isaac Kershner chairman, when Mr. Fay arose and made a speech of some two hours' length, in which he reviewed the circumstances of his becoming pastor and the opposition to him, and falsely accused Eld. Ladley and others of opposing his coming to Yellow Springs.

He also said he had done a great deal for the church; had obtained some $3,800 of good subscriptions for the liquidation of the church debt, &c.

Mr. Kiler having the subscription papers in his pocket requested the clerk to read them, which he did, when Eld. Fay arose to go out. Mr. Kiler earnestly requested him to remain, which finally he consented to do, when Mr. Kiler went on to show that Mr. Fay had not obtained $3,800, unless he counted both subscription lists, which was not admissable, for if the pledges on one paper are collected those on the other cannot be; and that the most that Mr. Fay had raised, aside from the Committee's subscriptions, is only $1,000, and in securing this he was aided by more than one individual!

It being now about dark the meeting adjourned to the next Saturday, the 12th inst.

Dec. 12*th*, 1857.—The First Christian Church met according to adjournment at 2 o'clock P. M., "to take into consideration the financial condition of the house and of the Building Committee in relation thereto."

Eli Fay was chosen Chairman and J. B. Weston Secretary, *pro tem*.

Mr. Kiler stated the liabilities of the Building Committee and how they were incurred—viz.: That when he was elected one of said committee and urged to accept the appointment, it was said that the debt was only $1,000, and that $3,000 had been raised by sale of pews to pay the debt and finish the house.

The Building Committee was at that time increased to ten persons, but some of them soon slipped their necks out, and the responsibilities were thrown upon four or five of them.

The debt is now $6,000. The committee are already sued for $600, and will, probably, be sued for $900 more before the 1st of April next.

The committee will be personally responsible for $2,000, and now offers the house to the church for $4,000.

If this proposition is not accepted and acted on, the committee will be obliged to close the chapel and sell it.

A. S. Dean arose and said that he did not believe the church could raise $4,000, that the only way to raise the money would be by a sale of the pews, and this he believed could be done. Indeed the pews had once been sold, and he believed that said sale was legal and is still binding. He remarked that this subject was thoroughly discussed in the spring of 1855, that he was the chairman of the committee to appraise the slips at that time and to sell them, and he would recommend the plan then adopted as the basis for present action.

The proposition to sell the pews was opposed by some, who thought that the church and friends should pay off the debt, and thus make the chapel a free house.

Mr. Fay did not believe the outsiders would subscribe for a free house; they would not pay out their money without receiving something in return; and, to obtain their aid, he would recommend the sale of the pews.

About "the church" much had been said, her ability, her numbers! but for his part, and he had taken much pains to observe, he did not believe there were 40 members all told; and, as to their ability, he could not, for the life of him, discover it! He did not believe the church could raise $4,000, and would, therefore, recommend the sale of pews.

Nearly all the members of the church were opposed to the selling of pews, and so was the Building Committee, (unless A. S. Dean be a member of said committee,) and nearly all the advocates of the measure were outsiders, or persons not connected with the church.

But the Building Committee must have money soon, or be compelled to foreclose the mortgage and sell the chapel.

They, therefore, concluded to waive their objections and make another trial of pew selling; and accordingly John Kershner moved the following:

"*Resolved*, That we recommend that funds for the payment of the debt on the Christian Chapel of Yellow Springs be raised by the sale of pews on the basis of resolutions adopted by the church in the spring of 1855, on which a former sale was made, and that a committee be appointed to appraise the pews."

A warm discussion of the resolution followed, pending which the church adjourned to meet in the vestry at 6 o'clock Monday evening, the 14th inst.

Dec. 14th.—The church met according to adjournment.

E. Fay, Chairman,
J. B. Weston, Clerk, *pro tem.*

Discussion on the preceding resolution was resumed.

Mr. A. G. Kiler stated that he wished it distinctly understood that the Building Committee would not hold themselves obligated to give deeds of pews unless the sales should amount to fully $4,000.

The resolution was amended by the movers by striking out the words —"funds for the payment of the debt on the Christian Chapel of Yellow Springs," and inserting "the sum of $4,000, to meet the proposal of the Building Committee."

"On motion of S. Richardson, the resolution was laid on the table."

"On motion of Isaac Kershner, voted that a committee be appointed to present a plan for raising funds to meet the proposal of the Building Committee."

"Voted that the Building Committee be empowered to appoint a committee in accordance with the foregoing resolution."

"The Building Committee appointed John Kershner, Wm. Mills and A. G. Kiler said committee."

A half hour or more was now consumed in miscellaneous speeches touching the church debt and the best manner of liquidating it, some opposing and others urging the Committee on Plan to report immediately.

Mr. Kiler thought it would require weeks to mature a good working plan; and Mr. Mills suggested that if they succeeded after months of thought and trial they might be satisfied.

But the general sense of the meeting seemed to be that a report be made that evening. The committee therefore retired, and in some ten minutes returned, when a skeleton report was presented to the meeting by Mr. Mills.

PLAN.

"1st. That an effort be made to sell the pews, as far as may be; and to lease the balance, provided the sum of $4,000 can be satisfactorily secured to the Building Committee."

"2d. That the pews be appraised by a committee as to their value by sale, and also by lease, per year."

"3d. That the pew-holders and lessees have the authority of employing and settling the pastor and passing such resolutions for the general regulation of the society as may be deemed advisable."

"4th. That the pastor be at all times a minister of good standing in the Christian community."

The reader will notice that the word "church" is studiously avoided; and that the phrase—"good standing in the Christian community" is very indefinite!

The report was received and the articles taken up one by one for adoption.

The first and second articles were adopted without much discussion, but by a very small majority, church members only voting.

Pending the discussion on art. 3d, the church adjourned to 6½ o'clock Thursday evening, Dec. 17th.

Dec. 17th.—Met according to adjournment. S. Richardson appointed Chairman. The evening was dark and stormy, the rain pouring in torrents, and as the Building Committee was not present, and the attendance small, adjourned to Monday evening, Dec. 21st, 6½ o'clock.

On Sabbath, Dec. 20th, Eld. Craig appeared in the pulpit of the chapel, and after the discourse, he requested the audience to remain, and called on Mr. Mann.

Mr. Mann stepped forward, and after a remark or two, was appointed chairman. Mr. Craig putting the motion from the pulpit.

Mr. Mann then stated that he had been authorized by Mr. Fay to submit two propositions to the congregation.

1st. A request, that the church will excuse him (Fay) from his pastoral duties for three months, more or less, to act as agent for Antioch College. The college is the great thing. Its prosperity should be paramount. If it can be freed from debt, the church will increase and flourish; but if the college is not saved, the church will retrograde, and doubtless also go down.

In making this request, therefore, Mr. Fay feels that he is following the path of duty, and in entering upon the work to which he is called, he believes that his labors will not only benefit the college but this church.

Of course the congregation excused Mr. Fay.

Mr Mann hoped that Mr. Fay's second proposition would not be accepted, and went on to pronounce a fulsome panegyric on the "eminent divine;" saying "that his ministrations had been remarkable satisfactory," that "we have received such edification, such comfort and instruction from him, as no other man in my whole acquaintance could have given us," &c !

Mr. Fay's second proposition is—that he will be satisfied with one half of his salary (*i. e.*, $400 instead of $800) if that amount can be made up to him; and that those who have subscribed and paid, can receive back one fourth of their money if they desire on account of his proposed absence for the three months next ensuing.

Mr. Mann hoped no person could have a heart to receive anything back.

Mr. Fay had now been pastor, or lecturer, for about nine months, and had received thus far but a few dollars for his services. Whether his labors were as highly appreciated by others as by Mr. Mann is very doubtful! or rather it is very certain that they were not, if Mr. M. believes the one half of his eulogistic declarations.

Whether Mr. Fay ever received the $400, we cannot say.

Monday Evening, Dec. 21*st.*—Met according to adjournment.

E. FAY, in the Chair,
J. B. WESTON, Sec. *pro tem.*

The discussion on the 3d art. of Committee's Report was resumed, and continued to a late hour.

The great question involved in this article is the disfranchisement of a large portion of the church by making a property qualification, or the ownership of a pew, the basis of a vote!

Eld. Jacobs opposed this principle and thought all church members and they alone should have the right to vote on all questions pertaining to the church.

Prest. Mann advocates the article as it stands in the report; thinks that the owners of pews should have the control, and they alone; and goes back to the times of our Puritan fathers to England, Rome and Egypt for examples and a law which he endeavored to apply to the case before the meeting! A large part of Mr. Mann's speech related to the distant past, when property or power was the basis of the right of suffrage; and what connection many of his remarks had with the case in hand we could not divine!

Eld. Jacobs replied—that we are not so far advanced as that yet; we are now where money makes right, and in half of a century we may be where might makes right, especially should Mr. Mann's doctrine prevail! He objected to Mr. Mann's assertion that "his own position —viz: that persons not members of the church shall have a right to vote by virtue of the money they may pay—is the highest principle of democracy."

He said that no democratic government would suffer any person, not being a citizen, to vote, notwithstanding the taxes he may pay for the support of said government, that in order to enjoy the right of suffrage, he must conform to the laws of naturalization established by such government.

Prest. Mann arose and with much scorn in the expression of his countenance and contempt in his bearing towards his opponent, he continued his remarks in about as lucid a strain and style as before.

Prof. Allen opposed the disfranchisement of the church or of any members of it. He believed a property qualification to be an unsuitable basis for church suffrage, and that the Congregational or Democratic form of church government is in harmony with the New Testament. He believed the church to be a divine institution, and maintained that *Christian character* or *the fitness to be a church member*, rather than any material possessions or outward accidents, was and is the true basis of church rights. He preferred a free house, or that the pews be rented from year to year, rather than sold; yet if that could not be, he would not object to any person or persons buying the pews or chapel entire, provided they would not attempt to buy the church or the rights of church members with it. Against such assaults he should then and forever protest. The prerogatives of the church are sacred and should be sacredly maintained.

The church is the bride, the Lamb's wife, she is Heaven-born, and should never allow her scepter to be dashed to earth and trampled in the dust.

Judge Mills supported the article. He thought that those who purchased pews should have the right to employ the pastor, and pass all other necessary regulations.

He could not see why those who will not purchase or lease pews should have the right to a voice in selecting the pastor; for if all the church members are allowed to vote, they can control the election of pastor and all other business; and for himself he could not aid on any such basis, and did not think that the outsiders generally would be willing to enter into any such an arrangement.

Isaac Kershner maintained that the church has rights peculiarly her own, rights which should not be infringed; and one of these is the right to vote on all questions relating to her existence and prosperity. He claimed that the church alone is fully able to raise the whole $6,000, and hoped she would do it.

J. E. Wilson doubted the ability of the church to pay the debt, and said the outsiders would not aid if all the church members are to have the right to vote. He believed the chapel would soon be sold at sheriff's sale, and then they could buy it in for $2,000 or $3,000.

John Kershner moved that the 3d section be so amended as to express that the members of the church, by virtue of their membership, be entitled to vote in matters therein contemplated.

J. B. Weston opposed the amendment and favored the article. He thought there were many members in our churches who ought not to vote ; persons who would not pay much for the support of the minister, or contribute to other expenses of the church or for the spread of the gospel.

Prof. Allen said it was no doubt true that many members in our churches were unfit for the positions which they filled ; they were lax, inefficient and neglectful of their duties ; but this was a reason why the church should exhort them to a more consistent life, should instruct and strengthen them, and if they still remained remiss to exclude them from the organization, rather than to refuse them the right of church suffrage.

So long as they are retained as members, and recognised in good standing, the right of voting ought not to be denied them.

After some further remarks the motion was put and lost. Affirmative, 3 ; negative, 6.

The question arose—Can a pew-holder have more than one vote ?

The third article appears to be indefinite on this point. Mr. Weston, therefore, put his head with Mr. Mann's while the debate went on.

If all the holders and lessees of pews were to have each a vote, nearly all the members of the church could have a voice, for several of those of limited means could unite and together purchase or lease a pew ; and, on the other hand, a man of wealth might purchase several pews and yet have but one vote.

Mr. Weston arose presently and moved that the third resolution or article be amended to read as follows—viz. :

3d. "That in employing and settling a pastor, and framing such regulations for the government of the society as may be deemed advisable, each pew shall entitle to one vote, which vote shall be cast by the owner or owners, lessee or lessees of such pew."

On the amendment quite a discussion arose.

Prof. Allen remarked that the amendment was much more objectionable than the original article. It makes a more deadly thrust at church rights, for a rich man can purchase several pews and have as many votes, while several poor men may buy or lease but one pew, and have but one vote between them, which is a virtual disfranchisement of all but one of them !

He was, therefore, opposed to the amendment.

On taking the vote the amendment was adopted. Affirmative, 5 ; negative, 1.

The section as amended was adopted. Affirmative, 6 ; negative, 1.

The reader will notice that the number of votes cast in these meetings is quite small, which results from two facts : 1st. Only church members were allowed to vote ; the proceedings in this state would otherwise be illegal. 2nd. Only a very few church members attended these meetings, some eight to ten persons, chiefly Mr. Fay's small faction. Nearly all the members had taken but little interest in meetings of any kind since Mr. Fay claimed to be pastor of the church.

The debate in these meetings, especially on the 3d article of the report, was earnest, and characterized on the part of some by an intolerant spirit. This was chiefly confined to persons not members of the church, who seemed determined to force the members into an arrangement depriving them of their rights, or otherwise compel the Building Committee to sell the chapel at Sheriff's sale, that they might bid it off at $2,000 to $2,500! Such was the ungentlemanly and unchristian spirit manifested by some of the citizens of Yellow Springs, Ohio!

Article 4th passed after amending it by striking out "community" and inserting "church," which last word, John Kershner said should have been in the original article, according to his understanding.

The chair appointed John Kershner, J. B. Weston and A. G. Kiler Committee of Appraisal, in accordance with the 2nd article of the report.

Adjourned to meet in the same place on Monday evening, Dec. 28th, at half-past 6 o'clock.

Monday, Dec. 28th, 1857.—"The church met according to adjournment."

"On motion of A. G. Kiler, voted to reconsider the vote adopting the 3d article of the committee's report as amended."

"On motion of Wm. R. King, *voted* that said article 3d be so amended as to express that the members of the church, not owning or leasing pews, by virtue of their membership be also entitled to vote in the matters contemplated in that article."

Mr. King had been absent from town for some time, and had not attended the several preceding meetings. Perhaps he had not been at home long enough to be posted by A. S. Dean.

"In answer to inquiry, Mr. Kiler stated, for the Building Committee, that for the sum of $4,000 they proposed to relinquish to the church all their right, title and interest in the house, reserving to themselves no seats or other rights whatever in the property of the house."

"On motion of W. R. King, *voted* to accept the proposal of the Building Committee, as made by Mr. Kiler, and that interest on that amount ($4,000,) be paid by the church from this date."

After some further desultory discussion, *voted* to adjourn, to meet at the same place on Saturday evening next, at half-past 6 o'clock.

J. B. Weston, Clerk *pro tem.*

Yellow Springs, Ohio.—*Jan. 2nd,* 1858.—The Christian Church met according to adjournment at half-past 6 o'clock P. M.

The house was organized by appointing J. B. Weston, President, and A. L. Allen, Recording Secretary.

The minutes of the last meeting were read. The Committtee on Appraisal of Pews then made a report.

On motion of W. H. Smith the report was received and the committee discharged.

A motion was then made by Mr. Kiler that the resolution or article reconsidered at a previous meeting on motion of himself, and subsequently amended on motion of W. R. King, now be adopted as then amended.

On calling for the final vote it was unanimously adopted.

In reference to a motion made by W. R. King at the previous meeting to accept the proposal of the Building Committee, Mr. Kiler then remarked that the Building Committee was now ready to receive proposals by bond or bonds from the church for the sum of $4,000. He was ready to go to Xenia or to any other place that night, if necessary, to draw up and enter into bonds with the church for the payment of the $4,000, or the church might appoint a committee to wait on them and transact the business.

After waiting some time and receiving no bids or proposals, or any intimation of any, Mr. Kiler made a short speech, at the close of which some one cried out, "Put up the house at public sale and we will buy it in for $2,000!"

Thus the whole matter seemed to be thrown back again upon the Building Committee.

After some further desultory discussion, on motion of John Kershner the meeting adjourned *sine die*. J. B. Weston, *Pres't.*

A. L. Allen, *Sec'y.*

Thus closed a series of the most peculiar meetings that we have ever attended. There were but a few church members at any of them. They were chiefly composed of persons who belonged to no branch of the church of Christ. These persons were the supporters of Eld. Fay, and they threatened the very existence of the Christian Church.

And why should they not? Mr. Fay himself, their chief, had been lecturing to them some nine months, and had *early* "preached" most of the church members away from his meetings.

Indeed when first elected, outsiders were allowed to vote; and at the end of his three months of trial he would not allow his name to be used for re-election on any other condition than that the congregation, and not the church only, should have the right to vote!

Thus after the first three months, however it may have been before, Mr. Fay, we think, was not the pastor of the church.

Moreover, he had neglected the ordinances of the church, and given no opportunity for persons to unite with it! His discourses were often most bitter against the various branches of the church, and far better calculated to please the multitude than edify the children of God. Indeed the Christian Chapel seemed more like a Sunday Theater than like a place for sincere, humble, Christian worship; and under such instruction one must soon come to despise and hate the true followers of Christ or to detest Mr. Fay, for "Ye cannot serve God and mammon."

What wonder, therefore, that, in the above-mentioned series of meetings ending Jan'y 2d, the outsiders should endeavor to bring the church under their control. They were highly pleased with Mr. Fay's doctrines (taken perhaps from Theodore Parker and other liberalists,) and were possibly under private instructions from Messrs. Fay, Dean, and Mann. Why should they not, therefore, struggle to disfranchise the members and take the very life of the church!

In view of these things, and especially to free our brethren of the Building Committee from the threatened necessity of selling their farms, or making other heavy sacrifices to meet the $6,000 church debt, some 23 friends met at the residence of Eld. D. F. Ladley, Jan'y 7th, at 2 o'clock P. M., to consult for the interests and prosperity of the Christian cause in Yellow Springs, Ohio. The meeting was regularly organized, and after appropriate, religious exercises, proceeded to business. The great object was a plan for successful action. It was thought that the money to free the church of debt could be most readily raised by subscription; but right here several of the most wealthy friends declared that they would not subscribe a single dollar for the First Christian Church; that there had been so much "pulling and hauling," passing resolutions at one meeting and rescinding them at the next, that they had no confidence in the body; that such discordant elements had found way into the church, that should they (?) now come forward and pay off the debt they feared that, like Antioch College, the church would soon be in debt again; but added they if the chapel can be a free house, if a new organization can be formed, and if such organization will elect its own pastor, and transact its own business, we will aid, andaid liberally.

There appeared, therefore, now to be but one way in which to obtain money sufficient to liquidate the church debt.

Taxation or assessment of property had been several times attempted, but as often failed. The sale of pews had been attempted, and on one occasion (Spring of 1855) a sale had actually been effected, yet not one single dollar could be collected. The plan of subscription for the First Christian Church had often been tried, and as often turned out a failure.

Indeed to have attempted to raise money for the First Christian Church would have been the height of folly, after Mr. Fay would not allow his name to be used by the church for re-election; but by the whole congregation!

His pretended election as pastor of the church, when hardly a church member voted for him, was very much like resolving the Franklin Convention into a *mass meeting*, and deeply offended the candid, honest men in our community, whether church members or not.

What course for successful action was there *then* left, especially when wealthy friends and brethren declared that they would not give one single penny to the First Christian Church? There seemed to be none, except on the conditions above specified. These were the only beams of light that flashed in upon the deep darkness. Here the Red Sea of angry contentions and intolerant oppositions, of rampant liberalism and usurping infidelity, opened, and the brethren and sisters, relying upon Israel's God, determined to go over on dry ground to the land of promise. They therefore adopted the following

PLAN OF SUBSCRIPTION:

"We, the undersigned, hereby promise to pay, provided an amount sufficient to satisfy the Building Committee can be raised, the sums attached to our names in this paper respectively to said Building Committee of the Christian Church for the purpose of enabling them to discharge the debts contracted in the erection of the Meeting House of the said church, on the following conditions—viz:

1st. Said Meeting House *shall be a free house*—that is, no seats shall be sold; although they may be rented annually for the support of the pastor.

2d. The pastor shall be elected in the manner hitherto usual in the Christian Churches in this State.

3d. That if the requisite amount can be raised, and the property secured, there shall be a new organization.

4th. An acquittance in full of all claims against the property shall be made out and recorded in legal form by the Building Committee."

After the adoption of the above plan, a committee of three was appointed to solicit funds and execute the plan.

Committee, { JOHN A. LAYTON,
IRA W. ALLEN,
THEO. W. DAWSON.

The committee-men met on the afternoon of the next day, looked over the ground carefully, and concluded that there would be no reasonable hope of success unless six or seven men would subscribe $300 each. They drove out of town just at evening, called on some friends, told them their conclusion, and wished them to put down $300 each.

That figure, they replied, was quite too high. They had not thought themselves able to give more than about one-half or two-thirds of that amount. Besides Antioch College may fail, or be entirely disconnected from the Christians, and then we shall wish to sell out and leave the place. Indeed we would now sell, if we could obtain anything like the value of our property.

The committee remarked that they still had some hope that Antioch would yet be redeemed to the Christians; and thought, if the friends here would take hold and pay off the $6,000 debt upon the church, that our sister churches throughout the country would take courage, raise $60,000, and buy back the College from the assignee, F. A. Palmer, of New York.

This idea gave courage, and four men pledged $1,200. On the day following $600 more were subscribed by two men; and in a few days nearly $4,000 were made available by men of means and integrity.

The Building Committee of three brethren subscribed $2,000, and thus nearly $6,000 were pledged on the simple conditions of the above plan. Success seemed already to hover over the Christian Banner! A future bright with promise, and all radiant with hope loomed up in the near distance; God grant that it may be realized!

It was thought advisable therefore to fulfil the conditions of the subscription; and accordingly "a new organization" was made on 22d of Jan., and incorporated as the "Second Christian Church of Yellow Springs, Green Co., Ohio." The church was organized by Eld. D. F. Ladley, assisted by Eld. S. Richardson, and consisted of 14 members, persons who had removed to this place from different parts of the Union, during the last five years, and all of whom save one had been members of the Christian Connection. None of them were members of the "First Christian Church" of this place. The organization was therefore "new" and satisfied one of the conditions of the "plan of subscription."

Jan. 23d, 1858.—The First Christian Church met according to notice, published in the "News Letter" of the Saturday previous. The meeting was fully attended, nearly all the members of the church being present. Nearly every seat in the large vestry was filled.

"On motion of S. Richardson, I. Kershner was appointed to the chair."

Prayer was then offered by Eld. Richardson.

"On motion of D. F. Ladley, N. H. Walbridge was appointed Assistant Secretary."

After some time, "On motion of A. G. Kiler, the following resolution was adopted:"

"*Whereas*, At a meeting of the First Christian Church of Yellow Springs, Greene Co., Ohio, held according to adjournment, on Dec. 28, 1857, on motion of W. R. King, it was voted to accept the proposal of the Building Committee, and that the interest on that amount (being $4,000) be paid by the church from this date, and

"*Whereas*, Said church has failed to fulfil said resolution or vote, therefore, be it

"*Resolved*, That said resolution or vote be and is hereby rescinded." Passed unanimously.

Later in the meeting—"On motion of John Kershner, the following resolution was adopted:"

Whereas, We the members of the First Christian Church of Yellow Springs, Greene Co., Ohio, on examination into our financial affairs, do find that as a church we are heavily in debt on our church property; and

Whereas, We are fully aware that we as a church should pay all our honest debts at the earliest moment; therefore

Resolved, "That our Trustees be and they are hereby authorized to sell the church property to the best advantage and as soon as possible, in order to liquidate the debt." Passed unanimously.

Eld. Ladley then made some remarks of a religious and encouraging nature.

Eld. Fay arose and requested the privilege of speaking. The President objected on the ground that Mr. Fay was not a member of the church, and the church had not invited any persons not members to speak that day. Mr. Fay said he was pastor of the church, and therefore had a right to speak; that his relation to the church was much more intimate than that of any member, and he claimed the right to be heard. The President remarked that if the church would so order he would not object to his speaking, but that he could not be heard without a vote of the church.

Eld. Richardson then moved the following:

"*Resolved*, That Eld. Fay have the privilege of speaking, as he expresses a desire to do so." Passed.

Mr. Fay then arose and made a speech of some length, the substance of which (taken down at the time) is as follows:

Eld. F. said that there had been conflicting elements in this community for a long time, in short two opposing parties. They differed—

1st. On the college question.

2d. In what manner a pastor should be elected.

3d. How many shall vote for a pastor.

4th. The position of the pulpit on the great questions of the day.

He then spoke of the Second Christian Church, which he called a "new enterprise," and said "in this new enterprise I heartily rejoice," because

1st. The Building Committee will be released.

2d. Something good may be effected. I bid it God speed.

"I will not oppose a single obstacle to the new organization, it can do its own business."

He then went on to say that he was the pastor of the First Christian Church, and yet he rejoiced in this new movement. 1st. For the sake of the Building Committee. 2nd. Because each man can now go his own way to his own place. He again alluded to the two parties and did not believe they could ever harmonize; did not think that affairs in this town could ever be brought into a state of unity. Yet if they are, said he, I will give of my means as freely and largely, in proportion to what I am worth, as any other man, to support the cause under this new banner.

If I have friends in this community, and I think I have many, judging by my audiences, which have been the largest ever assembled in this house, (and for these statements I can be excused as I am the pastor of this church;) if I have friends, I say, I hope they will, if possible, co-operate with this new movement. I bid them God speed.

All who can sail under this new banner, try it. If you succeed, I am the last man who will throw any embarrassment into this meeting or this community. I will stand aside and never say one word against it.

Go ahead. I bid you God speed. If you pay for this property I don't know what will become of the First Christian Church. I might hand in my resignation, but it might not avail anything, for I suppose the church will be ignored, perhaps become extinct. Don't know what I shall do with myself! Ha! ha! Will some of the brethren tell me?

After some further church business, on motion of Eld. Ladley,

Resolved, That we adjourn to meet at this place on next Thursday, 28th inst., at 10 o'clock A. M. D. F. LADLEY, Clerk.

Late in the afternoon of the same day the Trustees of the Second Christian Church, understanding that the First Christian Church had authorized its Trustees to sell the chapel, met said officers and made them an offer for the house. They accepted the offer, saying that it was a better bid than they had ever received for the house, and better than they could expect to receive if they should wait any longer. They expressed themselves entirely satisfied with the offer, and proceeded that afternoon to an office of a Justice of the Peace and executed a *Warrantee Deed* of the property of the First Christian Church to "the Trustees of the Second Christian Church and their successors in office for ever."

On the very next day, Sabbath, the 24th inst., Mr. Fay, notwithstanding his assertions in the above public speech, began to operate against the "new movement," as he called the Second Christian Church. He went out to the residence of John Kershner, but not finding him at home left a message with his wife—viz.: that he very much desired that Mr. Kershner would not accept of the offer of the Second Christian Church, &c.

Who can place confidence in such men?

A friend, in looking over the laws of Ohio, discovered one on reversionary interests. The attention of our counsel was called to this.

He thought the transfer of the property, as already effected by warrantee deed, a legal and sufficient one, yet, if we had any doubt about it, the transfer could also be made by permit of Court; that the one process would not invalidate the other. The case was somewhat complicated, yet he thought that no claim of any reversionary interest could ever be sustained, if any were made in future. It was thought best by some to obtain a permit of Court, and accordingly our counsel drew up a petition, which was signed by Judge Wm. Mills and the Trustees of the First Christian Church. Mr. Mills remarked that such a petition was not at all necessary, for he had sold the land to the First Christian Church and deeded it in such a way that there could be no reversionary interests claimed in it by any of his heirs. He examined the Ohio statute referred to and thought there was no necessity of following that in transferring the property in question; that he was perfectly willing, however, to sign the petition and did so.

Jan. 28th, 1858.—"The First Christian Church met according to adjournment. Isaac Kershner in the chair. Prayer by Eld. Ladley. The minutes of the last meeting were read and approved."

Eld. Ladley being in feeble health and somewhat weary from walking over to the chapel, in reading the minutes happened to omit the names of some of the movers of resolutions, when Mr. Mann took occasion to pick flaws and make objections to the minutes as read by Eld. Ladley.

Mr. Fay also had a word to say, but they effected nothing; for the minutes were in proper legal form, as the names of the movers of all the resolutions were on the book.

The Trustees, who were authorized at the previous meeting to sell the church property to the best advantage and as soon as possible, were called on for a report.

Said Trustees made a report of progress, which report on motion was accepted.

On motion of D. F. Ladley,

Resolved, That we adjourn to one week from next Tuesday, at 2 o'clock P. M.—viz., Feb. 9, 1858. D. F. LADLEY, Clerk.

Feb. 1st, 1858.—The aforementioned petition of the Trustees of the First Christian Church and William Mills to the Court of Common

Pleas was presented to said Court at Xenia. A. S. Dean was present and made, through his lawyer and his own testimony, some false claims, owing to which and to the Judges not being familiar with the statute, and also to the pressure of other business, the case was laid over for a further hearing.

In the meantime, however, a new Judge came to preside over the Court, and the time for receiving the petition registered for a later day of the session.

Our counsel informed us that A. S. Dean came to Xenia very early on the previous Thursday morning and called at his residence before he was up. Mr. Dean said he had come to consult with him about a certain matter; a church case; about the sale of some church property in Yellow Springs. Counsel told him that he could not talk with him on that subject.

A. S. Dean now gave counsel to understand that the Hon. Horace Mann had instructed him to consult with him on the matter. Counsel could not help that, he was not at liberty to talk with him on that subject.

A. S. Dean still persisted in talking, and gave our counsellor a long, sad story about affairs at Yellow Springs, throwing in a question now and then, which counsel did not take the trouble to answer.

After Mr. Dean had "said his say" he took his hat and left, none the wiser after his long effort to pump our counsellor!

Feb. 6th.—W. H. Smith (a student,) one of Mr. Fay's clique, broke into the chapel vestry through a window and opened the doors, when Mann, Fay and others came in and held a meeting, which they claimed to be a monthly meeting of the church! and that, too, when monthly meetings had fallen into disuse.

According to the records of the church there had been but one monthly church meeting since the 1st August, 1857, and that one was held Oct. 3d, 1857. The whole affair was, of course, illegal, for the house did not belong to them; and 1st, they broke into the house, and that, too, when it was known that the Second Christian Church had had the keys and possession of the chapel since the 24th of January.

2nd. The meeting was not legally called, no public notice having been given, and was known only to a very small minority of the members of the church. Besides, the regular legal meeting of the church had adjourned over from Jan. 28th to Feb. 9th.

But, notwithstanding all this, they proceeded to smuggle 18 or 19 persons into the First Christian Church! which was the first opportunity to join the church which Mr. Fay had given since his residence in

Yellow Springs; and this, even, some weeks after he had been excused to act as agent for the College. Why was he not off on his agency?

The manner, too, of receiving these persons was not a little strange. They were received without asking them any questions, not even whether they believed in the New Testament or no! and in the face of opposition! On such easy conditions one would suppose that Eld. Fay might have persuaded a larger number of his congregation to join "his society."

Mr. Kiler charged them with a violation of the laws of Ohio in breaking into the house, and intimated that he who comes in by any other way than through the door "is a thief and a robber."

Horace Mann arose and asked the chairman if he did not come in by the door? and said he had a right to the church for he owned a pew. Mr. Kiler asked him how much he had paid for his right? and charged home upon him that he had not paid a single dollar on the meeting house, which Mr. Mann did not deny, for it was a fact.

News of this remarkable revival and large accession to the church spread rapidly through town and country, reaching Cincinnati and other distant places with almost telegraphic speed.

Of course this secret underhanded movement was "for effect," to enlarge the small faction of the church which supported Eld. Fay, and, if possible, obtain votes enough to control the adjourned meeting to be held Feb. 9th, three days later.

Mr. Mann now moved that a new clerk be appointed; and, although there was no vacancy, the regular standing clerk not having resigned, and although Mr. Kiler protested against any such action, yet a new clerk was elected, after which they began to rescind the legal and orderly transactions of the two preceding meetings of Jan. 23d and 28th.

Eld. Richardson, on going by, saw that there was a meeting in the chapel. He went in, and observing the character of the assemblage gave battle.

Layton also learning of the meeting went in and contested their illegal and disorderly proceedings.

They (the factionists) passed resolutions rescinding all that was done in the meetings of Jan. 23d and 28th, save the one resolution instructing the Trustees to sell the church property "to the best advantage and as soon as possible," which they almost totally changed by an amendment.

Feb. 9th, 1858.—The First Christain Church met according to adjournment from the 28th ultimo, at 2 o'clock P. M.

Isaac Kershner in the chair, D. F. Ladley, church clerk.

After prayer by Eld. McWhinney, the chairman called for the minutes of the last meeting.

The clerk commenced to read when he was interrupted by Mr. Mann, who asked Eld. Ladley if he "was about to read the minutes as the clerk of the church." Mr. M. said that at the last meeting of the church, (Saturday, the 6th inst.,) owing to the absence of the clerk, "the church proceeded to elect another clerk in place of Mr. Ladley, and as the clerk then elected was now present, Mr. Mann took exception to Mr. Ladley's reading the minutes."

Why is it that Mr. Mann is so often desirous to have a special clerk? The reason is very evident in this case.

He wished to have the minutes of the spurious church meeting of the 6th inst. read and approved, and how could this be effected except through the counterfeit church clerk, Wm. M. King?

The Chair informed Mr. Mann that the meeting alluded to was illegal and he should not recognize it in any way.

Mr. Mann somewhat excited replied to the Chair, and again excepted to Eld. Ladley's reading the minutes.

After considerable sparring between Mr. Mann and others, the Chair requested the church clerk to proceed to read. Mr. Mann now remained in his seat and Eld. Ladley completed the reading of the minutes.

The report of the Trustees was then called for, on motion of Eld. Ladley, when the Trustees reported that they had sold the church property according to their instructions.

After the report was made Mr. A. S. Dean attempted to speak, but was stopped by the Chair, who said that outsiders could not be allowed to speak without permission of the church. Mr. Dean again attempted to speak, and was again interrupted by the chairman.

Mr. Dean persisted and said, "I have been implicated. You called on the Building Committee to report, and I am a member of that committee," when he was finally silenced by the Chair and kept his seat.

On motion of Eld. Ladley, the report of the Trustees was accepted by a unanimous vote.

Mr. Dean's statement, "You called on the Building Committee to report," is about as correct as most of his sayings. The Building Committee *had not been called on*, in this meeting, to make a report. The Trustees, and not the Building Committee, had been authorized to sell the church property, and they only were called upon to report.

Eld. Fay arose and requested permission to speak.

The Chair said Mr. Fay cannot be heard.

Eld. Fay asked if he could not be permitted to submit a single proposition. The Chair objected.

Mr. Mann arose and moved that Eld. Fay have liberty to submit a proposition.

Motion was lost. Affirmative 12; negative 38.

Mr. Mann arose and said that as Mr. Fay was debarred from speaking to his (Fay's) own church, he (Mr. Mann) "would read to the church some propositions which Mr. Fay had desired to present with the view of reconciling the differences which now divide the church." Mr. Mann went on to speak of the great desirability of harmony and good feeling in the church, and thought that the propositions which he was about to read might bring affairs into a state of unity. He deprecated divisions and dissensions and trusted that the differences might be harmonized.

ELI FAY'S PLAN.

"Propositions by which to liquidate the indebtedness of the First Christian Church in Yellow Springs, and also to harmonize all parties in sustaining it.

First. "The subscription raised by the Second Christian Church for the purpose of purchasing the church property, shall be so increased by the First Christian Church and its friends as to cover the entire indebtedness upon the property, exclusive of the just and equitable portion which the Building Committee should assume, which shall be determined by themselves and three other men to be chosen by the First Christian Church. The whole of the subscription thus increased shall be secured to the Building Committee on the conditions as to the payment of the subscription belonging to the Second Christian Church of Yellow Springs, when the Building Committee shall give to the First Christian Church of Yellow Springs a warrantee deed of the church property.

Second. "After the property shall be thus secured to the First Church, an opportunity shall be given to all suitable persons who desire it to unite with the First Church. Two months shall be deemed a sufficient time for that purpose; at the expiration of which a pastor shall be chosen by a majority of the church members present at a special meeting which shall be called for that purpose, due notice of which shall be given. This proposition shall not be considered as a precedent to control future action, but simply as a measure to meet present emergencies. (!)

Third. "The pews of the church shall be rented annually to defray the expenses of the church.

Fourth. "If these propositions shall not be accepted, we propose that, according to resolutions passed at our church meeting last Saturday, the Building Committee keep the sale of the church property an open question until the 20th instant; and that if during that time the First Christian Church shall make as good an offer as any other party, they shall be entitled to the property. The comparative value of the property shall be determined by a disinterested committee to be chosen by the Building Committee and the First Christian Church."

Messrs. Mann, Fay and Dean talk about harmony, peace, "unity," when they had done so much to distract and divide! when they had within a few weeks endeavored to disfranchise, if not utterly destroy the church!

What confidence could be placed in them, in their plans, or in their professions? They had never paid a dollar towards the debt on the chapel! They (Dean and Mann) had been endeavoring for nearly three years to force the church into the pew-selling arrangement; and opposed the raising of money by other plans. They had prevented the taking up a collection on the day of dedication, which at that time would have gone far towards liquidating the debt. They had for a long time been "stumbling blocks" and almost "insuperable barriers" to the advancement and prosperity of the church, and now Mann and Fay come forward with a plan, professedly to harmonize all parties!" Greater duplicity could not well be exhibited. There was in this plan no basis for the noble superstructure of harmony and Christian unity; and this they well knew or ought to have known.

Only a few days previous, Jan'y 23d, Mr. Fay said before a large audience, that "there had been conflicting elements in this community for a long time; in short, two opposing parties;" and affirmed his belief that these parties could never be harmonized; yet he now comes forward with "peace propositions!" Was there sincerity here? Were these the propositions of a conquered enemy suing for peace? or were they not rather an intriguing scheme to gain time, a stratagem to decoy the victors upon mines all ready for explosion?

The object was clearly to destroy the new organization, to break up the only successful arrangement by which the church was freed from debt, and the Building Committee from a crushing burden.

It was to make the whole matter an open question again; to roll the burden back upon the Building Committee that they might yet be forced to a sale of the pews, or to the only other alternative, to a sale of the property by the Sheriff. And this last would doubtless have been the result, had any considerable portion of the church accepted the specious and sophistical argument of Mr. Mann in favor of the adoption of Mr. Fay's plan.

Mr. Mann* certainly struggled powerfully to forestall the minds of the

* We regret exceedingly the course which Mr. Mann has taken since he joined the Christian Church. Had he manifested an interest in our weekly prayer meetings; had he attended our monthly church meetings and taken hold, heart and hand with us, he might have accomplished great good. And we would ask why Mr. Mann was not

audience, and on reading each portion of the plan, made lengthy comments and commendations; yet all to no purpose, for his motion, at the close of his speech, that the church reconsider its vote, and permit Mr. Fay to speak upon his propositions—was lost by an overwhelming majority as before!

It was well known by persons at a distance from Yellow Springs, that such conflicting forces had found way into the church, that such innovations had been allowed, that there was now no hope for peace except in a new organization. As one instance we give the following:

"This is to certify, that Eld. J. G. Reeder, one of the so-called self-constituted committee has frequently called at my house during the last three years, and on more than one occasion has said concerning church affairs here, that our only salvation would be to form a new organization.

"July, 1858. " John A. Layton."

But let us examine these so-called "peace propositions."

1st. "To liquidate the indebtedness of the First Christian Church." Was not the church already free from debt? The Trustees sold and deeded away the church property, Jan'y 23d, and received therefor money, notes, and approved subscriptions; and the members of the Building Committee, who were personally bound for the whole debt, approved of the sale.

2d. "To harmonize all parties in *sustaining it*," &c. Had Mann and Fay the slightest idea that "all parties" could ever be induced *to sustain* the First Christian Church? We think not. Several men of means had said that they would not subscribe a single dollar for the First Christian Church; and Mr. Fay's experience in circulating subscription papers had, doubtless, shown him that the debt could not be cancelled without their aid. Besides one of the express conditions of the plan on which the money had just been raised was that "*there shall be a new organization.*" How then, we ask, could the subscribers to this plan and this condition (who embraced nearly all the able and respectable members of the First Christian Church) now stultify themselves by accepting the propositions of Messrs. Fay and Mann!

The idea is supremely ridiculous, and was so regarded by candid men.

---

baptized, especially when he acknowledged that immersion is the true mode? Why has he not attended to the ordinance of the Lord's Supper, with the Church? Why has he not attended our prayer meetings, if his sympathies are so emphatically with the Christians as he has often publicly asserted? Why has he not attended our fellowship or monthly church meetings except when he has had some plan or scheme to accomplish?

Does Mr. Mann believe in practical Christianity as manifested by the Christian Connections?

Was Mr. Mann a frequent attendant at prayer meetings in Massachusetts; and did he exhibit a deep interest in practical piety? We ask for information.

Will Mr. Mann, or any one who knows the facts, give candid and truthful replies to the above questions?

4

3d. "The subscription raised by the Second Christian Church," &c. The Second Christian Church did not raise the subscription.

The money was pledged before the Second Christian Church had an existence, and was subscribed by members of the Christian, Methodist and Presbyterian Churches, and by those belonging to no branch of the church, and with the definite understanding that there should be a "new organization," one that should elect its own pastor and transact its own business.

This subscription was presented to Horace Mann, A. S. Dean, Austin Craig, H. A. Warriner and others connected with Antioch College; but they would not subscribe a single dollar, and yet they or some of them desired to control the church! If they wished to aid in liquidating the debt, why did they not then subscribe on a pledge which they were assured would be successful? Was it because they were determined to wrest the church, as we believe they had the college, from her denominational, her old Bible platform? and place her upon a sandy foundation?

The pernicious influence of the College was deeply regretted by good Christians of all the churches of the place; for the Christian Church was not only threatened, but the true interests of all denominations, pure and conservative Christianity herself.

There was great joy therefore when the money was raised, the Second Christian Church organized, and the chapel purchased for a free Christian House.

Of course, Mann, Fay & Co. would be delighted to add a few dollars to the successful subscription, if by that means they could bring back the chapel to the possession of the First Christian Church! but they were several weeks too late.

4th. "By themselves and three other men to be chosen by the First Christian Church."

Did Messrs. Fay and Mann intend to insult the Building Committee, after they had so deeply injured them? Of course Mann, Dean, and others were to be perfectly free to pay what they pleased, but the members of the committee who had "borne the burden in the heat of the day," who had been oppressed with a $6,000 church debt, must be instructed by a Church Committee how much they ought to give!

Would Mr. Mann have the Building Committee men subscribe more than $666 67 each, or $2,000 together, the amount which they actually did pledge? Was not this sufficiently liberal, when himself and others better able to give largely than the committee-men, had not paid a single dollar to diminish the church debt! Let these gentlemen come forward and pay handsomely, before they talk about instructing the Building Committee in liberality.

5th. "When the Building Committee shall give to the First Christian Church of Yellow Springs a warrantee deed of the church property."

After the First Christian Church has sold and deeded away "the church property" and the Building Committee men have expressed their satisfaction with the transaction; what then Messrs. Fay and Mann? Would you have the sale vitiated, the money reverted to the subscribers, and the $6,000 debt thrown back upon the Building Committee? God forbid.

6th. "An opportunity shall be given to all suitable persons who desire it, to unite with the First Christian Church."

Do Mann and Fay consider all the 19 individuals whom they smuggled into the church on Feb. 6th "suitable persons?" If so, better take in the whole community.

Of course, the election of a pastor "by a majority of the church menbers" under such circumstances, even, ought not to be "considered as a precedent to control future action!" "but simply as a measure to meet present emergencies!"

Ever after this first election the pastor will, doubtless, be chosen by the congregation or the community!

7th. "Of course Mann, Dean and Fay are very willing that the pews should be rented to meet the annual expenses of the church, after others had paid the $6,000 debt, especially if the lessees only have votes!"

8th. But should the above plan not be accepted, Mr. Fay offers another, viz:—"that the Building Committee keep the sale of the church property an open question until the 20th inst." according to resolutions passed at the spurious church meeting of Feb. 6th by said Fay and his co-laborers.

Does Mr. Mann suppose that the church will be so stupid as to recognize the proceedings of an illegal meeting as valid, and coercive of her action?

Besides what right has the Building Committee to keep the sale an "open question," even had the Trustees not sold the chapel? Jan'y. 23d the First Christian Church instructed *her Trustees* to sell the church property "as soon as possible," but not the Building Committee.

9th. What Mr. Fay means by "the comparative value of the property shall be determined," &c. we do not understand. What has "the comparative value of the property" to do in the case?

Be that more or less, must not the whole church debt be paid?

Such were the so-called "peace propositions" of Eld. Fay; but did they contain any elements of peace, of sincerity, or of honesty?

Eld. Ladley said that it is singular that persons will now put forth efforts to accomplish that which is already accomplished; that these propositions (of Mr. Fay) came too late; that this house is sold, a deed is made out for it, and a consideration already, perhaps, in hand. The work is accomplished, and the debt liquidated. Mr. L., referring to those who complain of the sale, said: These men have paid nothing out of their pockets; they ought not to complain. The Second Christian Church organized here has no new banner. They have rehoisted one, under which some have rallied, and more will.

Mr. Mann replied—"We did not know the church property had been sold until we heard it here this afternoon," &c.

Here Eld's. Fay and McWhinney officiously volunteered some remarks contrary to the rules of the meeting.

Eld. McW. had doubtless been brought over from Enon, to aid Messrs. Fay and Mann!

J. F. Crist arose, and said that many of these remarks here this afternoon were made for effect; that it was well known there was a certain party here headed by Mr. Mann, which had always thwarted the Christian Church. Now, said Mr. Crist, we have here a rallying against that party; and this will go much further than Yellow Springs; it will spread through the Christian Denomination.

I've heard down at Cincinnati, said Mr. Crist, the news that there has been a *glorious revival* here! That nineteen new converts were added to the church last Saturday! Mr. Crist said that these were not genuine additions to the church, but that those members were brought in for effect.

(Mr. Crist was here interrupted.) He proceeded to say that nine or ten months ago this party elected a certain pastor, and that three-fourths of the church were disaffected at this. Fay was elected by a small *minority*, without the church having had sufficient notice that there was to be an election. The strife now going on will result in good.

Mr. Mann's remarks commendatory of, and in connection with, Mr. Fay's propositions were quite lengthy and intended to affect the feelings and carry the votes of church members.

He endeavored to work on the sympathies of the Building Committee, and to excite their feelings of self interest by showing how much more money they would receive if these propositions were adopted. During the whole speech, and especially during these remarks, Mr. Fay eyed the committee men with most searching eagerness, apparently expecting every moment to see them yield to Mr. Mann's magic power, surrender to his specious logic, repudiate their endorsement of the recent sale of the chapel, and throw the whole thing back upon the church and themselves! But Mr. Fay watched in vain, and all of Mr. Mann's labored efforts were in vain; for John Kershner arose and said "the Trustees have sold this house to the Second Christian Church of this place according to their instructions, have executed a warrantee deed for the same, and they intend to stand to the sale." The Building Committee remained firm. Not a single muscle relaxed. They had endorsed the sale and they would stand to it, and why not? They knew that all the Horace Manns, A. S. Deans, and Eli Fays in the country would not pay them as much as they have received for the church property. They knew that they had received nearly *four times as much available means* as had ever before been pledged to the liquidation of the debt. They knew, too, that if this sale should be invalidated, they would never again receive so good an offer, that the property would be thrown back upon their hands, and that they would probably be compelled to sell it at Sheriff's sale.

Besides, they had sold to the friends of the Christian Denomination, to the friends of a free but genuine Christianity, and to the foes of irreligion and infidelity.

Every consideration, therefore, of interest as well as of duty, notwithstanding Mr. Mann's specious sophisms, called on them to stand to the sale; and this they were fully and uncompromisingly determined to do.

Indeed it is difficult to catch old foxes after you have several times endeavored to trap them.

The First Christian Church having sold her property, freed herself from debt, and now completed her business. Thomas Kershner moved the following:

"*Whereas,* We the first Christian Church of Yellow Springs, Ohio, through our Trustees, have sold the property of the church in order to pay the debt thereon, and

Whereas, We as a church are now without a chapel, or any suitable place in which to meet for worship, therefore,

Resolved, That this church be and is hereby *dissolved.*"

Mr. Mann desired to see the resolution. The Clerk handed it to him. He looked it over carefully, then jumped from his chair and poured forth a sweeping, excitable speech of some five to ten minutes.

He protested against the resolution, and declared that it would be impossible to dissolve the church so long as any member objects; the law would not permit it; and he defied the whole world to take from him his church rights and privileges without his consent.

Mr. Mann's sweeping declarations, and almost phrenzied asseverations, however, did not convince the church of the illegality or impropriety of passing the resolution.

Before taking his seat, Mr. Mann requested that counsel be taken from ministers present, mentioning Eld's. McWhinney, Craig and Weston; and accordingly moved that these ministers be invited to address the meeting, before taking the vote on the resolution.

The chairman objected. He said that this is strictly a business meeting of the church. The gentlemen called on for speeches are not members of this organization, and hence have no legal or moral right to speak in this meeting without an invitation or vote of the church.

He was sorry to be under the necessity of refusing permission to outsiders to speak; yet he must do so unless otherwise ordered by the church.

Mr. Mann then moved that Eld. McWhinney be allowed to speak.

Motion lost by a vote of nearly 3 to 1.

He then moved that Eld. Craig be allowed to speak, and afterwards that Eld. Weston speak; but each motion was lost by a heavy majority of nearly 3 to 1, the vote in the affirmative being 13, in the negative about 40.

Elder Fay—"Mr. Chairman, may I take one look at this corpse before you proceed to bury it?"

Chair—"I can't allow Mr. Fay to speak."

Elder Fay said: "I now give notice, as pastor of this church, that it is not disbanded, and cannot be."

Eld. McWhinney now forced himself upon the meeting in a few fire-eating remarks aimed at Eld. Ladley.

Then followed two of Mr. Fay's clique (members of the church,) one a student, W. H. Smith, the other a workman in the factory, Mr. Twist, whose speeches were full of border ruffian invective.

Eld. D. F. Ladley arose, and in his usual calm, collected manner spoke to the resolution. He thought the resolution a proper one under the circumstances. The church had sold her entire property, had now no place for worship; and moreover a large share, doubtless nearly all of the members, wished to leave the church, and hence the resolution to dissolve the organization.

He believed such a step to be warranted and legal, and did not see that it would do injustice to any one. It would place all on the same level; and each one "could then go his own way to his own place."

If any wished to unite with the Second Christian Church, they could do so.

If any wished to unite with other churches, they could then have the privilege; and if others desired to organize a new church, they would undoubtedly have a right so to do. Believing the resolution therefore to be legal, as well as just and equitable, he should vote for it.

The motion on the resolution was now put, and passed unanimously. Affirmative 34, negative none.

The *First Christian Church* of Yellow Springs, Green co., Ohio, *was* therefore *declared dissolved.*

Messrs. Mann and Fay now announced that the First Christian Church is not dissolved and cannot be, and requested the members and friends to remain. Most of the members however left. Mr. Fay took the chair.

A majority of the Trustees of the Second Christian Church, owning the house being present, announced that no meeting could be held in the chapel without their permission.

Mr. Fay said he had money enough to pay a fine, if necessary, and he preferred to pay a good fine rather than not to speak for ten minutes.

The Trustees protested against any meeting in their house that evening. A. S. Dean declared—"any man who interrupts does so at his peril," and dropped a hint about "funerals."

Mr. Mann took his seat at the table and employed his pencil busily in drafting resolutions. Mr. Fay went on with his mercurial speech, throwing out sweeping and reckless assertions. * * * * "As the pastor of the First Christian Church in Yellow Springs, I now give notice that this church is not disbanded, nor is there any power on earth which can disband it according to the usuages or the profession of the Christian denomination."

Let the reader not be deceived. The usages of the Christian Denomination are different from those of most, if not all others, branches of the church of Christ.

Each one of our churches is congregational or democratic, and supreme to control its own affairs. Our Conferences are simply advisory bodies, made up of free and independent churches. Our United States or General Convention (quadrennial) is also purely an advisory body, made up of delegates from our various Conferences. It has no power to dictate to or control any Conference in its action; just as the Conference has no right or prerogative to control any church. Our churches are, therefore, free, independent, democratic bodies or corporations, transacting all their business by a majority vote of the members present at any regular or legal business meeting of the same. Every member is entitled to one vote and but one.

Such at least are the general usages of our denomination; and if any single sister church has any special regulations conflicting with the above general rules, we are not advised of them.

In view of the above, therefore, we ask why a unanimous or even a majority vote cannot dissolve one of our churches?

We see no reason why the power which creates cannot destroy; why the power which organizes cannot disorganize; why our churches cannot dissolve by a majority vote even as well as organize and transact other business by such vote.

That a corporate body can be dissolved no one will pretend to deny.

A church is an incorporate body. A church can, therefore, be dissolved.

Moreover, Mr. Kershner did not offer said resolution hastily or thoughtlessly. Counsel was taken of several ministers of the Denomination as well as of able lawyers, and the almost universal opinion was that our churches can dissolve by a majority as well as by a unanimous vote.

Let Mann, Fay and Dean make as many reckless assertions as they will to further selfish interests and carry out selfish schemes, we still firmly believe in the omnipotence of truth and the final triumph of justice!

Mr. Fay further said, "We have accepted the Holy Scriptures as our only rule of church government; and there is not an example between the lids of the Bible of such an attempt as that which we have just witnessed; nor is there a sentence which can be so tortured as to countenance this attempt. The Bible gives no authority to disband a church."

"The Holy Scriptures our only rule of church government." How does this declaration harmonize with some of Mr. F.'s statements in his 'Incognito' articles? Elds. John Ross and O. E. Morrill, of New York, can doubtless answer."

We would ask Mr. Fay if the Bible declares that a church organization cannot be dissolved?

Do the Sacred Scriptures teach that churches were not organized on the democratic principle, and that a majority vote was not competent to control?

Do they teach that churches were incorporated bodies, and that they can never be dissolved so long as one member objects?

We cannot believe that any sane, well-informed man will contend that Christ and his apostles had the Ohio statute laws, that the churches of that day were incorporated according to said laws and could not be dissolved; or that the churches as they existed at that time could not be dissolved.

Did not "the Amen, the faithful and true Witness," declare to the church of the Laodiceans, "I will spew thee out of my mouth?"

We believe that the First Christian Church of Yellow Springs, Ohio, both as a corporate body and as an association of professing Christians, was dissolved on the 9th of February, 1858, and that such dissolution was both advisable and necessary.

Mr. Fay also said, "I offered my propositions for pacification in good faith." If Mr. F. offered his plan in good faith, what will be thought of his statements on the 23d January, when he declared that he believed that the two parties could never be harmonized? Did he make both speeches "in good faith?" or were his "God speeds" on that occasion a mockery, and his declaration that "he would not oppose a single obstacle to the new organization" a lie? Why does Mr. Fay make a declaration one day and belie it the next?

Mr. Fay, about a year previously, had said a considerable privately about forming a new organization "of the right sort of men," yet now he pretends that he desires peace and "fusion."

But read the following:

CARD.

"This is to certify, that some time in the Spring of 1857 I was standing under the awning in front of the Post-office, when Mr. Fay came along and said he wanted to speak to me in private. We stepped to one side, and Mr. Fay remarked there was going to be a 'new organization' and that I was too good a man to be lost."

"I replied by saying, 'What do you mean, sir?'

"He said that they were going to get up a 'new organization' and wished me to go with them, but that it must be kept secret!

"July, 1858. "JOHN A. LAYTON."

J. B. Weston then arose and made quite an excitable speech, directly in the face of another protest of the proprietors of the house, in which he endeavored to show that the dissolution of the church was not legal. He affirmed that "no final action in the matter of the sale has been reported," which is a direct denial of the report of the Trustees of the First Christian Church made but an hour or two before, and which Mr. Weston himself heard, for he was sitting within a few feet of the Trustees who made the report. Why did Mr. Weston allow himself to be so carried away with excitement?

He also said, "If every member of the church, with the exception of only one person, should vote to dissolve the church, that one person protesting against it, the church could not be dissolved."

Because a very few members opposed the resolution to dissolve the church therefore Mr. W. declares the dissolution illegal. Does Mr. Weston know more about law than men who have given their lives to the study and practice of it? Able lawyers of the State of Ohio have given their opinion that there is nothing in law (common or statute) to prevent such dissolution, and when they were informed of the customs and usages of the Christian Denomination, they saw no reason, in an ecclesiastical point of view, why a majority vote was not competent to dissolve one of our churches.

"But Mr. Weston said that this whole thing was as unprecedented and unwarrantable in its nature as it was unchristian in its conception."

So Mr. Weston said an hour or so before, just as the vote to dissolve had been taken, to Bro. David Jewell, who voted for the resolution, "Nobody but a black-hearted hypocrite could take part in such a proceeding." Bro. Jewell pleasantly checked Mr. Weston, and hoped he would not allow himself to become too much excited.

Deacon Jewell is one of our most candid, thoughtful and reliable men.

Eld. A. Craig followed in some brief remarks, when Eld. McWhinney gave vent to his pent up feelings. And why not? After he had come over from Enon to defend Mann and Fay in church affairs, as he had previously in College affairs, it would certainly be rather unpleasant to be compelled to return without "freeing his mind." His speech, however, was desultory and composed of assertions.

The resolutions which Mr. Mann had drafted were passed, appointing committees to obtain the keys of the chapel, &c.

Prof. Allen supposing that these individuals had now given vent to their envious and seditionary feelings, arose and remarked that he had nothing to say, on the present occasion, touching the action of the First Christian Church, and would now add nothing to the protest of the present proprietors against the disorderly and illegal proceedings just witnessed; but he would repel the unjust insinuations and charges against the Second Christian Church. He was a member of that church, was acquainted with its proceedings, and knew the charges to be without foundation in truth. He remarked that the money to clear the chapel of debt could be raised only on condition that there should be a "new organization," that the Second Christian Church had been formed to comply with that condition, that it is based on the old Christian platform, "the Bible our rule of faith and practice," that it harbors no hard feelings towards any church in the place, intends to do its own business, and to observe the glorious precept, "Do unto others as ye would they should do unto you."

Eld. Fay then made a second speech, after which A. S. Dean mounted a seat and poured forth a torrent of foul-mouthed personalities, such that even J. B. Burrows would not insert them in his scurrilous "Yellow Springs News Letter."

"A resolution was then proposed that the vote empowering the committee to sell the church property be rescinded."

What did Mr. Mann mean by this resolution? The church had not instructed the Building Committee to sell the property, but the

Trustees; and the Trustees had fulfilled their instructions and made their report, which was unanimously accepted by the church. Why, therefore, this illegal, disorderly meeting, and this resolution to rescind what had never been done?

"If the blind lead the blind, both shall fall into the ditch."

"A committee of three was appointed to wait upon Eld. Ladley and in the name of the First Christian Church demand the book of church records."

Thus a few excited, disorderly persons continued to give vent to their bitter and envious feelings, until they exhausted themselves for the day and adjourned to the 20th inst., at which time their committees were requested to report.

On the 12th of February, towards evening, Wm. M. King and Mr. Harrington broke into the chapel, when L. G. Fessenden, S. M. Davis, Birch and sons, Twist and others, came in, and taking possession of the large melodeon used by the choir carried it away.

Soon after Mann and Fay, followed by their disciples, came in. Mr. Fay took the chair and called on the Committee on "Keys" to report.

L. G. Fessenden reported that he could not obtain the keys of the chapel.

Mr. Fay reported for the Committee on Church Book that they had called on Eld. Ladley, but he refused to give them the book; that he asked Eld. L. his reasons for refusing to comply with the committee's request and also asked him to arbitrate; but Eld. L. replied that he had nothing more to say at present on that subject, but he would be happy to see the committee-men when they had anything pleasant to say.

Wm. M. King moved the following:

"*Whereas* John Kershner and wife and others voted to disband the church, therefore—

"*Resolved*, That said John Kershner and others be and are hereby suspended from this church until they make reparation." Adopted.

Mr. Fay arose and said that he held a statement in his hand, by a student of the college, which he trembled to read. That that statement contained a charge of abusive and profane language against a member of the First Christian Church, (one of those embraced in the above resolution,) and had he known that said church contained such a member he would not have preached to it! Mr. Fay then read the statement, which was signed by J. W. Eddy.

Mr. Eddy then said that there was one person who heard the conversation; thinks J. B. Burrows was the man.

Mr. Fay said he understood that Mr. Lewis was also present and heard the improper language alluded to.

Mr. Fay calls on Mr. Burrows to state what he knows about the matter.

Mr. B. responds in a few remarks; thinks the gentleman did use profane language.

Mr. Lewis was then called on and corroborated the statement of Eddy in part.

Mr. Mann then asked what is customary in such cases.

Mr. Jewell arises and asks if it is customary to suspend a man from the church and try him afterwards?

Mr. Fay said the Bible rule is, "Moreover if thy brother shall trespass against thee, go and tell him the fault between thee and him alone," &c.; but this case is different. This is a public offence, and the mildest course would be to appoint a committee to wait upon the accused.

Mr. Mann moved that a committee of three be appointed to attend to the matter. Carried.

Committee appointed, { MR. FESSENDEN, " DENORMANDIE, " LEWIS.

Mr. Fessenden was excused from acting on the committee at his urgent request. Perhaps visions of lost music students loomed up before him. Not one of said committee has lisped the matter to the accused!

But the reader asks who is this Mr. Eddy? He is an eccentric young man and is thought to be extremely odd, if not of unsound mind. The Professor of Logic and Belles Lettres in the College remarked that he was frequently under the necessity of stopping Mr. Eddy and silencing him from reading his essays, on account of their infidel statements and vituperation of the Bible.

J. B. Burrows was the editor of the short-lived and scurrilous "Yellow Springs News Letter."

Mr. Lewis is a shoemaker, one of Fay's clique.

Such were the men who brought forward or abetted the above charge.

Who would not respect himself the more for being accused by such persons? and who would not be suspicious of himself if praised by them?

Eld. Jacobs, writing on this matter, speaks briefly of the occurrences of the 12th February, and then says:

"On the next day I was in a store where several persons were talking over the doings of the preceding evening. I stated that the proceedings of that meeting were much like the proceedings of an inquisition; that the actors on that occasion appeared to exhibit a desire to crush the accused, who was not present, and therefore could not answer for himself. His offence had been concealed for two months or more, but now at this crisis it is published to the world, and after the accused had declared by his vote he would act no longer with them!

"I further said that a Christian should endeavor to restore a brother in the spirit of meekness when he knows of his transgression; and if he says nothing to the offender privately to restore him, he should not bring the matter before the public. The doings of last evening looked as if certain persons wished to despitefully use and persecute the accused.

"Becoming somewhat excited at these remarks, Mr. Lewis, who was sitting near by, jumped up and said, 'Gentlemen, I will tell you just how it is. I heard the abusive language alluded to about two months ago. I said nothing to any one about it; but Mr. Eddy informed Mr. Mann of it two or three days ago, and he (Mann) had it brought forward.' "JESSE JACOBS."

The gentleman thus attacked and vilely accused was absent, but on learning the charge pronounced it false.

He says he used ungentlemanly language to Mr. Eddy on account of his frequent insults to him in his office, but no profane terms. Is not the above one indication, at least, that there are no depths to which Mr. Mann will not stoop to accomplish his schemes; no instruments he will not employ to traduce the characters of those who dissent from or oppose his views and plans?

Mr. Fessenden moved that an Executive Committee of five be appointed to attend to the business and guard the interests of the church.

Committee appointed,
- MR. DENORMANDIE,
- " FESSENDEN,
- " TWIST,
- " BUSS,
- DR. WARRINER.

Mr. Buss excused on request.

Mr. Fessenden excused on his urgent request and Mr. Birch was appointed in his place.

Mr. Mann moved that the Executive Committee have power to fill vacancies. Passed.

Mr. Fay requests the Executive Committee to remain a moment after adjournment. Adjourned.

The Executive Committee, after the audience had mostly dispersed, ordered the Trustees of the Second Christian Church out of the house.

The Trustees gave the committee to understand that they owned the chapel and that they should take care of it. The committee left and the Trustees locked up the house.

Next day, Feb. 13th, the Trustees of the Second Christian Church drove to Xenia to obtain counsel touching the disorderly course of W. M. King and his co-laborers, Fay, Dean and others. Said King made a false affidavit before Justice Shroufe, swearing that the book of church records is his own personal property, and a writ of replevin was issued for seizure of said book wherever found, and summoning Eld. D. F. Ladley to appear on the 16th inst. before said justice to answer the action of Wm. M. King.

The book, however, disappeared, and could not be found.

On their way home from Xenia the Trustees of the Second Christian Church were met by the constable, who served writs of replevin on them, summoning them to appear on the 16th before Justice Shroufe!

The present proprietors of the house had now an excellent opportunity for bringing a legal action against King and others, as they had a few days later against Burrows and others; but they concluded to stand simply on the defensive, and suffer if need be in the cause of truth and justice, and on arriving at home they placed a watch in the chapel in accordance with the counsel of able lawyers, which was kept up for some days; and since which the disciples of Fay and Mann have not disturbed the premises.

On the next day (Sabbath) the proprietors of the chapel recalled the permission which they had previously given to the Sunday School of the late First Christian Church to hold their meetings in the chapel.

They regretted exceedingly to take this step, but those connected with and sustaining said school had broken into the chapel and held the disorderly meetings above specified, and besides their counsellor had advised them to withdraw their permission.

On the 16th, the persons summoned, appeared before Justice Shroufe, but as the plaintiff did not appear, the action was set aside. Indeed how could said plaintiff have appeared and held up his head in the presence of the court, after breaking into a chapel and aiding in carrying off a melodeon, after his false oath before Justice Shroufe, and when the original writ had been greatly changed by interlineations after it left the office of the Justice. After all these and other things could said King look any honest man in the eye! Had he appeared on that occasion he would have been covered if possible with still deeper contempt and disgrace.

As it was, said King, Mann and others were in Xenia to attend court, expecting that the petition of Wm. Mills and the Trustees of the late First Christian Church would be presented that day.

On the preceding evening, Mr. Twist had been dispatched, it is said, to West Liberty for Fay and McWhinney, who had just been making speeches in behalf of Antioch College and the proposed "Joint Stock Company," to the citizens of that town, and had closed their meeting by informing said citizens that they would call on them the next day for stock subscriptions.

The next day came but no Fay and McWhinney were to be found or heard of! Had they been abducted? or had they gone up in the chariot of their college eloquence?

Said Fay and McWhinney passed, according to report through Yellow Springs by night and turned up in Xenia before daylight of the 16th and spent the day lounging about that town instead of taking the stock subscriptions of the good people of West Liberty some 30 miles distant! In the morning of the same day there was quite a rush of Fay's disciples from Yellow Springs to Xenia. Wm. M. King who broke into the chapel, and Horace Mann, driving down in company in single carriages. The exodus however turned out to be "a wild goose chase."

The 16th was, it is true, the day appointed by court in which the First Christian Church might represent her petition; but said church had previously disbanded, and, of course, no petition could be presented, nor was it necessary. But the counsel of Mr. Fay's clique, not fully posted, had informed them that said petition would be before the court again on the 16th inst., and hence the rush of the so-called Fayites. They had their labor for their pains, for after watching the court all day, and hearing of no church petition, they returned by night, completely crest-fallen, to Yellow Springs. What a pity this had not been the first day of April!

These proceedings damaged them greatly, their prestige was gone! They were now comparatively quiet, and it was said that they did not want the chapel, that they would build a new and better one, &c.

Mr. Harrington, had a few weeks previously opened a Commercial College in Yellow Springs, and engaged Wm. M. King as one of the teachers. They had, it is said, quite a number of students, and were doing very well; but after they broke into the Christian chapel on the afternoon of the 12th, and King had got out a writ of replevin for Eld. Ladley, the community became so disgusted and outraged, that the students left the Commercial School and it was broken up.

Soon after Mr. Harrington and two other members of Mr. Fay's clique purchased or leased Eld. Fay's nursery, and are now endeavoring to make a living by *nursing fruit trees.* We hope the trees will grow straight, and that the fruit will not be poisonous!

On the 18th Feb. Eld. Maple, editor of the *Gospel Herald,* wrote a long letter to Eld. Austin Craig, in which he stated what was not true and broke the most sacred obligations of friend to friend.

A few days later, a so-called "convention for the redemption of Antioch College" was held in Stafford, N. Y. An examination of the minutes shows that there were ten actors in that meeting, and that *the* five who managed and controlled the convention went from this place and vicinity and were members of Mr. Mann's clique! And one, if not more, of the remaining five persons was a coadjutor of Mann and Fay!

Let any one acquainted with the facts read the minutes of that meeting, and say if ever a convention was more partizan.

Of course, Mr. Mann's clique—viz., "Dean, Fay & Co.," which Maple had pronounced—a "little, scheming, selfish, greedy clique," had full swing, and blew off a large amount of gas. They spoke of a plot which "more than two years ago," they said, "was in existence to effect the removal of Mr. Mann from the presidency of Antioch College." * * * "that in furtherance of this plot, the Christian Church in Yellow Springs had been divided, and an attempt made to destroy the First Christian Church there," in confirmation of which Eld. Maple's letter was read and an extract from it published as a portion of the minutes of the convention, which contains the following, viz:—

"The sole object of this Second Christian Church organization is the removal of Mr. Mann and the present faculty."

1st. Concerning the plot, spoken of we know nothing.

2d. The division in the church was caused by the plottings of Mann, Dean, Fay and others, as the history of the church shows.

3d. The First Christian Church of Yellow Springs was dissolved on Feb. 9th, 1858, by a unanimous vote of its members—viz., Affirmative 34. Negative none.

4th. The charge of Eld. James Maple against the Second Christian Church of Yellow Springs, is false, as the following documents will show.

Statement of Eld. Ladley and Snow Richardson, who organized the "Second Christian Church of Yellow Springs, Green Co., Ohio."

"To whom it may concern:—We, the undersigned, having attended the preparatory meetings of the organization of the Second Christian Church of Yellow Springs, did by request, on the 22d day of January,

1858, organize said Second Christian Church at the house of D. F. Ladley, and neither at that time nor at any other time did we hear it intimated that this organization was to interfere with or effect Mr. Mann or the College in any way.

"YELLOW SPRINGS,
April, 1858."

Signed { D. F. LADLEY,
SNOW RICHARDSON."

STATEMENT OF THE MEMBERS OF THE SECOND CHRISTIAN CHURCH.

"We, the undersigned, members of the organization of the Second Christian Church, of Yellow Springs, which was organized at the house of Eld. D. F. Ladley, on the 22d day of January, 1858, in view of the erroneous and false statements as published in the *Gospel Herald* of April 15th, '58, feel it to be duty to ourselves and to the cause of Christ to make a statement of facts, viz.: that we attended the preparatory meetings to said organization, and that we never heard at any of those meetings one word said about removing Mr. Mann from the Presidency of Antioch College, or that this organization would affect said college; and that the assertion made in the *Gospel Herald* of April 15th, to wit: "The sole object of this Second Christian Church organization is the removal of Mr. Mann and the present Faculty," is without foundation in truth; yea, is absolutely *false*.

Signed
E. LAWRENCE,
A. M. LAWRENCE,
G. W. JONES,
ELEANOR JONES,
JESSE JACOBS,
T. A. LAWRENCE,
SAMANTHA JONES,
E. J. LAWRENCE,
S.G. JONES,
JOHN A. LAYTON,
IRA W. ALLEN,
W. H. DOHERTY,
T. W. DAWSON."

"YELLOW SPRINGS, O., April, 1858."

The above are the names of all the original members of the Second Christian Church save one, a lady. None of these were members of the First Christian Church, and only five of them ever had been; four of the five withdrawing on account of selling the pews in the spring of 1855, and the other at the time Mr. Fay was chosen by the "congregation," June, 1857.

During the month of Feb., much excitement was stirred up in town by A. S. Dean, Eli Fay, Horace Mann, and a few others, by means of false charges against the Second Christian Church.

Some of these charges were :—

1st. That the members of the Second Christian Church voted in the meetings of the First Christian Church and controlled her action.

This charge is incorrect and malicious. Some of the members of the Second Christian Church, it is true, attended some of the meetings of the First Christian Church, but they took no part in them, either in speaking or voting. They were simply spectators, which cannot be said of some who were not members of either church.

2d. It was said that the Second Christian Church was established on a pro-slavery basis, and was opposed to the First Christian Church on account of her anti-slavery sentiments.

There is not even the shadow of truth in this. We did not hear the word slavery mentioned in connection with the church until our enemies harped upon "that word" to gain sympathy for their clique.

3d. That the object of the Second Christian Church was to overthrow Antioch College.

It was said by some of the Soliciting Committee, early in Jan'y. to some persons who declined subscribing much towards the church debt because of the assignment of the College and the strong probability that it could not be redeemed to the Christian Denomination, that, if the brethren in Yellow Springs will subscribe and pay the $6,000 to clear the chapel of debt, the sister churches of the denomination may perhaps be encouraged to raise money, lift the college out of the mire, and place it upon a secure foundation; that if this should be the result, their property would rise materially in value, and return to them, doubtless, more than the amount of their subscriptions to the church. This is directly the of opposite the charge.

The charge is therefore untrue. The statements on the preceding pages prove this. The individual members of the Second Christian Church have always and constantly desired the prosperity of Antioch College as intended by the Marion Convention; and they will do as much to establish it upon that basis as any other church of equal ability. We therefore repel with indignation and pity the untrue charges against the Second Christian Church which wily enemies have circulated through the country in print and by letter.

The second Christian Church occupies no sectarian ground, but is organized on the old Christian platform, "The Bible our rule of faith and practice," upon the broad, free, inspiring principles of the Sacred Scriptures. She will cherish no feelings of unchristian rivalry or opposition towards any church or any denomination.

JOHN KERSHNER, A. G. KILER, BENAJAH WILSON.	Trustees of the late First Christian Church.
THOMAS KERSHNER, JOHN KERSHNER, A. G. KILER.	Building Committee of the late First Christian Church.
D. F. LADLEY,	Clerk of said late First Christian Church.

The above persons were members of the First Christian Church from the day of its organization, January 19th, 1852, to its dissolution, February 9th, 1858, and were in office most of the time.

J. A. LAYTON, IRA W. ALLEN, T. W. DAWSON.	Trustees* of the Second Christian Church.
JESSE JACOBS,	Clerk of Second Chhris Church.
E. LAWRENCE,	Treasurer of Second Christian Church.

*The Trustees of the Second Christian Church never belonged to the First Christian Church, and are not personally acquainted with its entire history, yet to the best of their belief the following is a true statement.

www.ingramcontent.com/pod-product-compliance
Lightning Source LLC
LaVergne TN
LVHW020231110826
845151LV00003B/888

9781425530884